YOTSUBA&!

2

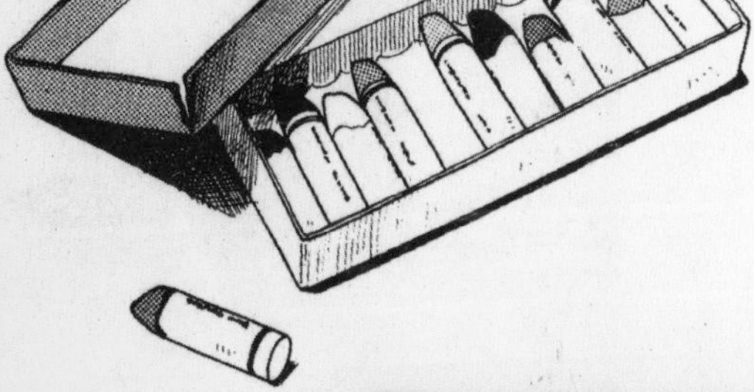

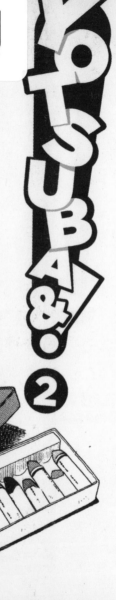

KIYOHIKO AZUMA

TABLE OF CONTENTS

YOTSUBA&!

KIYOHIKO AZUMA

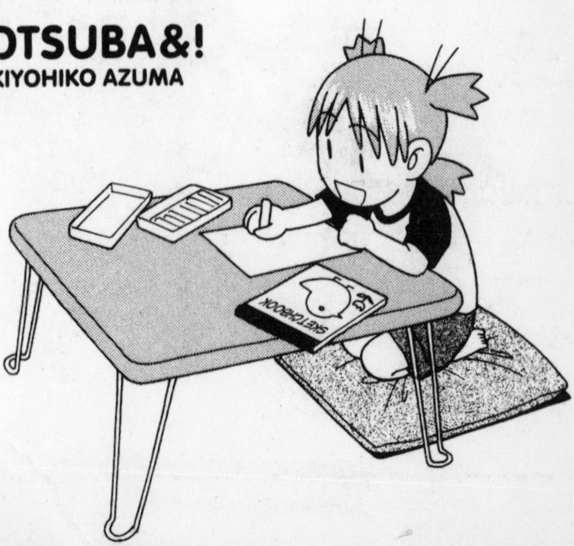

SKETCHBOOK

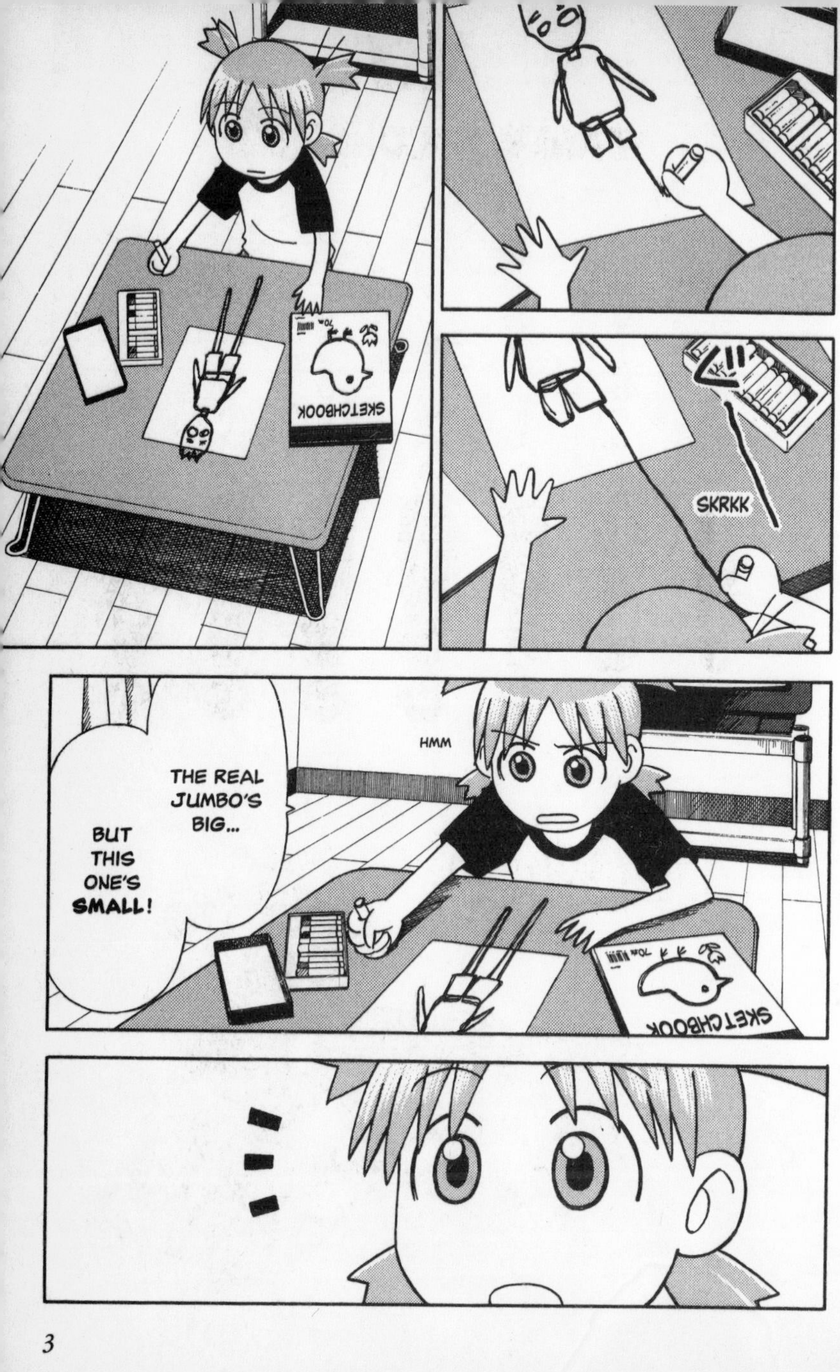
SKRKK
HMM
THE REAL JUMBO'S BIG... BUT THIS ONE'S SMALL!

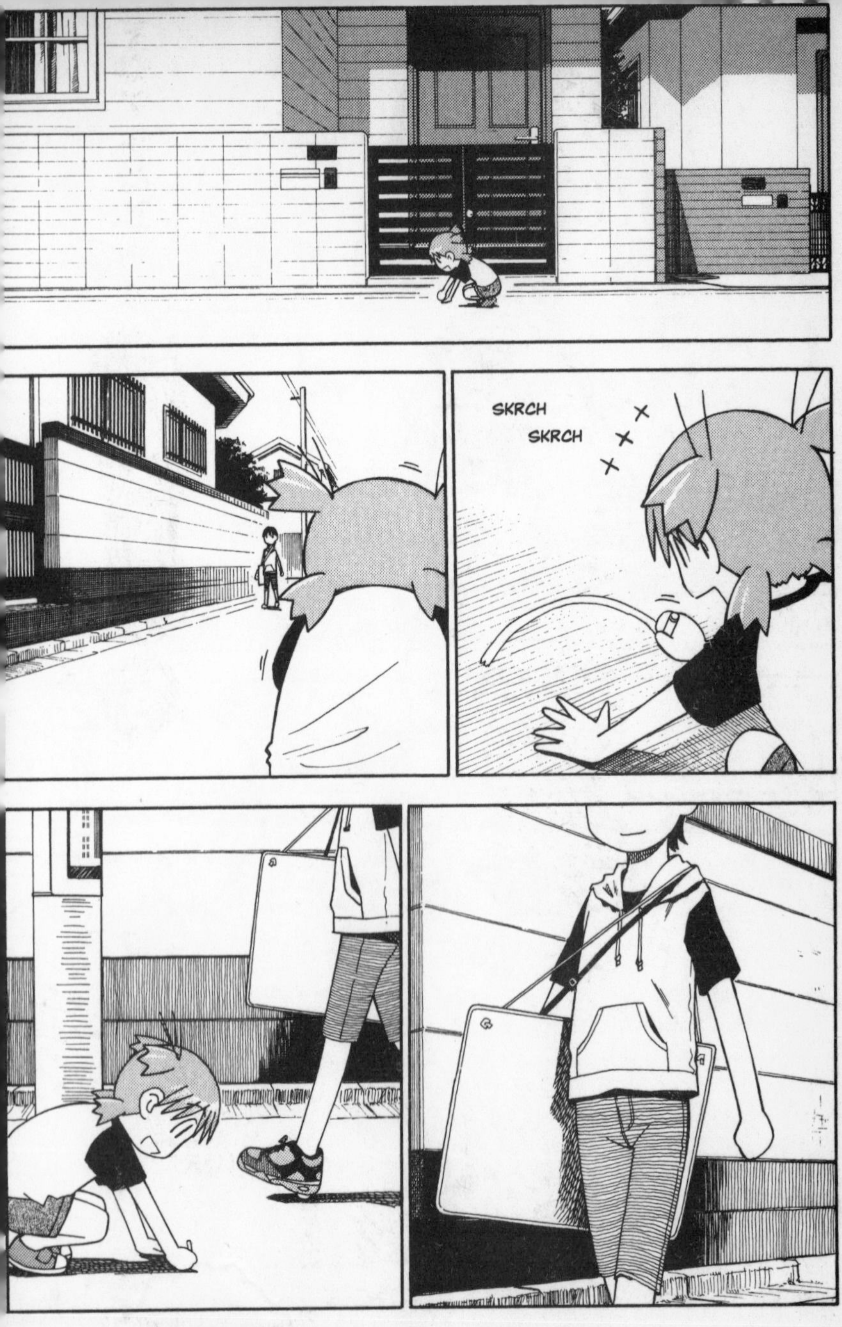
SKRCH
SKRCH

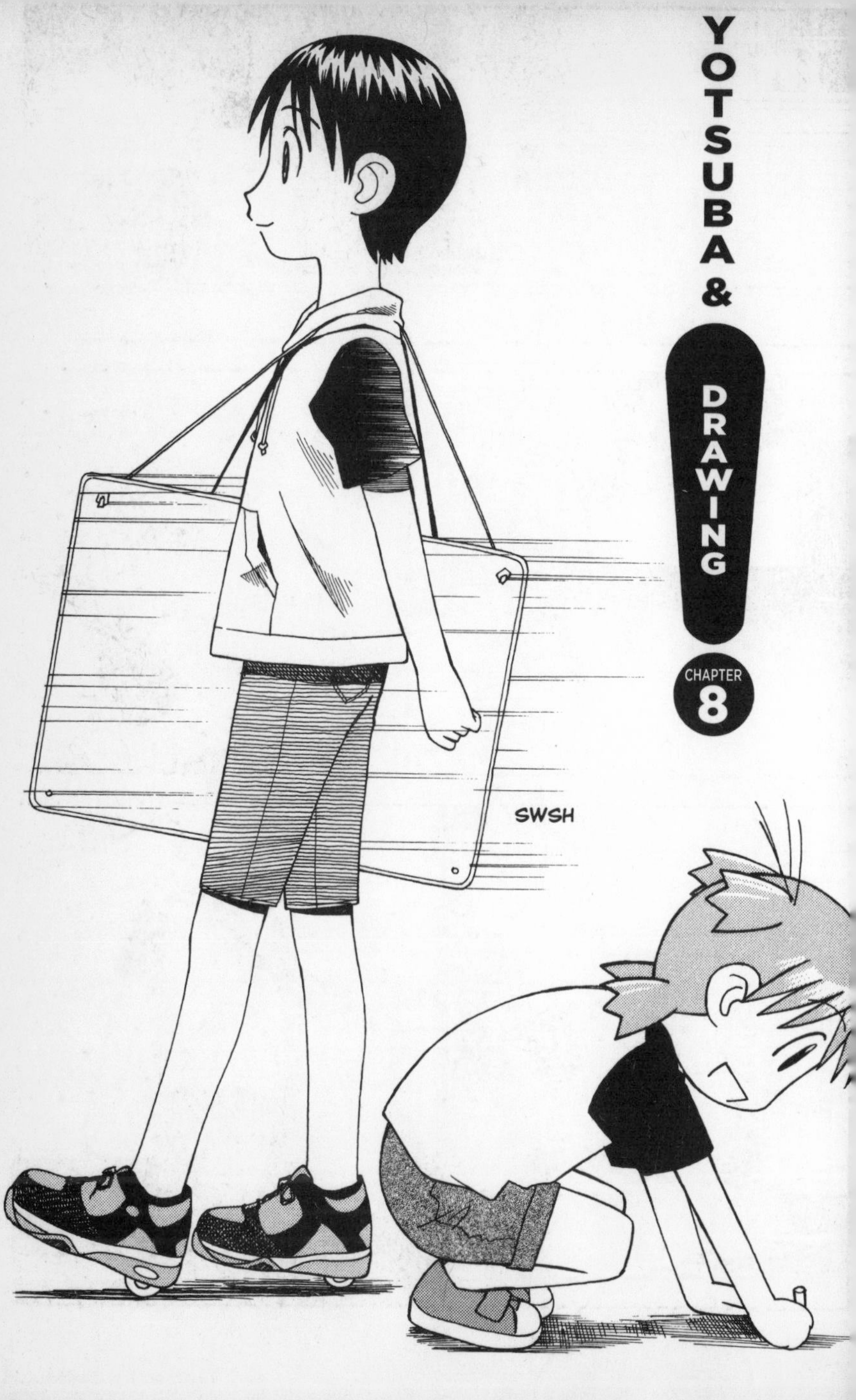
YOTSUBA &
DRAWING!
CHAPTER 8
SWSH

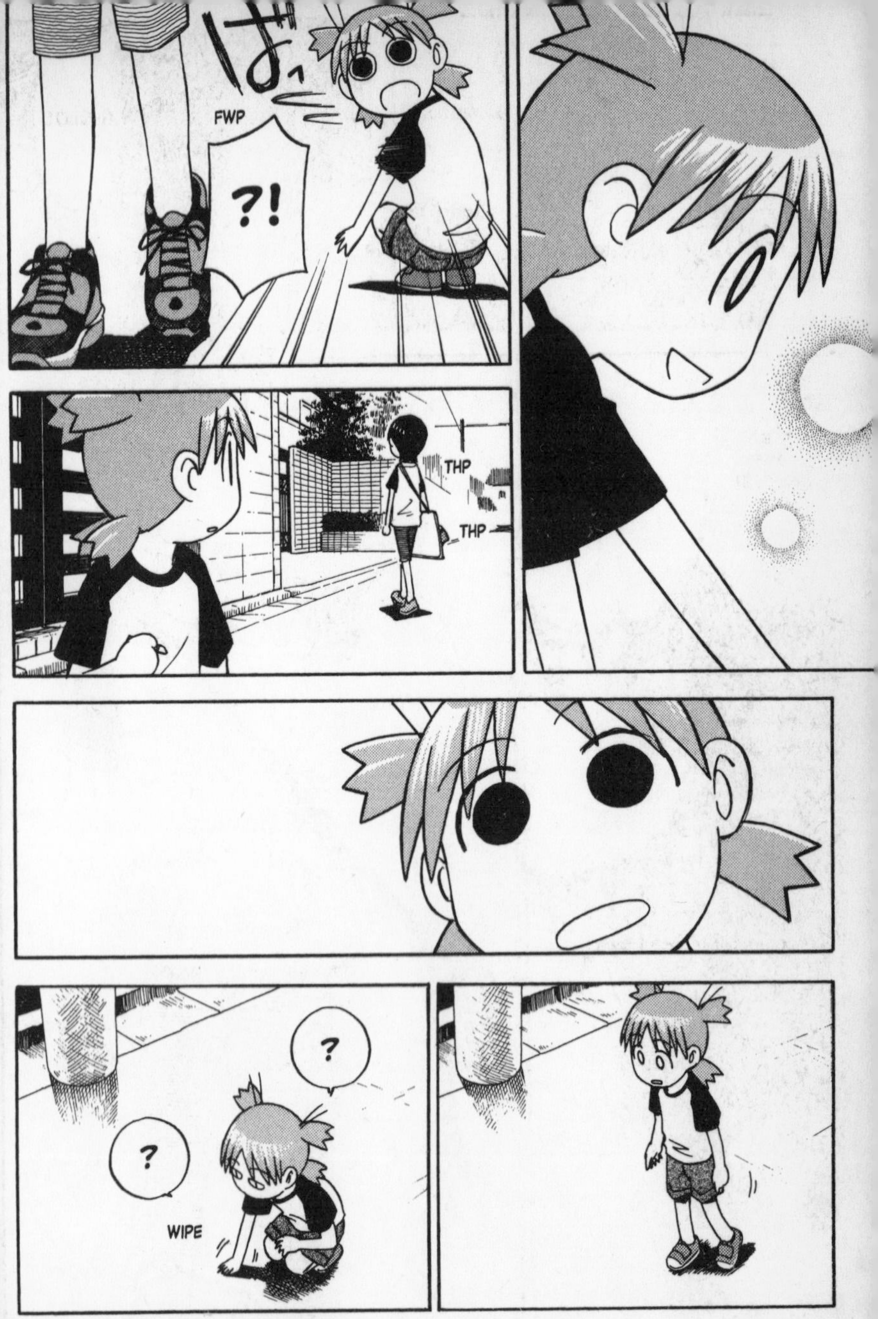
ばっ
FWP
?!
THP
THP
?
?
WIPE

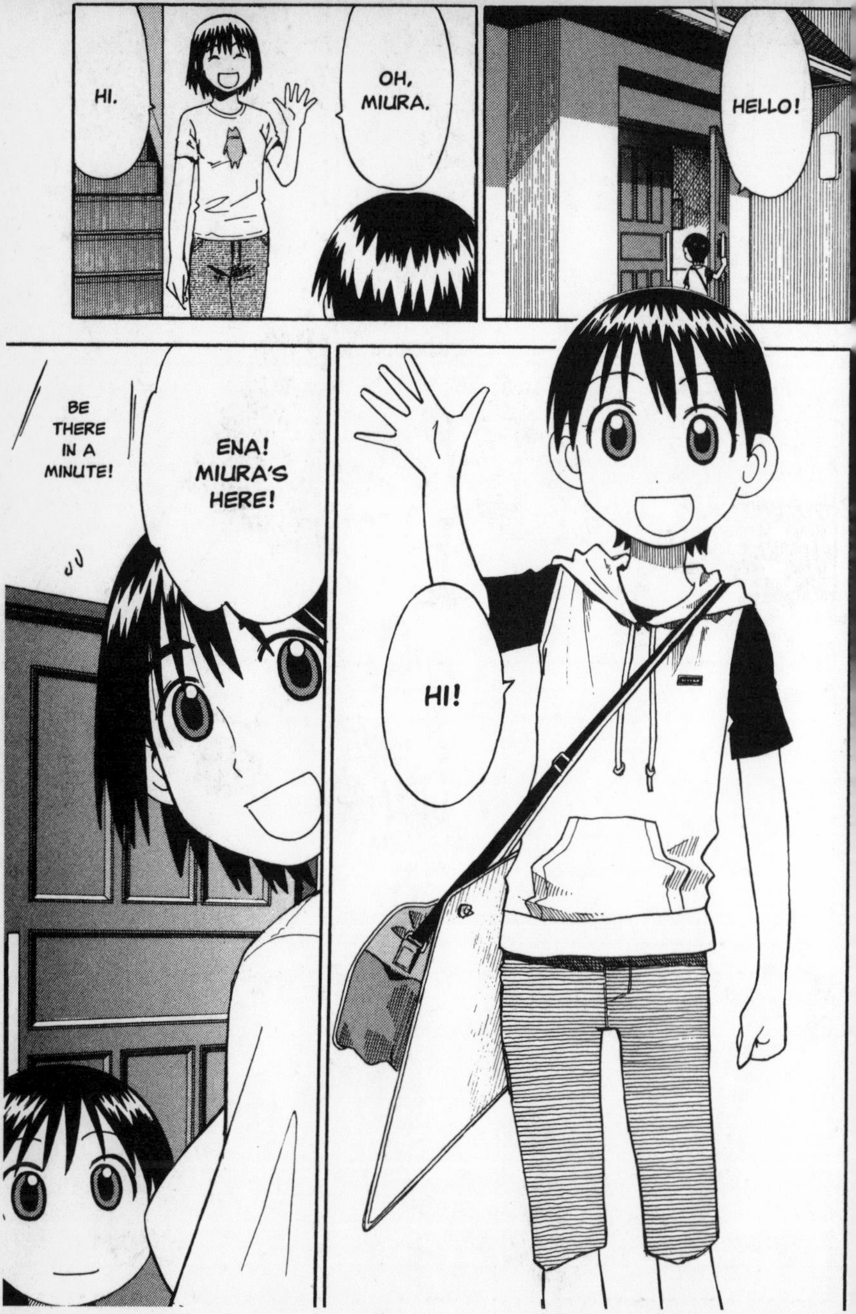
HELLO!
OH, MIURA.
HI.
HI!
ENA! MIURA'S HERE!
BE THERE IN A MINUTE!

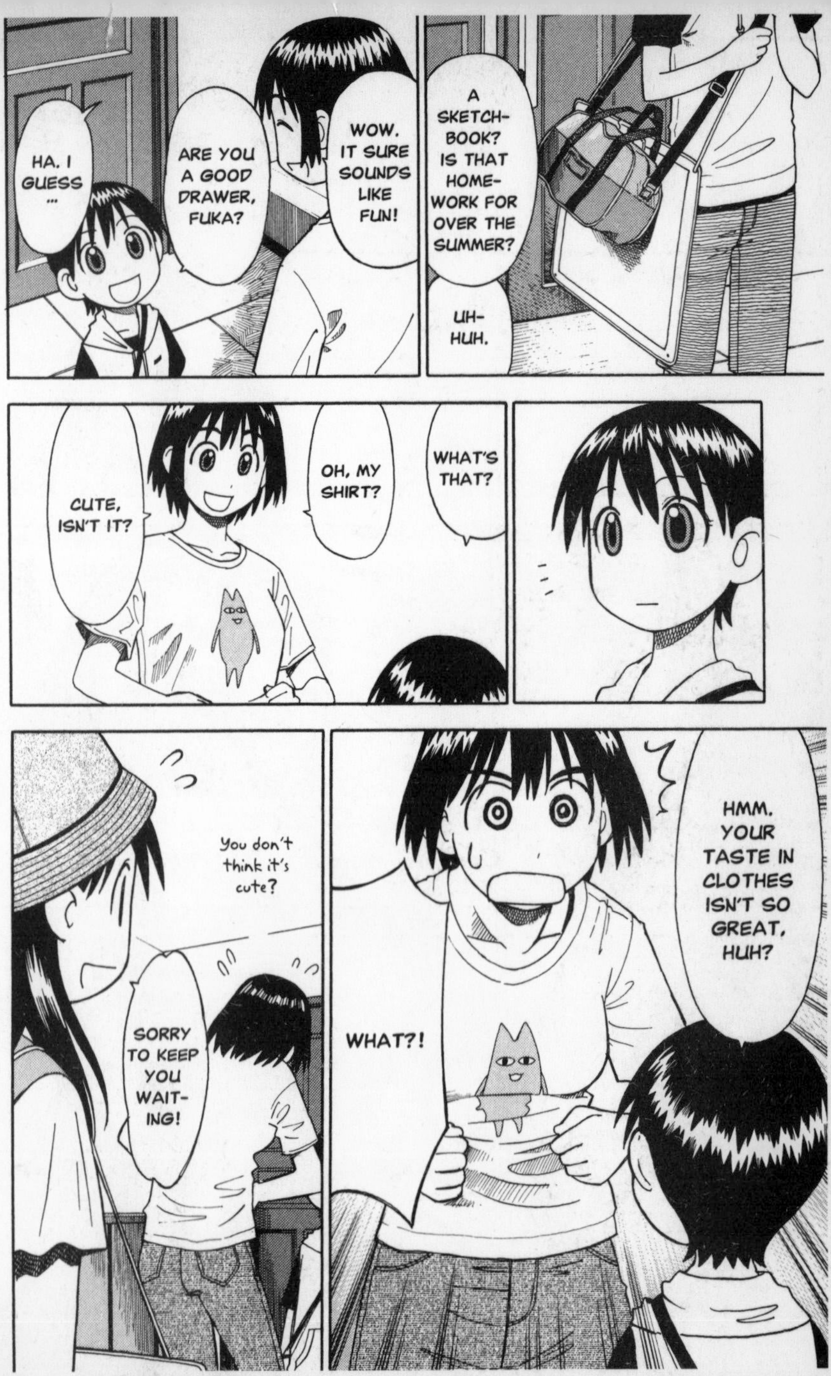
A SKETCHBOOK? IS THAT HOMEWORK FOR OVER THE SUMMER?
UH-HUH.
WOW. IT SURE SOUNDS LIKE FUN!
ARE YOU A GOOD DRAWER, FUKA?
HA. I GUESS ...
WHAT'S THAT?
OH, MY SHIRT?
CUTE, ISN'T IT?
HMM. YOUR TASTE IN CLOTHES ISN'T SO GREAT, HUH?
WHAT?!
You don't think it's cute?
SORRY TO KEEP YOU WAITING!

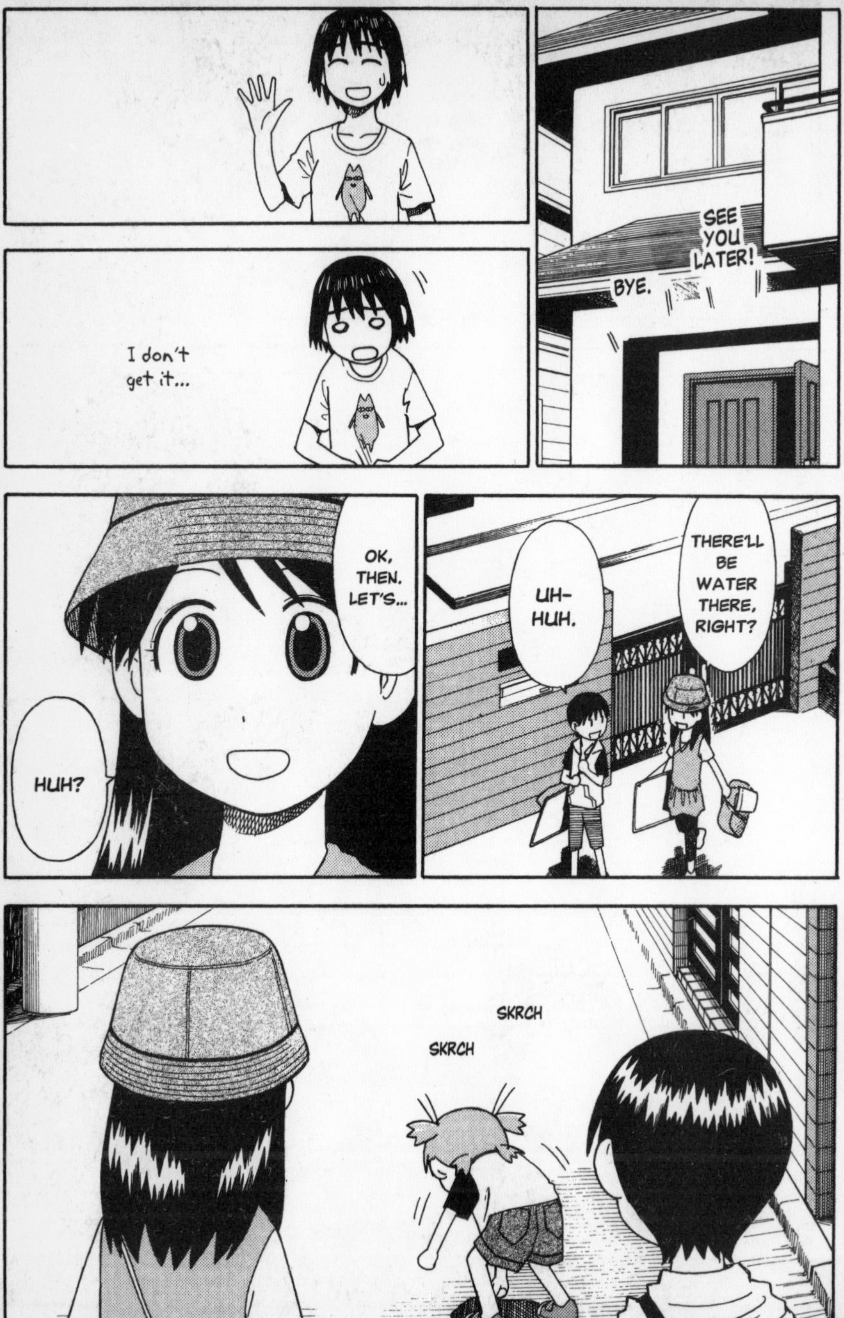
SEE YOU LATER!
BYE.
I don't get it...
THERE'LL BE WATER THERE, RIGHT?
UH-HUH.
OK, THEN. LET'S...
HUH?
SKRCH
SKRCH

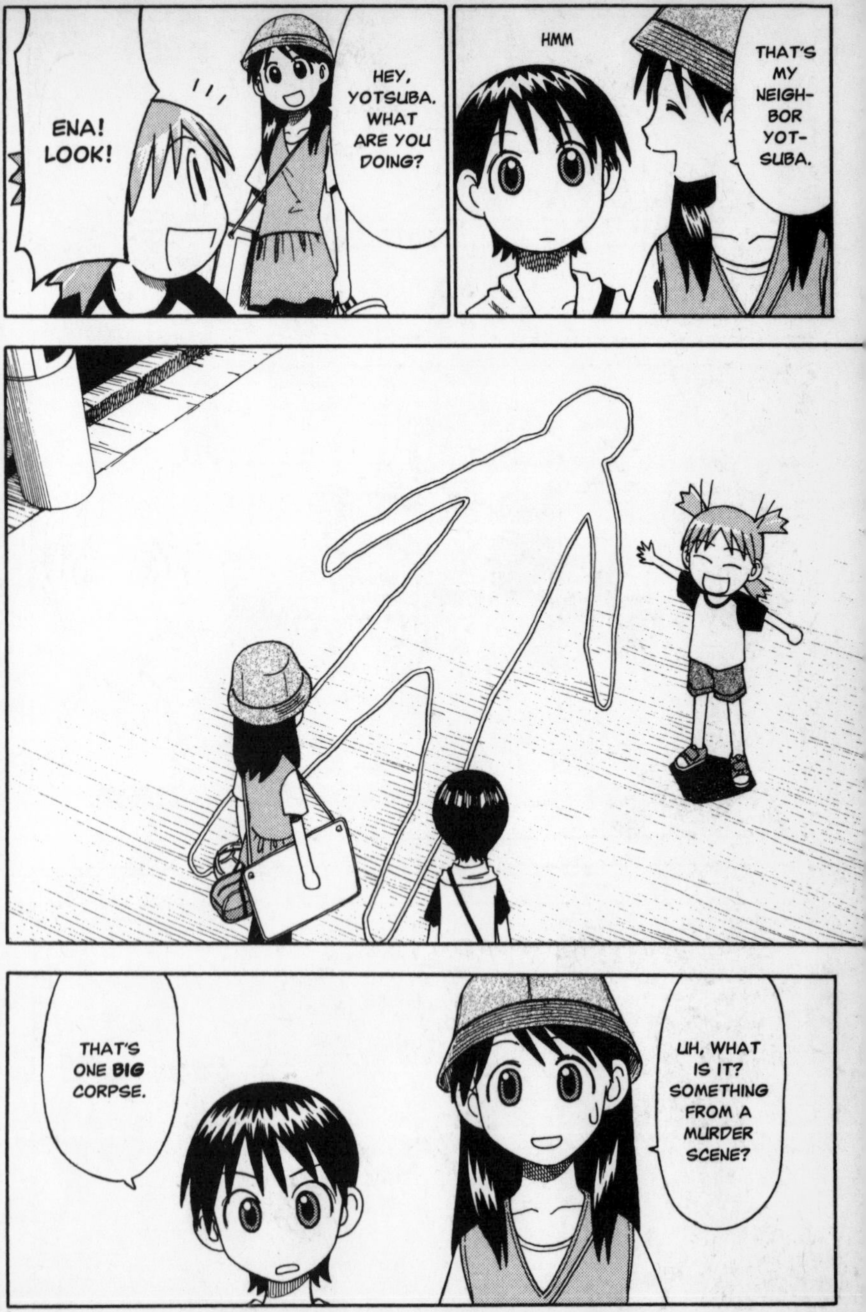

ENA! LOOK!
HEY, YOTSUBA. WHAT ARE YOU DOING?
HMM
THAT'S MY NEIGHBOR YOT-SUBA.
UH, WHAT IS IT? SOMETHING FROM A MURDER SCENE?
THAT'S ONE **BIG** CORPSE.

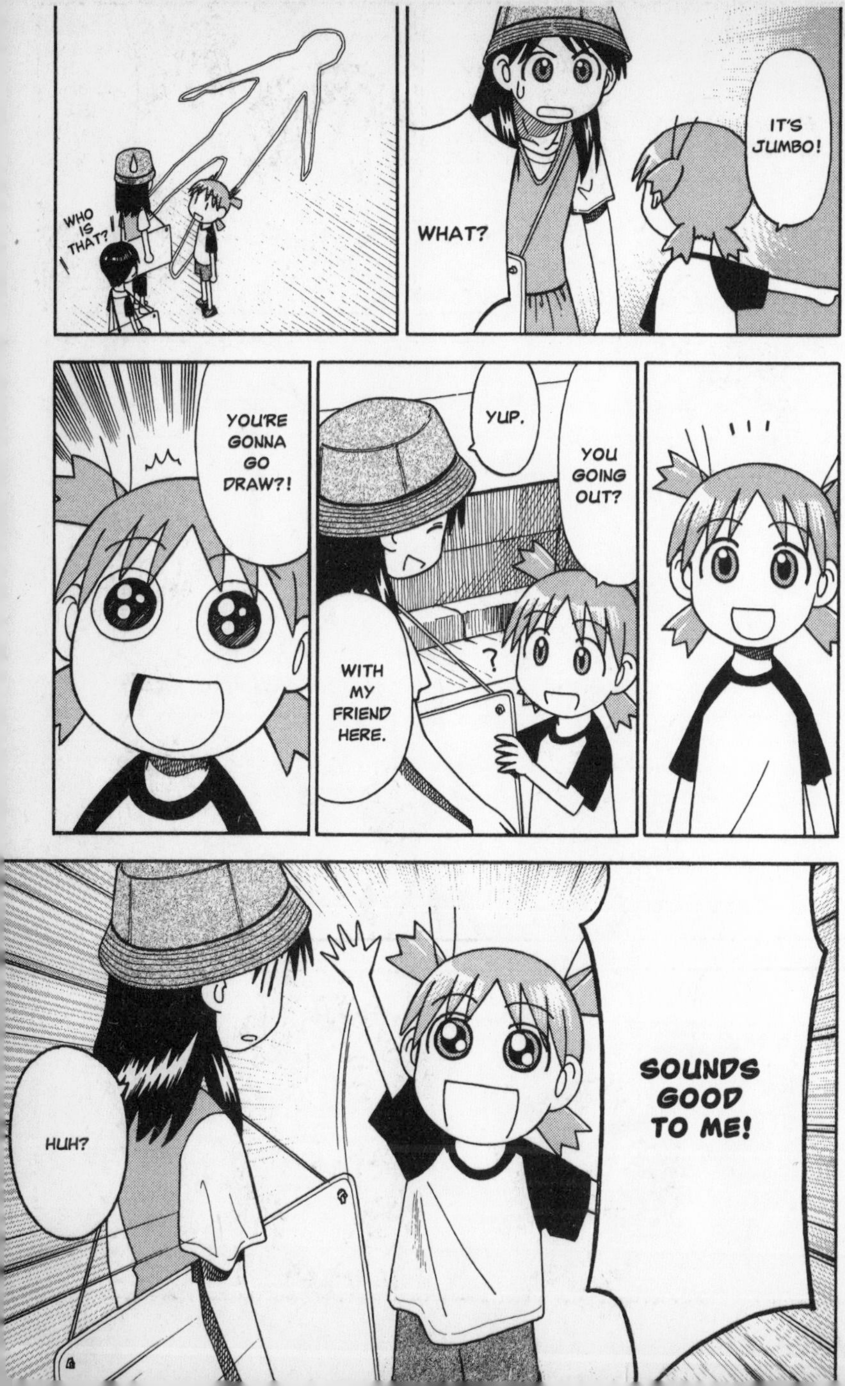
IT'S JUMBO!
WHAT?
WHO IS THAT?
YOU GOING OUT?
YUP.
WITH MY FRIEND HERE.
YOU'RE GONNA GO DRAW?!
SOUNDS GOOD TO ME!
HUH?

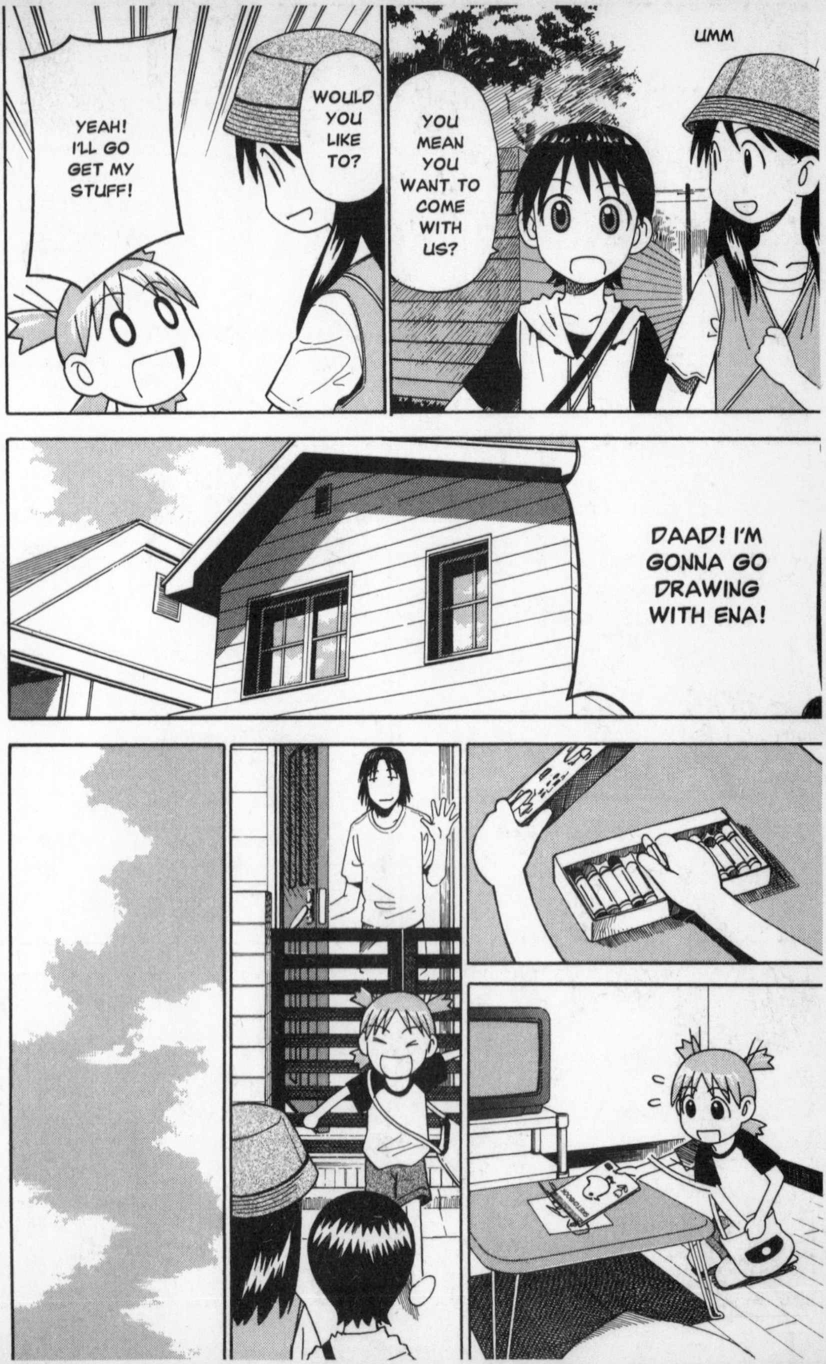
UMM
YOU MEAN YOU WANT TO COME WITH US?
WOULD YOU LIKE TO?
YEAH! I'LL GO GET MY STUFF!
DAAD! I'M GONNA GO DRAWING WITH ENA!

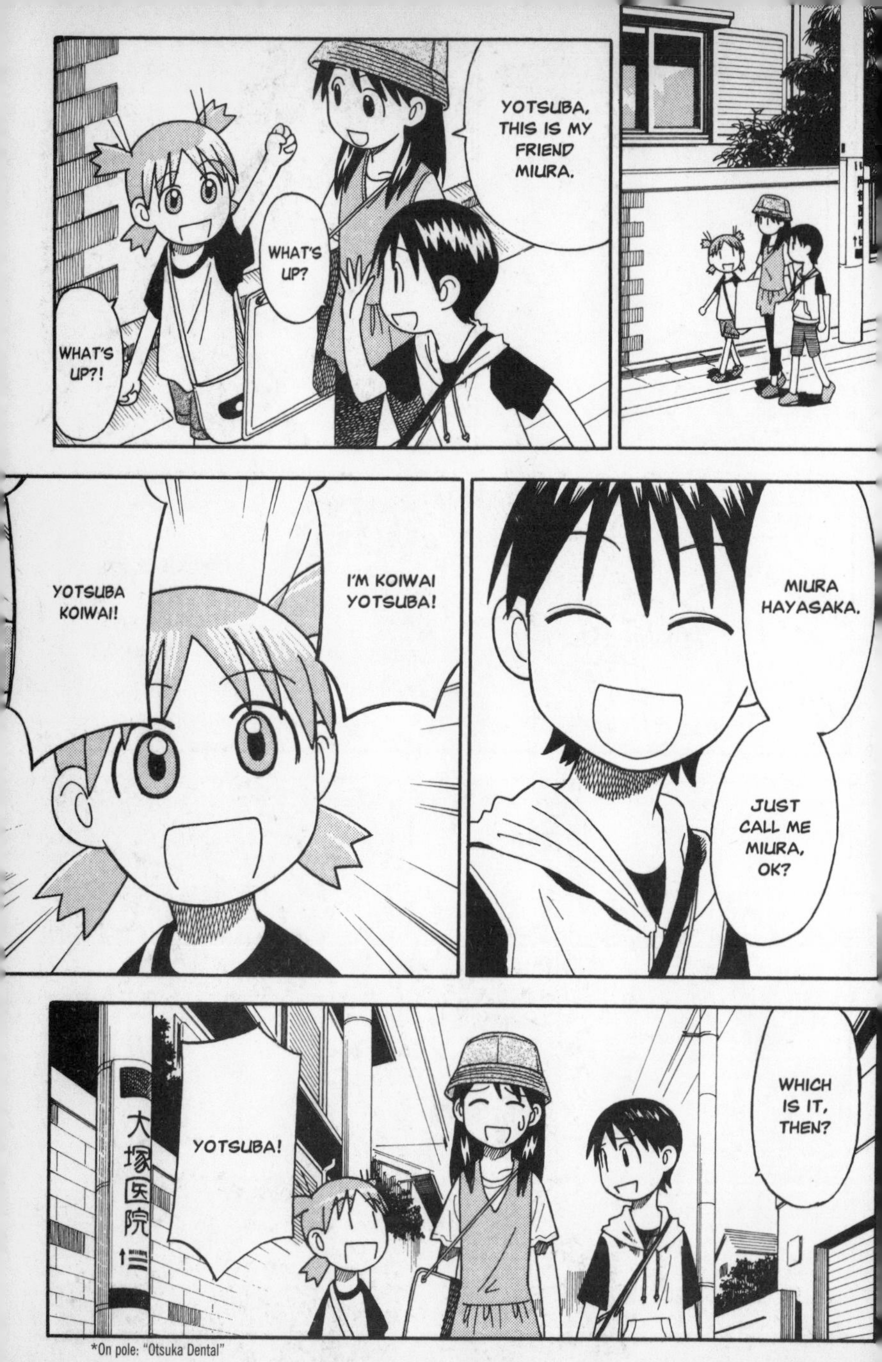

YOTSUBA, THIS IS MY FRIEND MIURA.
WHAT'S UP?
WHAT'S UP?!
MIURA HAYASAKA.
JUST CALL ME MIURA, OK?
I'M KOIWAI YOTSUBA!
YOTSUBA KOIWAI!
WHICH IS IT, THEN?
YOTSUBA!
大塚医院

*On pole: "Otsuka Dental"

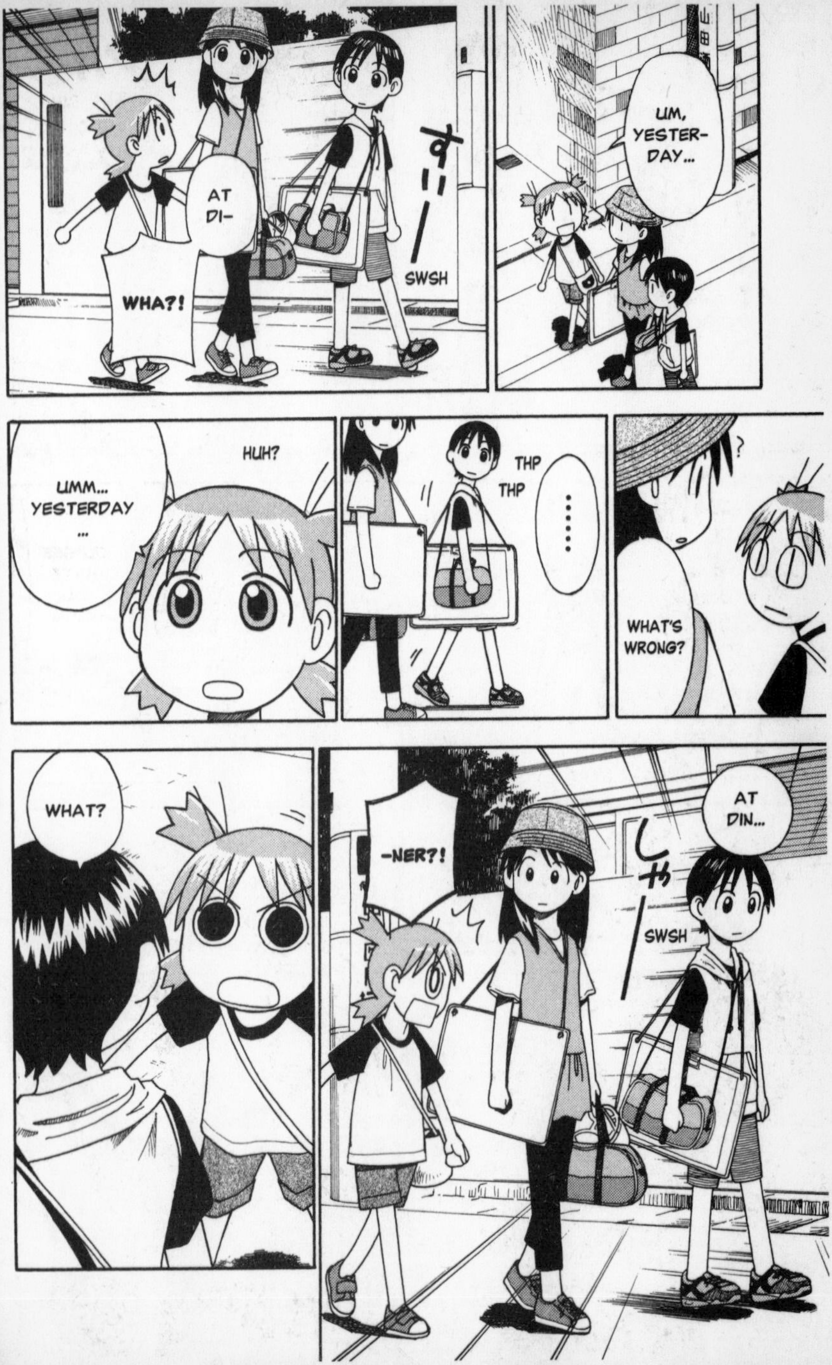

UM, YESTER-DAY...
AT DI-
WHA?!
SWSH
WHAT'S WRONG?
THP
THP
......
UMM... YESTERDAY ...
HUH?
AT DIN...
SWSH
-NER?!
WHAT?

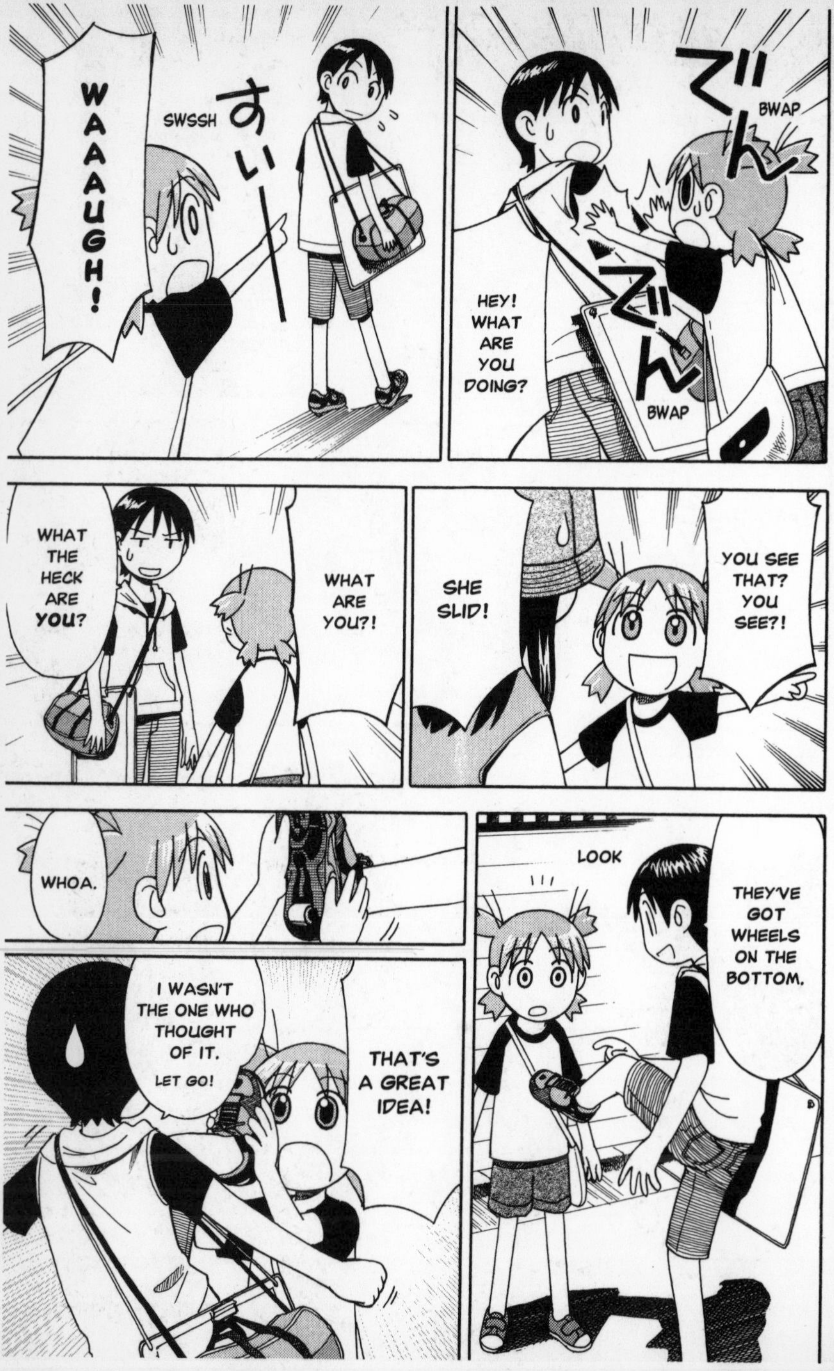

でんでん
BWAP
HEY! WHAT ARE YOU DOING?
でんでん
BWAP
WAAAAUGH!
すい
SWSSH
YOU SEE THAT? YOU SEE?!
SHE SLID!
WHAT ARE YOU?!
WHAT THE HECK ARE YOU?
LOOK
THEY'VE GOT WHEELS ON THE BOTTOM.
WHOA.
THAT'S A GREAT IDEA!
I WASN'T THE ONE WHO THOUGHT OF IT.
LET GO!

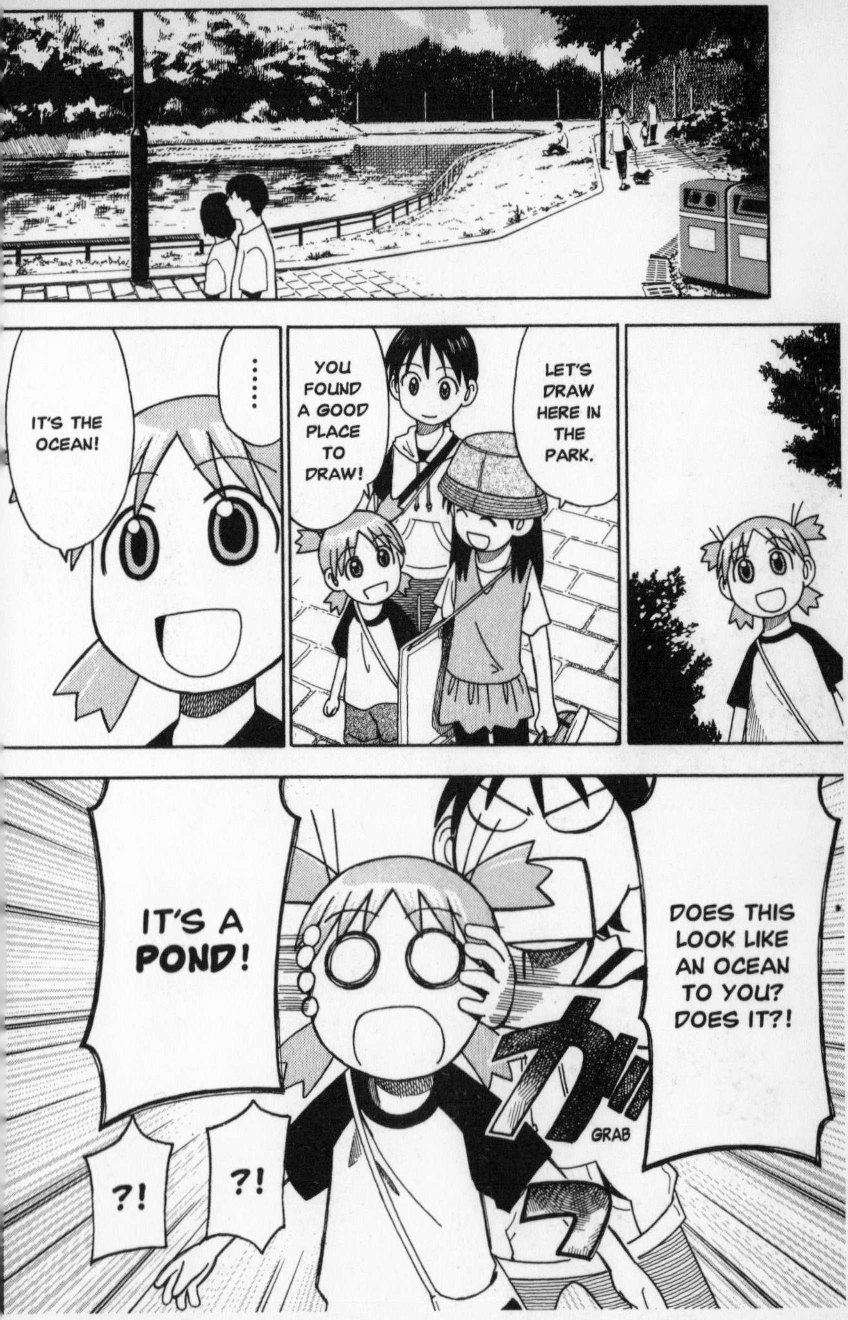

LET'S DRAW HERE IN THE PARK.
YOU FOUND A GOOD PLACE TO DRAW!
......
IT'S THE OCEAN!
GRAB
DOES THIS LOOK LIKE AN OCEAN TO YOU? DOES IT?!
IT'S A POND!
?!
?!

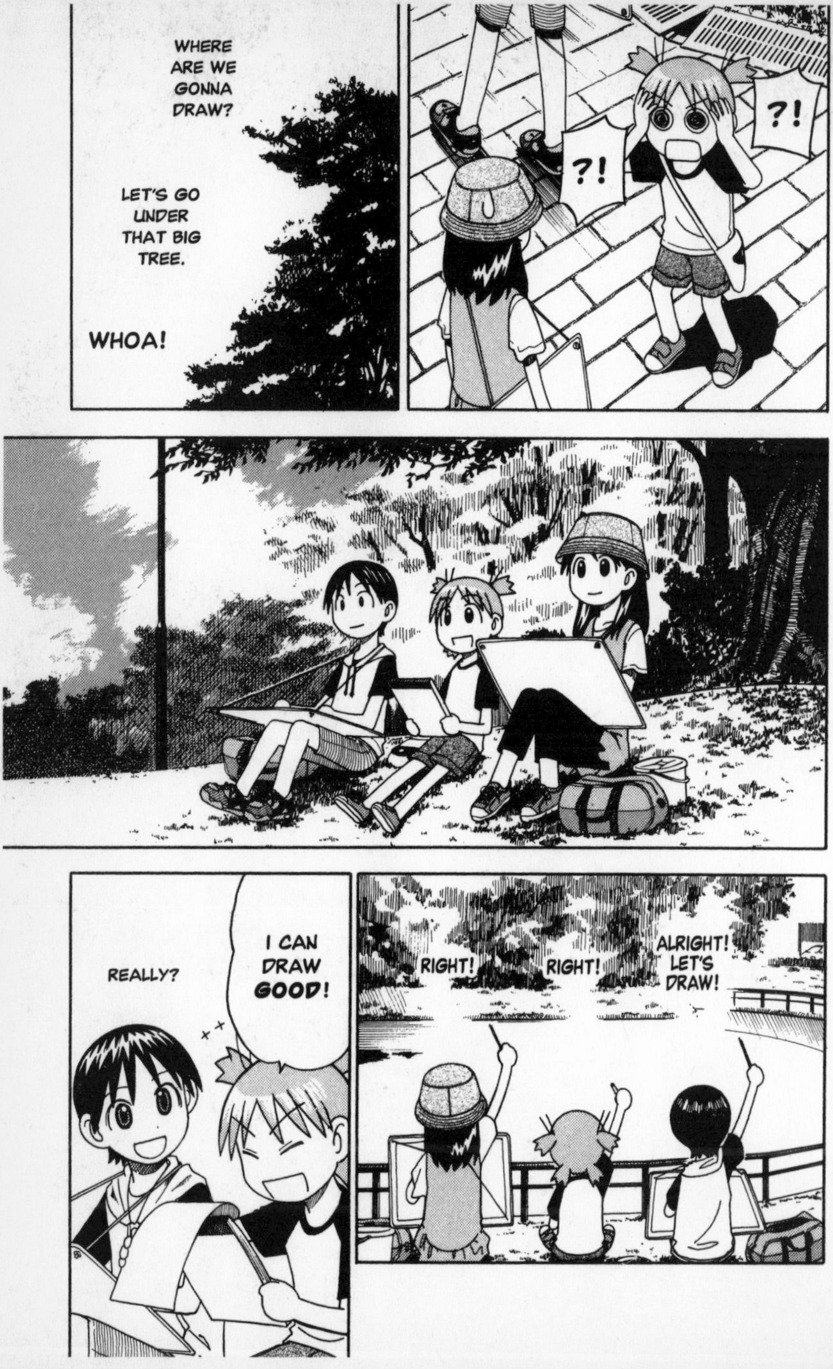
?!
?!
WHERE ARE WE GONNA DRAW?
LET'S GO UNDER THAT BIG TREE.
WHOA!
ALRIGHT! LET'S DRAW!
RIGHT!
RIGHT!
I CAN DRAW **GOOD**!
REALLY?

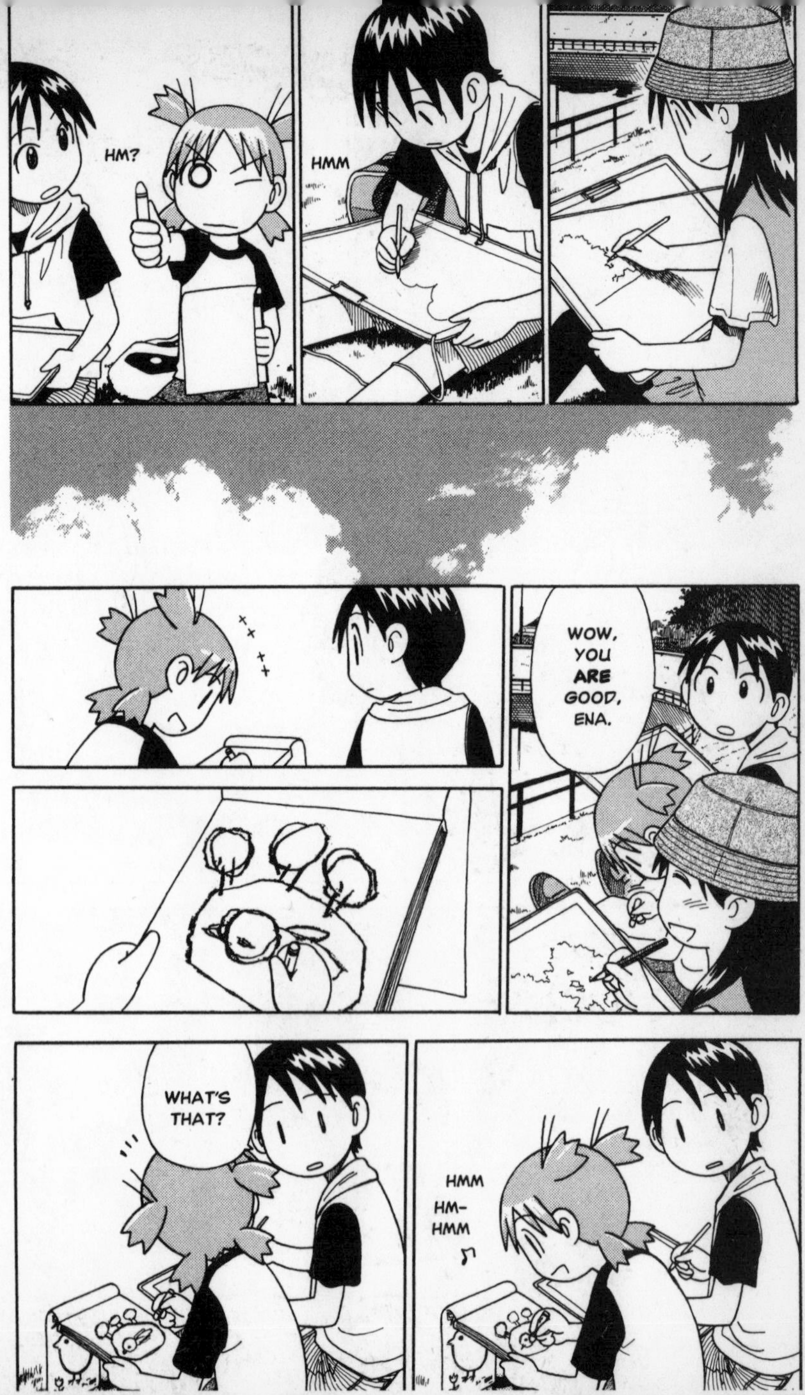
HM?
HMM
WOW, YOU ARE GOOD, ENA.
WHAT'S THAT?
HMM HM-HMM

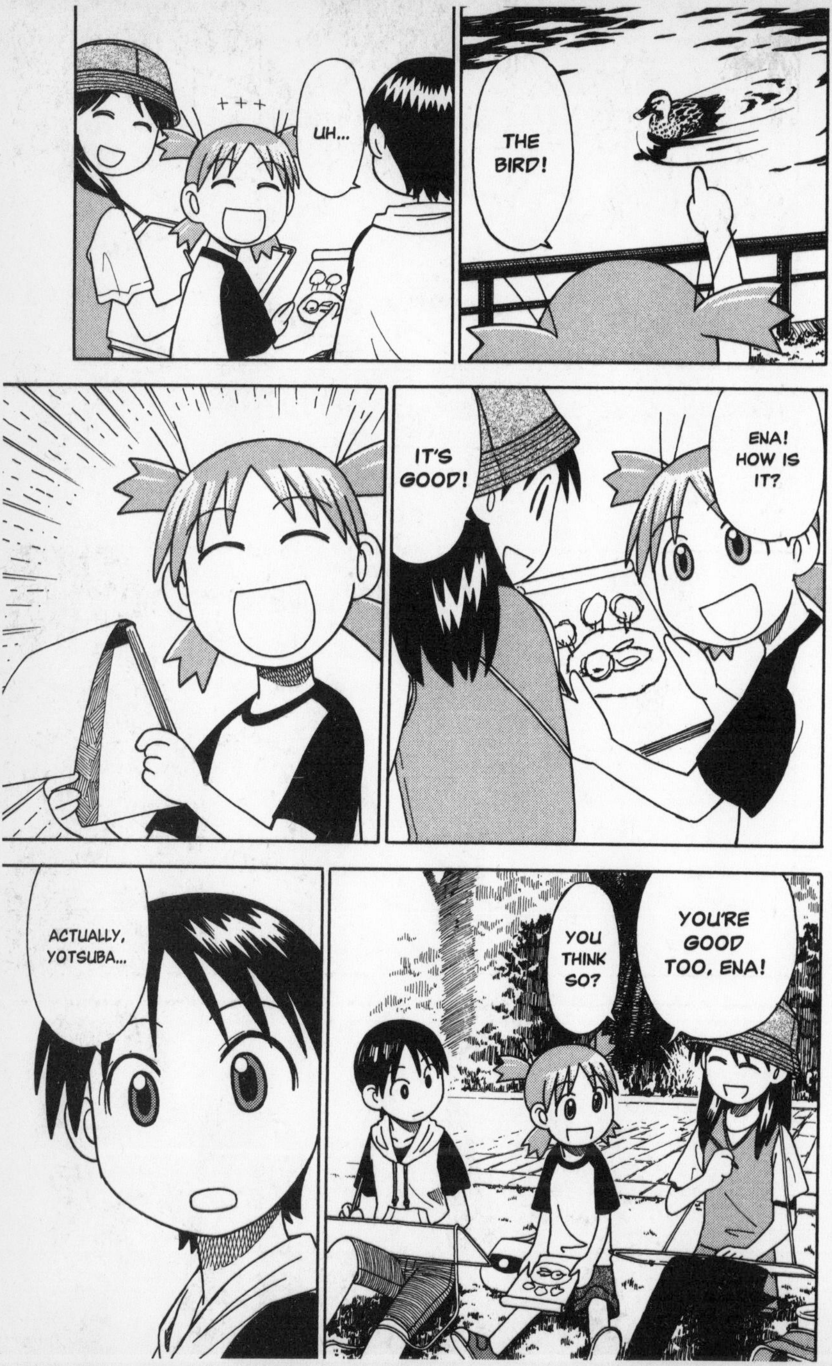
THE BIRD!
UH...
ENA! HOW IS IT?
IT'S GOOD!
YOU'RE GOOD TOO, ENA!
YOU THINK SO?
ACTUALLY, YOTSUBA...

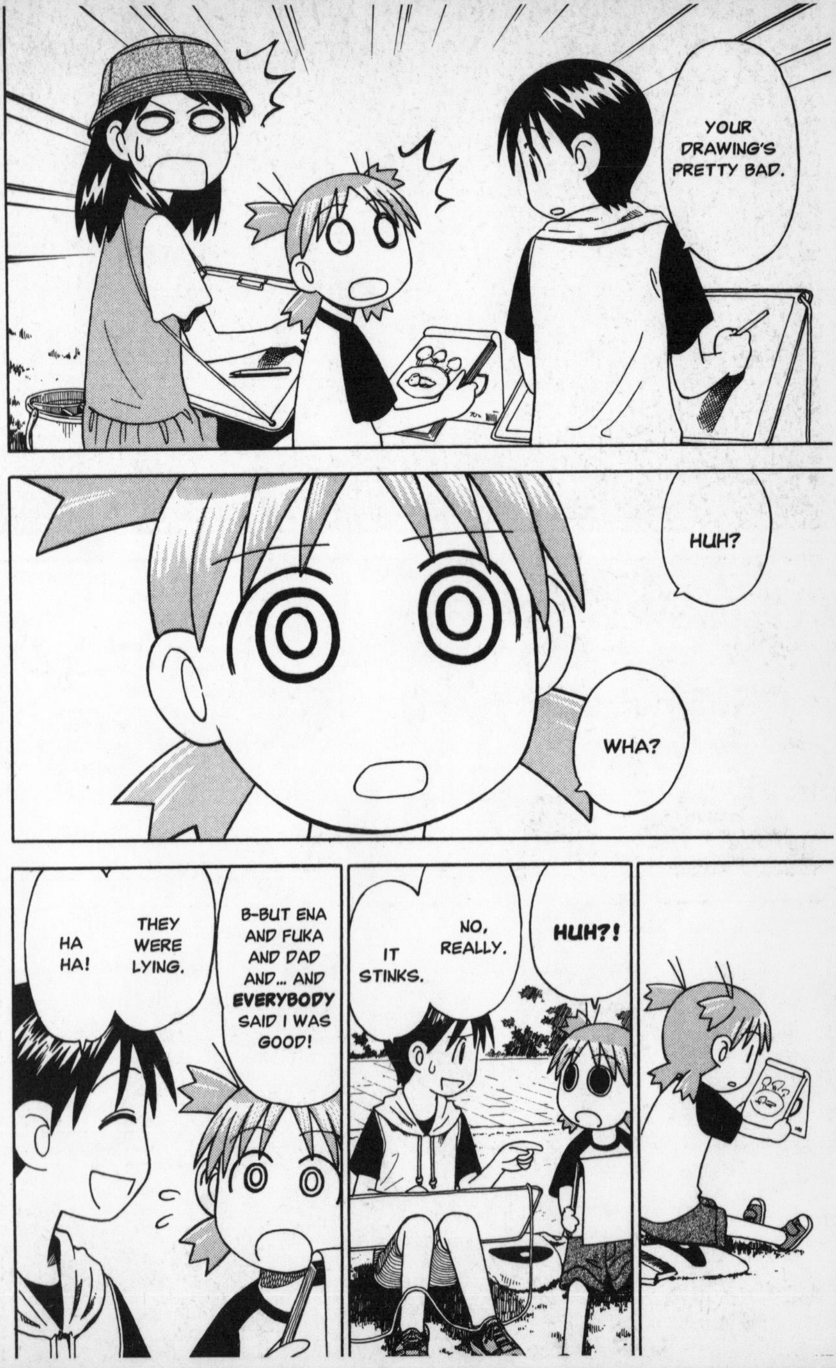
YOUR DRAWING'S PRETTY BAD.
HUH?
WHA?
HUH?!
NO, REALLY.
IT STINKS.
B-BUT ENA AND FUKA AND DAD AND... AND EVERYBODY SAID I WAS GOOD!
THEY WERE LYING.
HA HA!

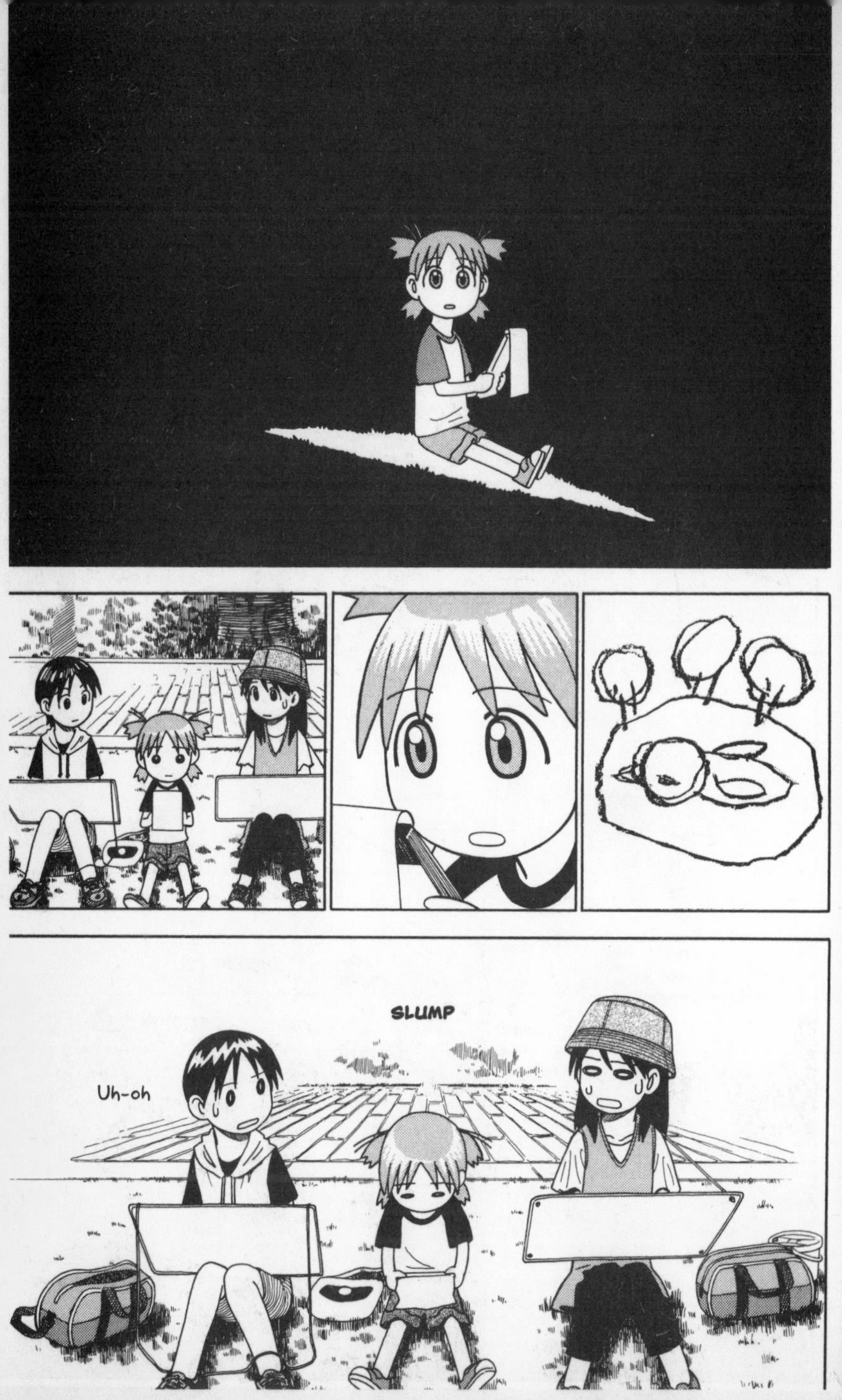
SLUMP
Uh-oh

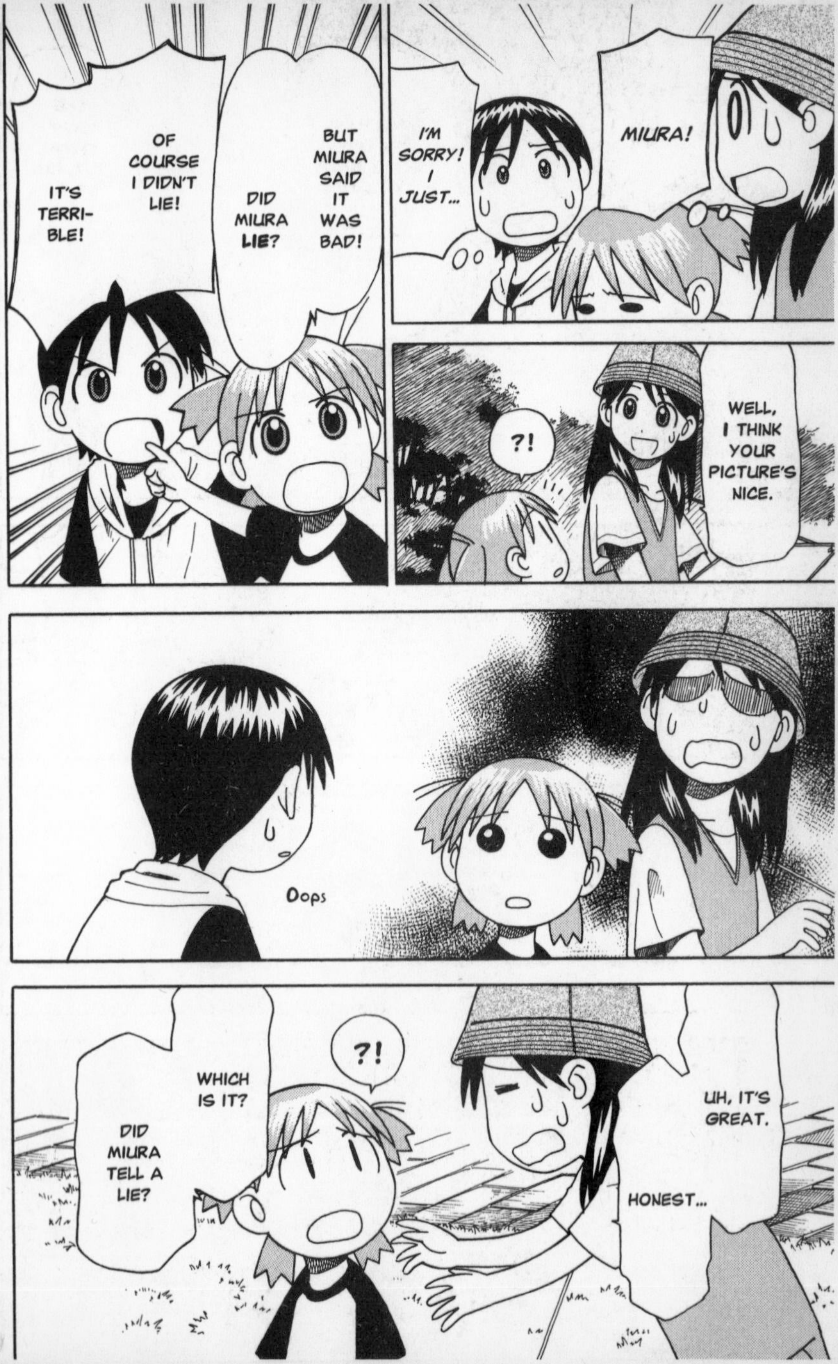
IT'S TERRIBLE!
OF COURSE I DIDN'T LIE!
DID MIURA LIE?
BUT MIURA SAID IT WAS BAD!
I'M SORRY! I JUST...
MIURA!
?!
WELL, I THINK YOUR PICTURE'S NICE.
Oops
DID MIURA TELL A LIE?
WHICH IS IT?
?!
UH, IT'S GREAT.
HONEST...

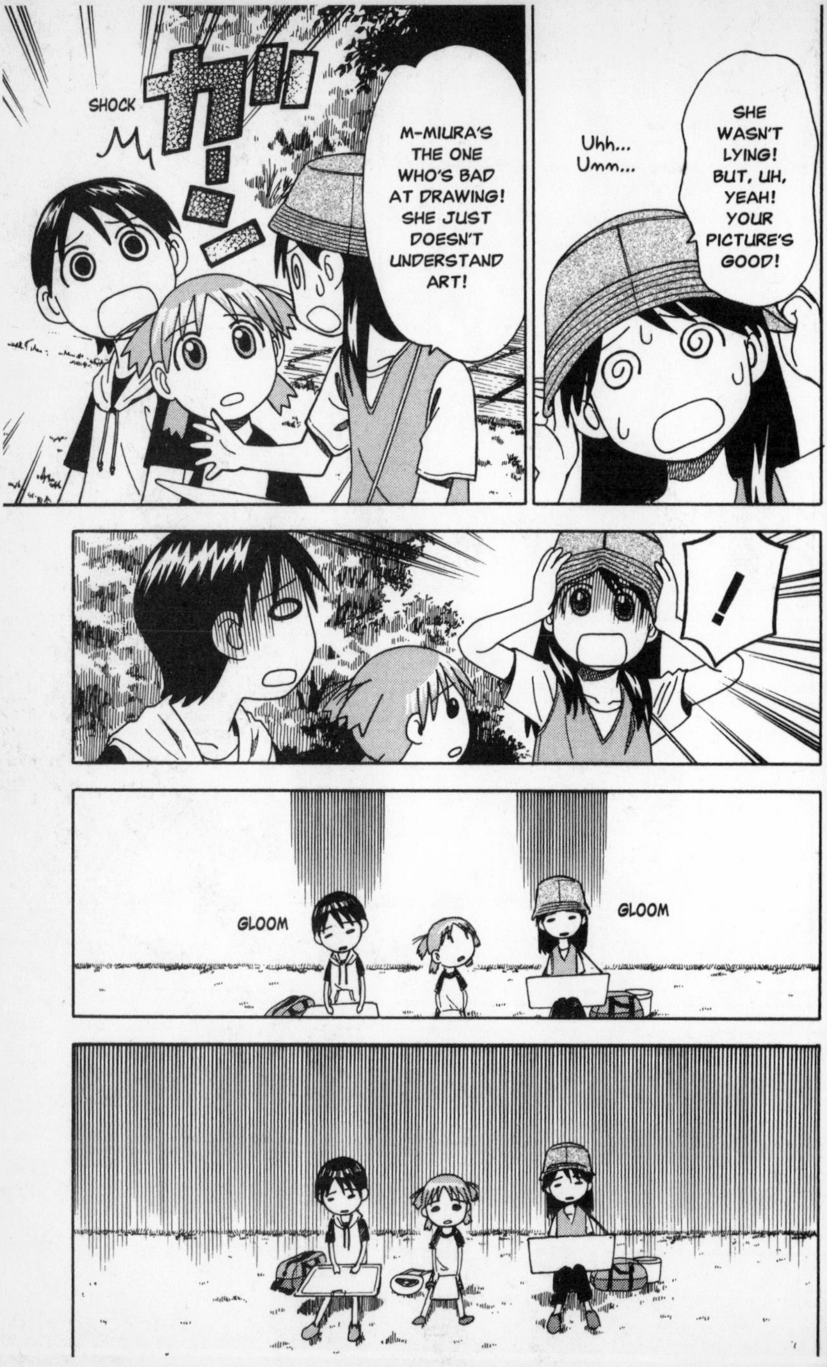
Uhh... Umm...
SHE WASN'T LYING! BUT, UH, YEAH! YOUR PICTURE'S GOOD!
SHOCK
M-MIURA'S THE ONE WHO'S BAD AT DRAWING! SHE JUST DOESN'T UNDERSTAND ART!
!
GLOOM
GLOOM

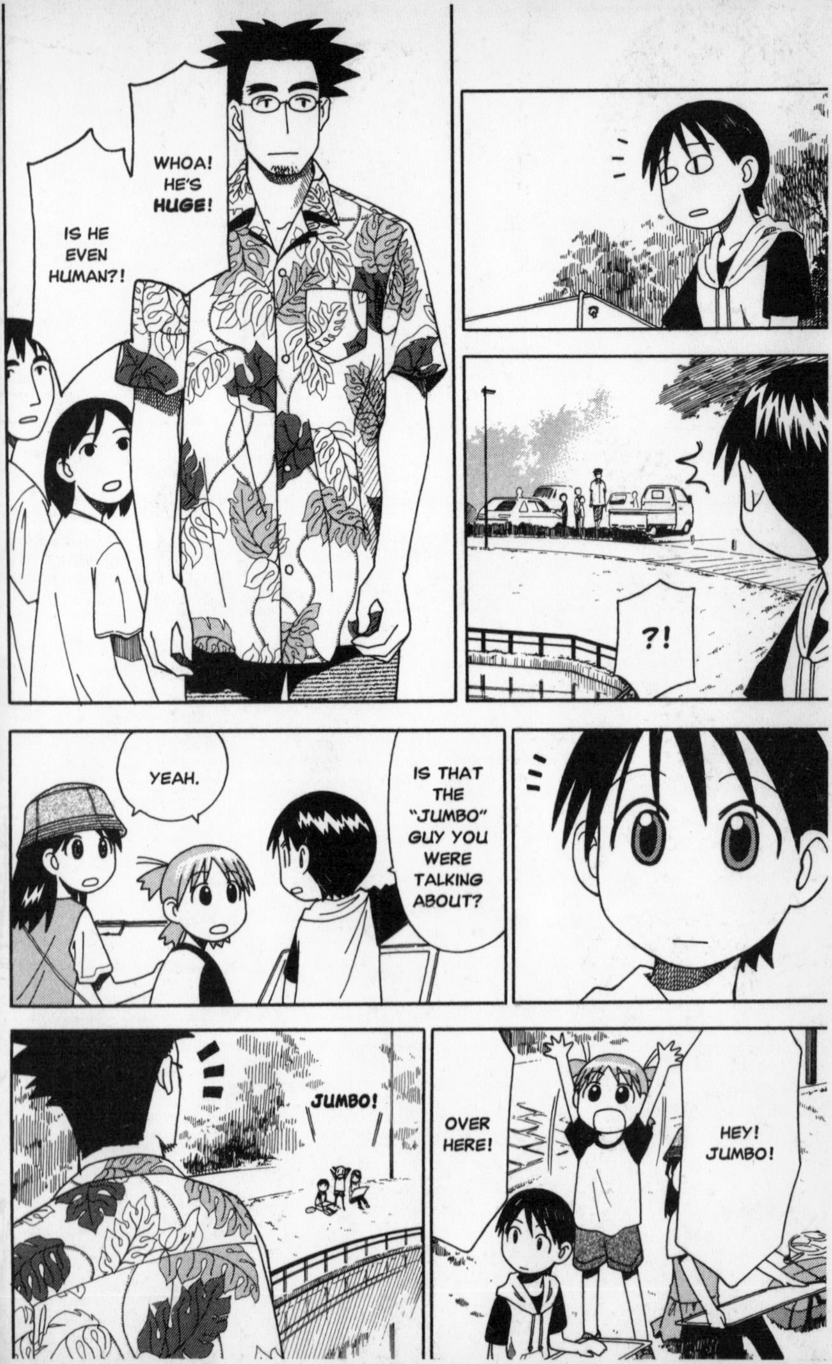

?!
WHOA! HE'S **HUGE**!
IS HE EVEN HUMAN?!
IS THAT THE "JUMBO" GUY YOU WERE TALKING ABOUT?
YEAH.
HEY! JUMBO!
OVER HERE!
JUMBO!

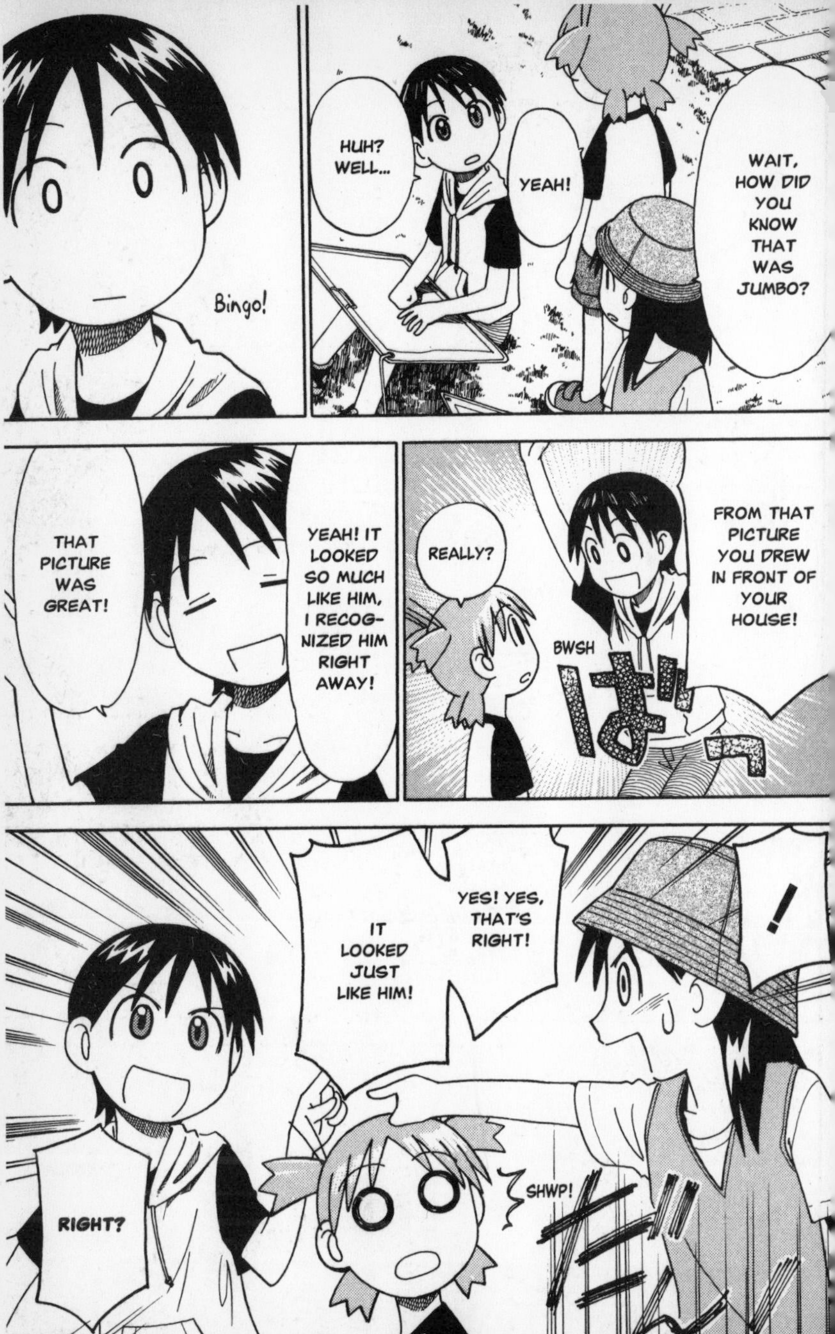
WAIT, HOW DID YOU KNOW THAT WAS JUMBO?
YEAH!
HUH? WELL...
Bingo!
FROM THAT PICTURE YOU DREW IN FRONT OF YOUR HOUSE!
BWSH
ぱっ
REALLY?
YEAH! IT LOOKED SO MUCH LIKE HIM, I RECOG-NIZED HIM RIGHT AWAY!
THAT PICTURE WAS GREAT!
!
YES! YES, THAT'S RIGHT!
IT LOOKED JUST LIKE HIM!
SHWP!
RIGHT?
TWITCH

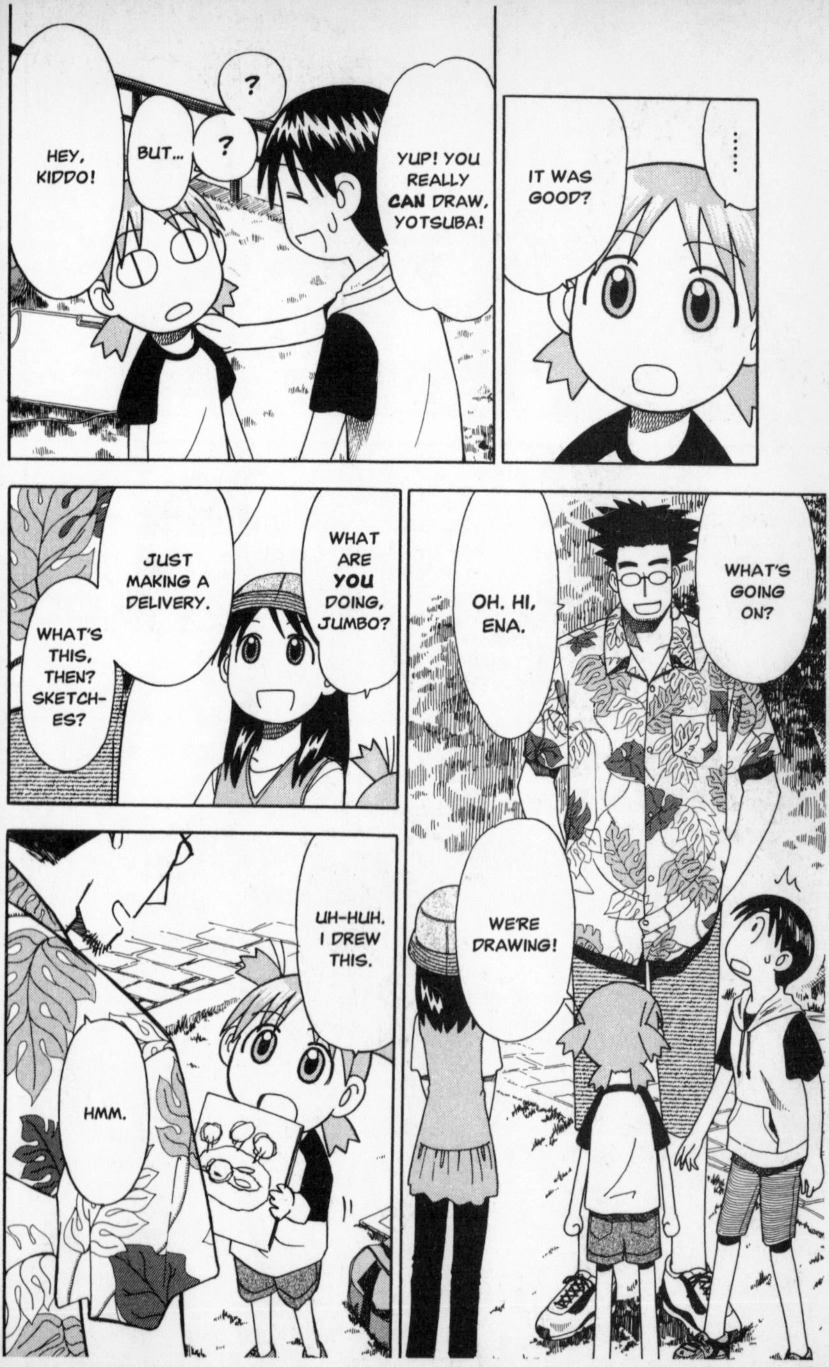
......
IT WAS GOOD?
YUP! YOU REALLY CAN DRAW, YOTSUBA!
?
?
BUT...
HEY, KIDDO!
WHAT'S GOING ON?
OH. HI, ENA.
WHAT ARE YOU DOING, JUMBO?
JUST MAKING A DELIVERY.
WE'RE DRAWING!
WHAT'S THIS, THEN? SKETCHES?
UH-HUH. I DREW THIS.
HMM.

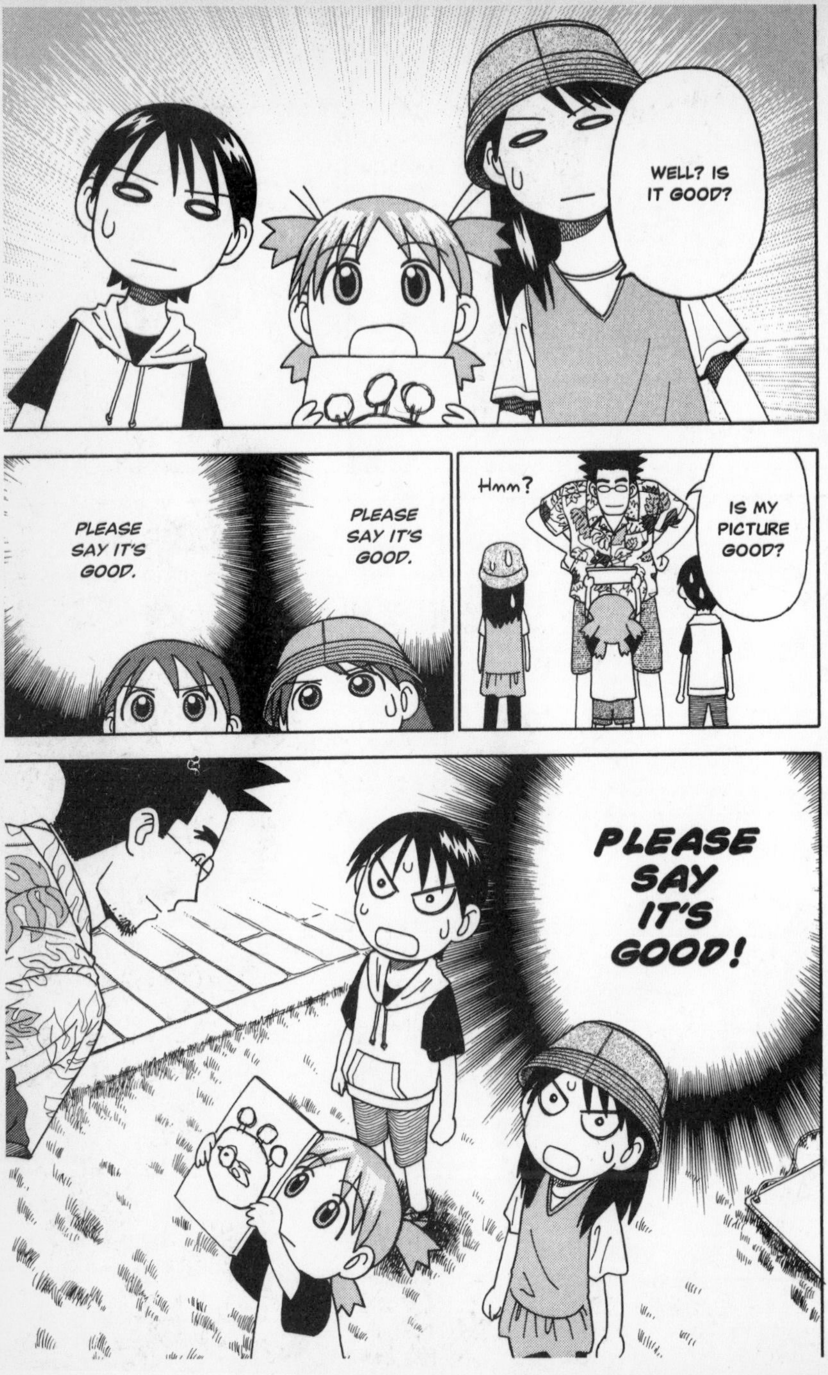

WELL? IS IT GOOD?
PLEASE SAY IT'S GOOD.
PLEASE SAY IT'S GOOD.
Hmm?
IS MY PICTURE GOOD?
PLEASE SAY IT'S GOOD!

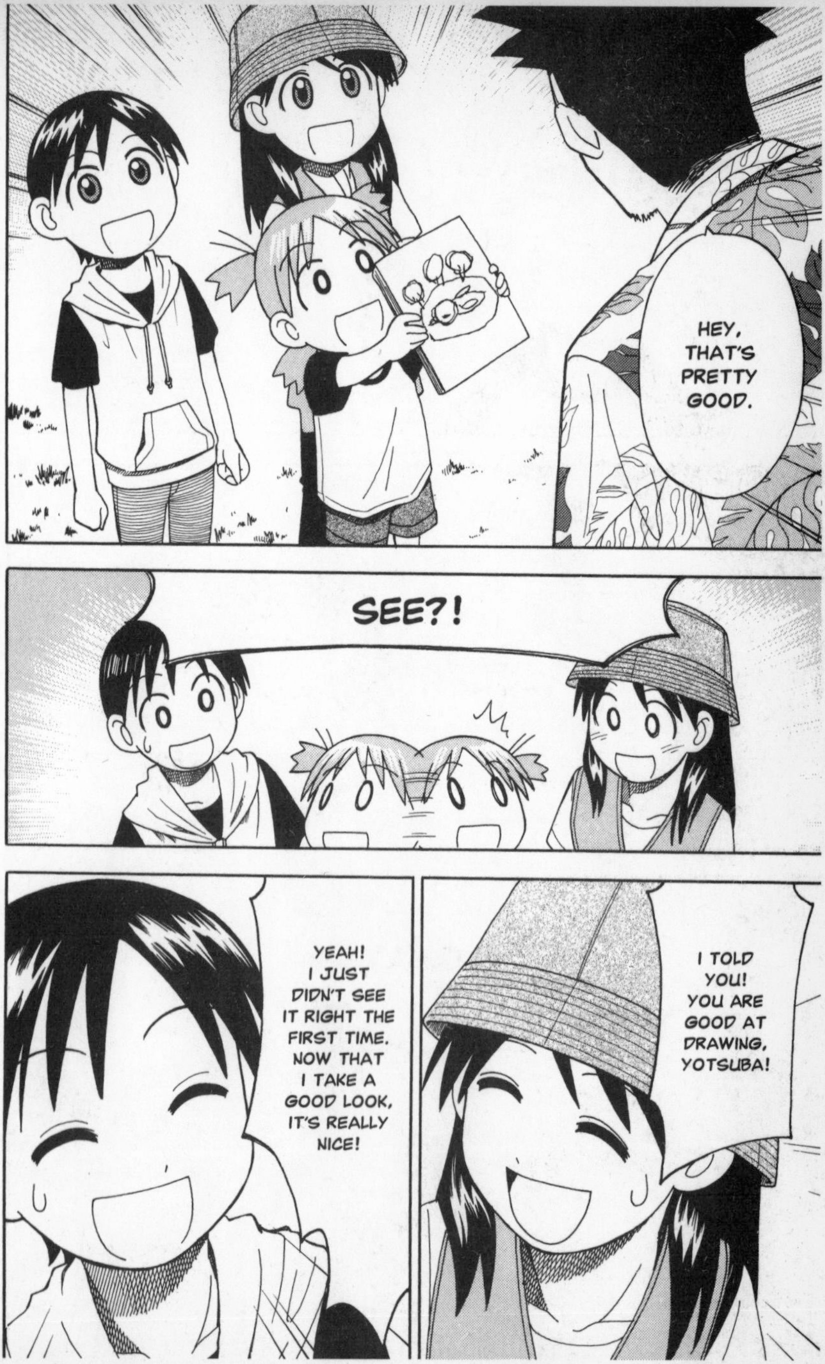
HEY, THAT'S PRETTY GOOD.
SEE?!
I TOLD YOU! YOU ARE GOOD AT DRAWING, YOTSUBA!
YEAH! I JUST DIDN'T SEE IT RIGHT THE FIRST TIME. NOW THAT I TAKE A GOOD LOOK, IT'S REALLY NICE!

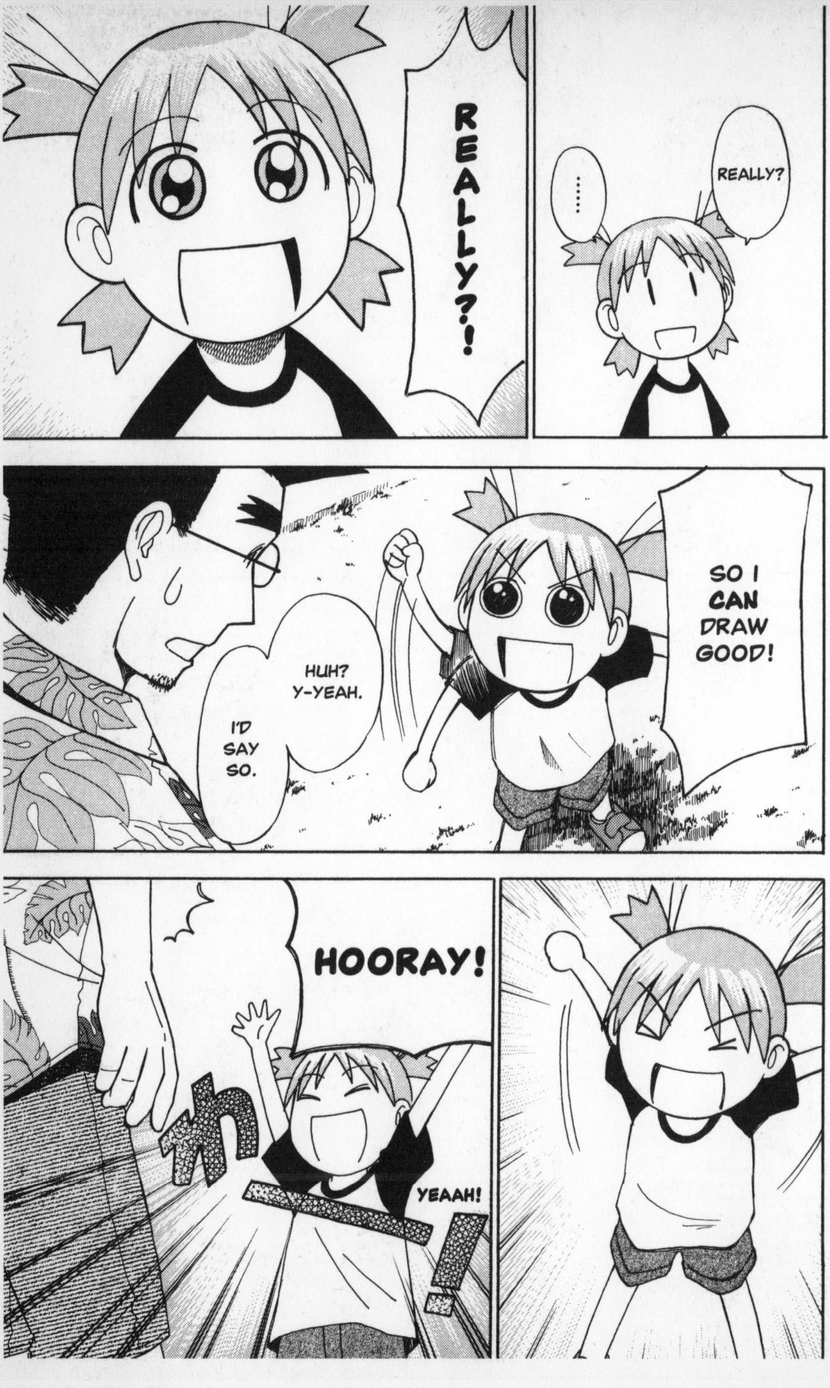

……
REALLY?
REALLY?!
SO I CAN DRAW GOOD!
HUH? Y-YEAH.
I'D SAY SO.
HOORAY!
YEAAH!

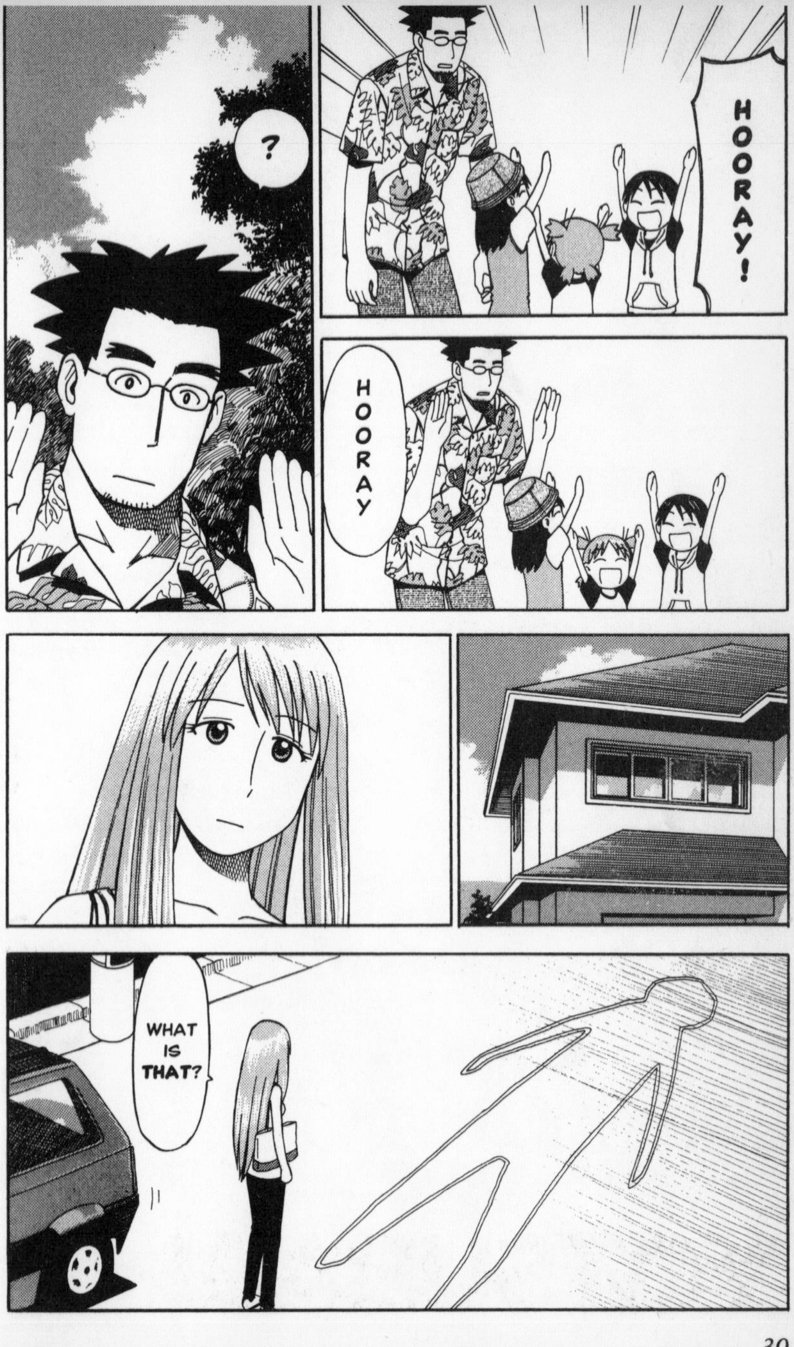
HOORAY!
HOORAY
?
WHAT IS THAT?

YOTSUBA&!

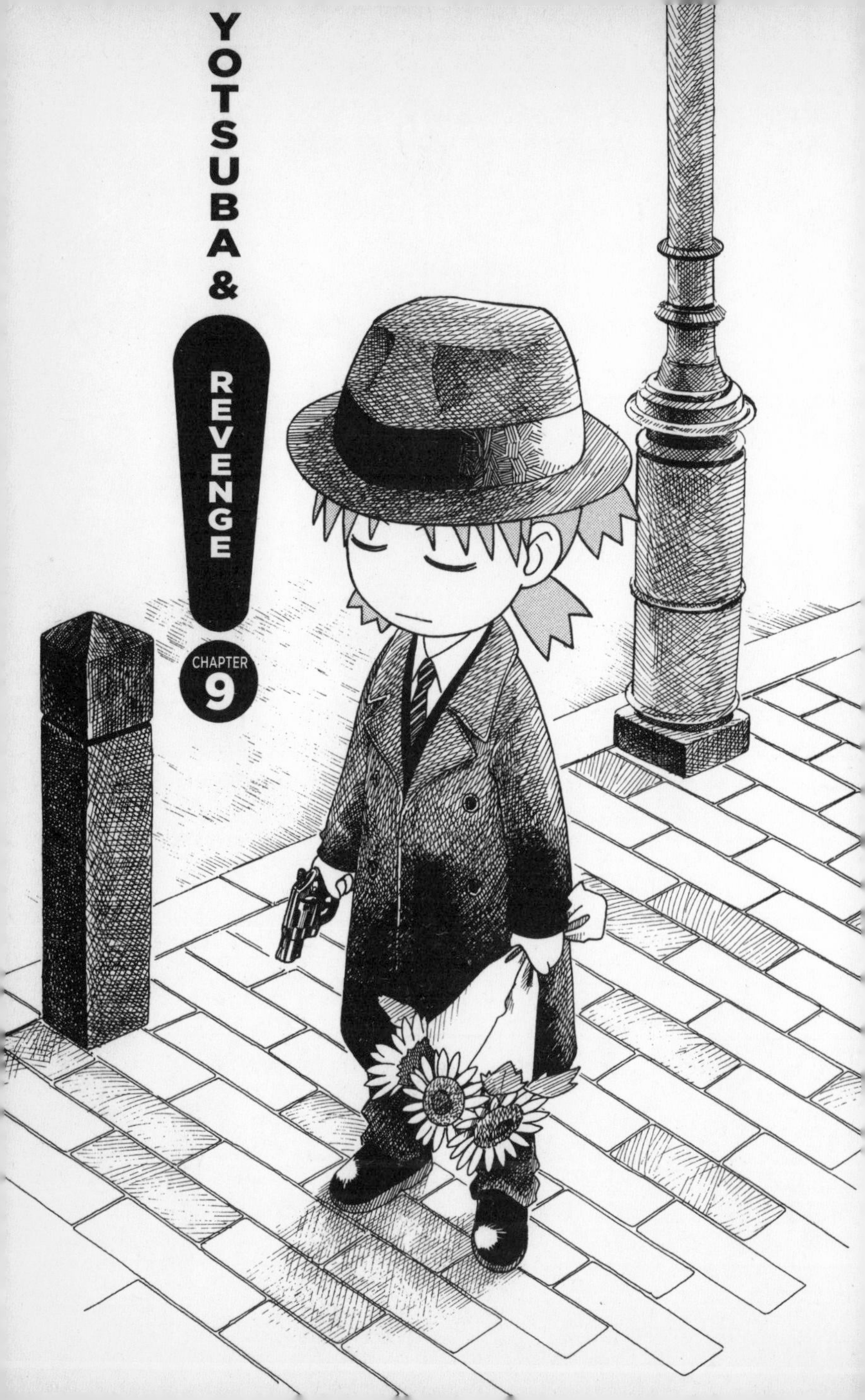
YOTSUBA &
REVENGE
CHAPTER 9

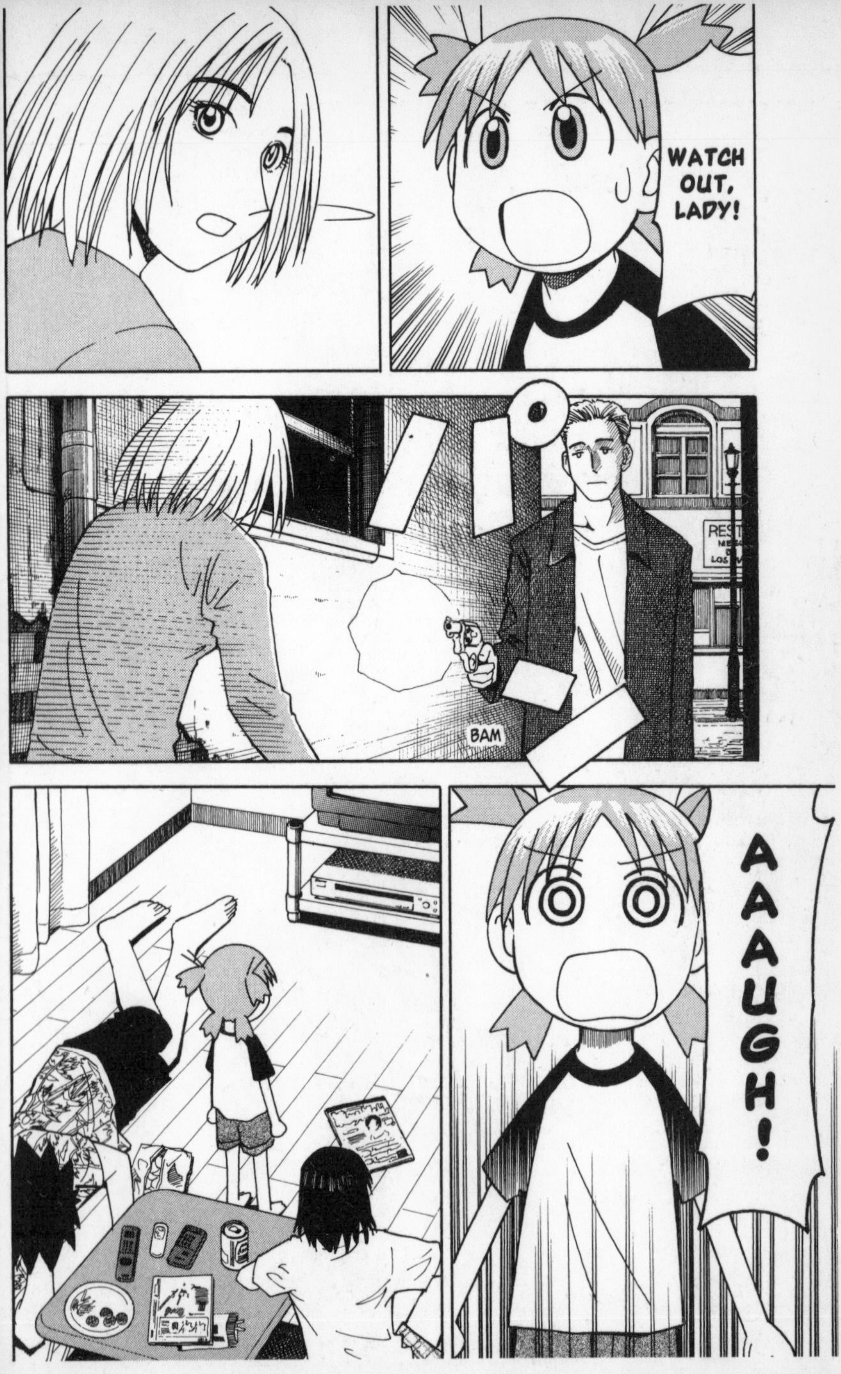
WATCH OUT, LADY!
BAM
AAAUGH!

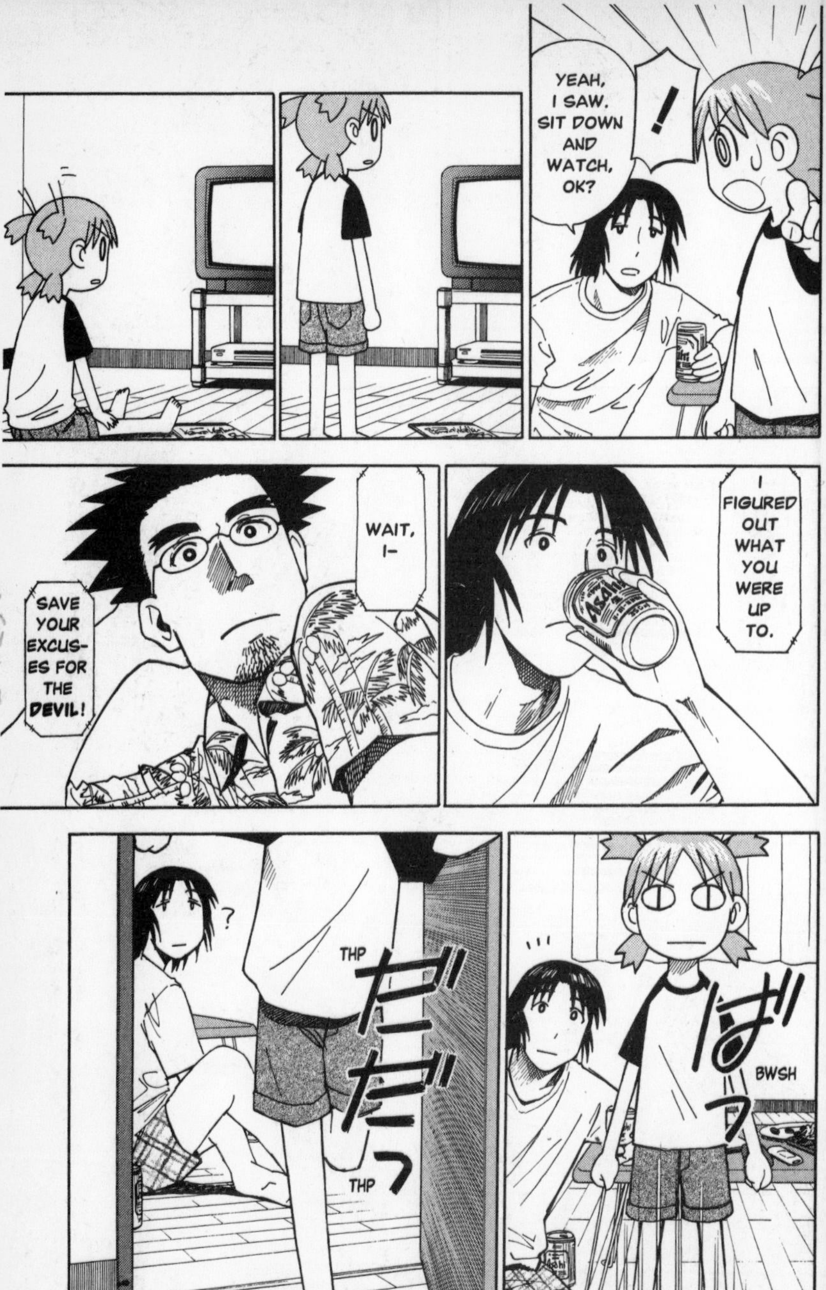
!
YEAH, I SAW. SIT DOWN AND WATCH, OK?
I FIGURED OUT WHAT YOU WERE UP TO.
WAIT, I-
SAVE YOUR EXCUSES FOR THE DEVIL!
BWSH
THP
THP

You can tell me in hell

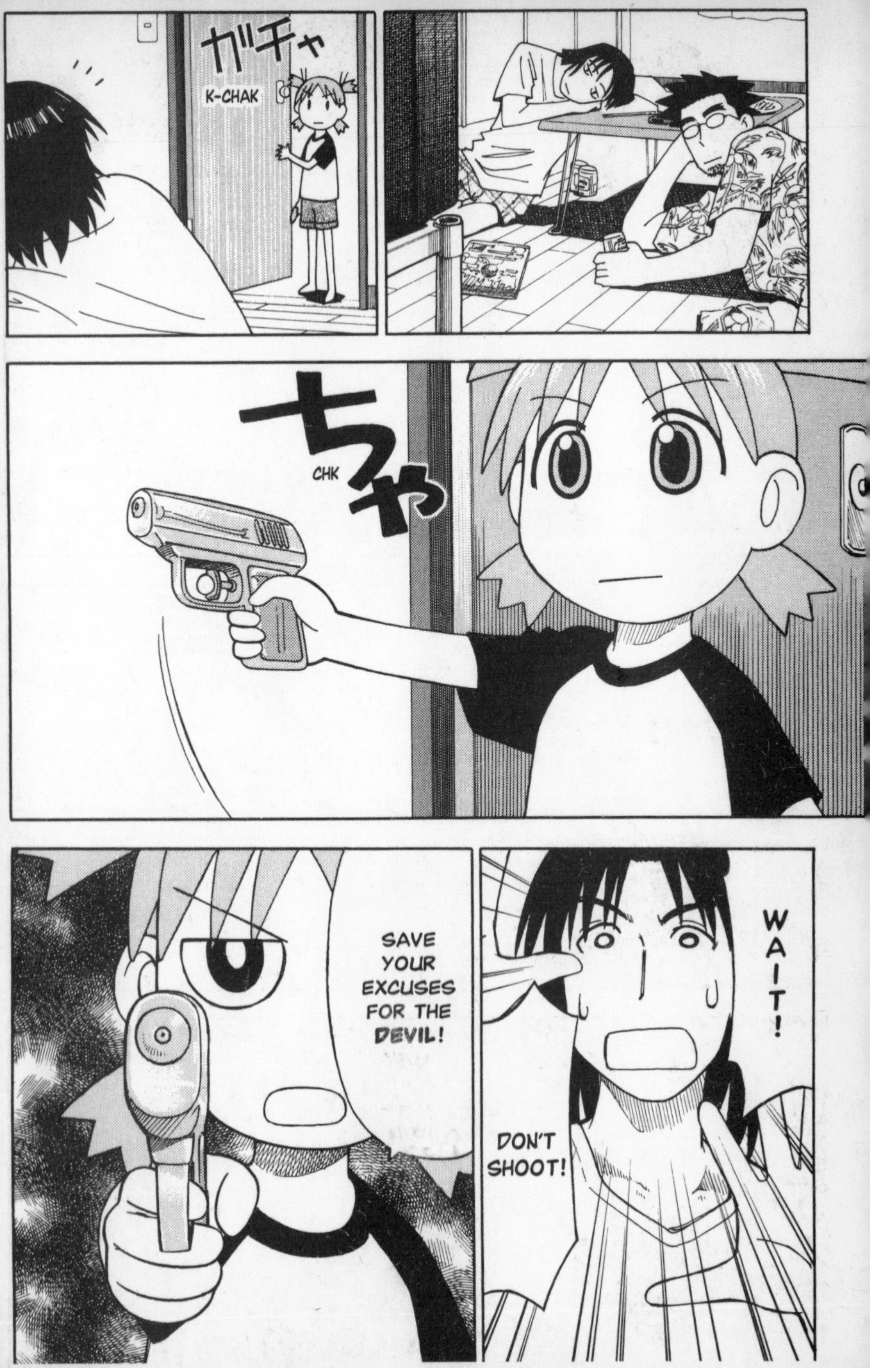

ガチャ
K-CHAK
ちゃ
CHK
WAIT!
DON'T SHOOT!
SAVE YOUR EXCUSES FOR THE DEVIL!

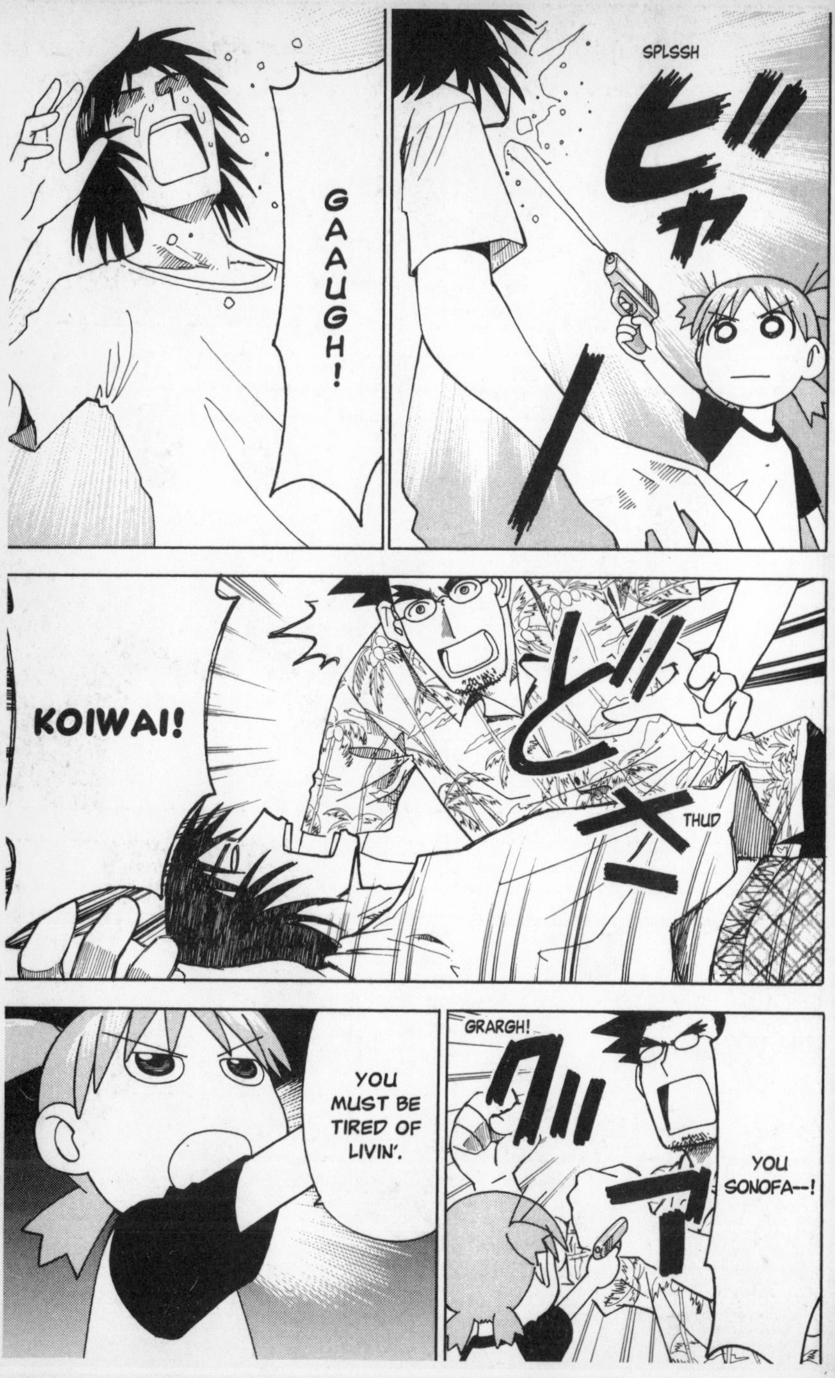
SPLSSH
GAAUGH!
KOIWAI!
THUD
GRARGH!
YOU SONOFA--!
YOU MUST BE TIRED OF LIVIN'.

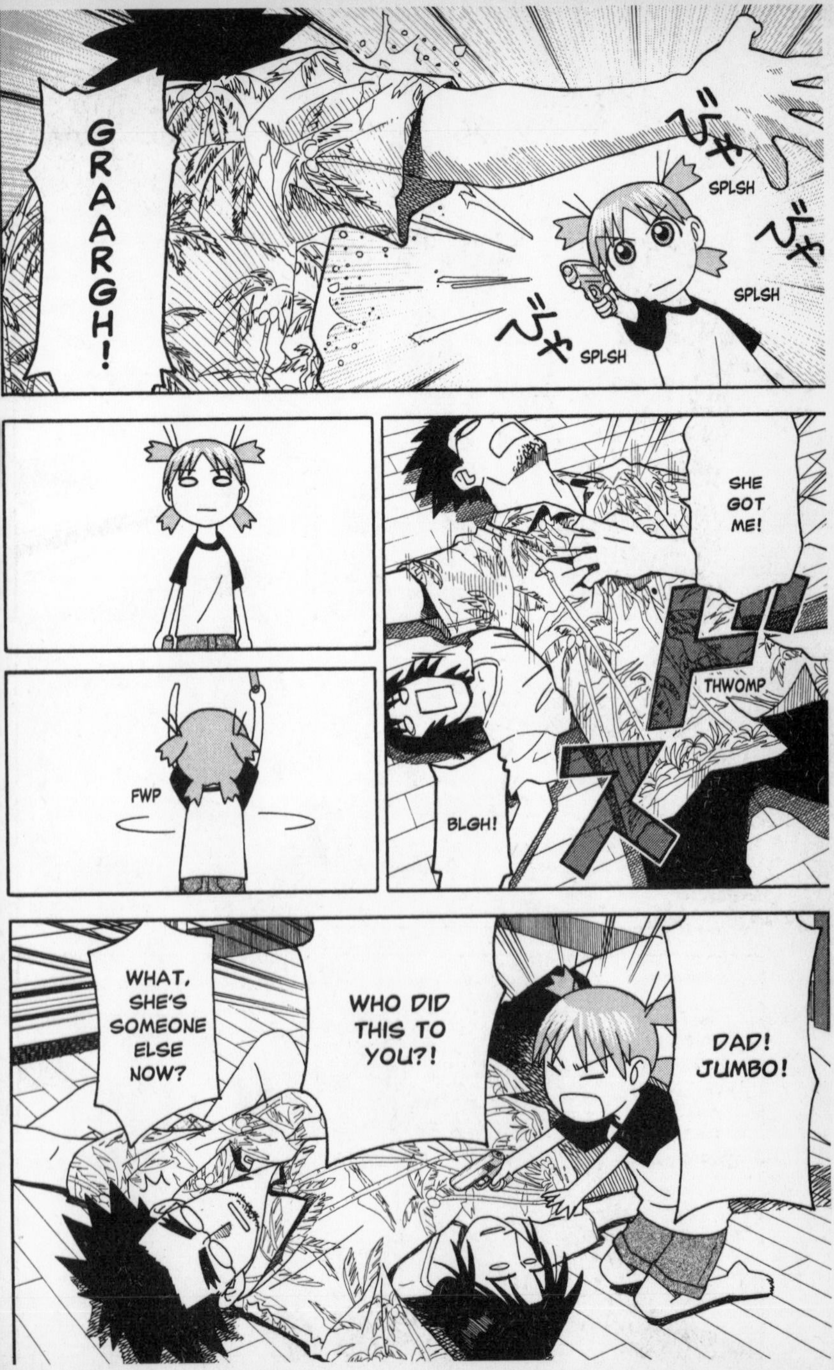

びゃ
SPLSH
びゃ
SPLSH
びゃ
SPLSH
GRAARGH!
SHE GOT ME!
THWOMP
BLGH!
FWP
DAD! JUMBO!
WHO DID THIS TO YOU?!
WHAT, SHE'S SOMEONE ELSE NOW?

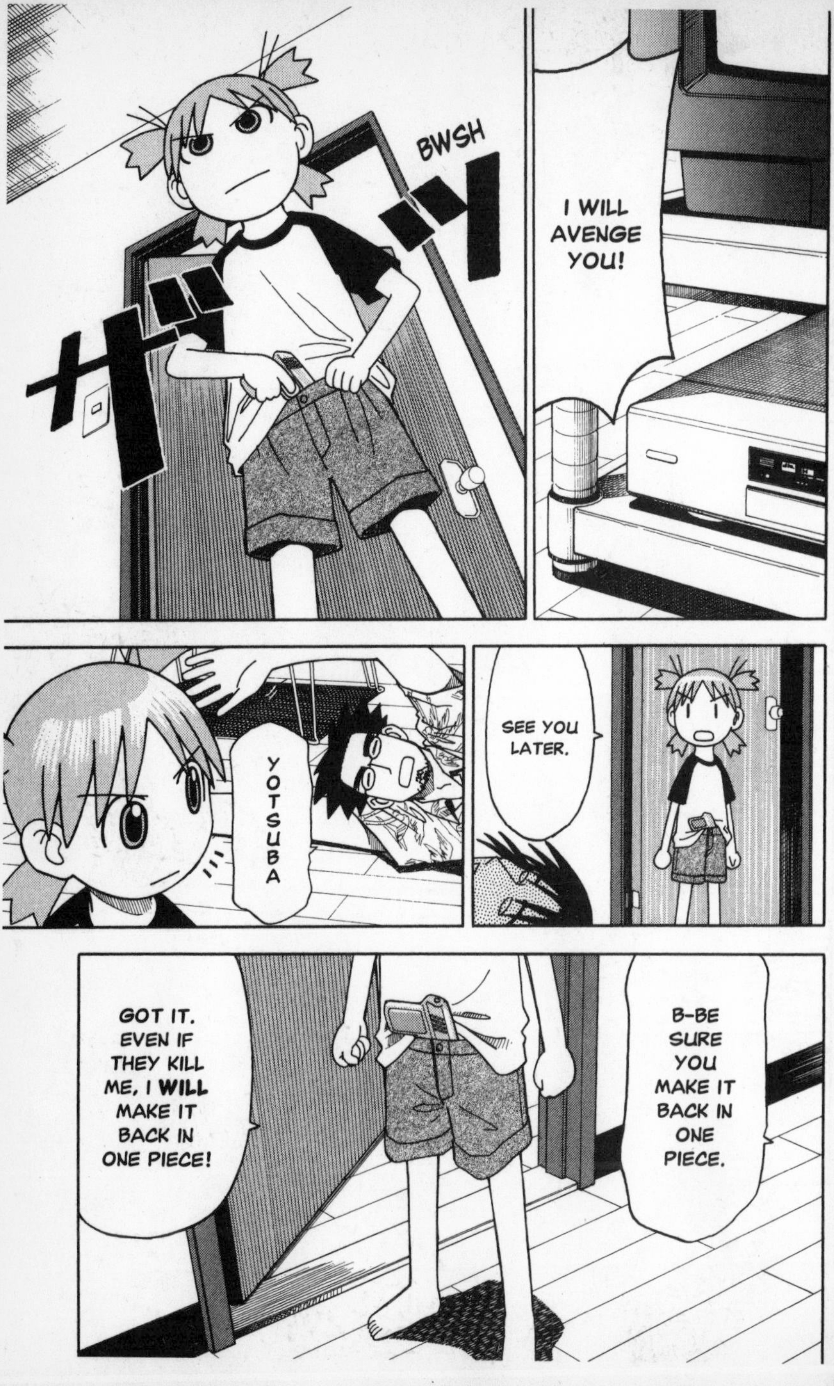
I WILL AVENGE YOU!
BWSH
SEE YOU LATER.
YOTSUBA
B-BE SURE YOU MAKE IT BACK IN ONE PIECE.
GOT IT. EVEN IF THEY KILL ME, I **WILL** MAKE IT BACK IN ONE PIECE!

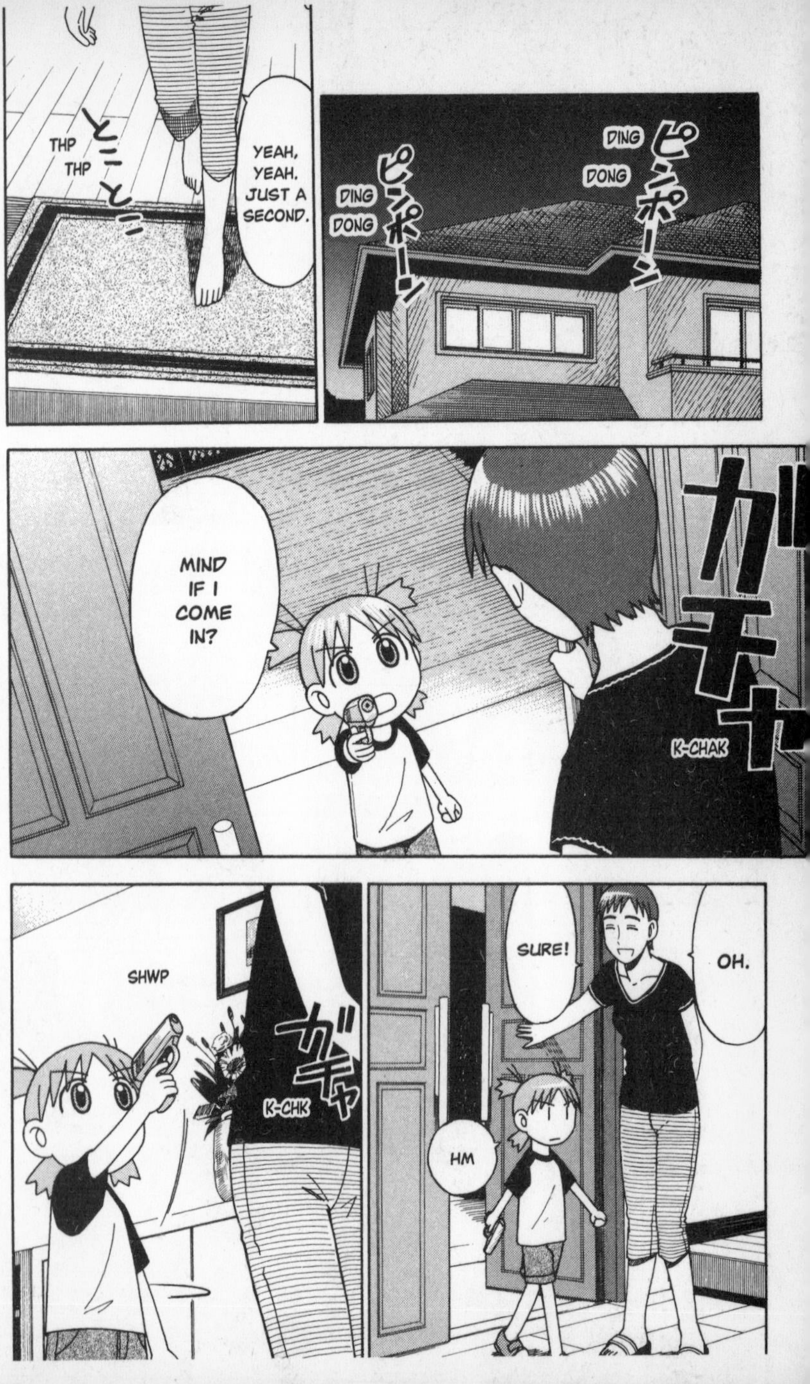

ピンポーン
DING DONG
ピンポーン
DING DONG
YEAH, YEAH. JUST A SECOND.
THP THP
ガチャ
K-CHAK
MIND IF I COME IN?
OH.
SURE!
HM
K-CHK
SHWP

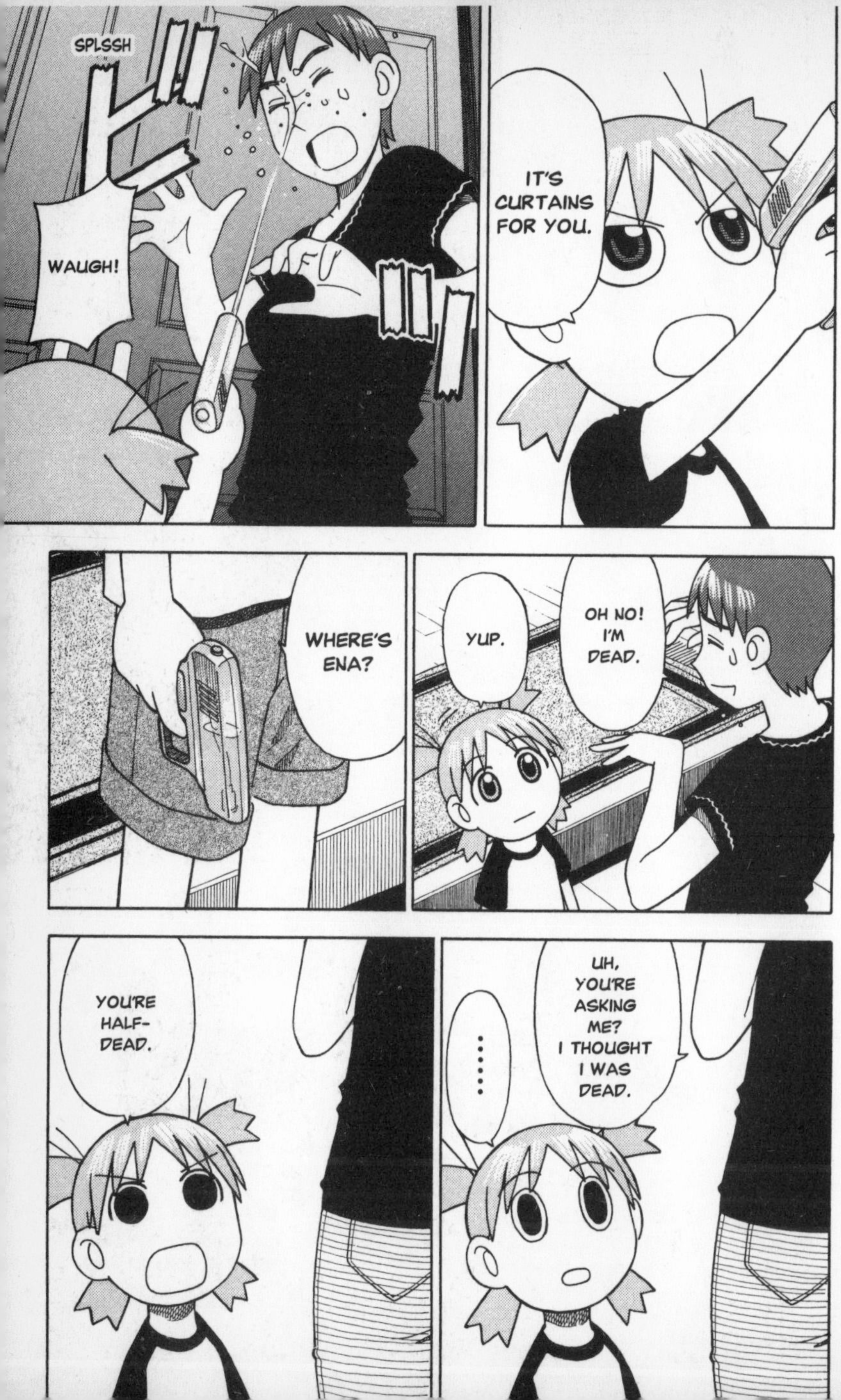
IT'S CURTAINS FOR YOU.
SPLSSH
WAUGH!
OH NO! I'M DEAD.
YUP.
WHERE'S ENA?
UH, YOU'RE ASKING ME? I THOUGHT I WAS DEAD.
......
YOU'RE HALF-DEAD.

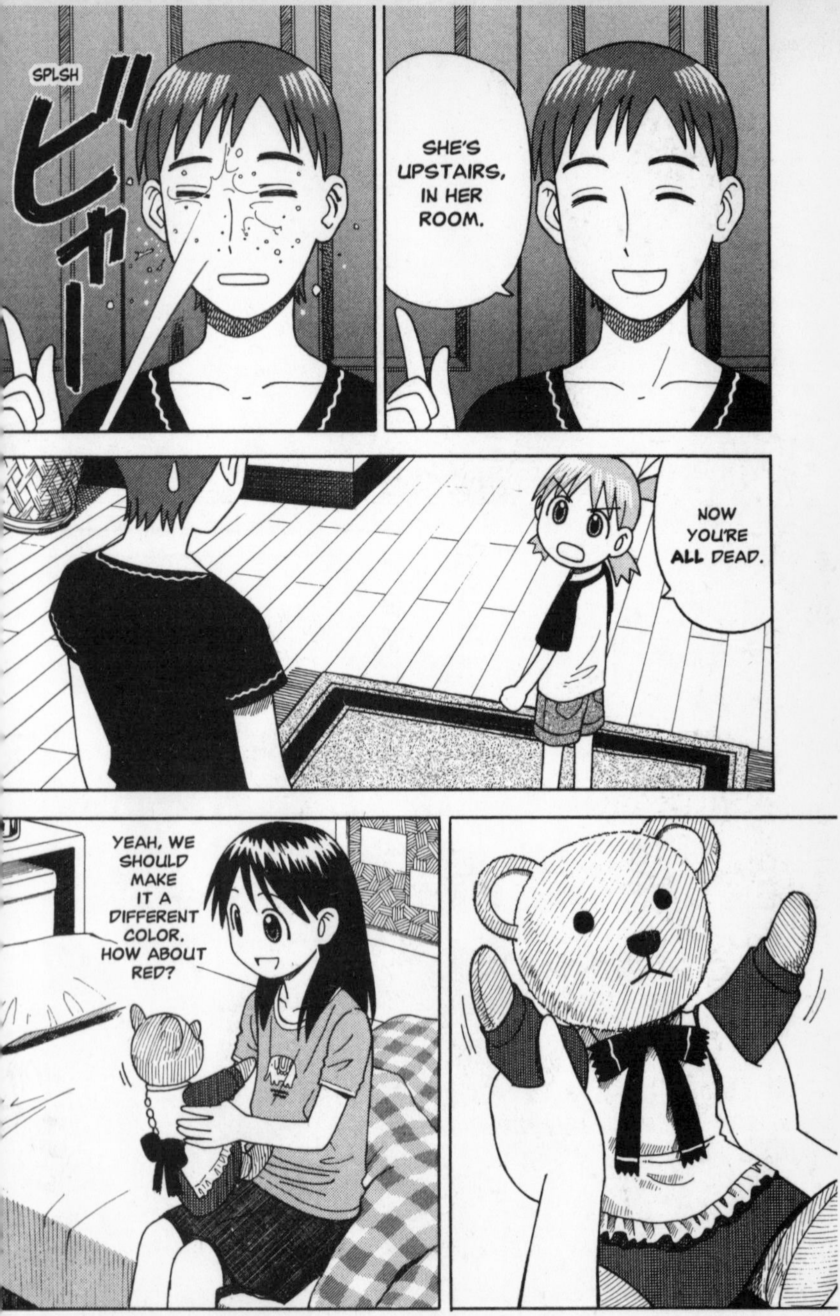
SHE'S UPSTAIRS, IN HER ROOM.
SPLSH
NOW YOU'RE ALL DEAD.
YEAH, WE SHOULD MAKE IT A DIFFERENT COLOR. HOW ABOUT RED?

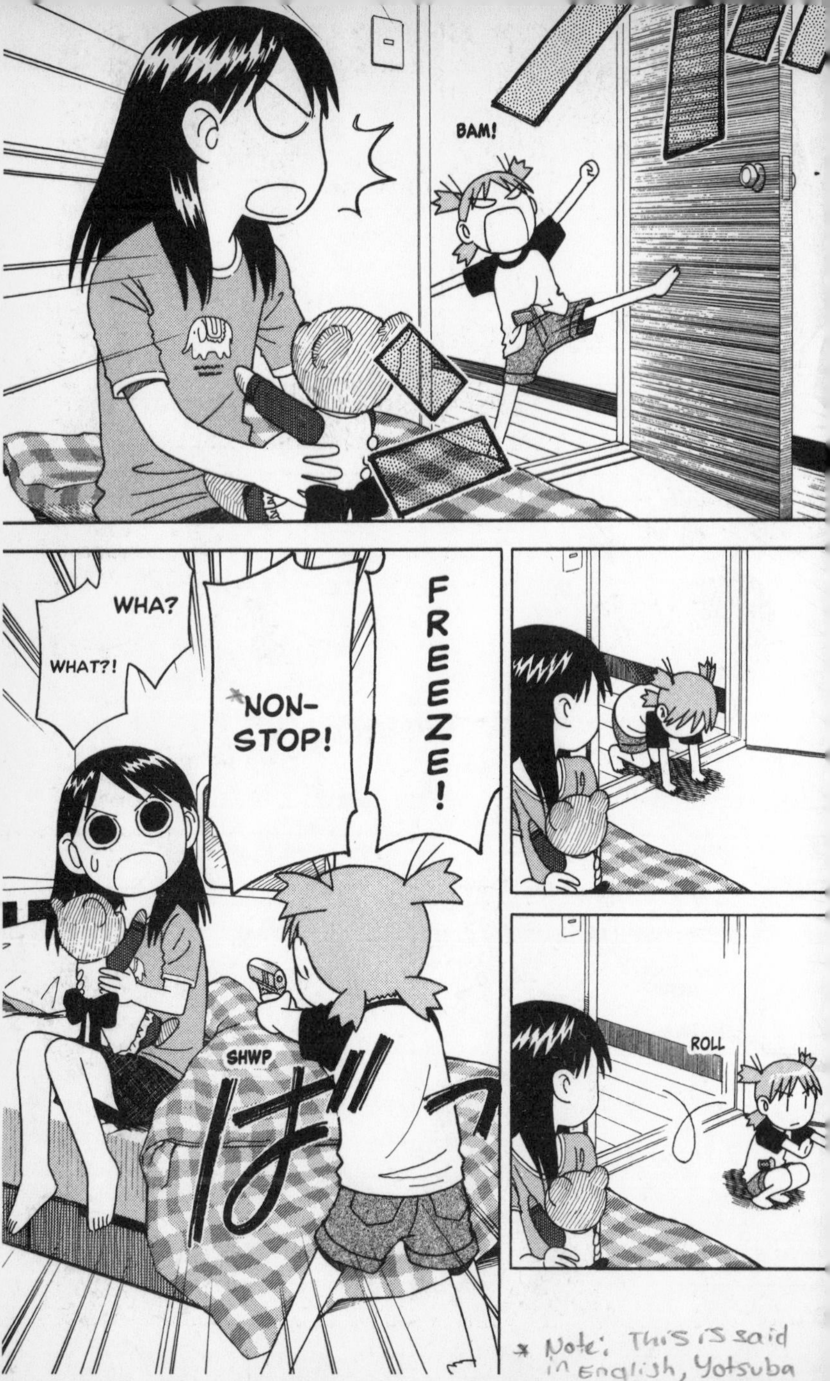
BAM!
ROLL
FREEZE!
*NON-STOP!
WHA?
WHAT?!
SHWP

* Note: This is said in English, Yotsuba obviously doesn't know what non-stop means.

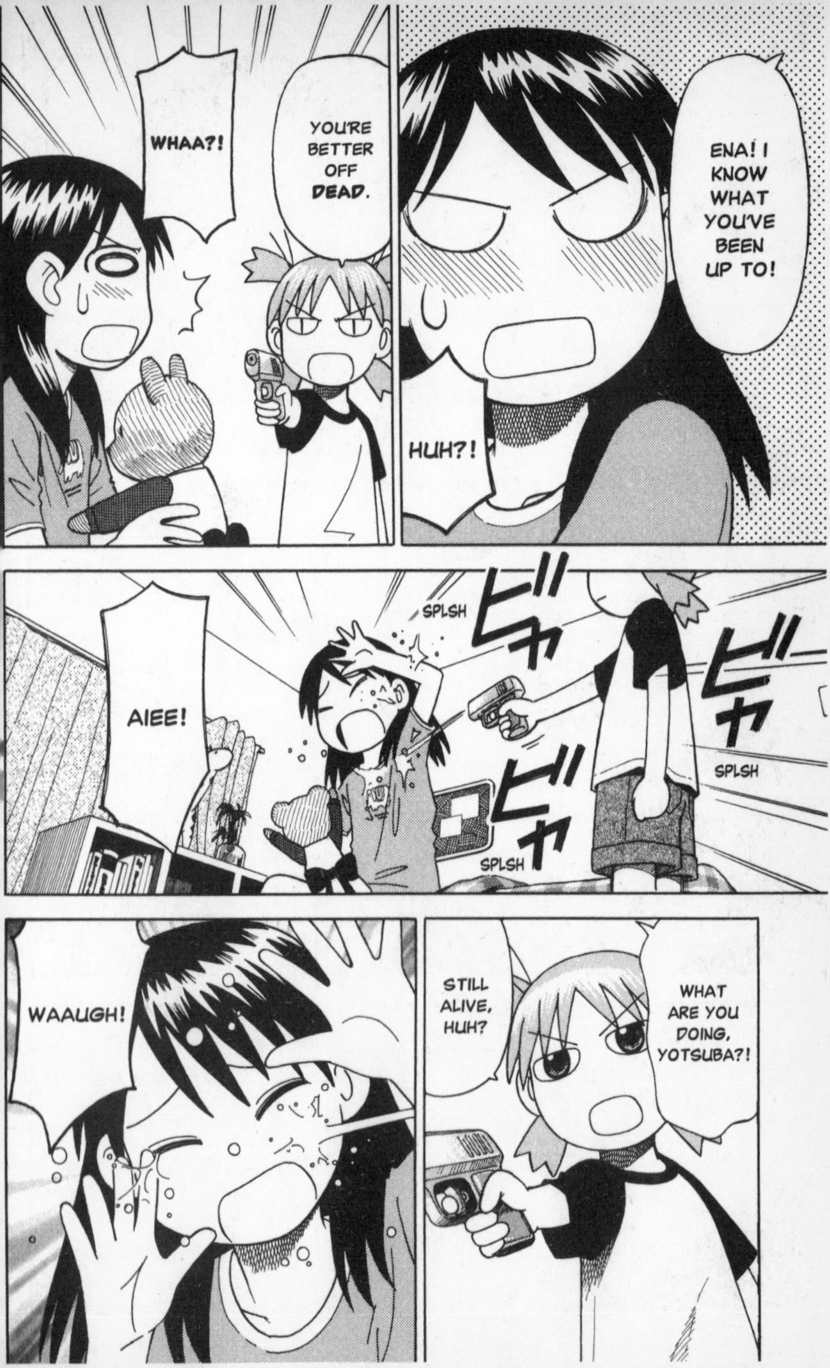
ENA! I KNOW WHAT YOU'VE BEEN UP TO!
HUH?!
YOU'RE BETTER OFF DEAD.
WHAA?!
ビシャ
SPLSH
ビシャ
SPLSH
ビシャ
SPLSH
AIEE!
WHAT ARE YOU DOING, YOTSUBA?!
STILL ALIVE, HUH?
WAAUGH!

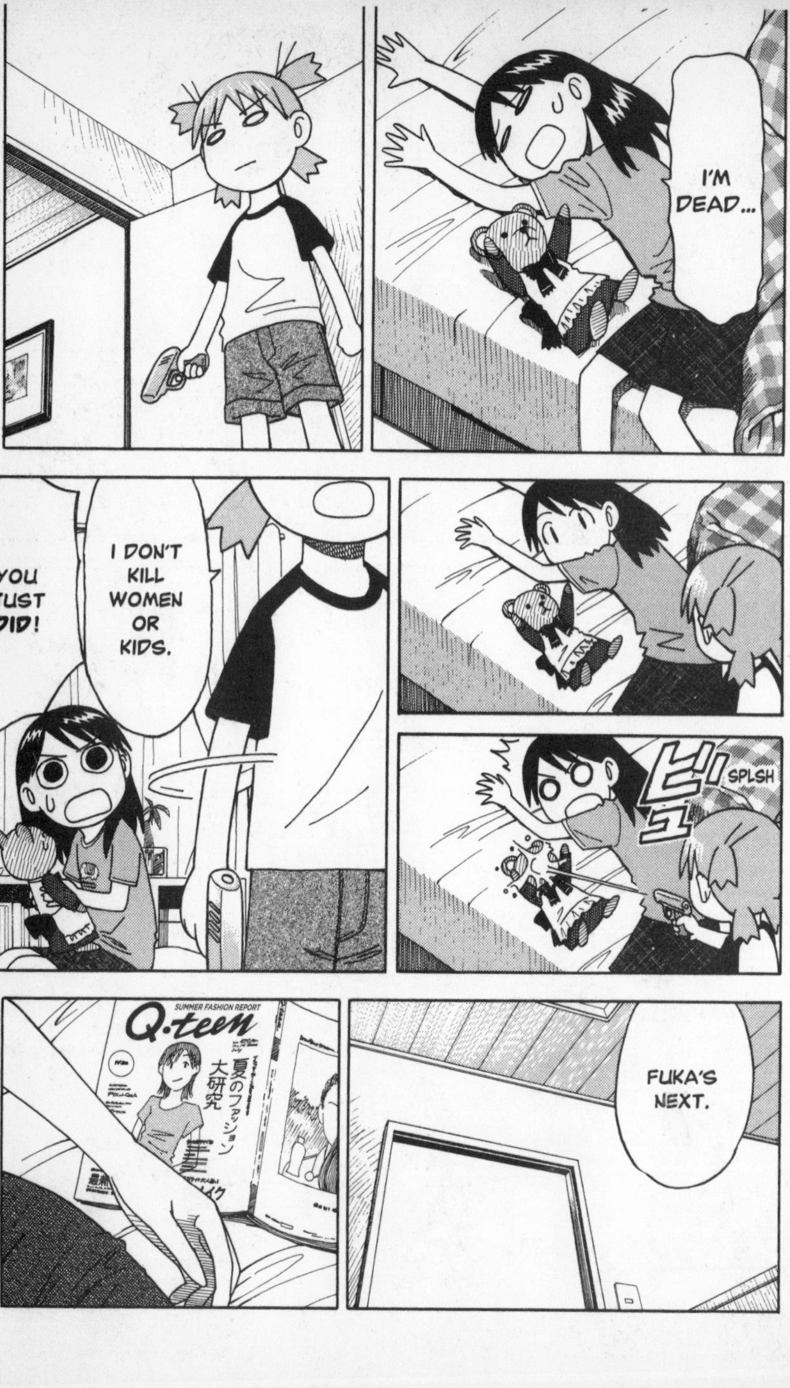
I'M DEAD...
ビュ
SPLSH
I DON'T KILL WOMEN OR KIDS.
YOU JUST DID!
FUKA'S NEXT.
SUMMER FASHION REPORT
Q-teen
夏のファッション大研究

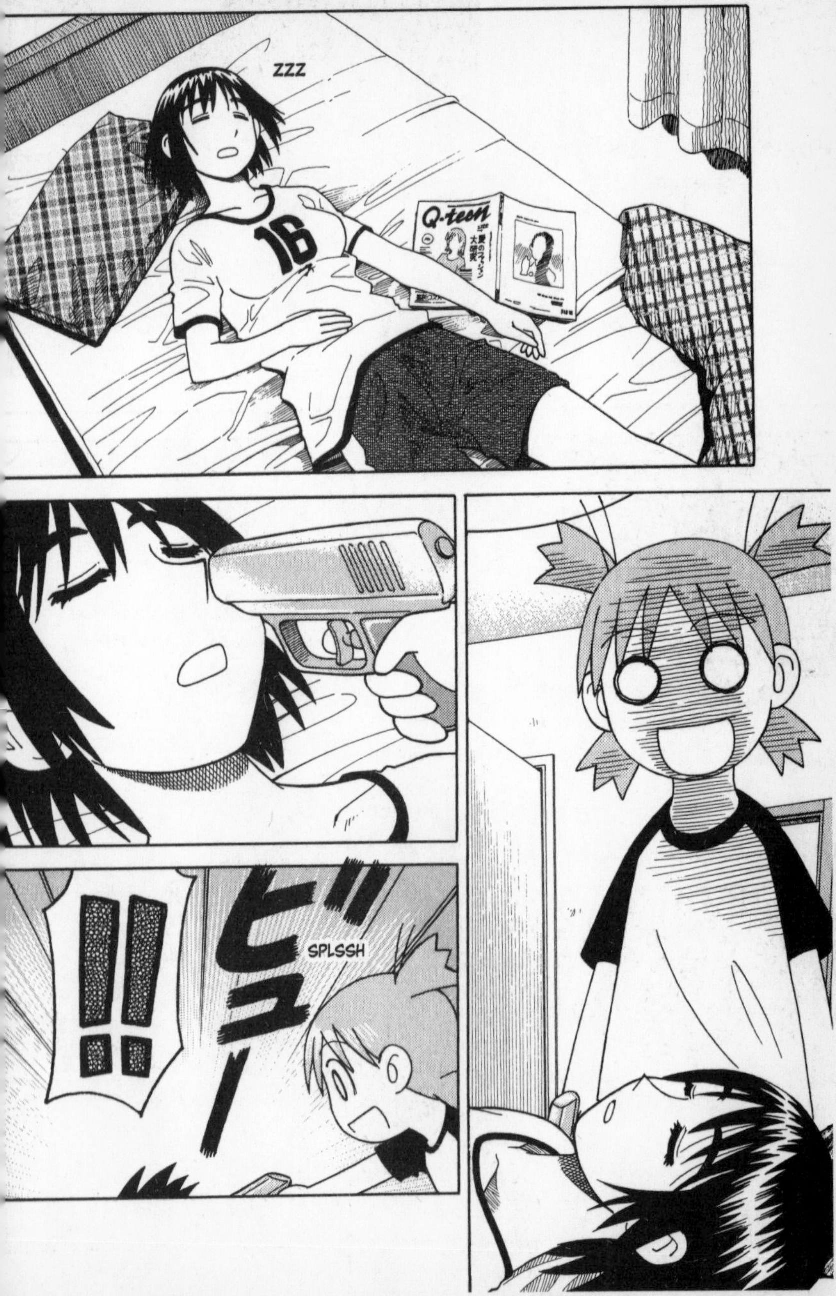
ZZZ
Q-teen
!!
ビュー
SPLSSH

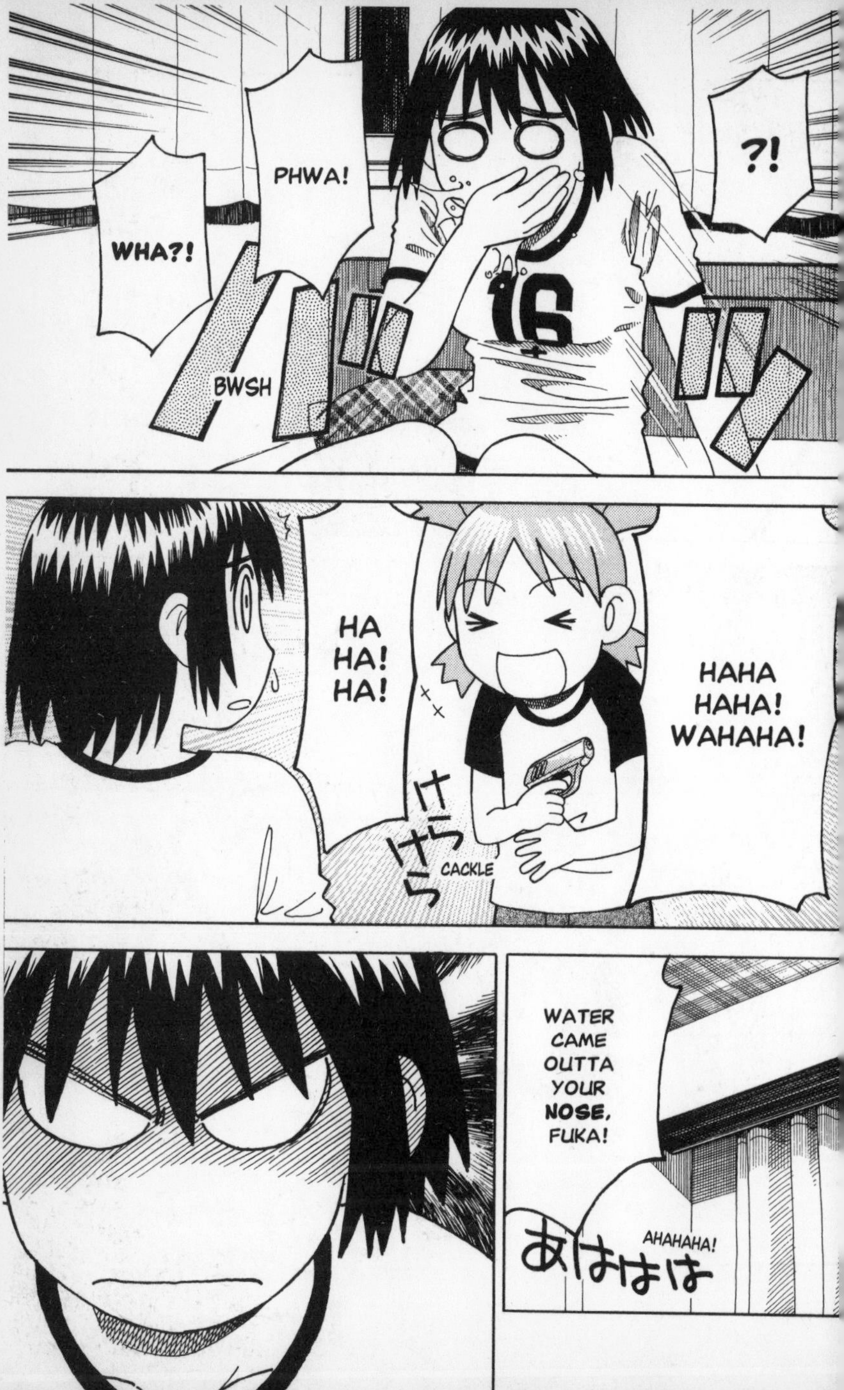
?!
PHWA!
WHA?!
BWSH
HAHA
HAHA!
WAHAHA!
HA
HA!
HA!
けらけら
CACKLE
WATER
CAME
OUTTA
YOUR
NOSE,
FUKA!
あははは
AHAHAHA!

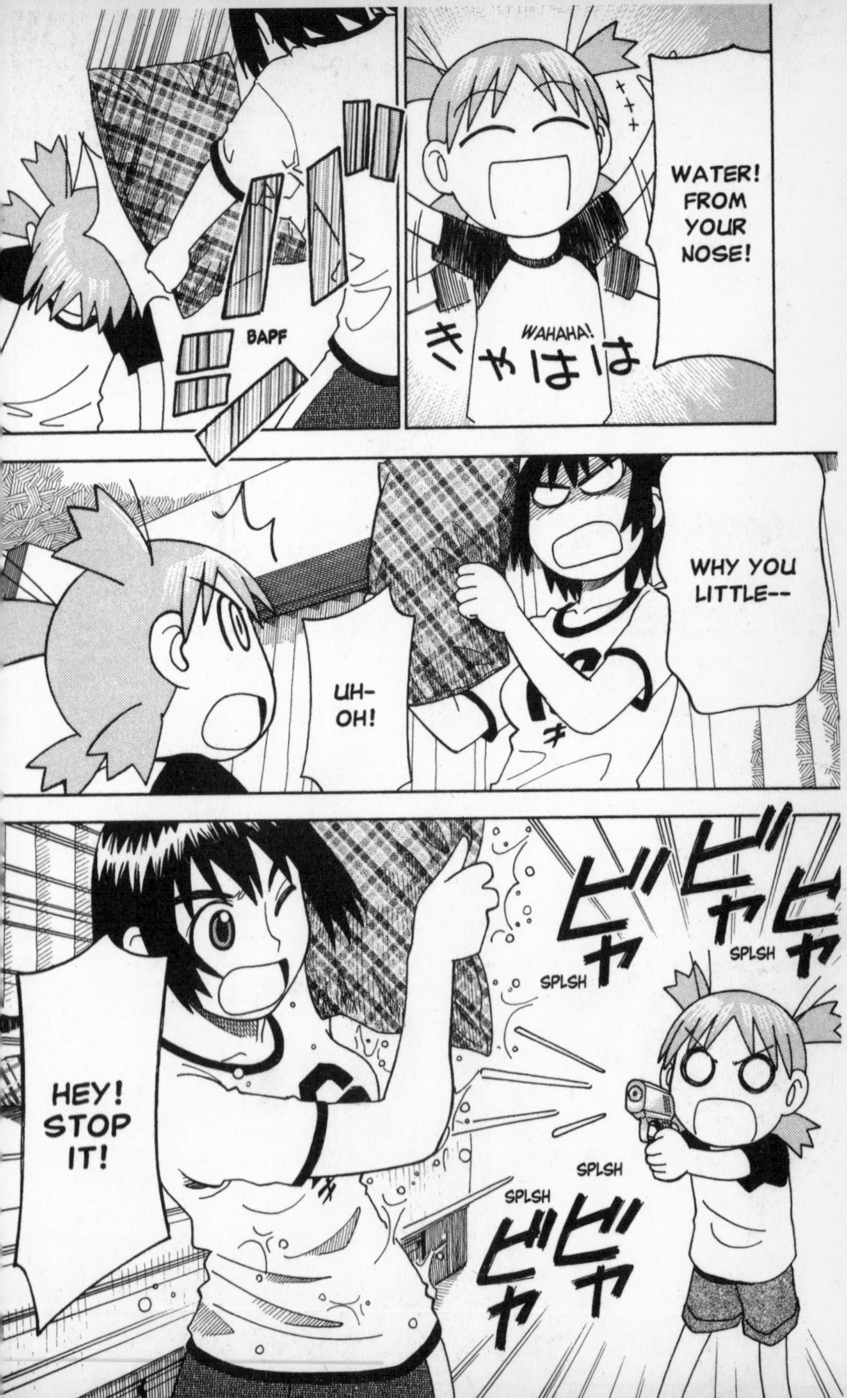
WATER! FROM YOUR NOSE!
WAHAHA!
きゃはは
BAPF
WHY YOU LITTLE--
UH-OH!
SPLSH
SPLSH
HEY! STOP IT!
SPLSH
SPLSH

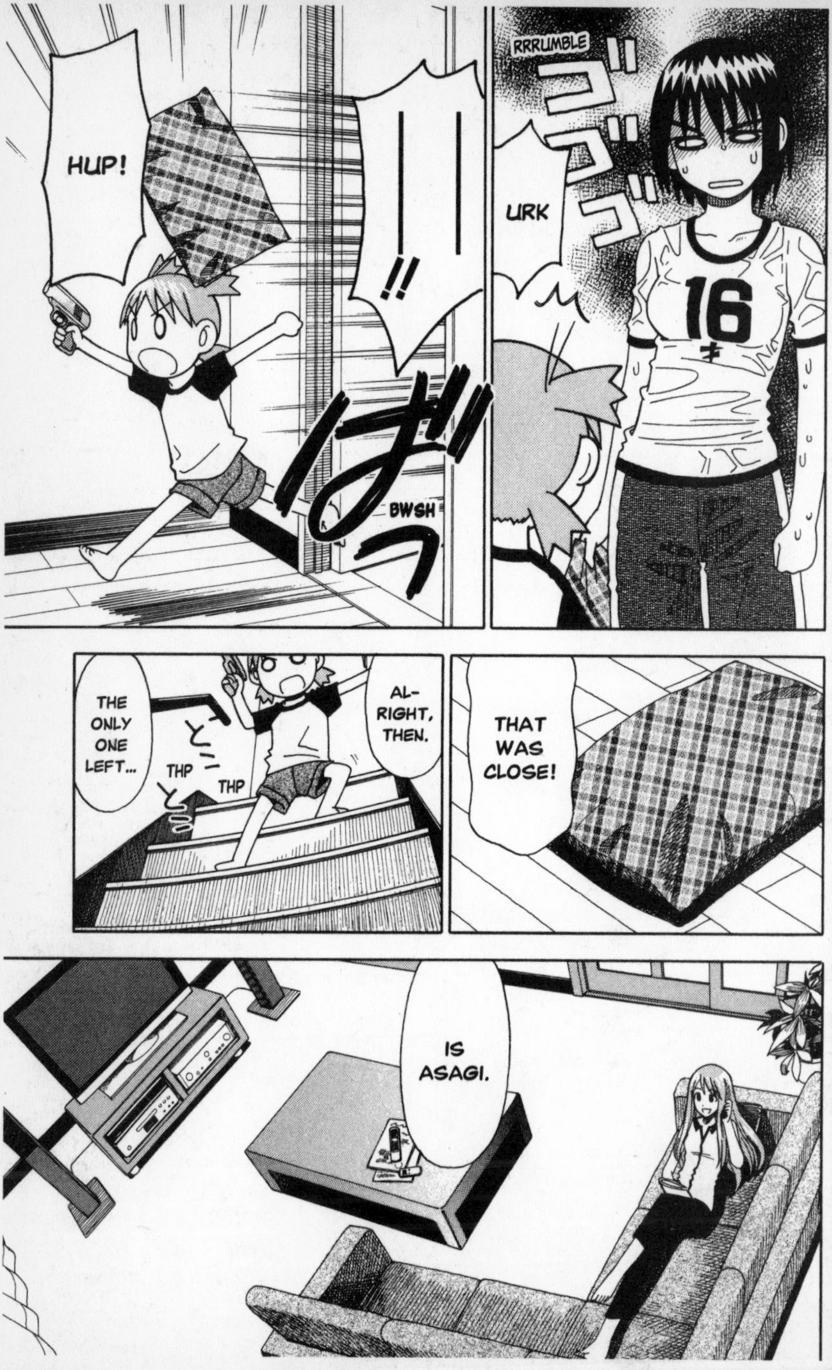
RRRUMBLE
URK
!!
BWSH
HUP!
THAT WAS CLOSE!
AL-RIGHT, THEN.
THE ONLY ONE LEFT...
THP
THP
IS ASAGI.

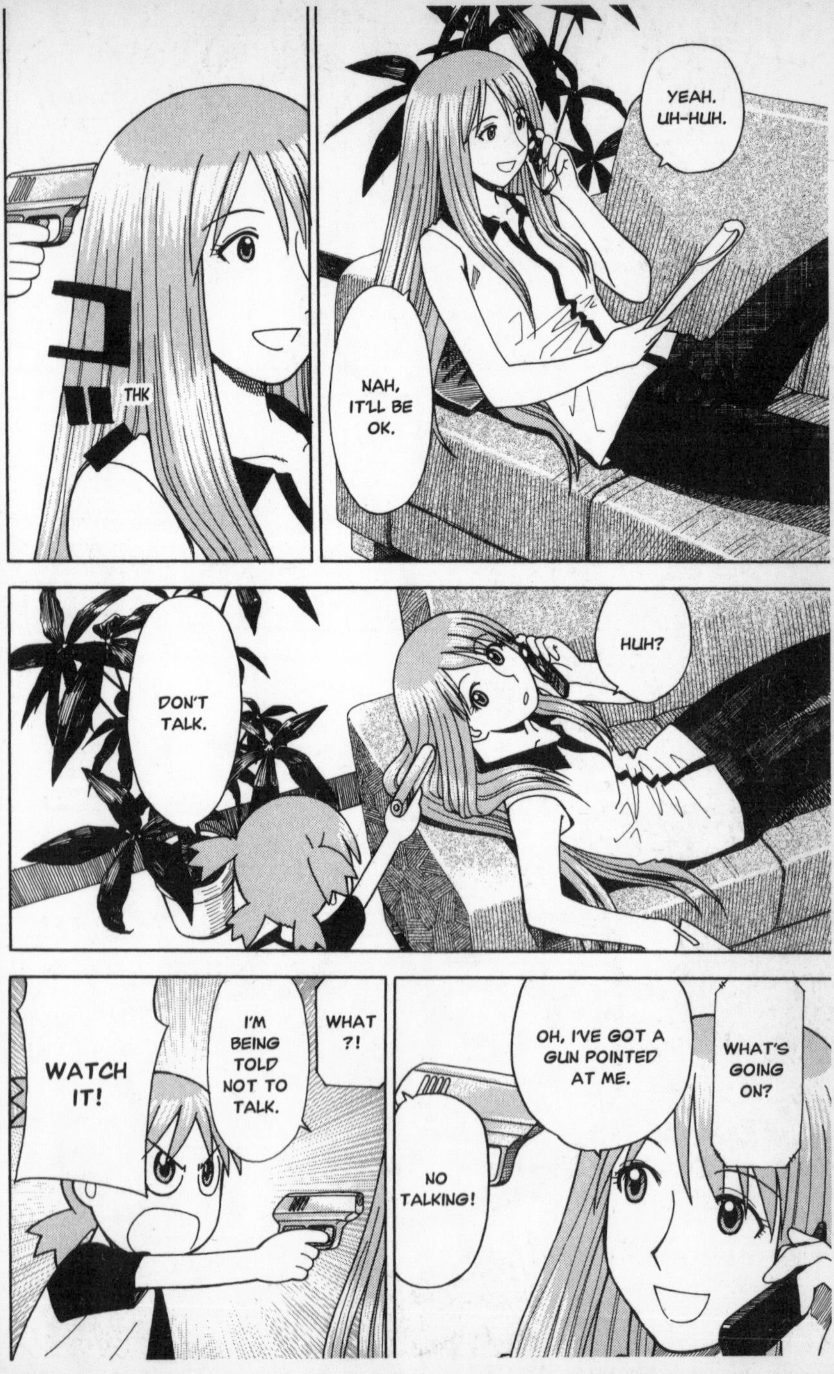
YEAH. UH-HUH.
NAH, IT'LL BE OK.
THK
HUH?
DON'T TALK.
WHAT'S GOING ON?
OH, I'VE GOT A GUN POINTED AT ME.
NO TALKING!
WHAT ?!
I'M BEING TOLD NOT TO TALK.
WATCH IT!

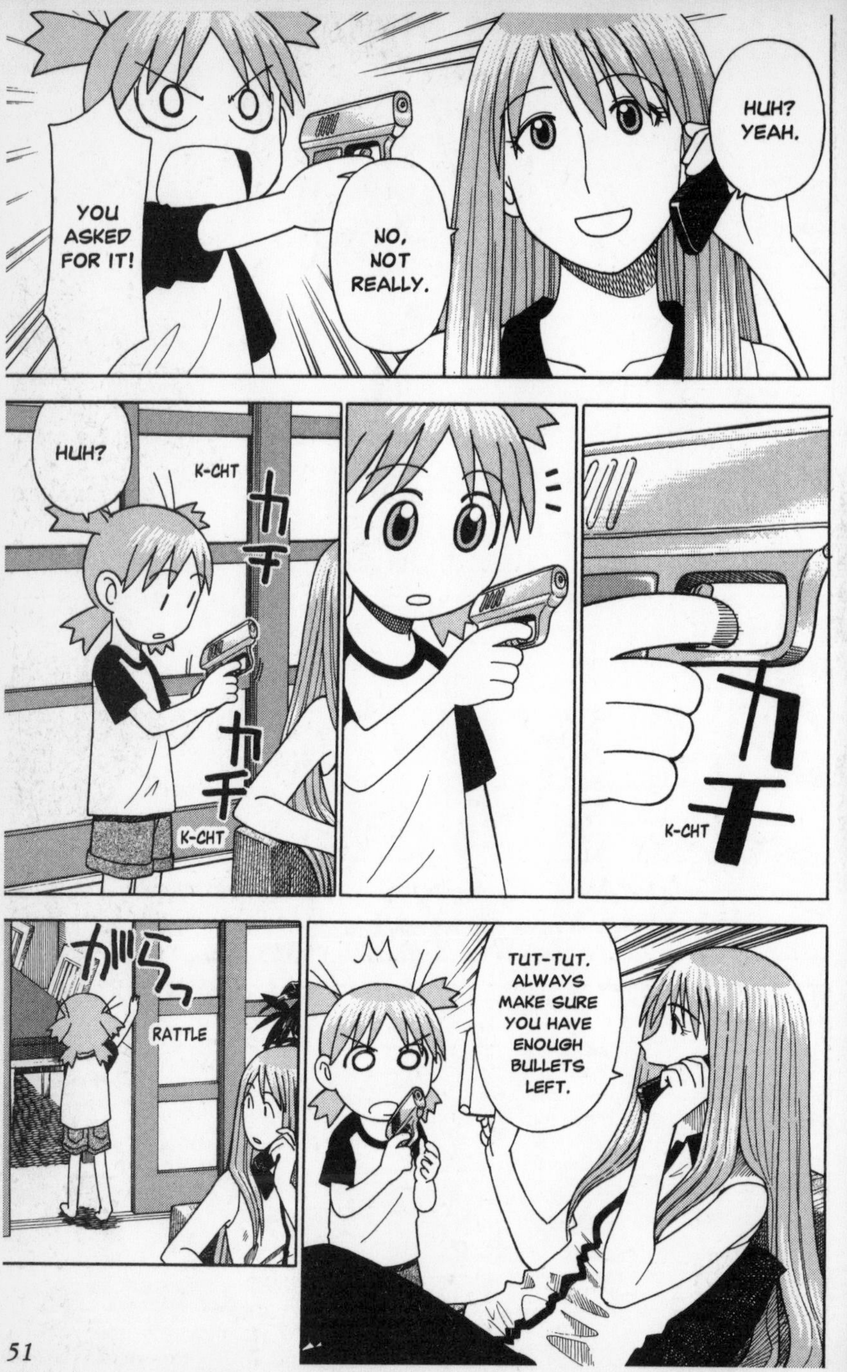
YOU ASKED FOR IT!
NO, NOT REALLY.
HUH? YEAH.
HUH?
K-CHT
カチ
カチ
K-CHT
カチ
K-CHT
がらっ
RATTLE
TUT-TUT. ALWAYS MAKE SURE YOU HAVE ENOUGH BULLETS LEFT.

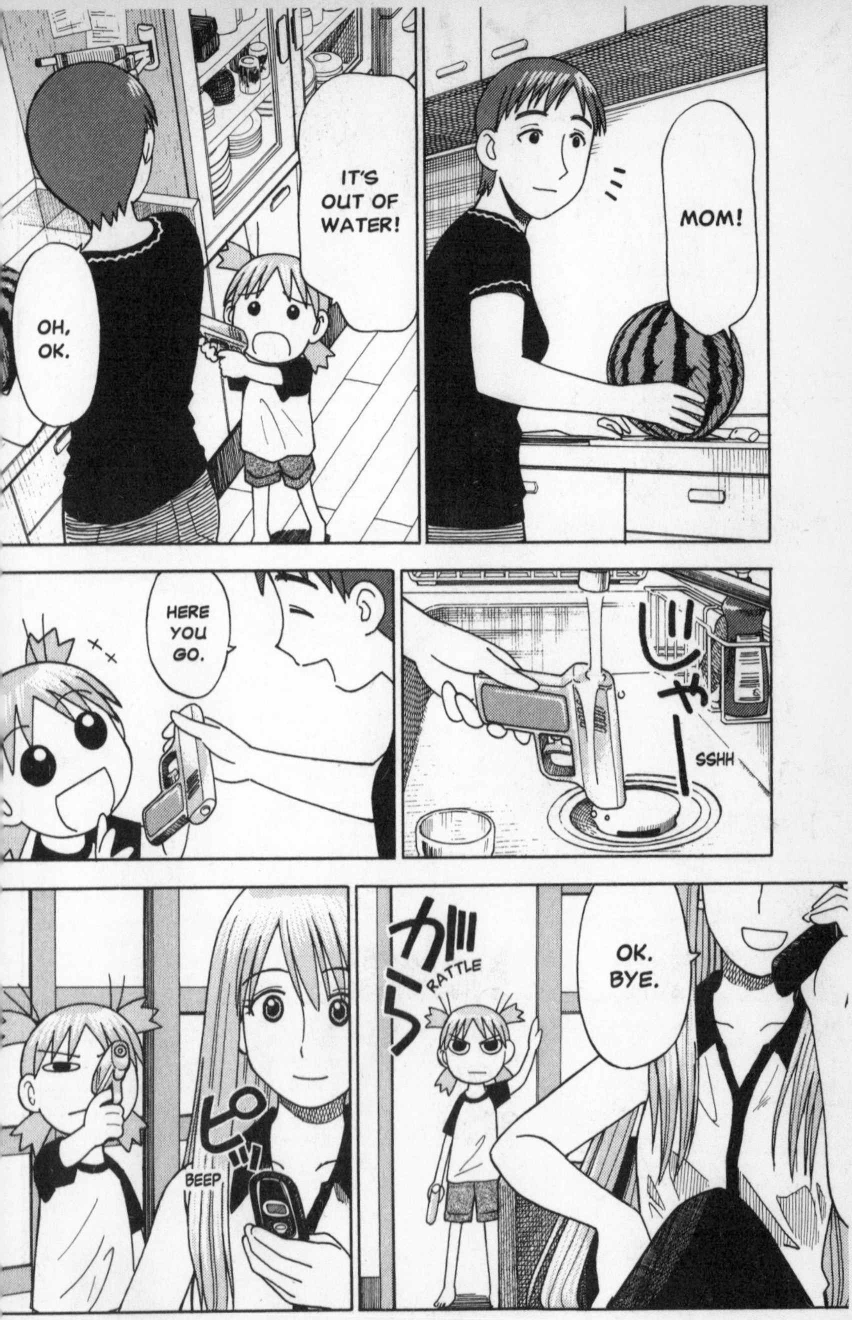
MOM!
IT'S OUT OF WATER!
OH, OK.
SSHH
HERE YOU GO.
OK. BYE.
RATTLE
BEEP

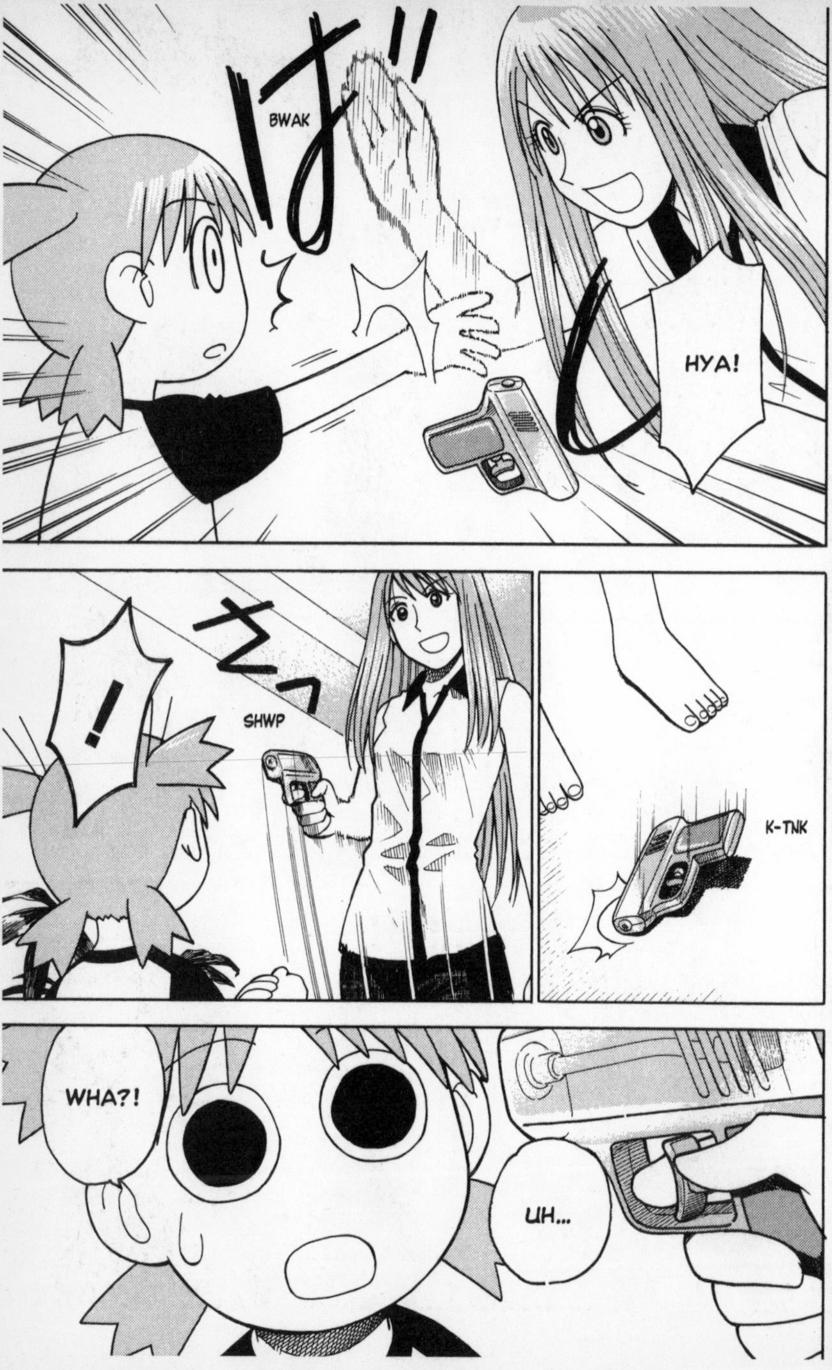

HYA!
BWAK
K-TNK
SHWP
!
UH...
WHA?!

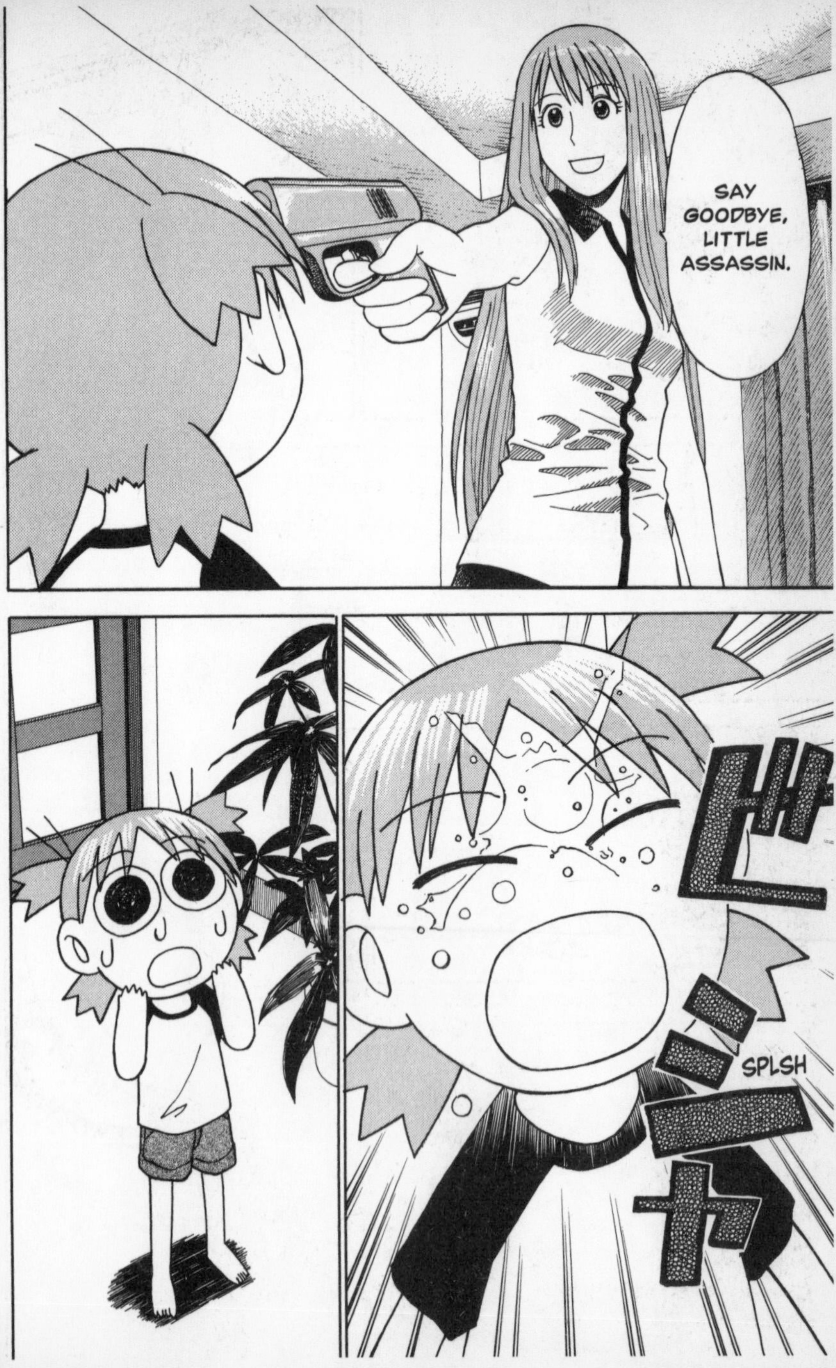
SAY GOODBYE, LITTLE ASSASSIN.
SPLSH

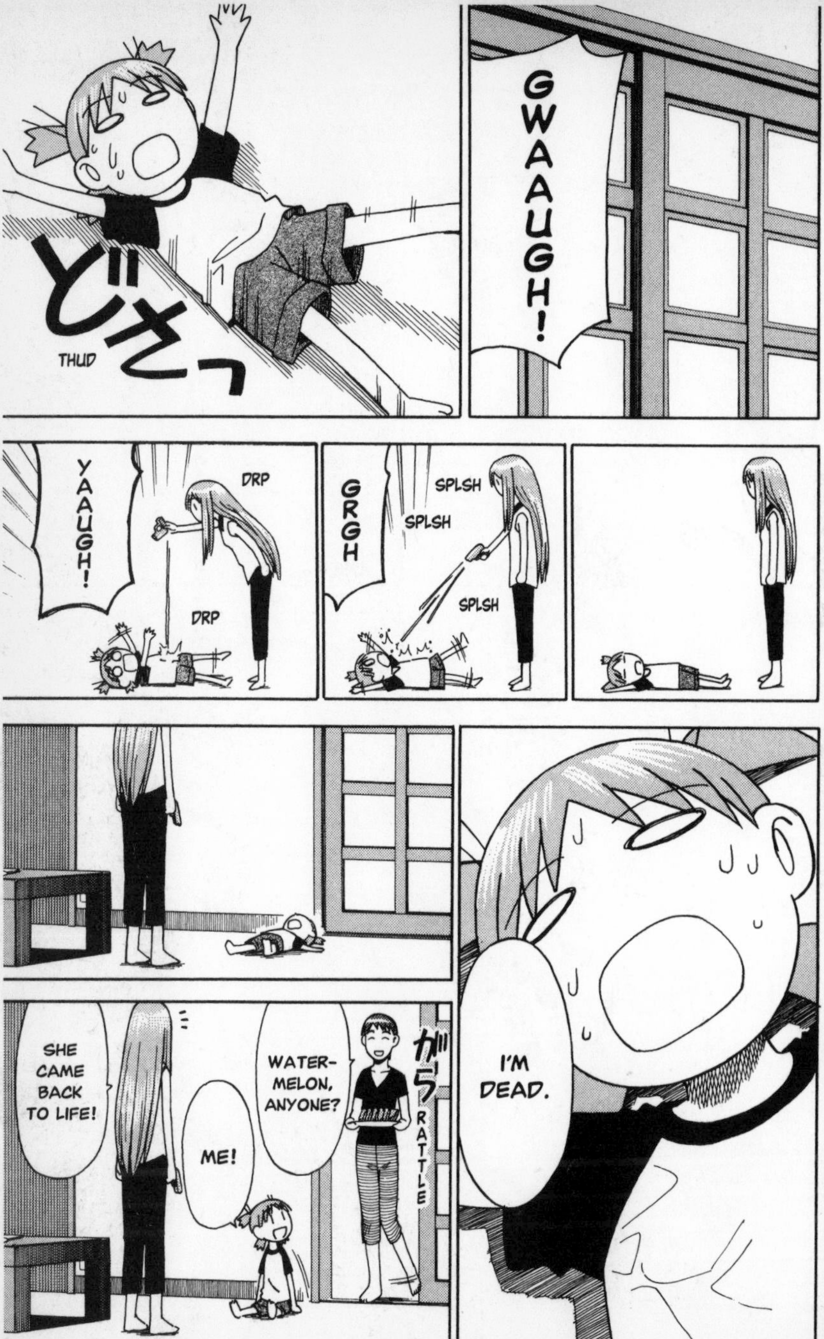
GWAAUGH!
どさっ
THUD
GRGH
SPLSH
SPLSH
SPLSH
YAAUGH!
DRP
DRP
I'M DEAD.
がら
RATTLE
WATER-MELON, ANYONE?
ME!
SHE CAME BACK TO LIFE!

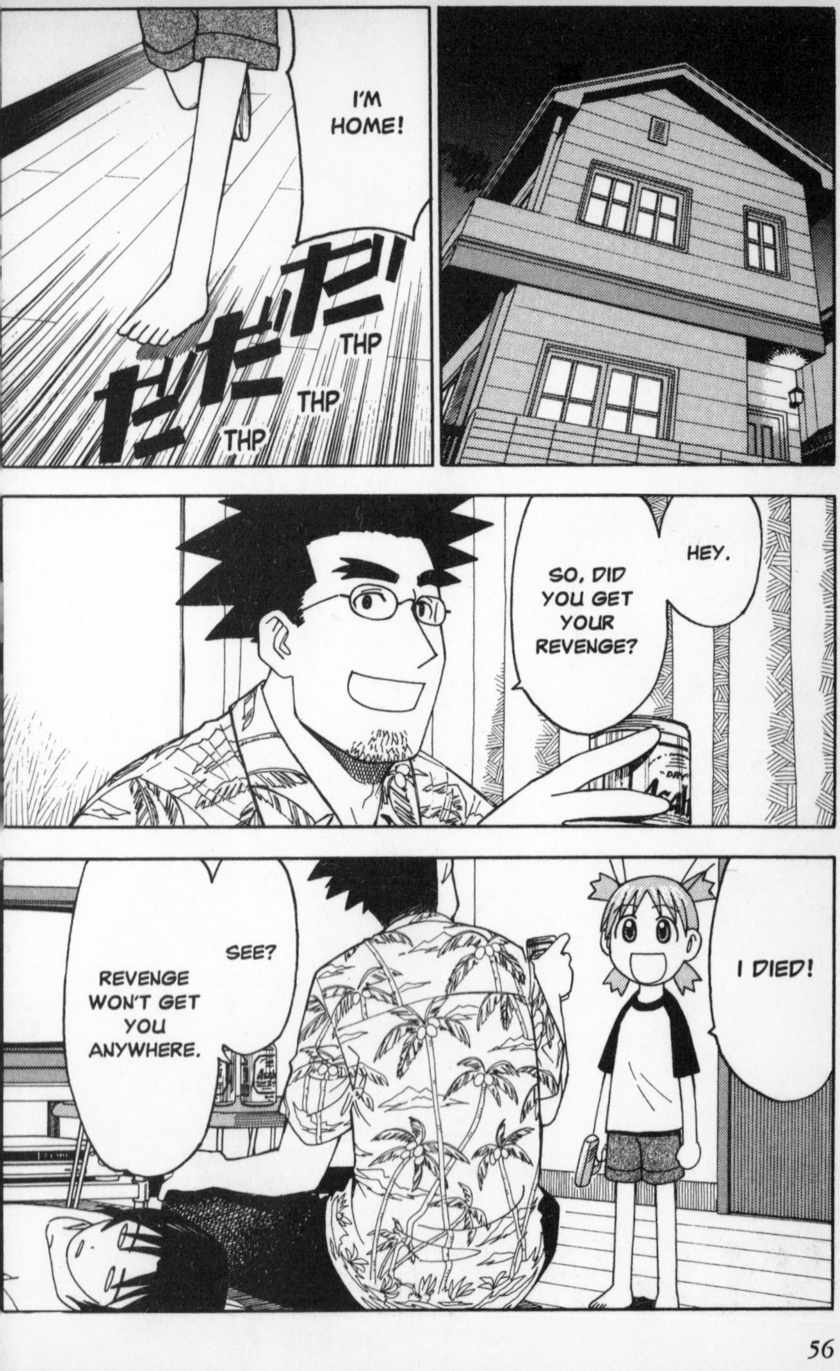
I'M HOME!
だだだ
THP
THP
THP
HEY.
SO, DID YOU GET YOUR REVENGE?
I DIED!
SEE?
REVENGE WON'T GET YOU ANYWHERE.

YOTSUBA&!

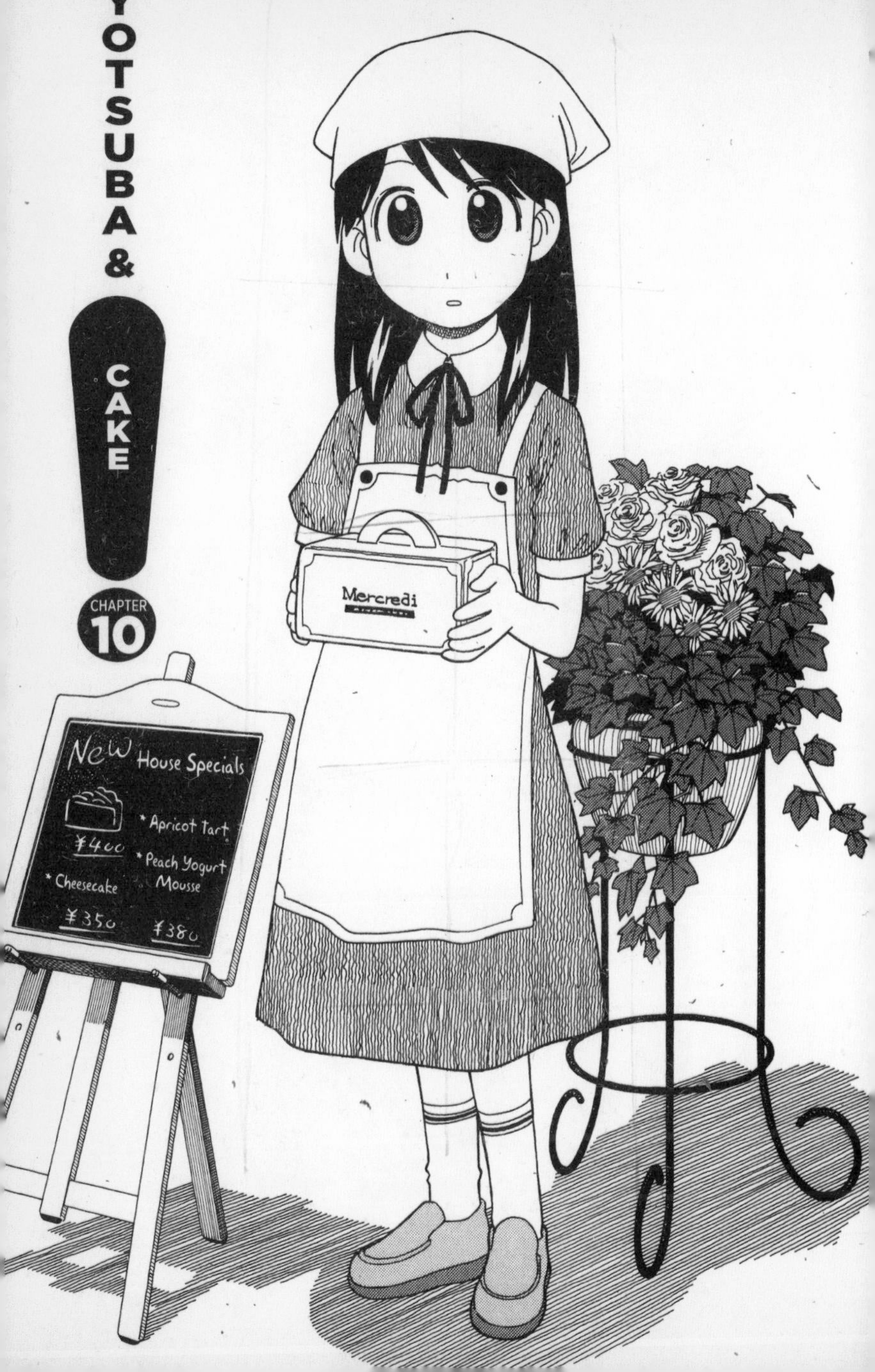
YOTSUBA & CAKE!
CHAPTER 10
New House Specials
* Apricot tart
¥400
* Peach Yogurt Mousse
* Cheesecake
¥350
¥380
Mercredi

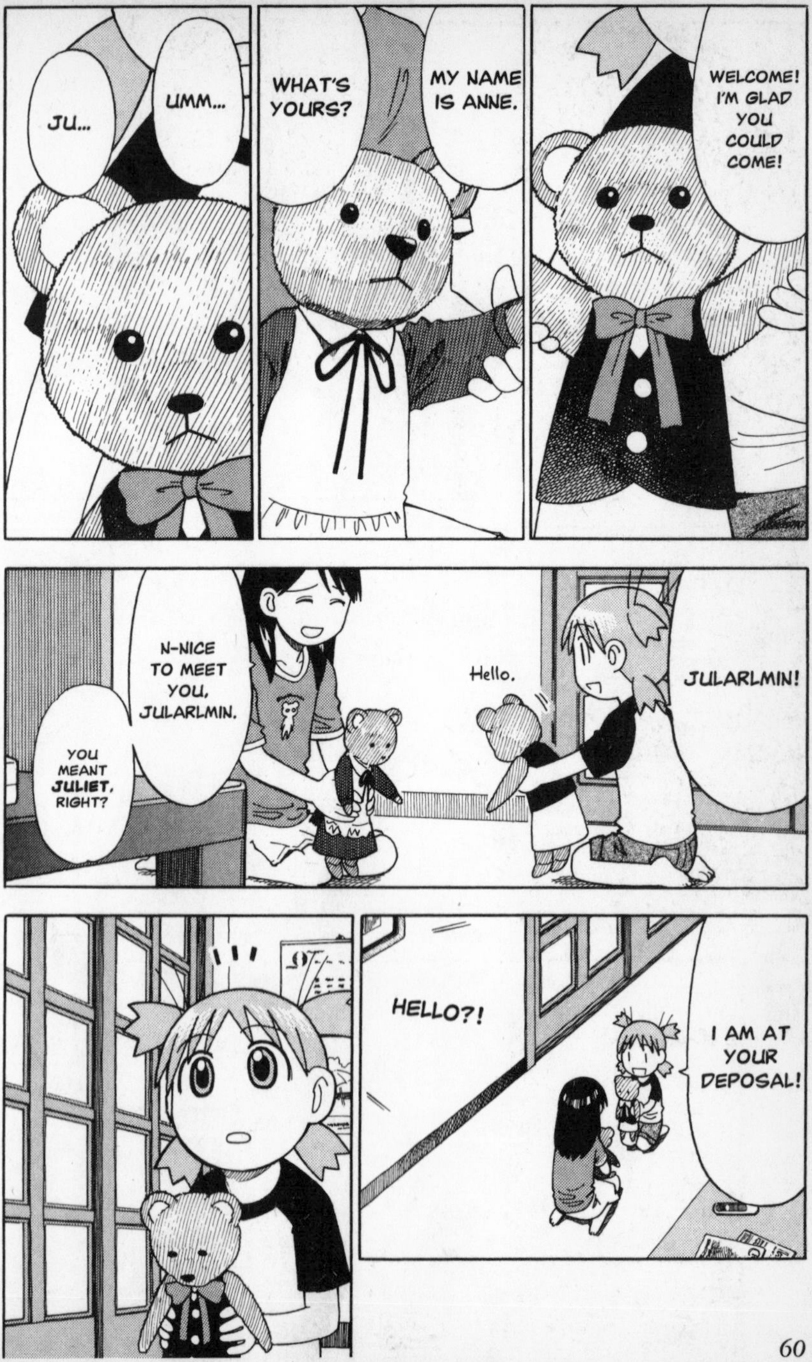
WELCOME! I'M GLAD YOU COULD COME!
MY NAME IS ANNE.
WHAT'S YOURS?
UMM...
JU...
JULARLMIN!
Hello.
N-NICE TO MEET YOU, JULARLMIN.
YOU MEANT JULIET, RIGHT?
I AM AT YOUR DEPOSAL!
HELLO?!

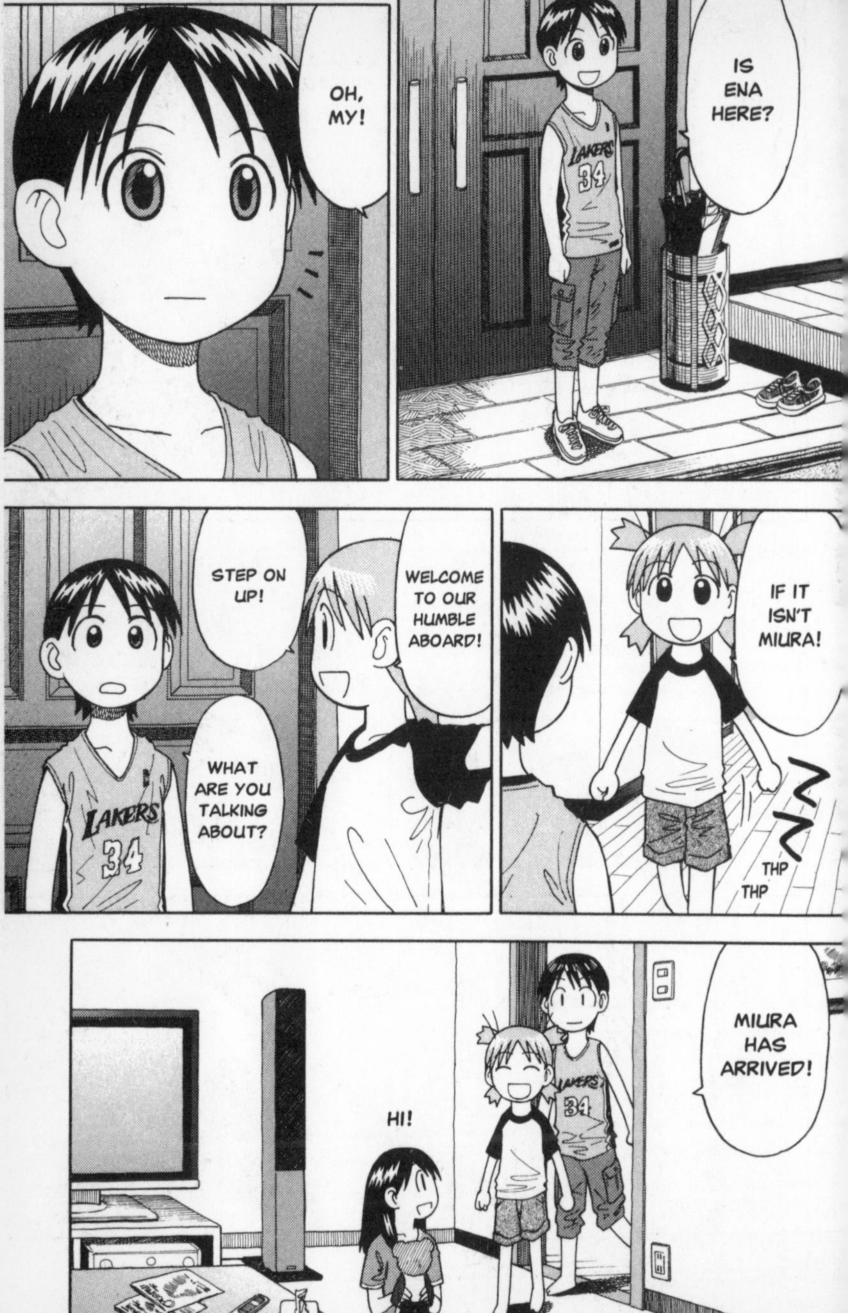
IS ENA HERE?
OH, MY!
IF IT ISN'T MIURA!
THP THP
WELCOME TO OUR HUMBLE ABOARD!
STEP ON UP!
WHAT ARE YOU TALKING ABOUT?
MIURA HAS ARRIVED!
HI!

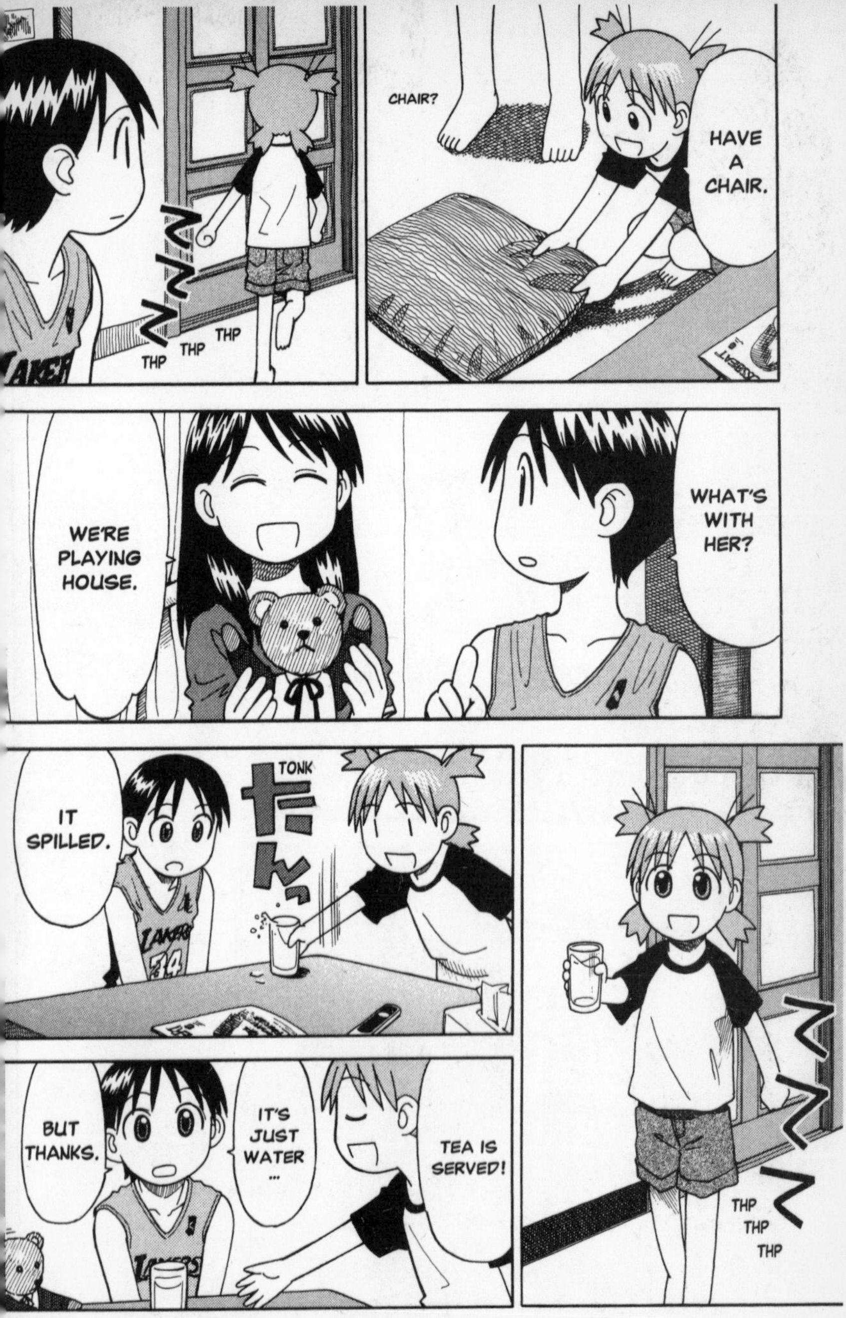
HAVE A CHAIR.
CHAIR?
THP THP THP
WHAT'S WITH HER?
WE'RE PLAYING HOUSE.
THP THP THP
TONK
IT SPILLED.
TEA IS SERVED!
IT'S JUST WATER ...
BUT THANKS.

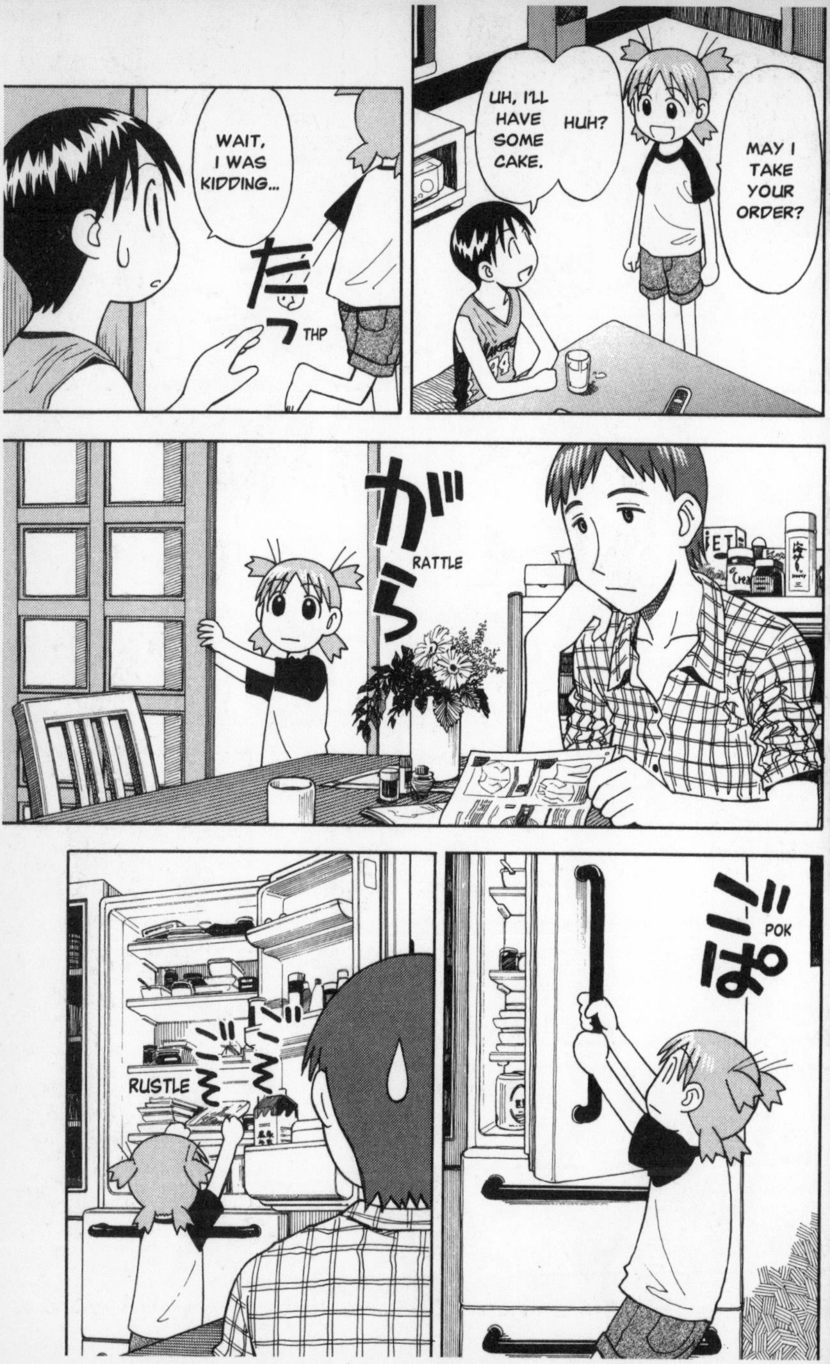
MAY I TAKE YOUR ORDER?
HUH?
UH, I'LL HAVE SOME CAKE.
WAIT, I WAS KIDDING...
たっ
THP
がら
RATTLE
POK
RUSTLE

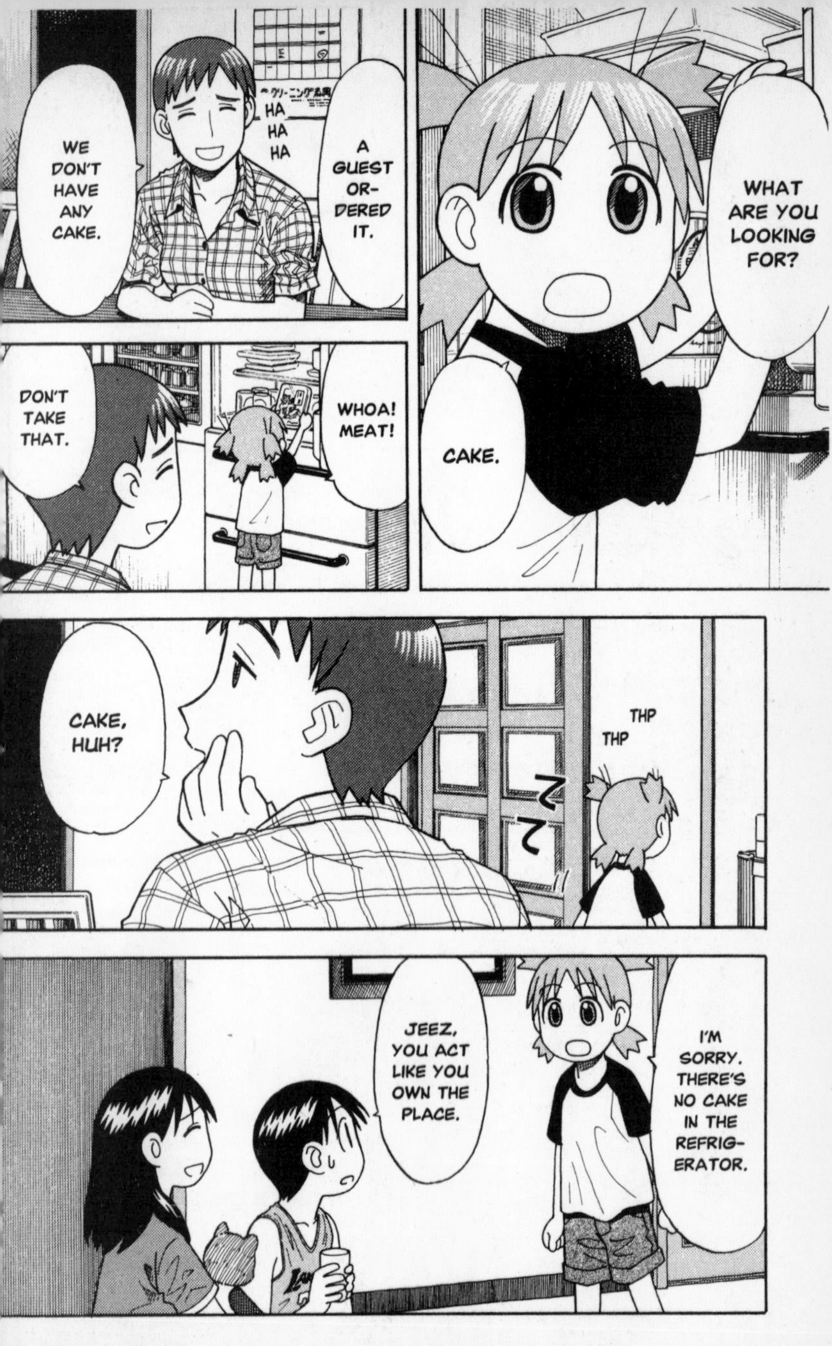
WE DON'T HAVE ANY CAKE.
A GUEST ORDERED IT.
HA HA HA
DON'T TAKE THAT.
WHOA! MEAT!
WHAT ARE YOU LOOKING FOR?
CAKE.
CAKE, HUH?
THP THP
JEEZ, YOU ACT LIKE YOU OWN THE PLACE.
I'M SORRY. THERE'S NO CAKE IN THE REFRIGERATOR.

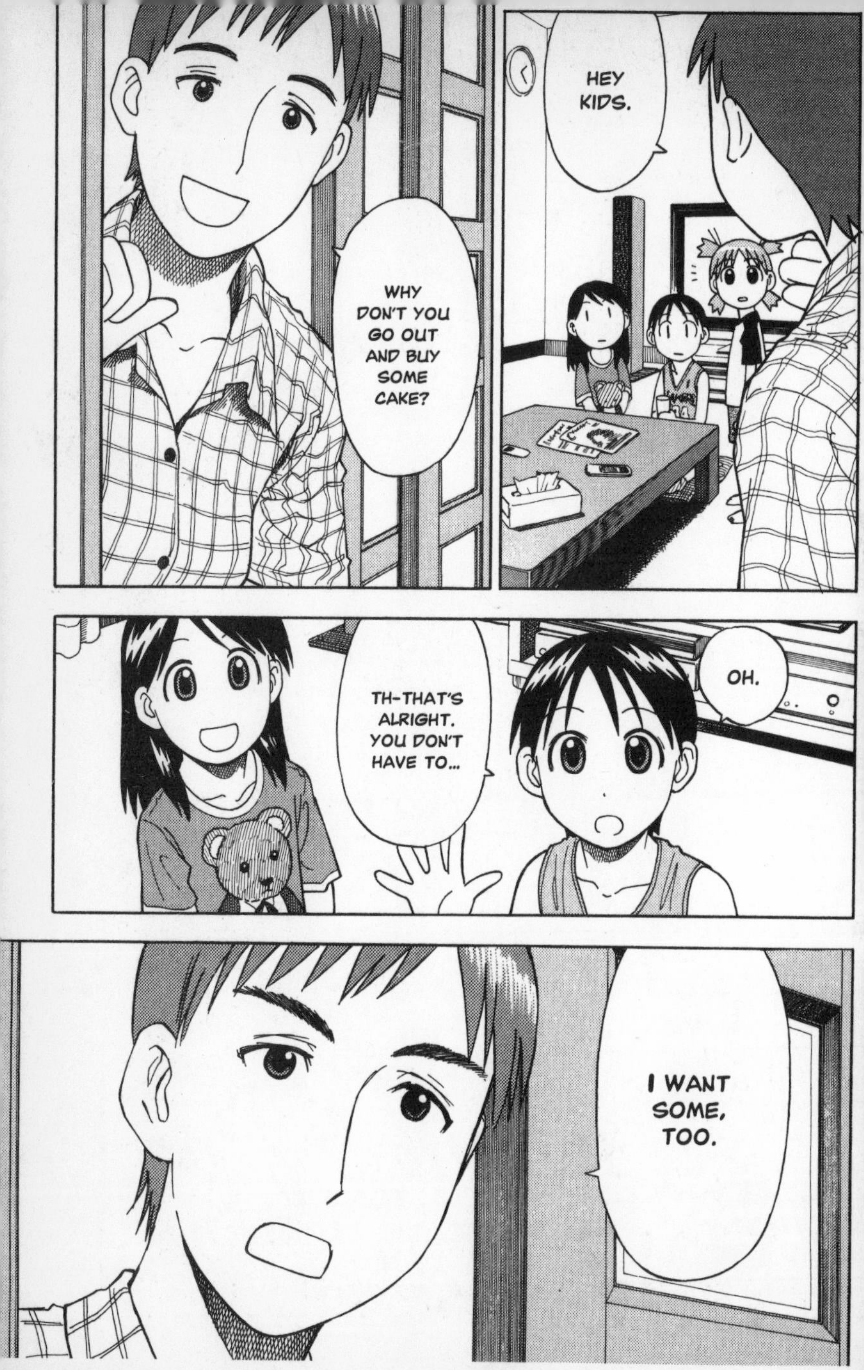
HEY KIDS.
WHY DON'T YOU GO OUT AND BUY SOME CAKE?
OH.
TH-THAT'S ALRIGHT. YOU DON'T HAVE TO...
I WANT SOME, TOO.

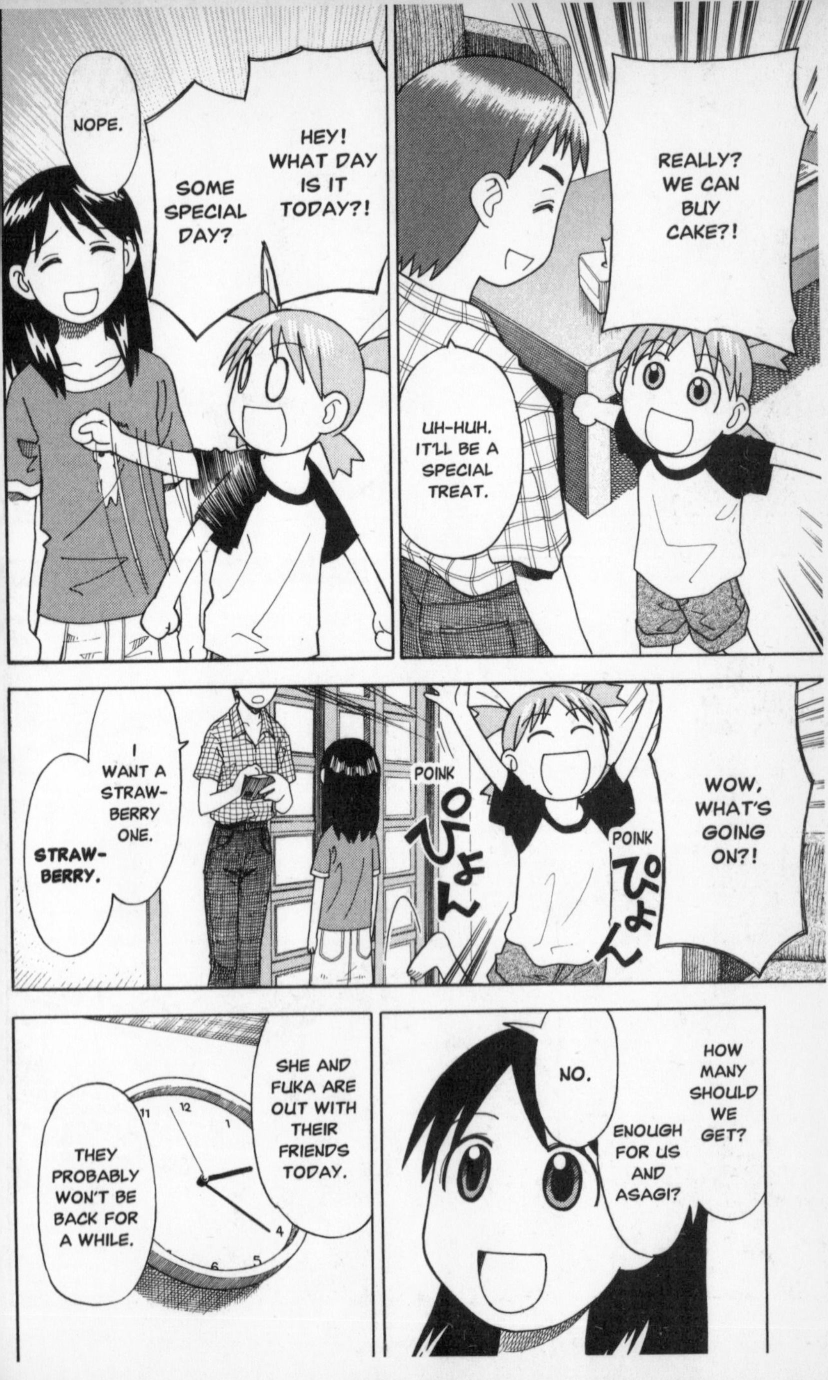
REALLY? WE CAN BUY CAKE?!
UH-HUH. IT'LL BE A SPECIAL TREAT.
HEY! WHAT DAY IS IT TODAY?!
SOME SPECIAL DAY?
NOPE.
WOW, WHAT'S GOING ON?!
POINK
ぴょん
POINK
ぴょん
I WANT A STRAWBERRY ONE.
STRAWBERRY.
HOW MANY SHOULD WE GET?
ENOUGH FOR US AND ASAGI?
NO.
SHE AND FUKA ARE OUT WITH THEIR FRIENDS TODAY.
THEY PROBABLY WON'T BE BACK FOR A WHILE.

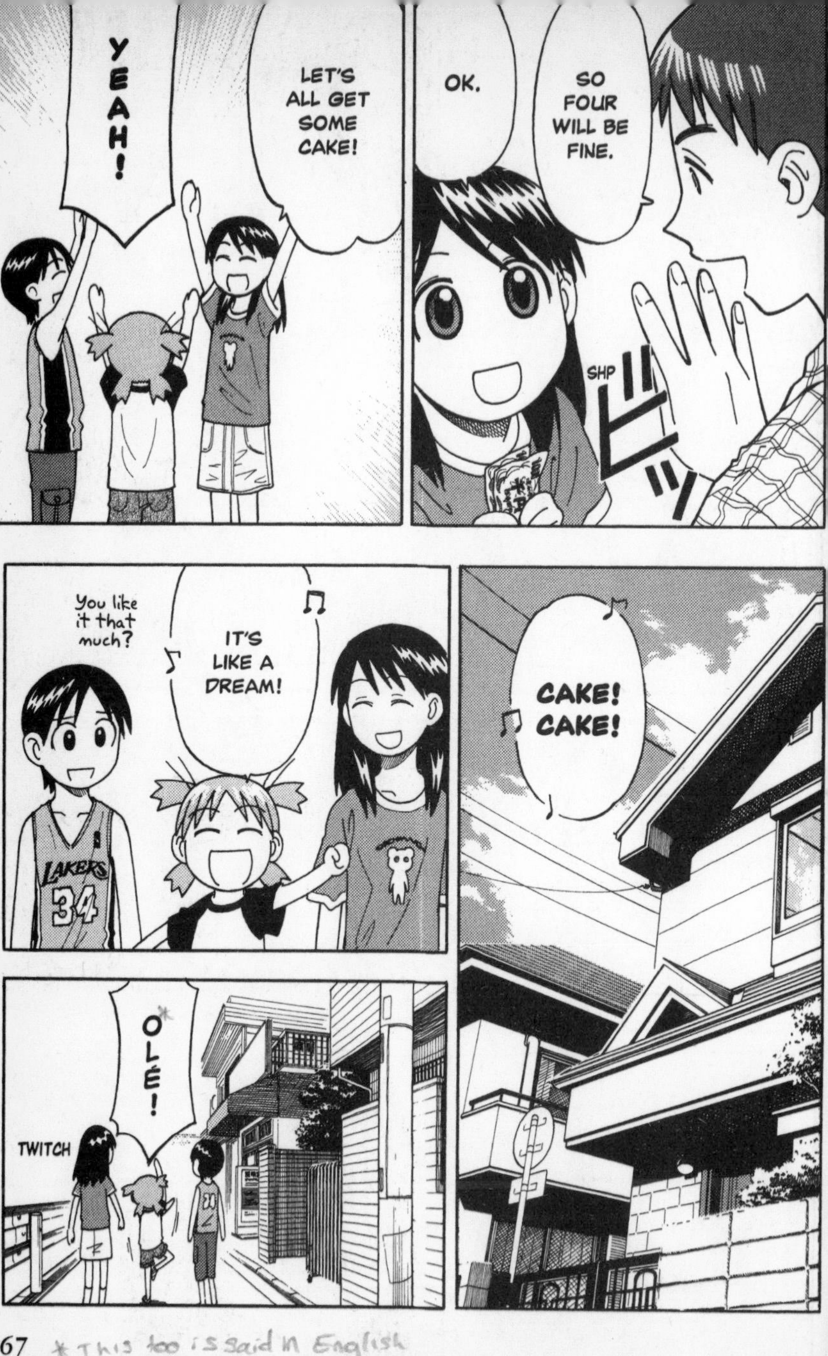
SO FOUR WILL BE FINE.
OK.
SHP
LET'S ALL GET SOME CAKE!
YEAH!
CAKE! CAKE!
IT'S LIKE A DREAM!
You like it that much?
OLÉ!*
TWITCH

* This too is said in English

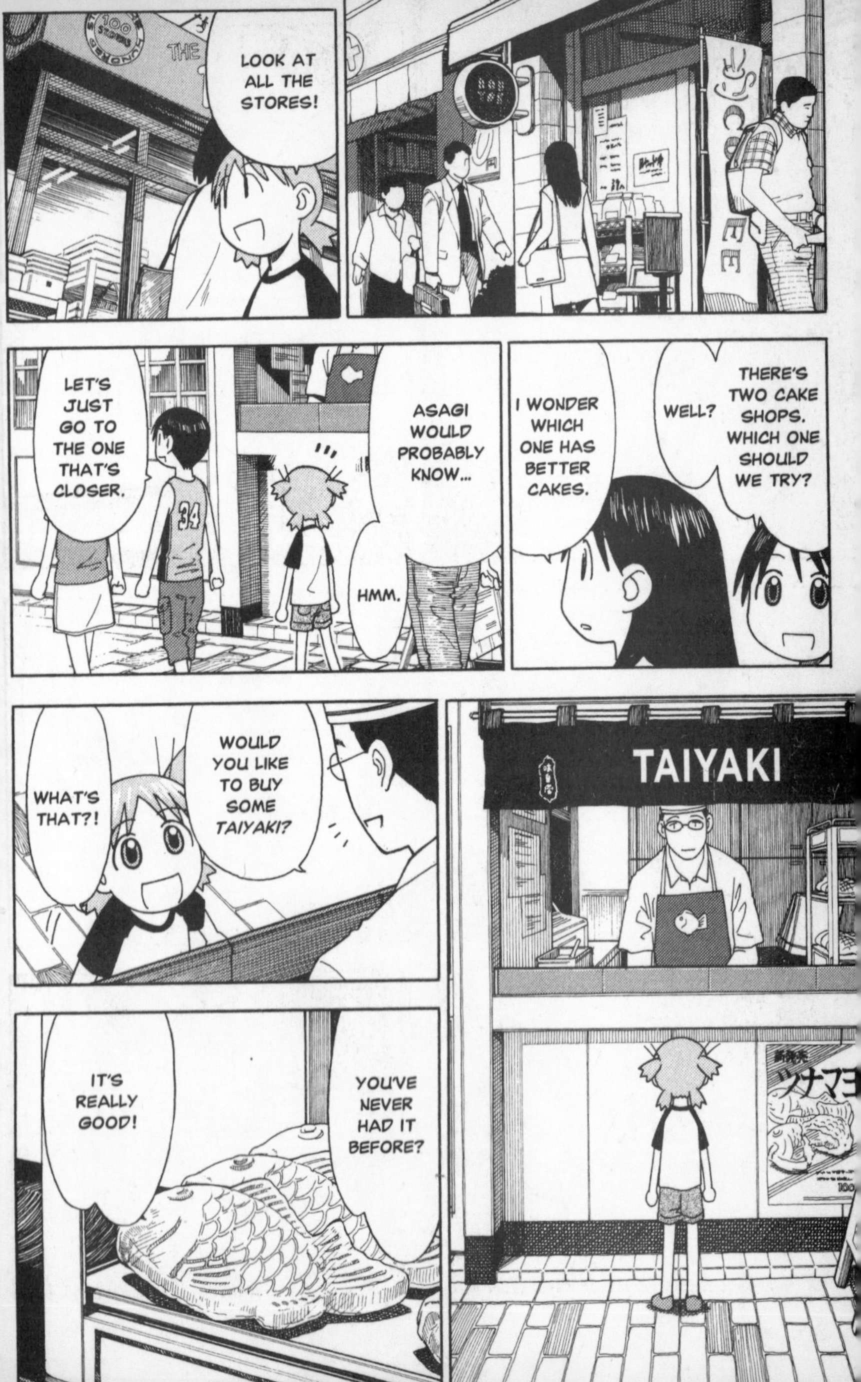
LOOK AT ALL THE STORES!
THERE'S TWO CAKE SHOPS. WHICH ONE SHOULD WE TRY?
WELL?
I WONDER WHICH ONE HAS BETTER CAKES.
ASAGI WOULD PROBABLY KNOW...
HMM.
LET'S JUST GO TO THE ONE THAT'S CLOSER.
TAIYAKI
WOULD YOU LIKE TO BUY SOME *TAIYAKI?*
WHAT'S THAT?!
YOU'VE NEVER HAD IT BEFORE?
IT'S REALLY GOOD!

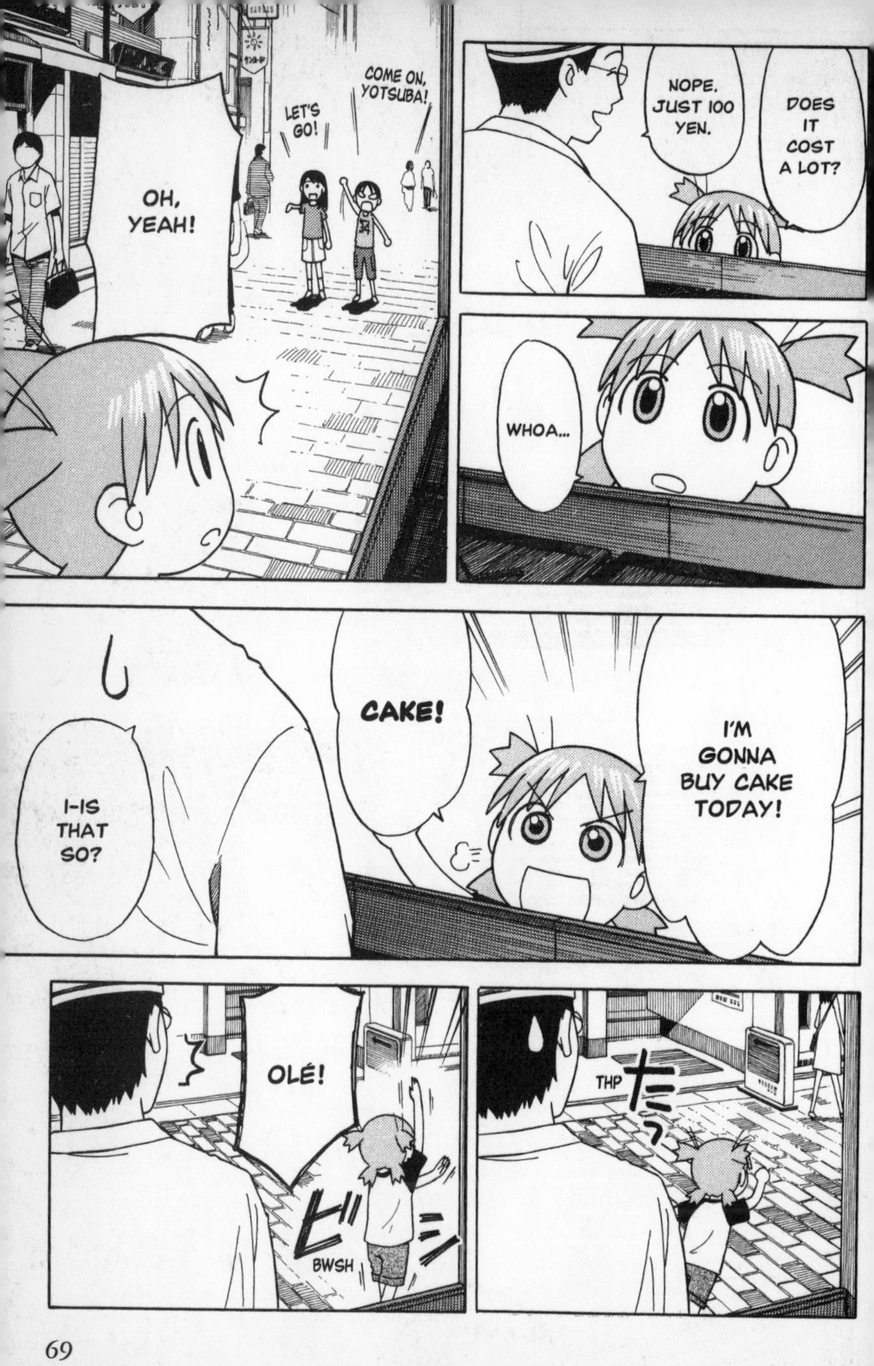
DOES IT COST A LOT?
NOPE. JUST 100 YEN.
WHOA...
COME ON, YOTSUBA!
LET'S GO!
OH, YEAH!
I'M GONNA BUY CAKE TODAY!
CAKE!
I-IS THAT SO?
THP
OLÉ!
BWSH

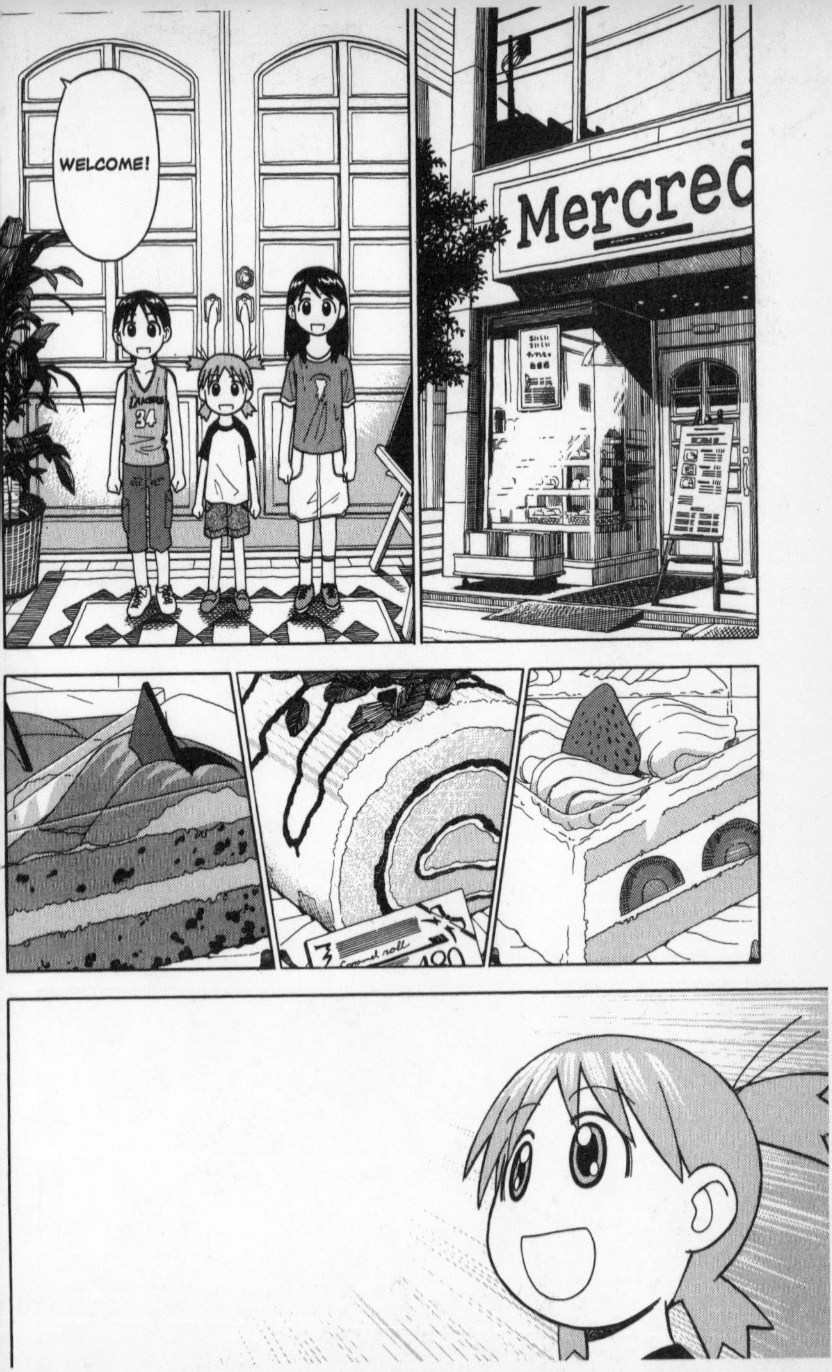
WELCOME!
Mercred
Caramel roll
480

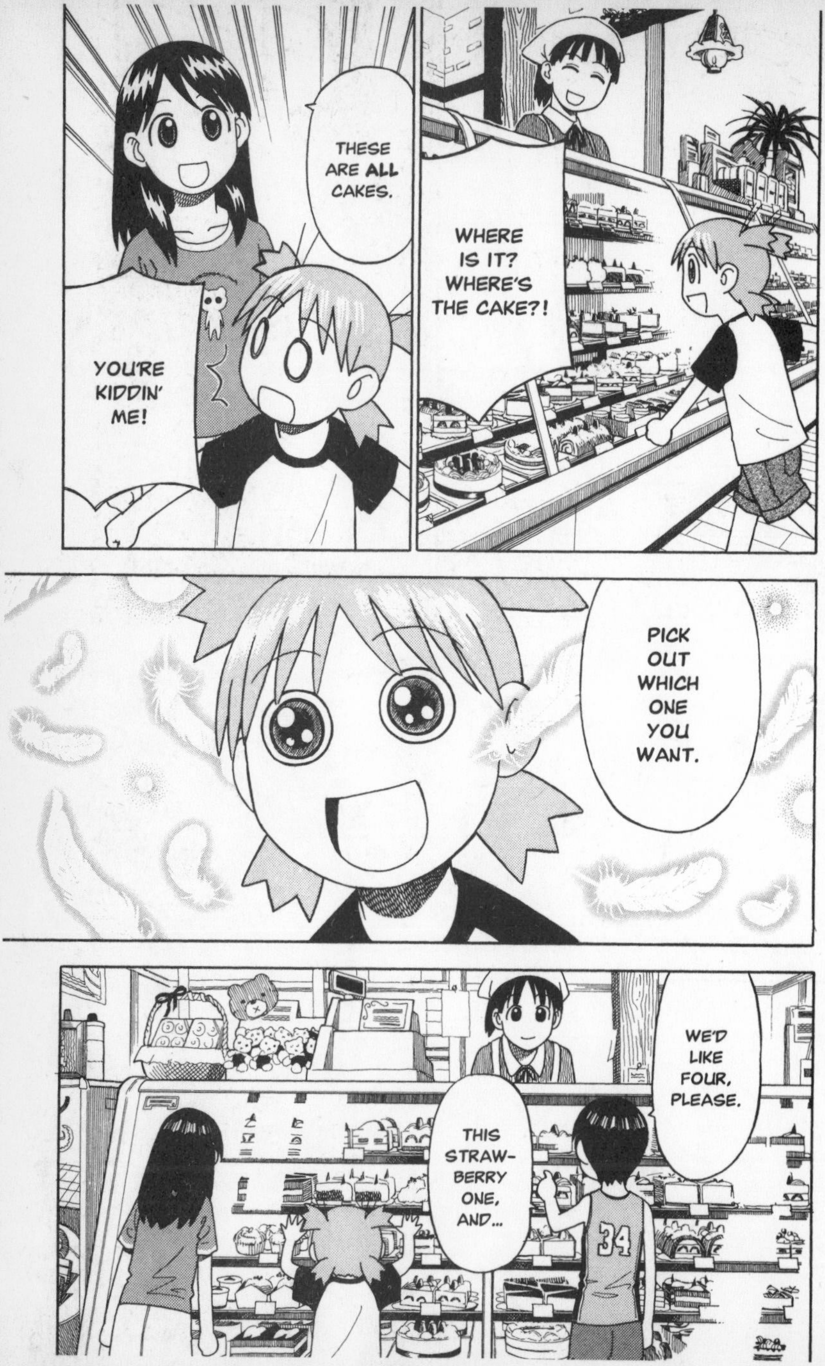
WHERE IS IT? WHERE'S THE CAKE?!
THESE ARE ALL CAKES.
YOU'RE KIDDIN' ME!
PICK OUT WHICH ONE YOU WANT.
WE'D LIKE FOUR, PLEASE.
THIS STRAW-BERRY ONE, AND...

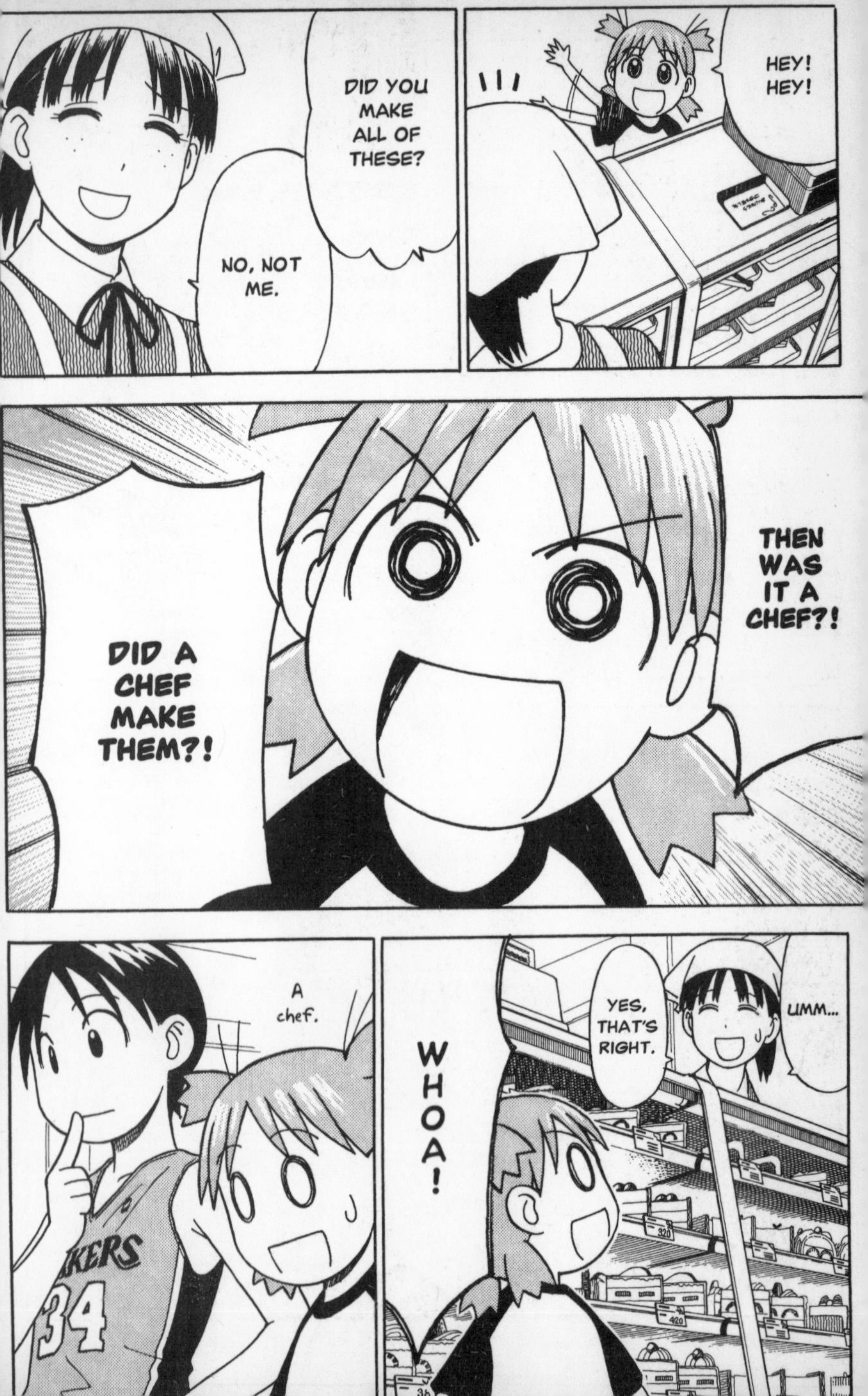
HEY! HEY!
DID YOU MAKE ALL OF THESE?
NO, NOT ME.
THEN WAS IT A CHEF?!
DID A CHEF MAKE THEM?!
UMM...
YES, THAT'S RIGHT.
WHOA!
A chef.

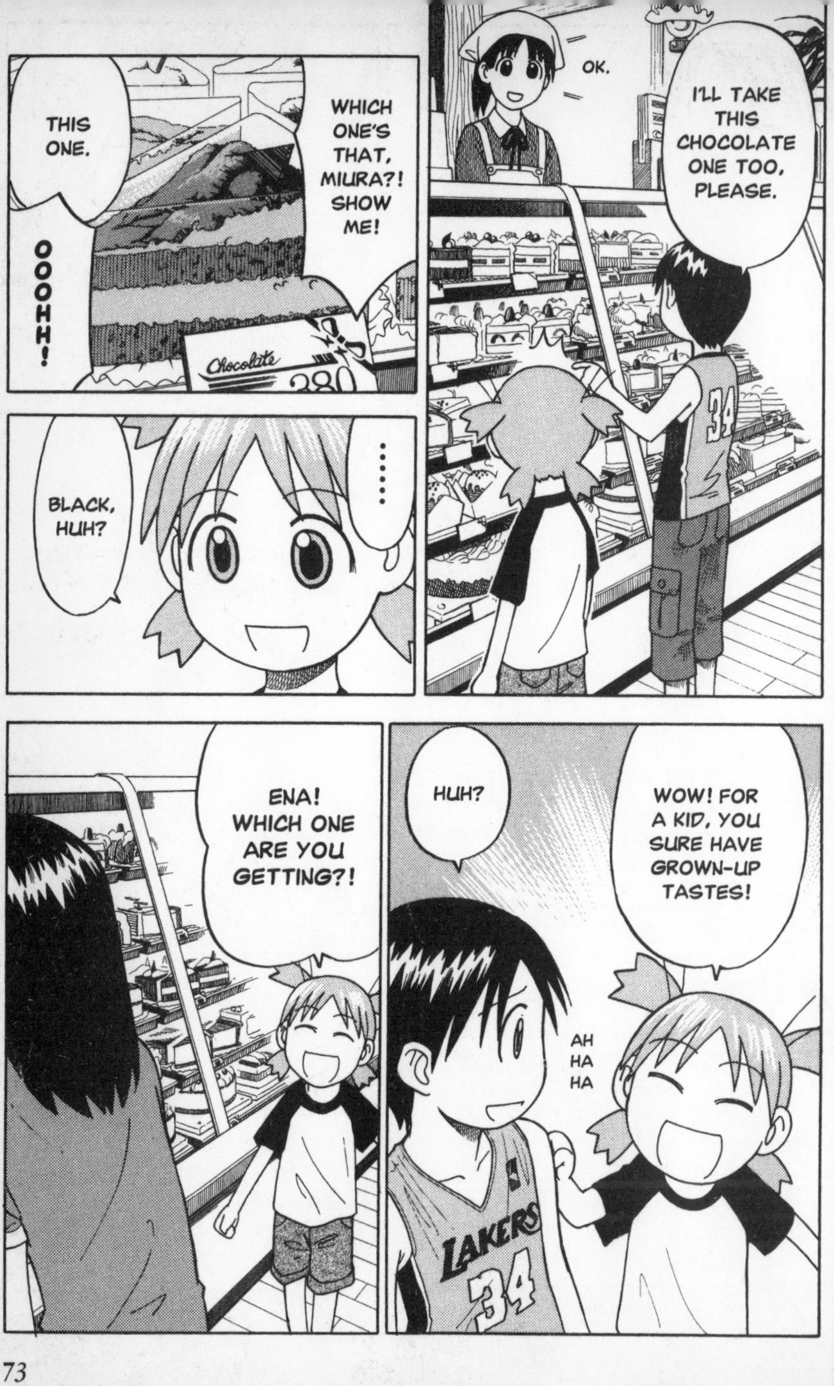

I'LL TAKE THIS CHOCOLATE ONE TOO, PLEASE.
OK.
WHICH ONE'S THAT, MIURA?! SHOW ME!
THIS ONE.
OOOHH!
Chocolate
280
......
BLACK, HUH?
WOW! FOR A KID, YOU SURE HAVE GROWN-UP TASTES!
HUH?
AH HA HA
LAKERS
34
ENA! WHICH ONE ARE YOU GETTING?!

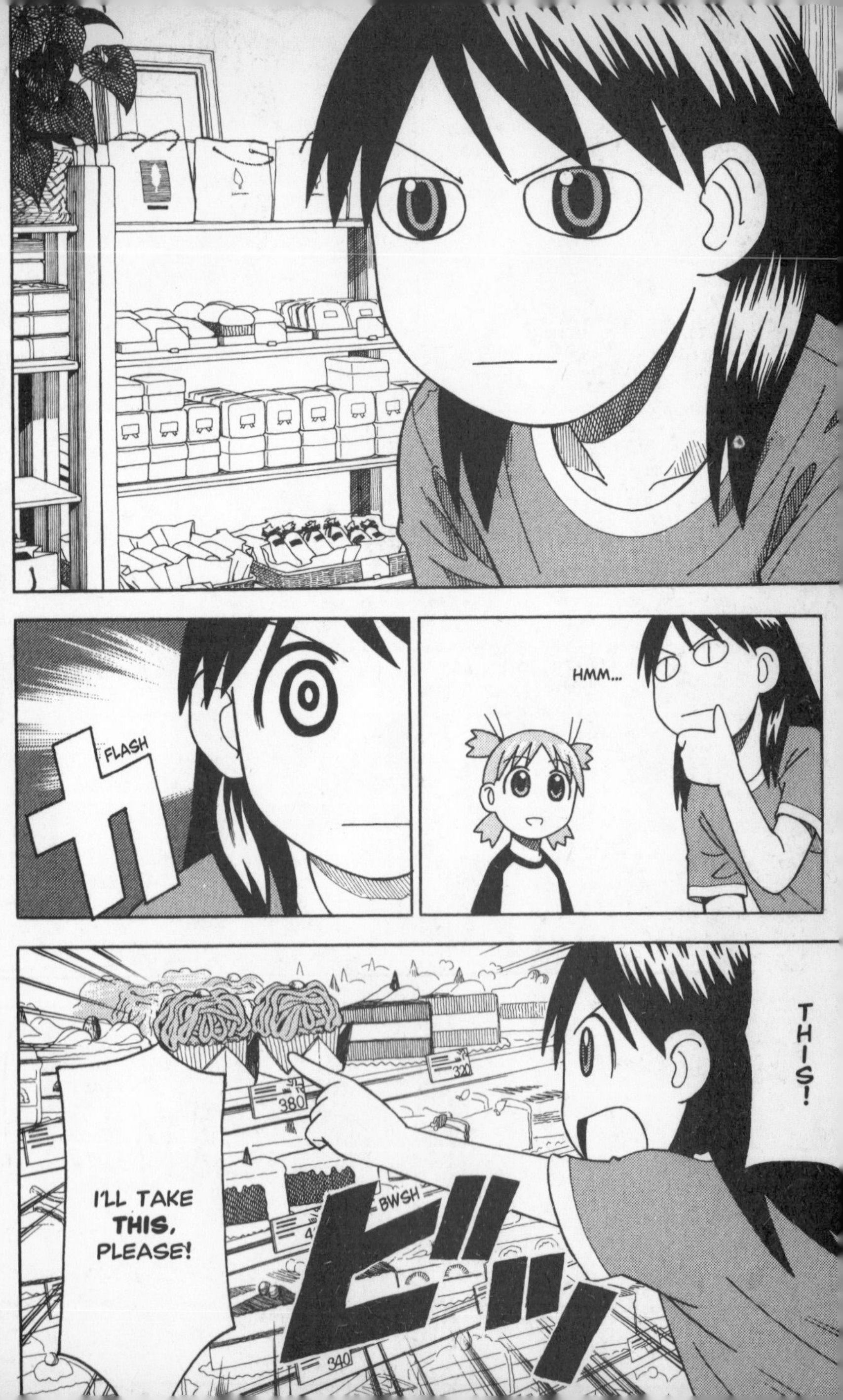
HMM...
FLASH
THIS!
I'LL TAKE THIS, PLEASE!
BWSH

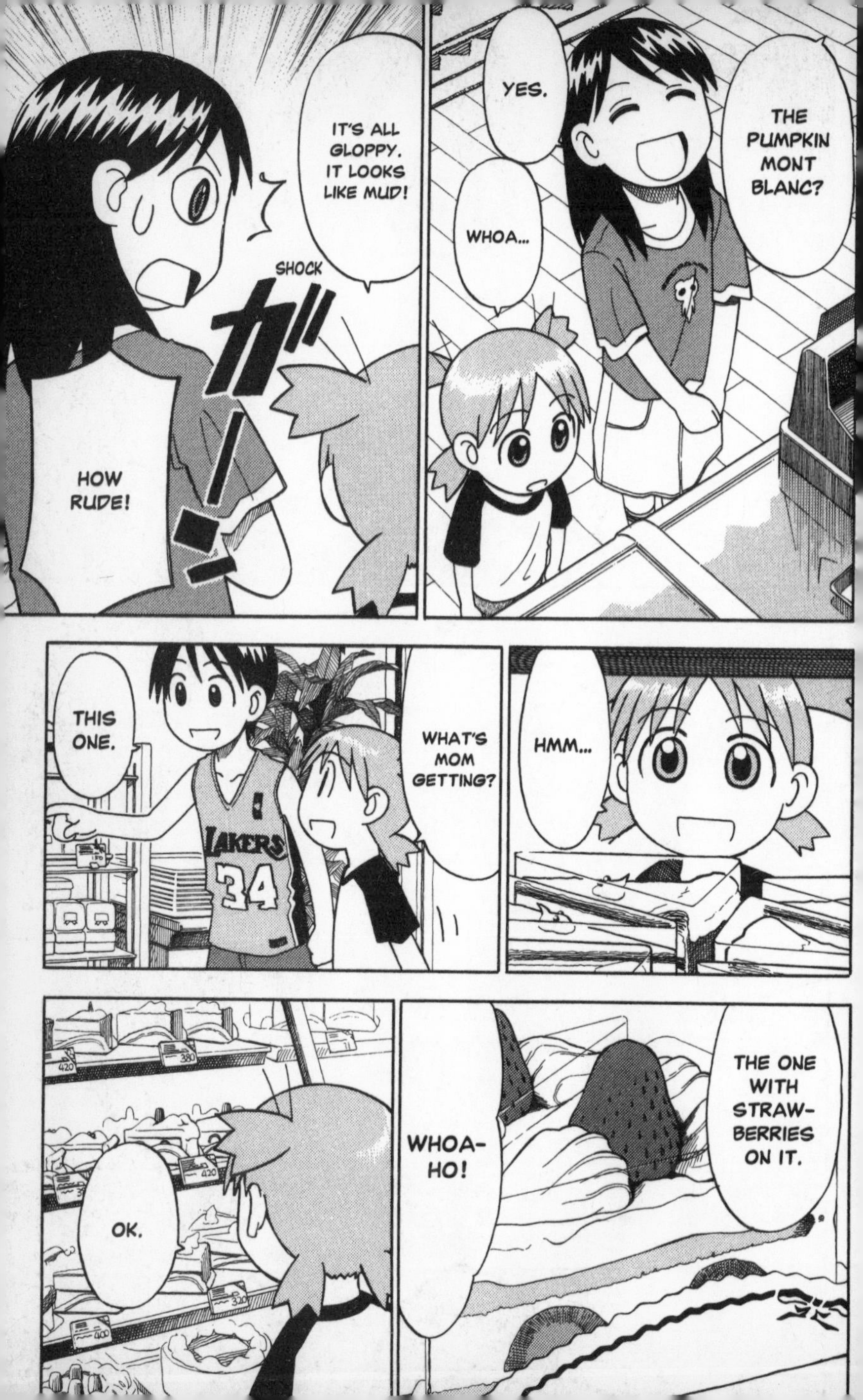
THE PUMPKIN MONT BLANC?
YES.
WHOA...
IT'S ALL GLOPPY. IT LOOKS LIKE MUD!
SHOCK
HOW RUDE!
HMM...
WHAT'S MOM GETTING?
THIS ONE.
THE ONE WITH STRAW-BERRIES ON IT.
WHOA-HO!
OK.

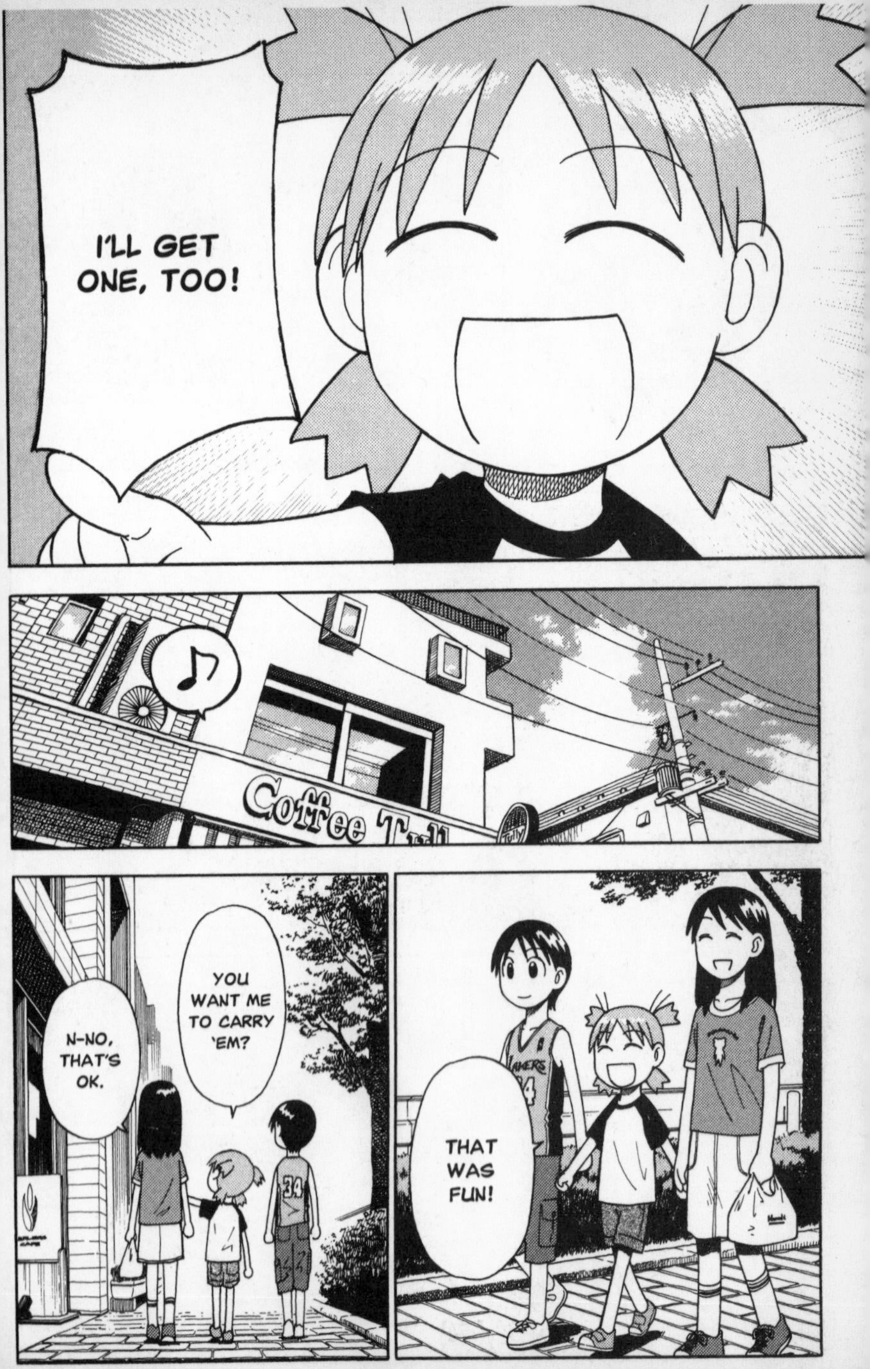
I'LL GET ONE, TOO!
♪
Coffee
THAT WAS FUN!
YOU WANT ME TO CARRY 'EM?
N-NO, THAT'S OK.

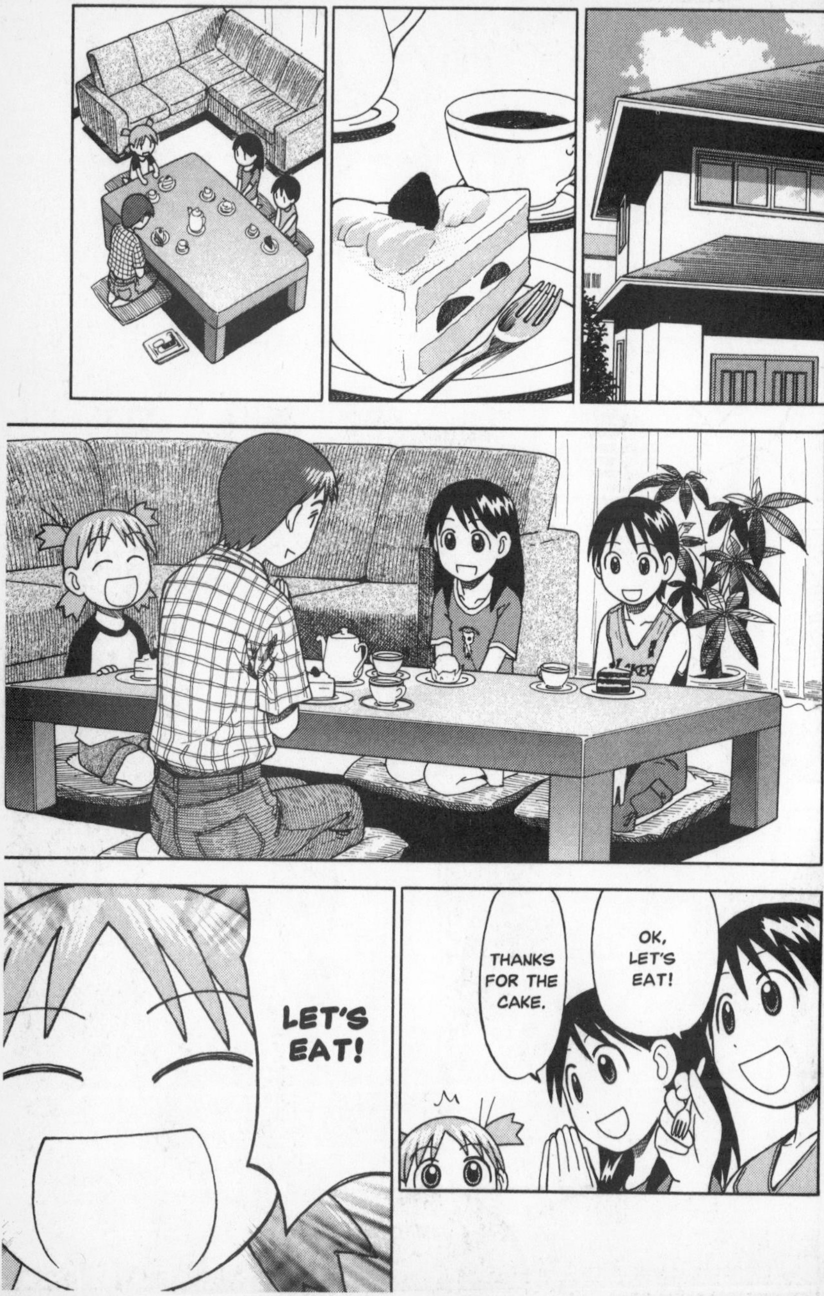
OK, LET'S EAT!
THANKS FOR THE CAKE.
LET'S EAT!

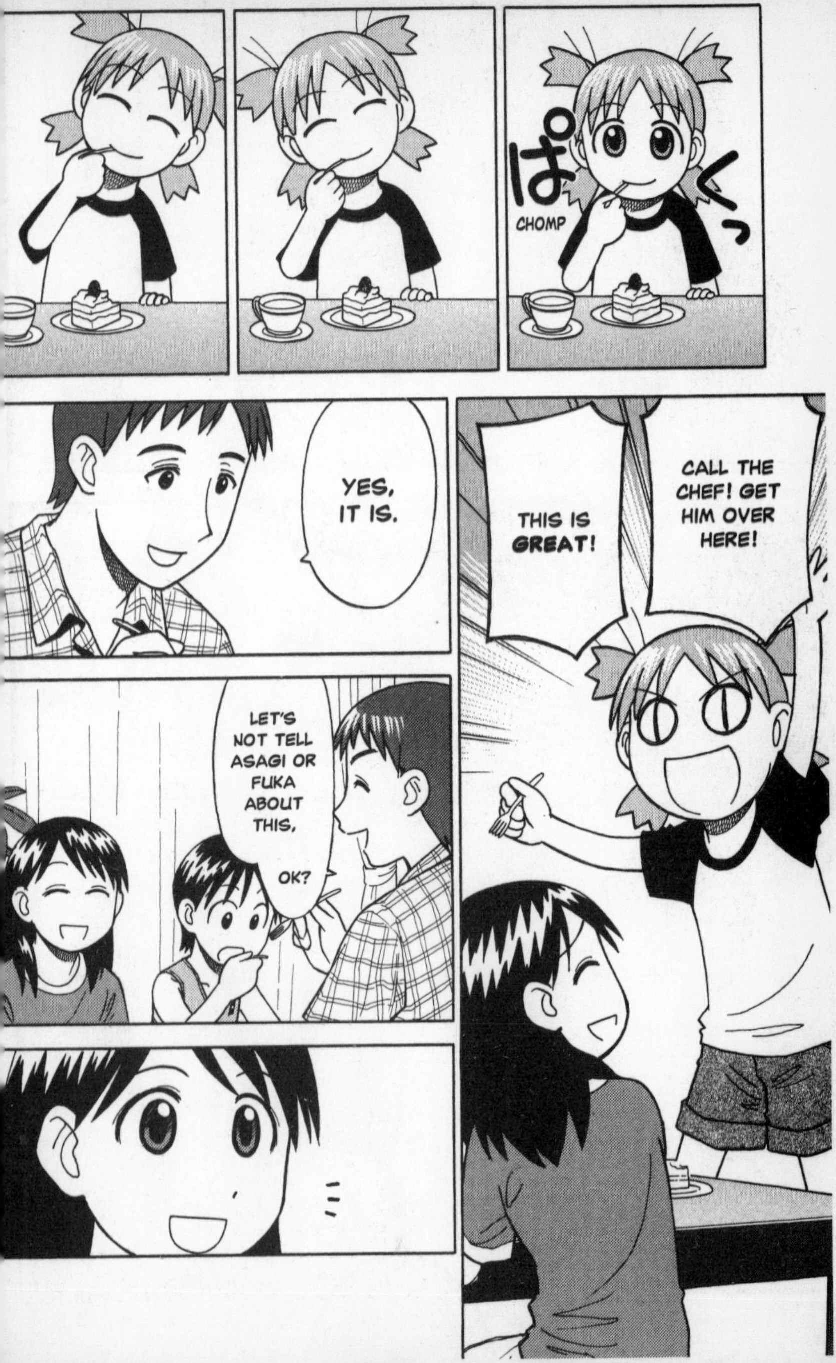

ぱくっ
CHOMP
CALL THE CHEF! GET HIM OVER HERE!
THIS IS GREAT!
YES, IT IS.
LET'S NOT TELL ASAGI OR FUKA ABOUT THIS,
OK?

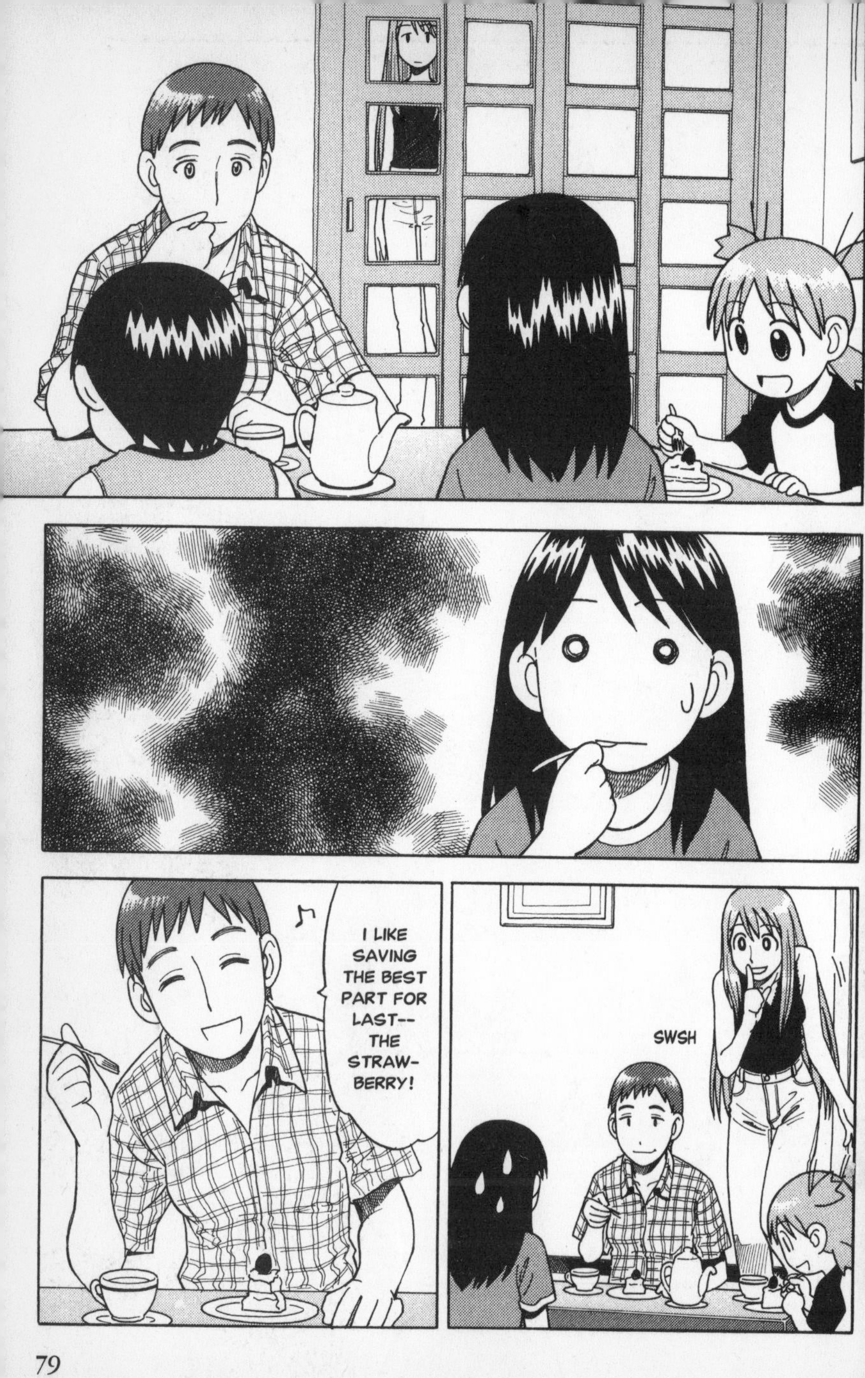
I LIKE SAVING THE BEST PART FOR LAST-- THE STRAW-BERRY!
SWSH

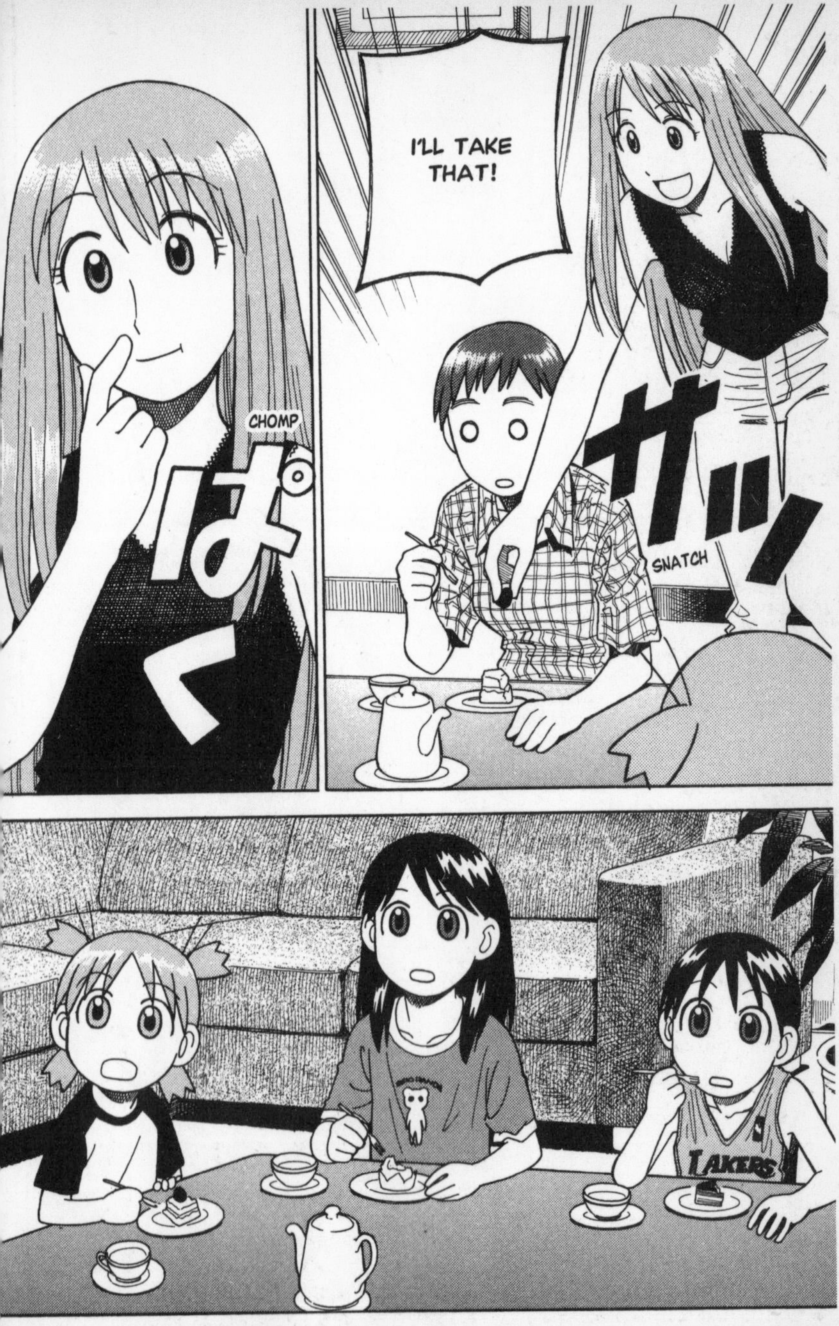
I'LL TAKE THAT!
サッ
SNATCH
ぱく
CHOMP
LAKERS

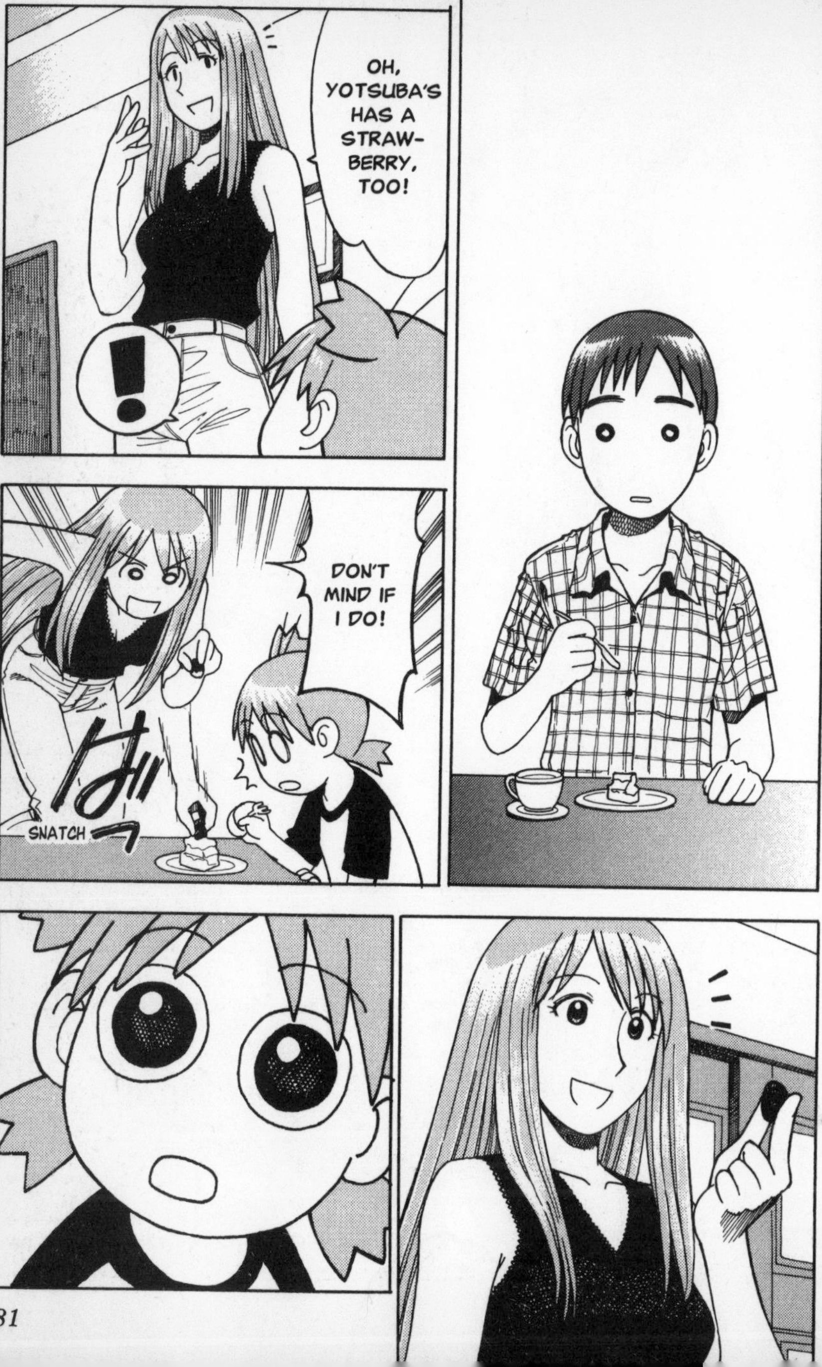
OH, YOTSUBA'S HAS A STRAW-BERRY, TOO!
!
DON'T MIND IF I DO!
SNATCH

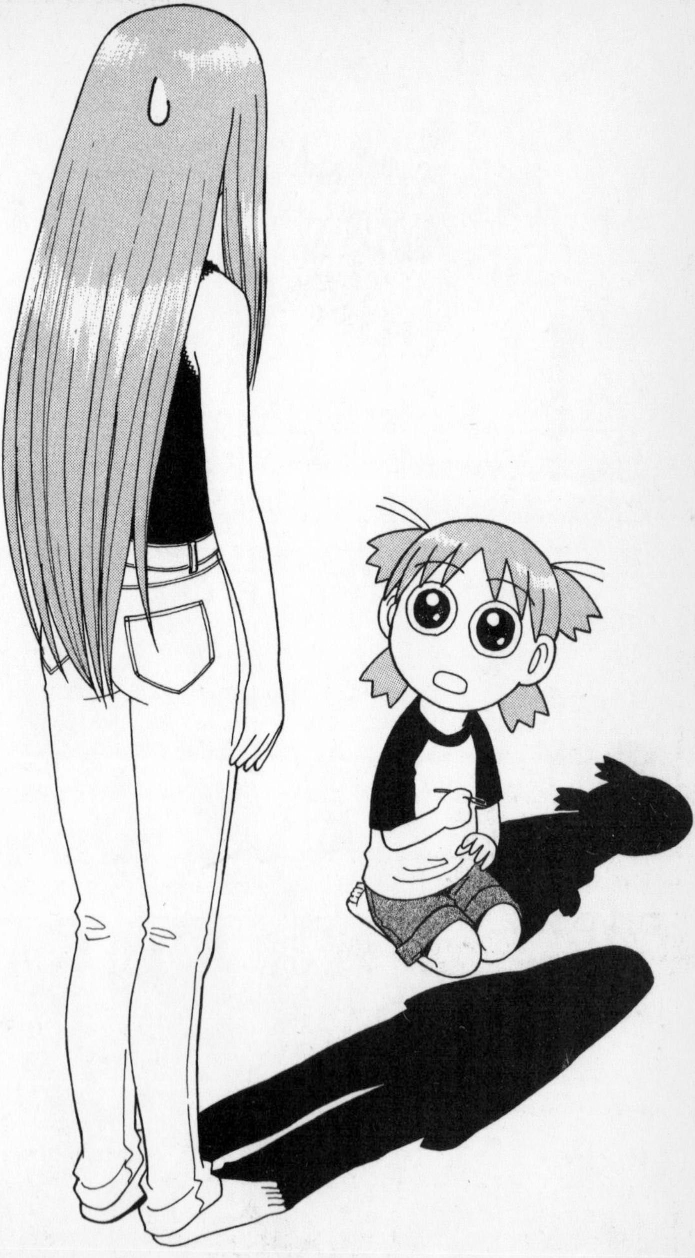

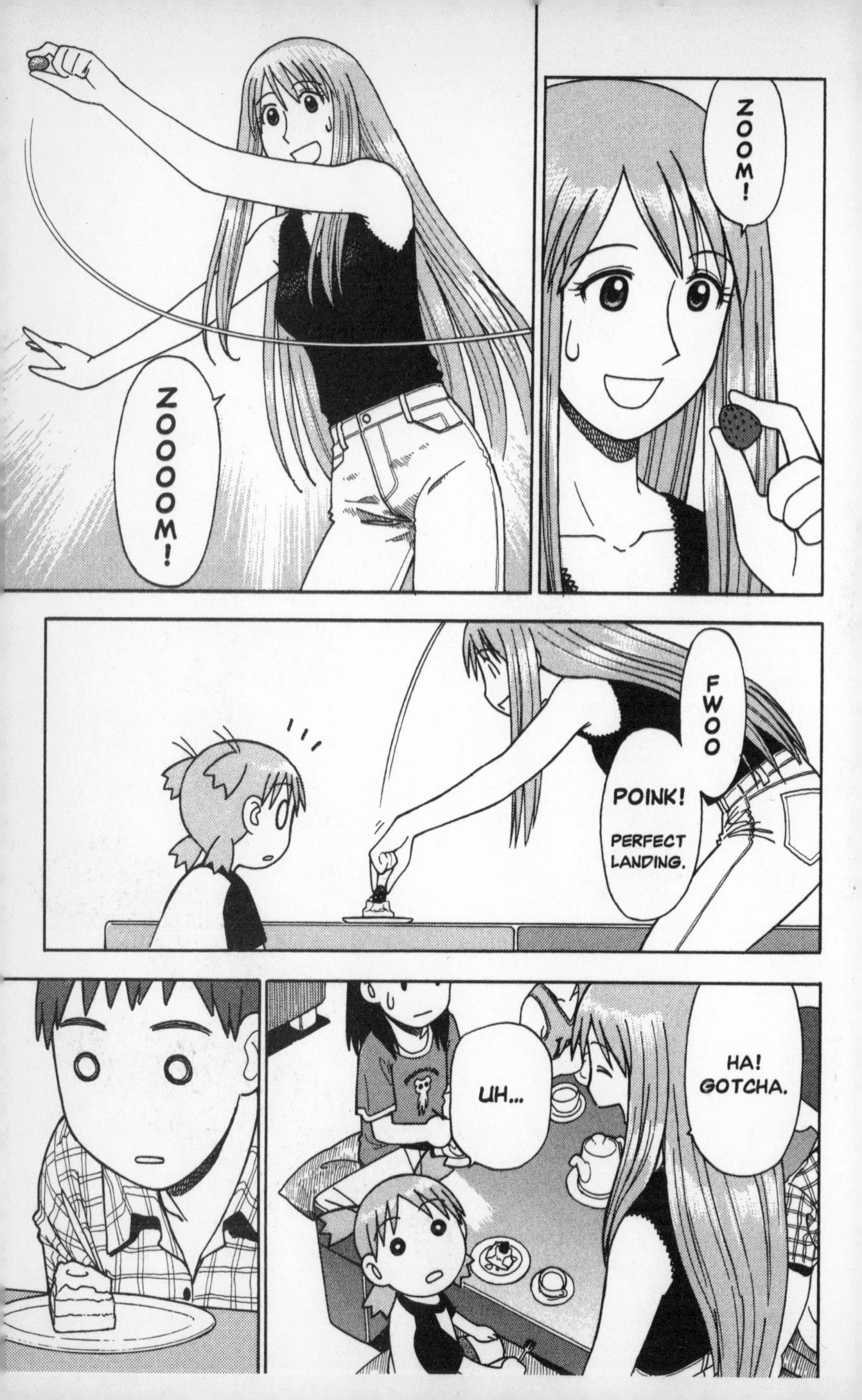
ZOOM!
ZOOOOOM!
FWOO
POINK!
PERFECT LANDING.
HA! GOTCHA.
UH...

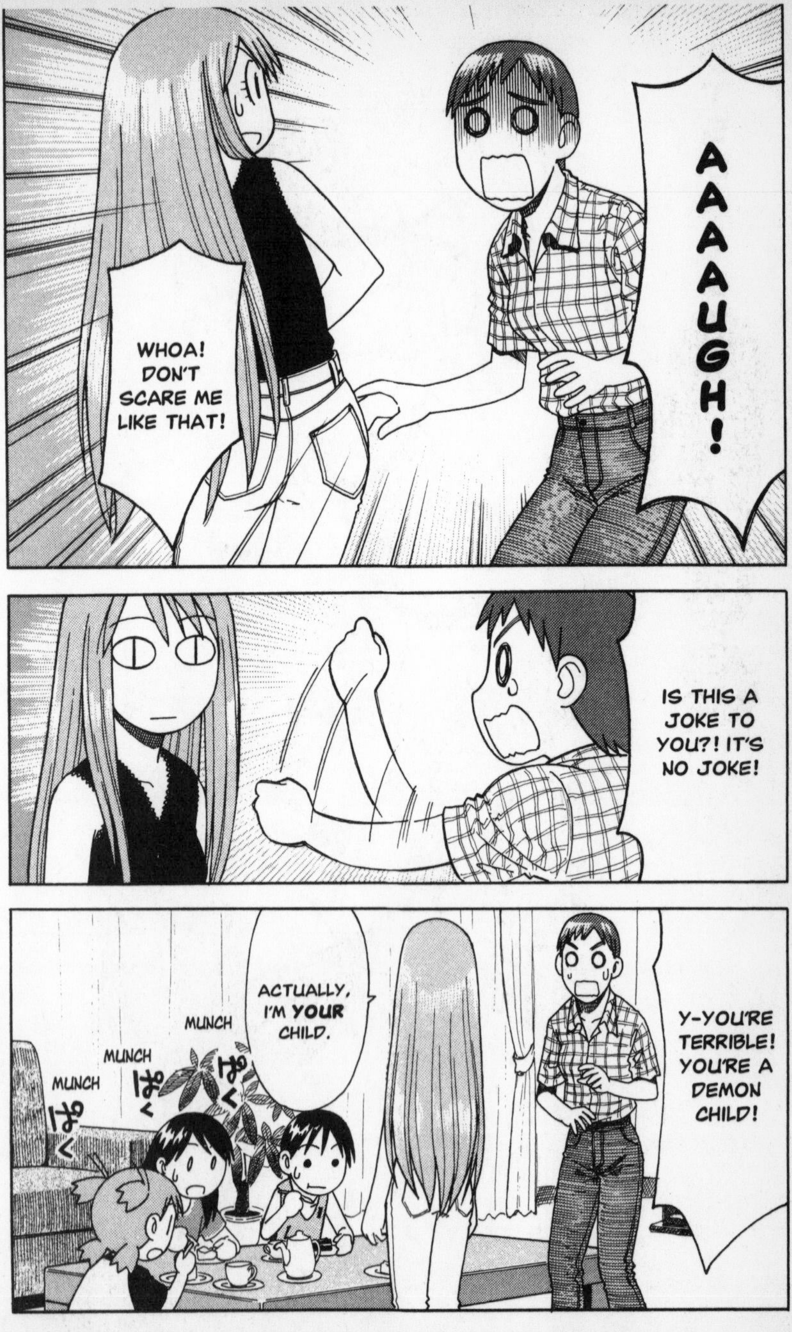
AAAAUGH!
WHOA! DON'T SCARE ME LIKE THAT!
IS THIS A JOKE TO YOU?! IT'S NO JOKE!
Y-YOU'RE TERRIBLE! YOU'RE A DEMON CHILD!
ACTUALLY, I'M **YOUR** CHILD.
MUNCH
ぱく
MUNCH
ぱく
MUNCH
ぱく

YOTSUBA & NO BOTHER

CHAPTER 11

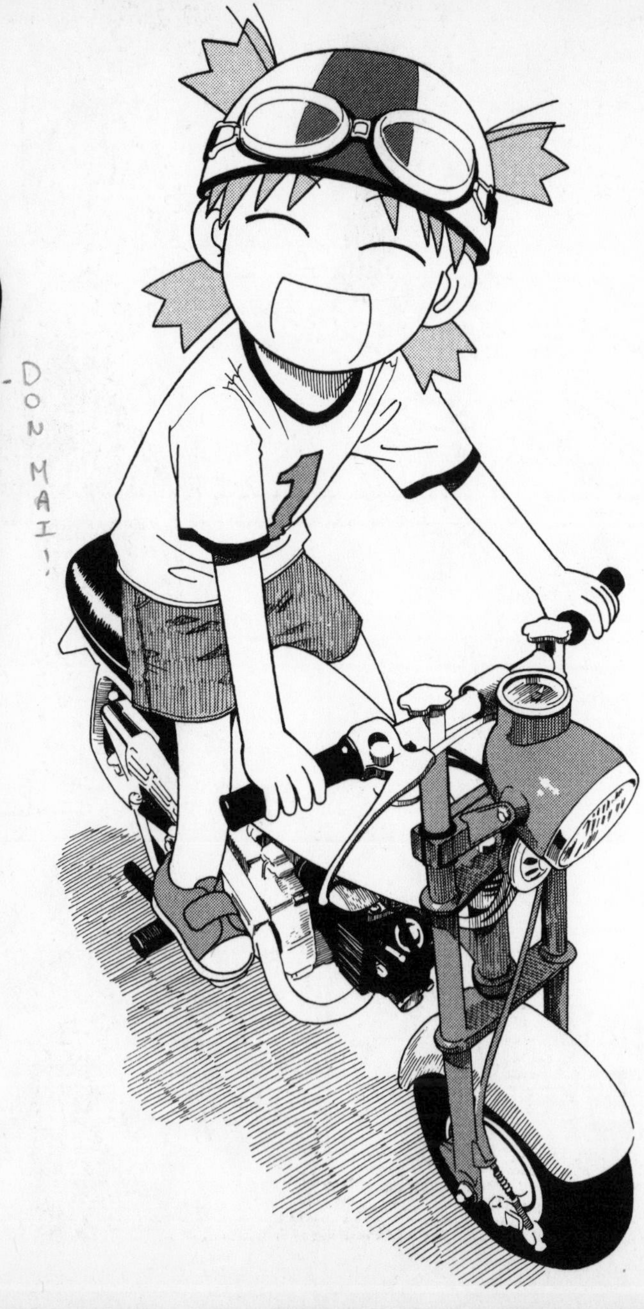
DON MAI!

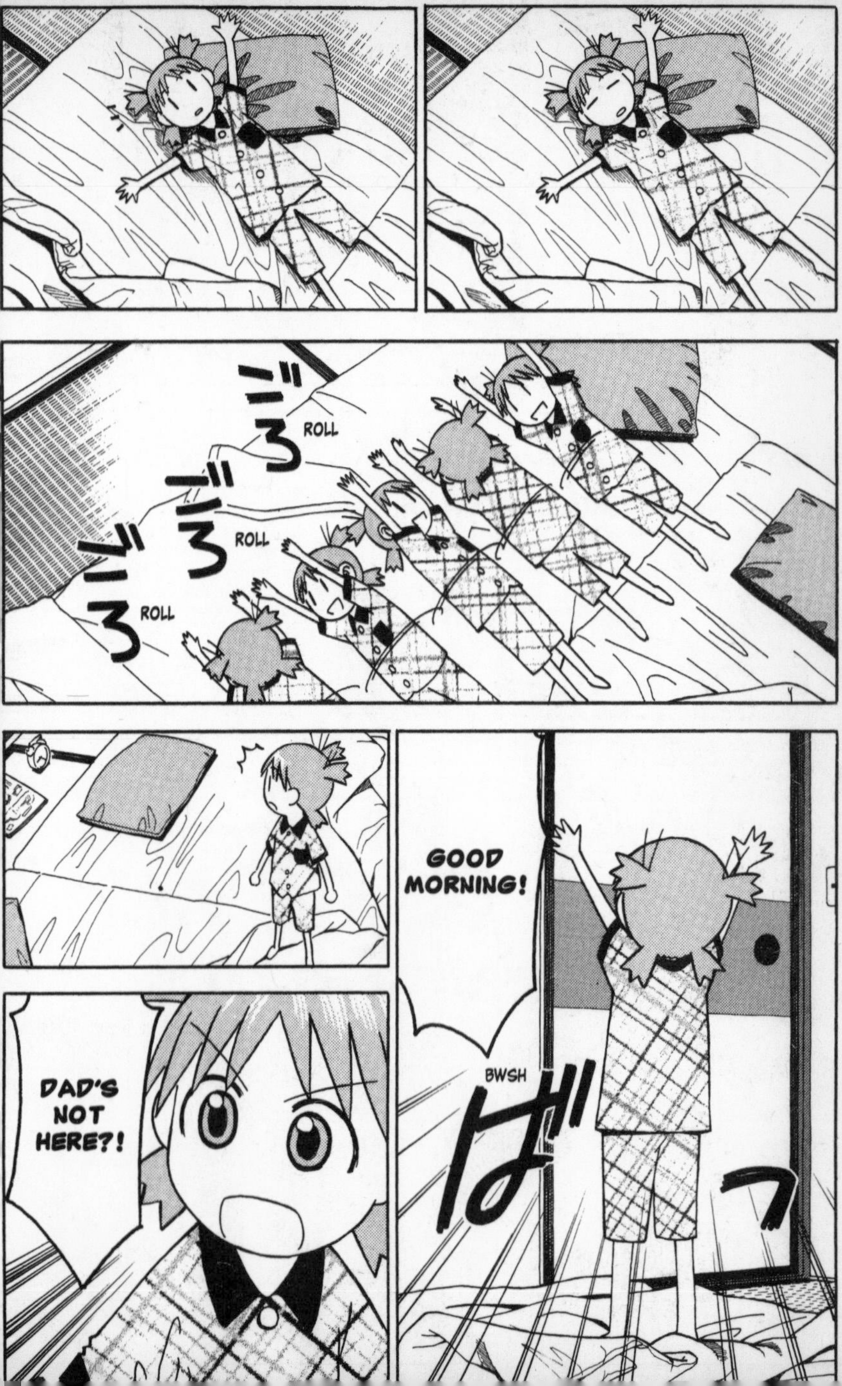

ごろ
ROLL
ごろ
ROLL
ごろ
ROLL
GOOD MORNING!
BWSH
ばっ
DAD'S NOT HERE?!

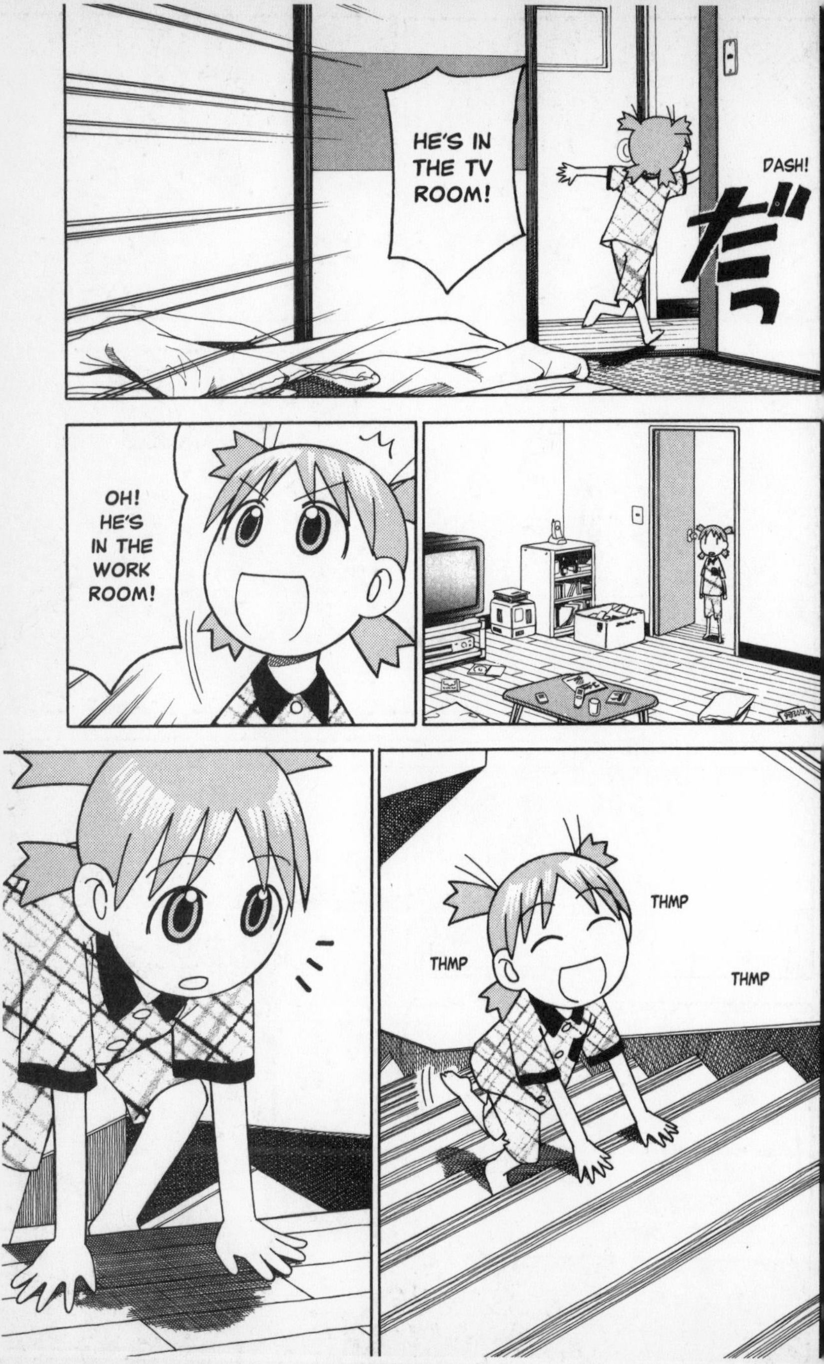
DASH!
ダッ
HE'S IN THE TV ROOM!
OH! HE'S IN THE WORK ROOM!
THMP
THMP
THMP

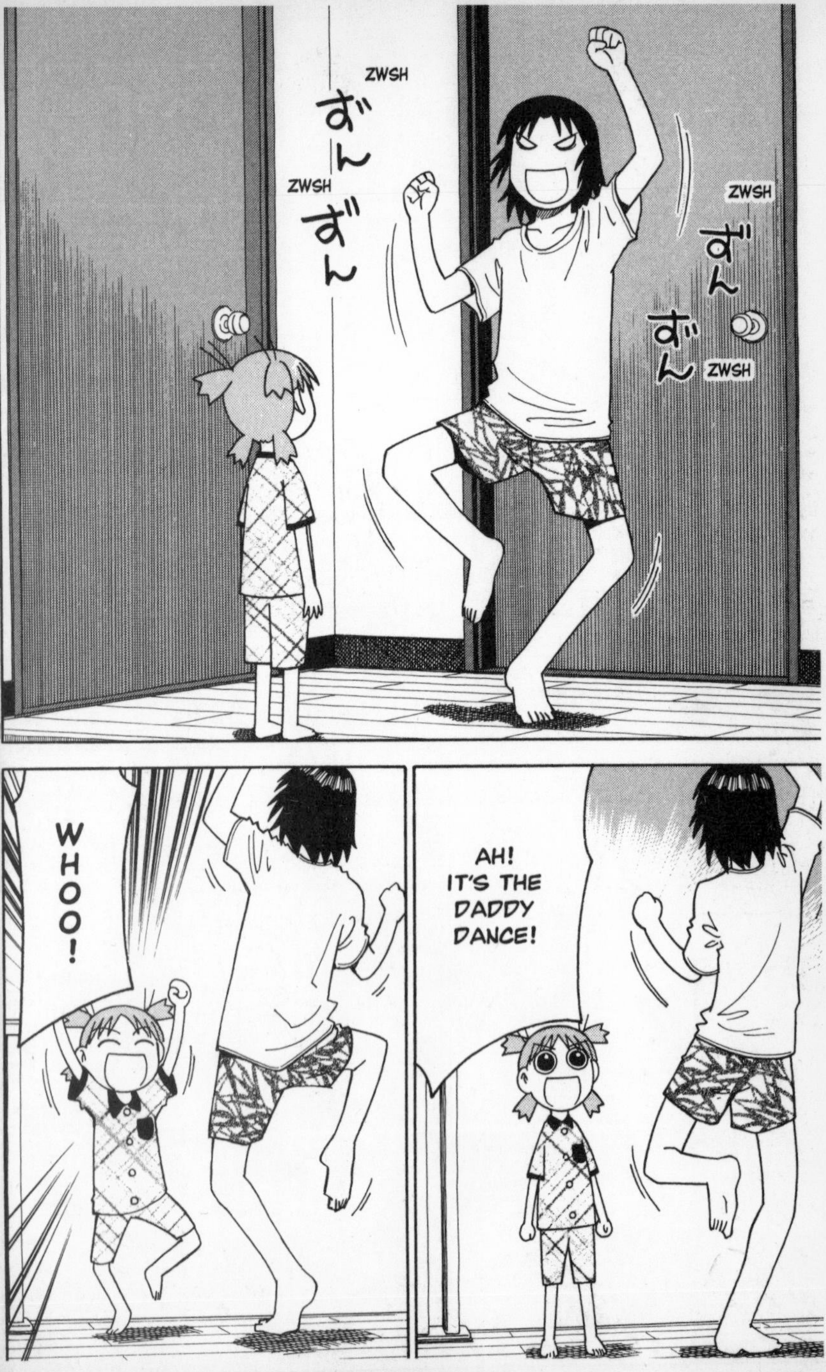
ZWSH
ずん
ZWSH
ずん
ZWSH
ずん
ZWSH
ずん
AH! IT'S THE DADDY DANCE!
WHOO!

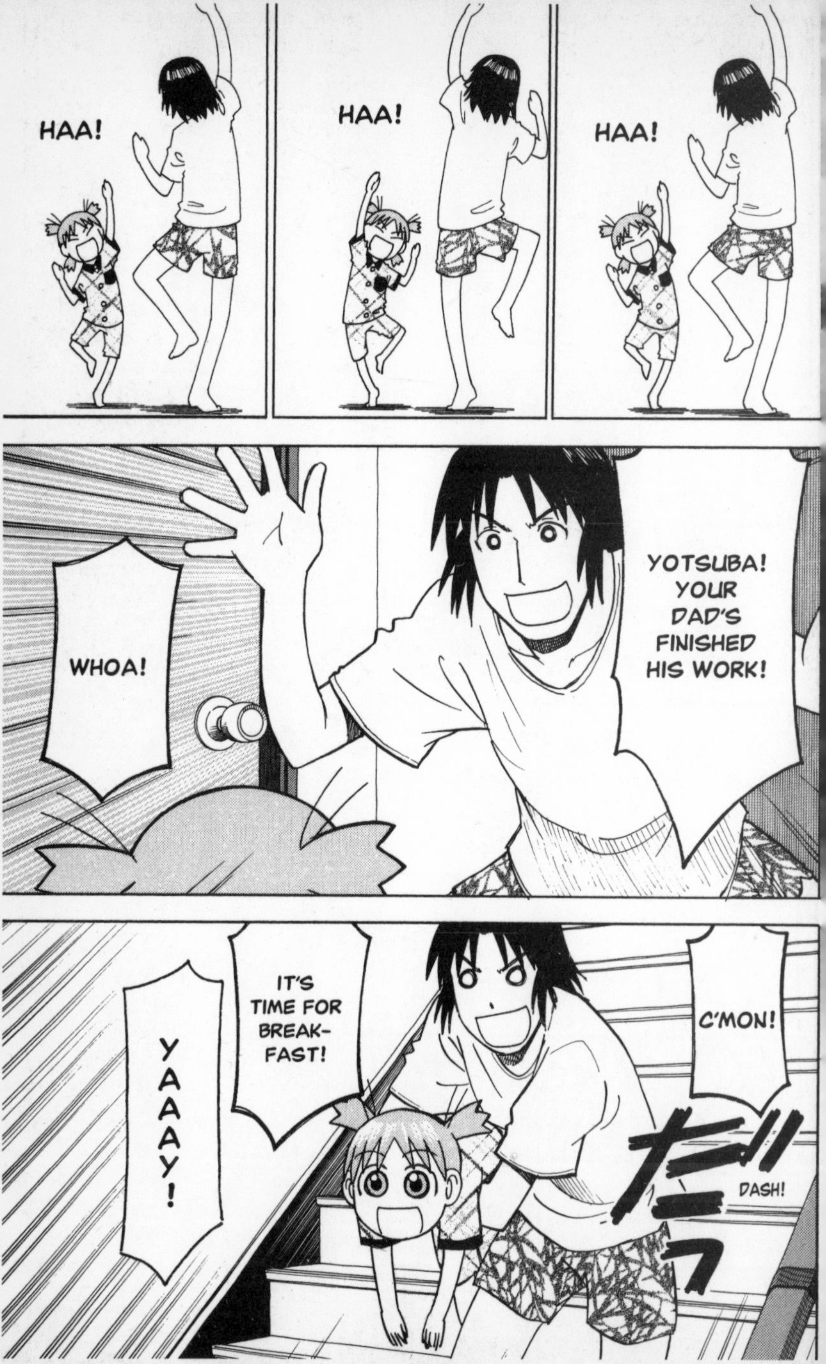
HAA!
HAA!
HAA!
YOTSUBA! YOUR DAD'S FINISHED HIS WORK!
WHOA!
C'MON!
DASH!
IT'S TIME FOR BREAK-FAST!
YAAAAY!

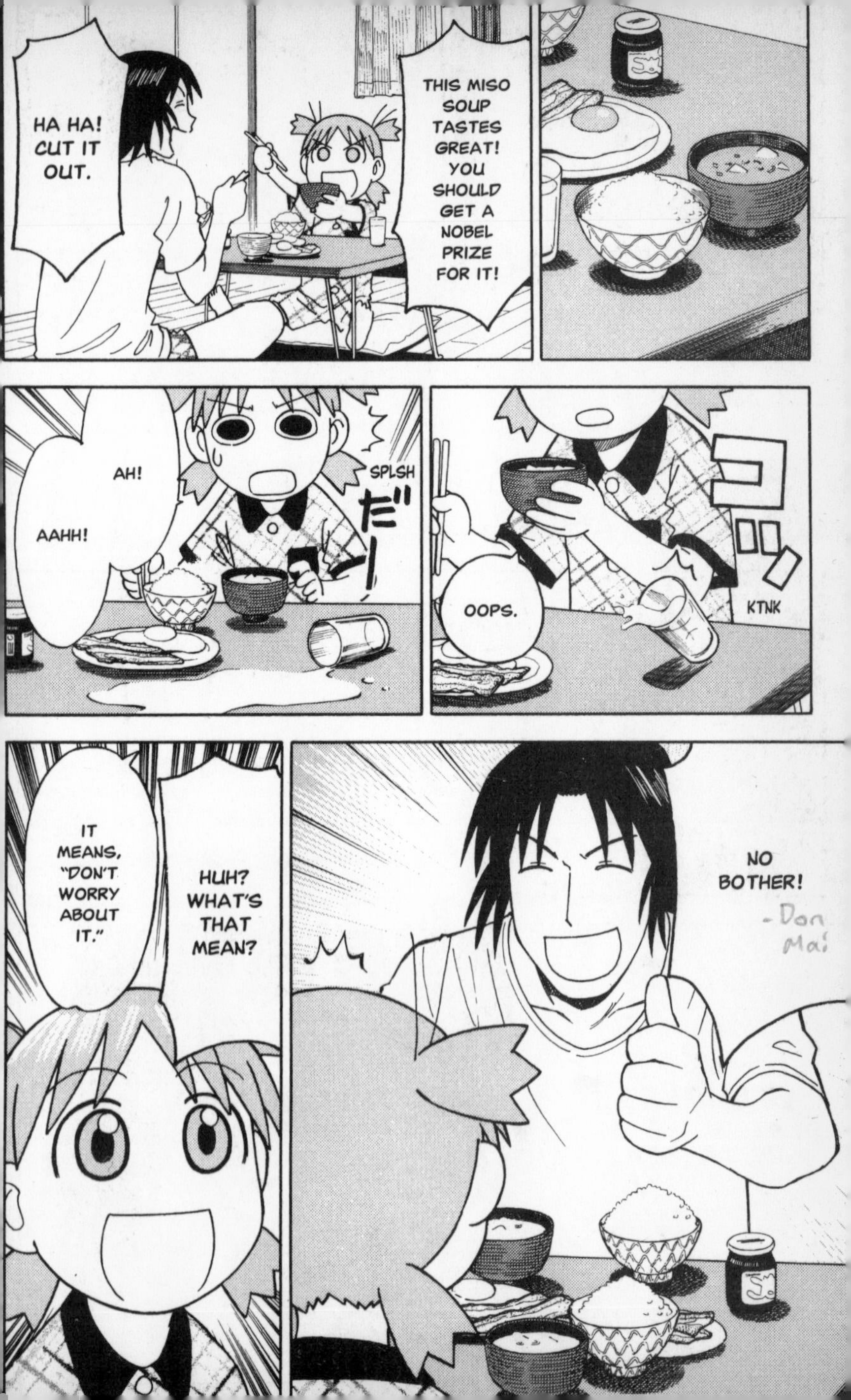

THIS MISO SOUP TASTES GREAT! YOU SHOULD GET A NOBEL PRIZE FOR IT!
HA HA! CUT IT OUT.
OOPS.
KTNK
SPLSH
AH!
AAHH!
NO BOTHER!
-Don Mai
HUH? WHAT'S THAT MEAN?
IT MEANS, "DON'T WORRY ABOUT IT."

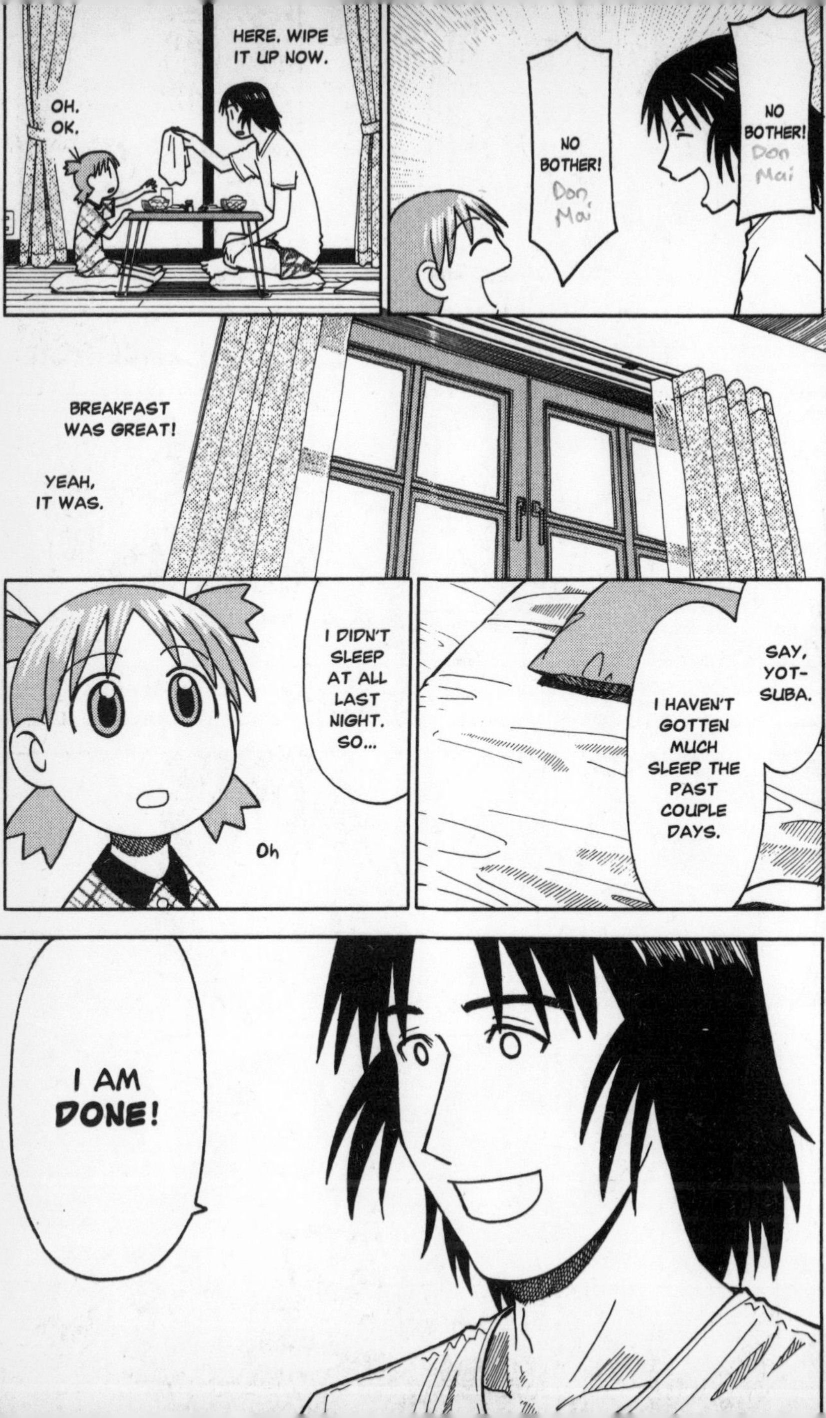
NO BOTHER! Don Mai
NO BOTHER! Don Mai
HERE. WIPE IT UP NOW.
OH. OK.
BREAKFAST WAS GREAT!
YEAH, IT WAS.
SAY, YOT-SUBA.
I HAVEN'T GOTTEN MUCH SLEEP THE PAST COUPLE DAYS.
I DIDN'T SLEEP AT ALL LAST NIGHT. SO...
Oh
I AM DONE!

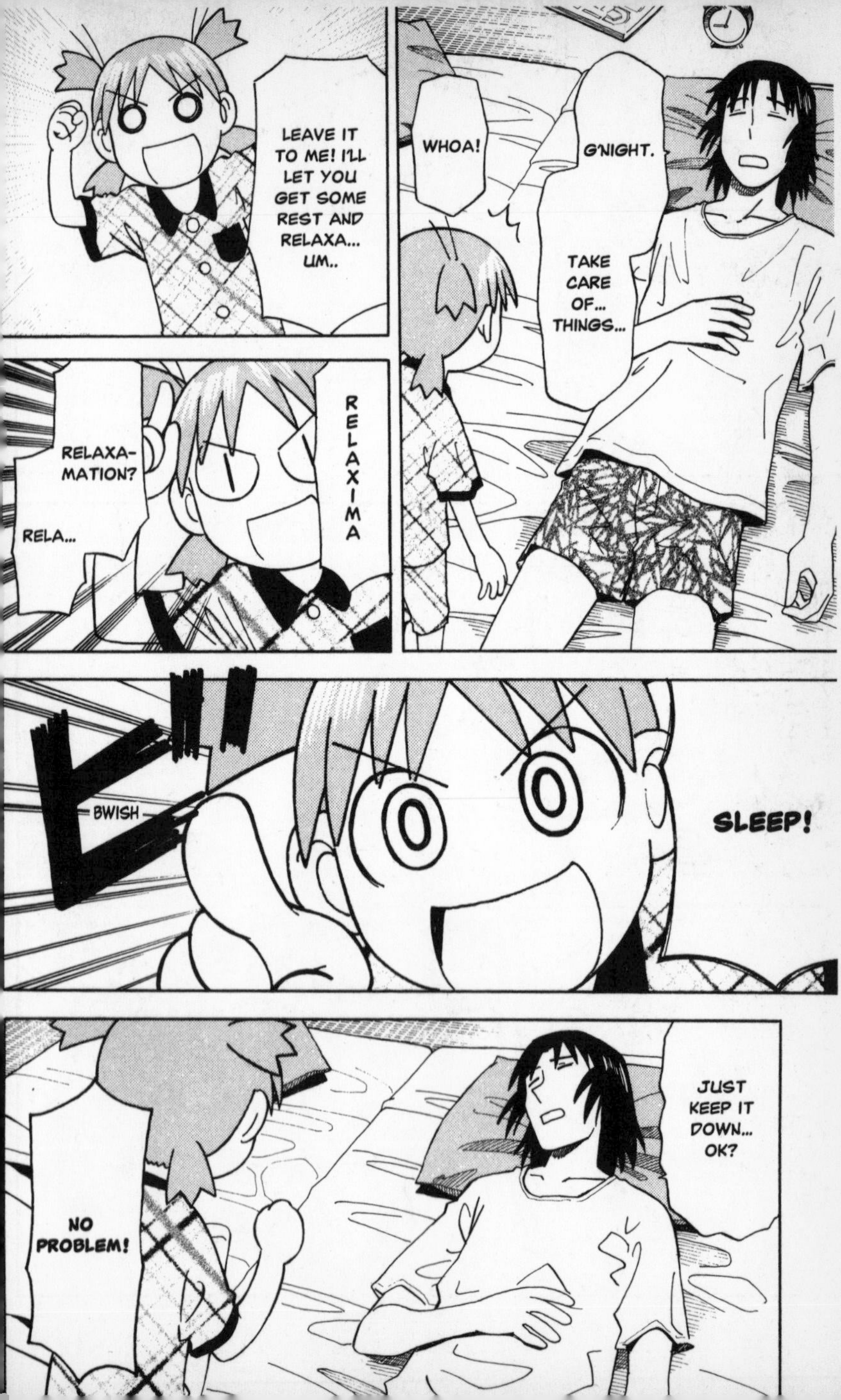
LEAVE IT TO ME! I'LL LET YOU GET SOME REST AND RELAXA... UM..
RELAXIMA
RELAXA-MATION?
RELA...
WHOA!
G'NIGHT.
TAKE CARE OF... THINGS...
BWISH
SLEEP!
JUST KEEP IT DOWN... OK?
NO PROBLEM!

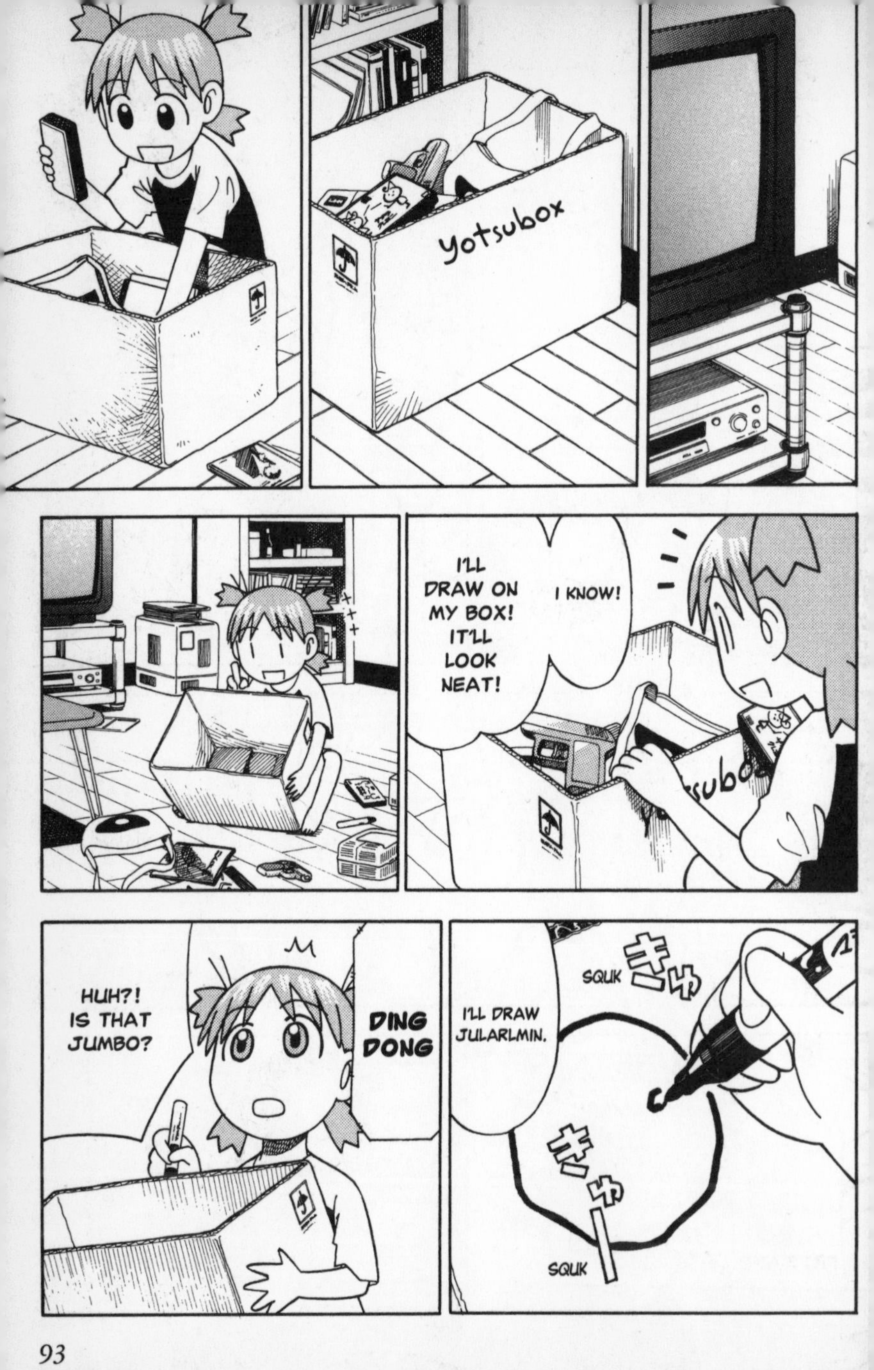
yotsubox
I KNOW!
I'LL DRAW ON MY BOX! IT'LL LOOK NEAT!
I'LL DRAW JULARLMIN.
SQUK
きゅー
SQUK
きゅー
DING DONG
HUH?! IS THAT JUMBO?

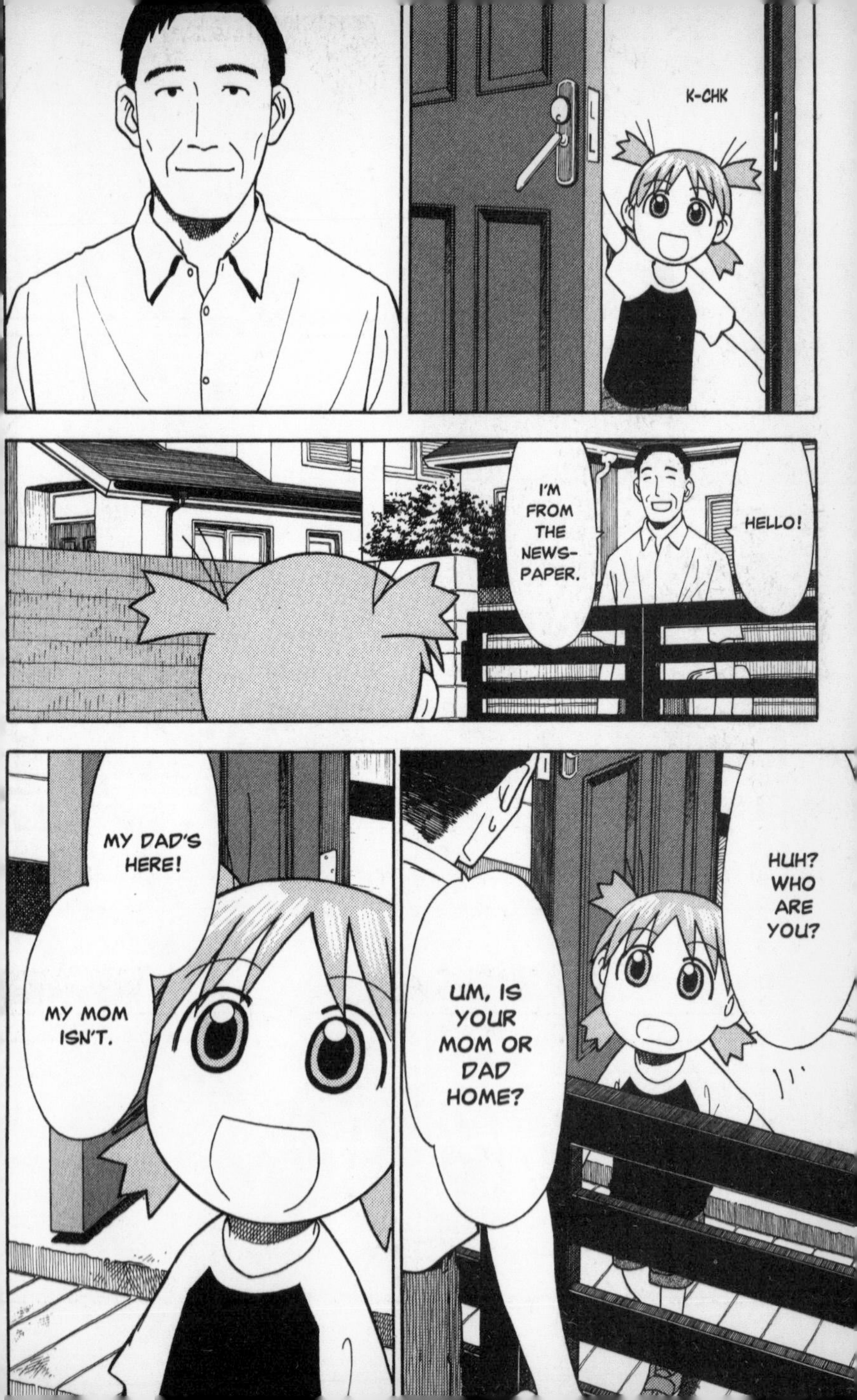
K-CHK
HELLO!
I'M FROM THE NEWS-PAPER.
HUH? WHO ARE YOU?
UM, IS YOUR MOM OR DAD HOME?
MY DAD'S HERE!
MY MOM ISN'T.

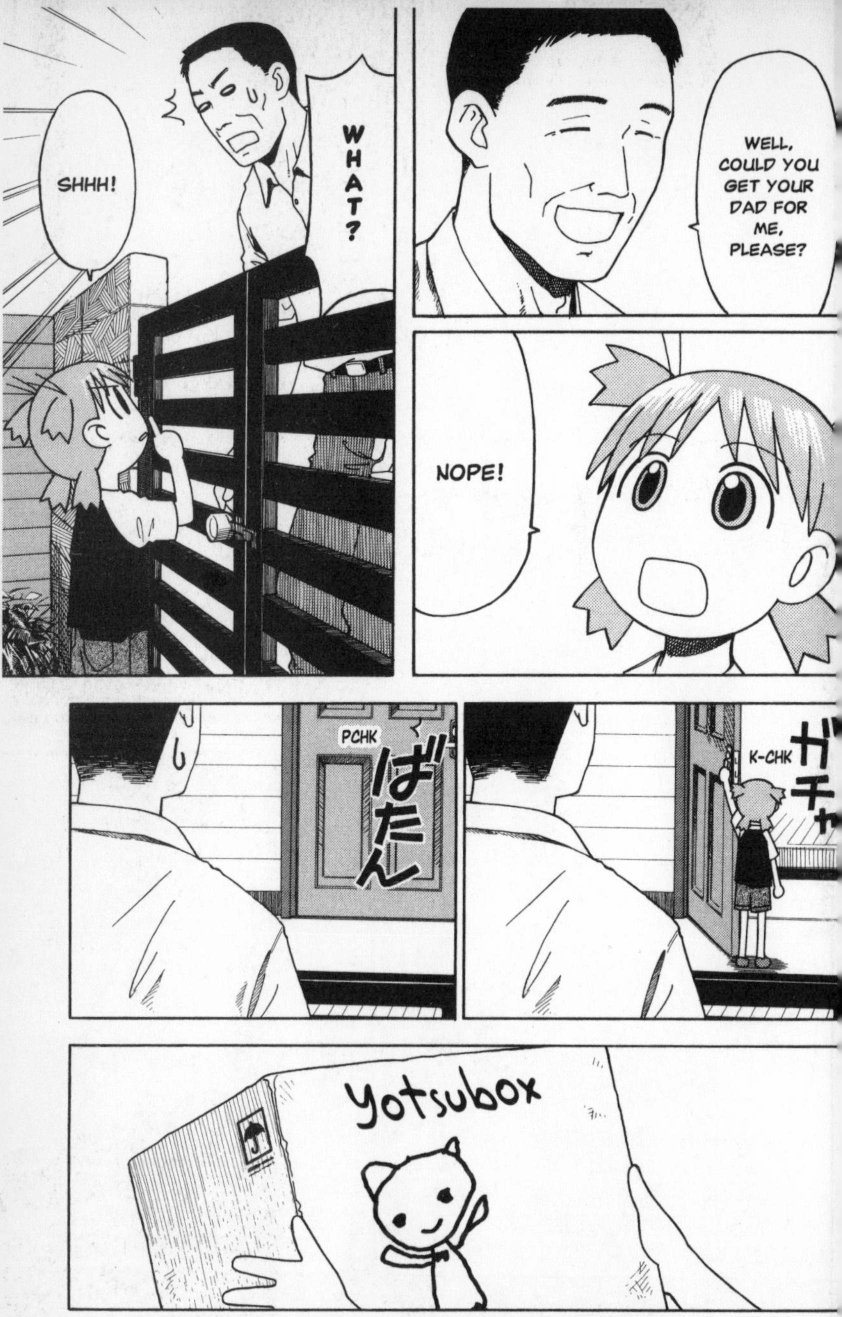
WELL, COULD YOU GET YOUR DAD FOR ME, PLEASE?
NOPE!
WHAT?
SHHH!
K-CHK
ガチャ
PCHK
ばたん
yotsubox

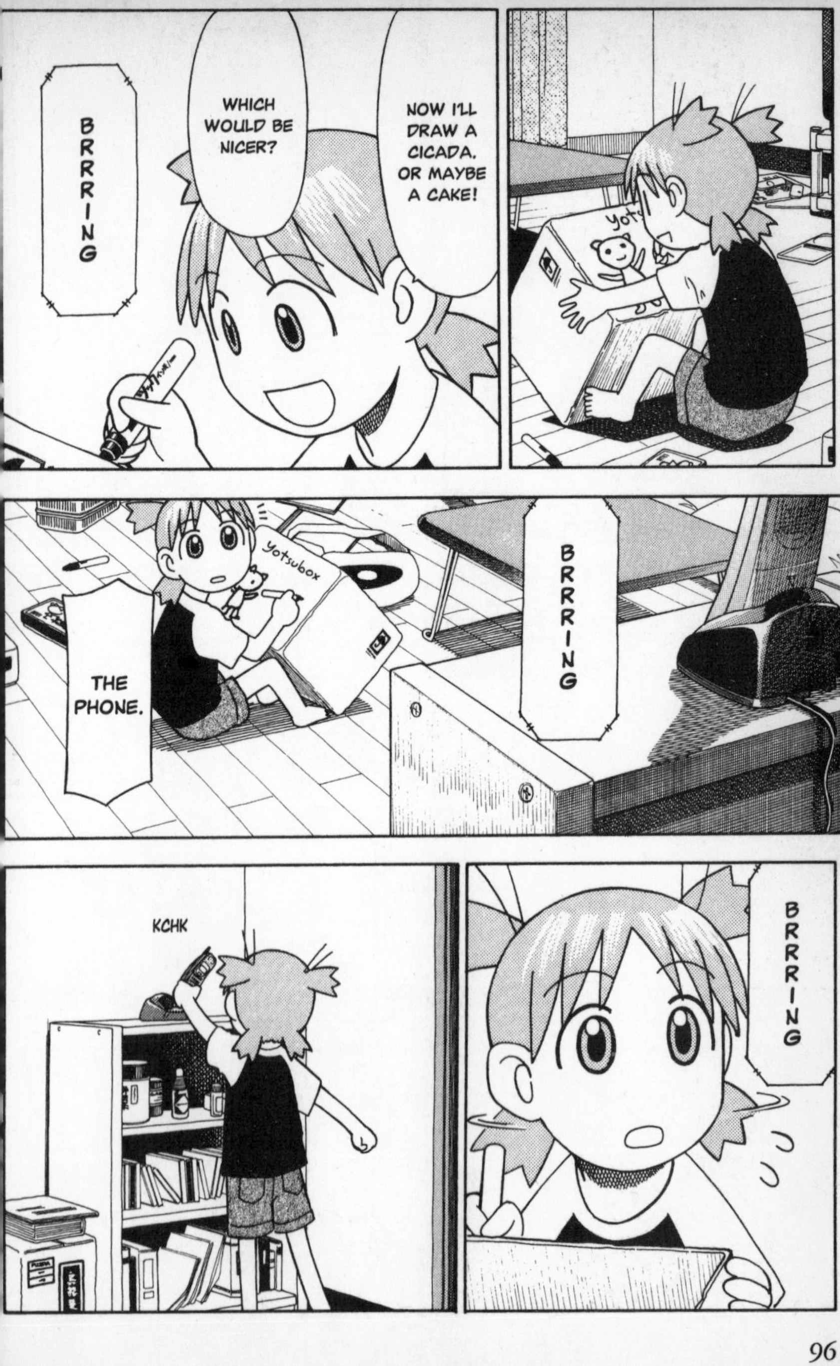
NOW I'LL DRAW A CICADA. OR MAYBE A CAKE!
WHICH WOULD BE NICER?
BRRRING
yotsubox
BRRRING
THE PHONE.
BRRRING
KCHK

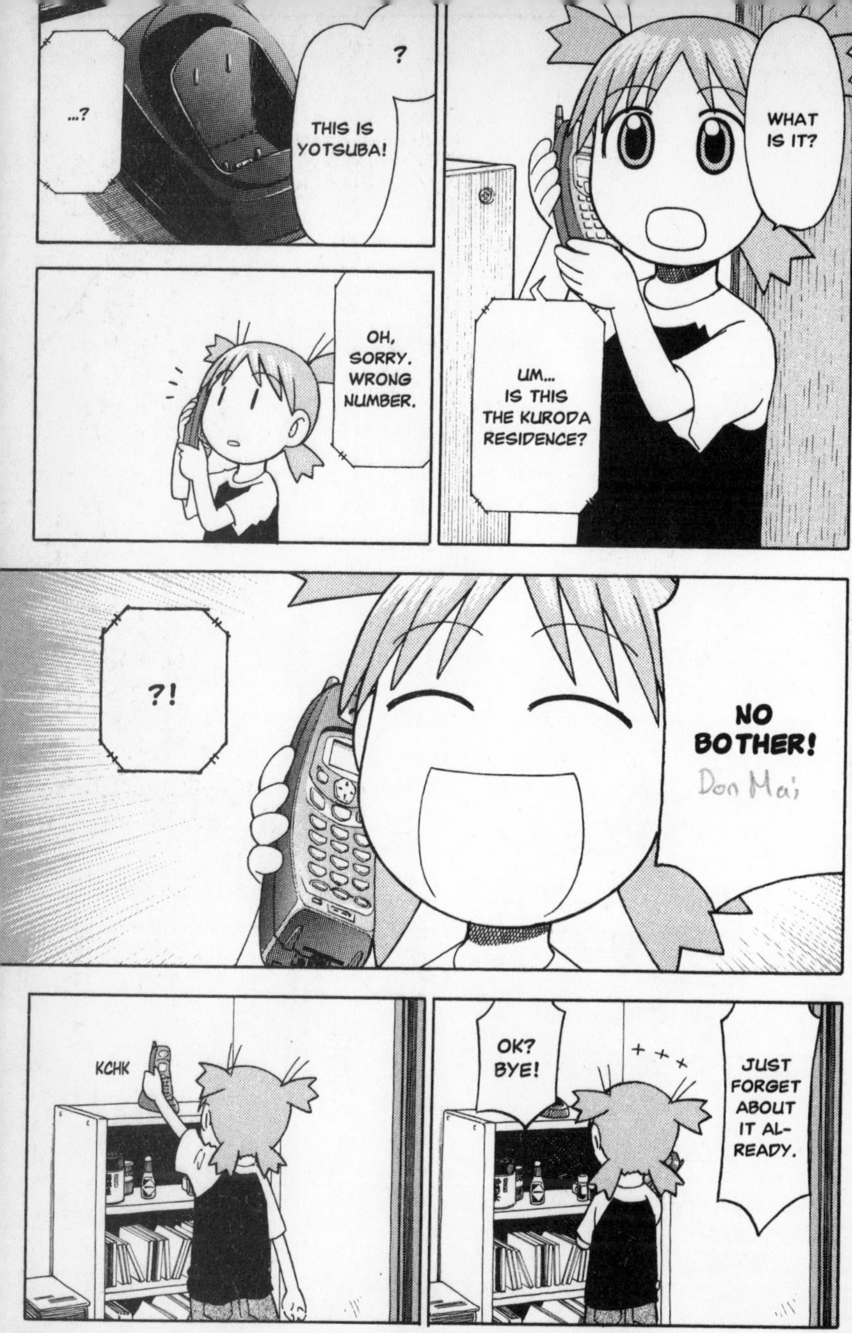
WHAT IS IT?
?
THIS IS YOTSUBA!
...?
UM... IS THIS THE KURODA RESIDENCE?
OH, SORRY. WRONG NUMBER.
NO BOTHER!
Don Mai
?!
JUST FORGET ABOUT IT AL-READY.
OK? BYE!
KCHK

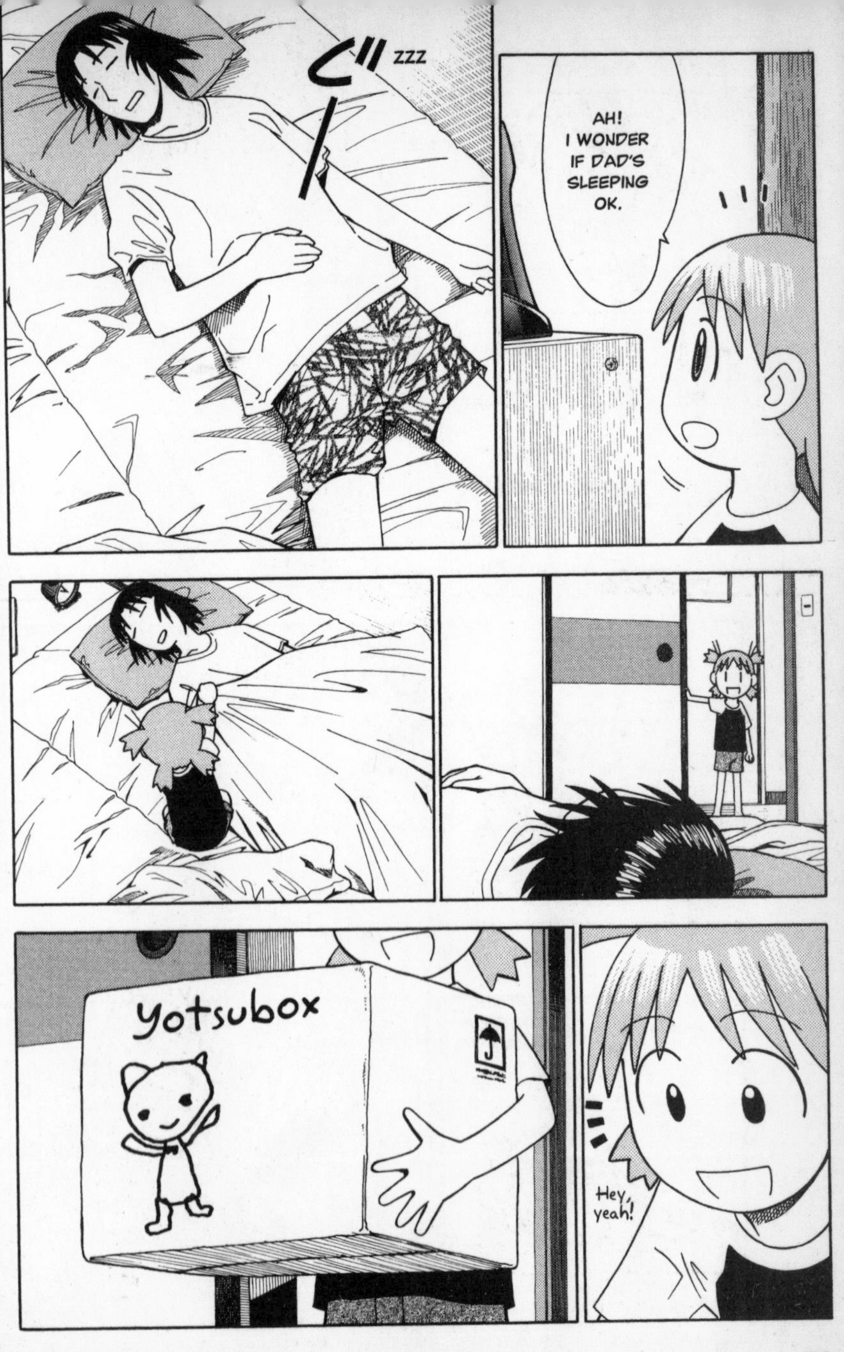
ZZZ
AH! I WONDER IF DAD'S SLEEPING OK.
yotsubox
Hey, yeah!

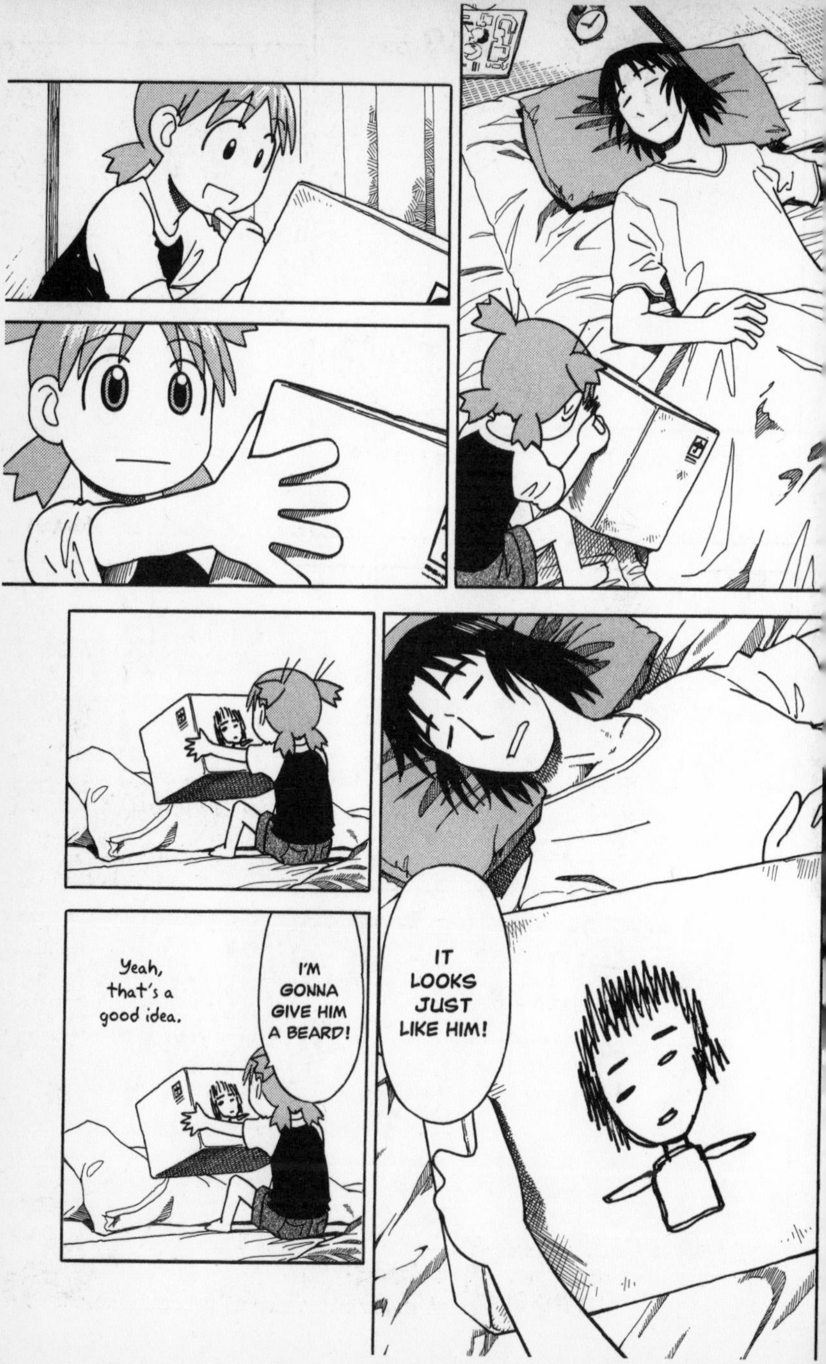
IT LOOKS JUST LIKE HIM!
I'M GONNA GIVE HIM A BEARD!
Yeah, that's a good idea.

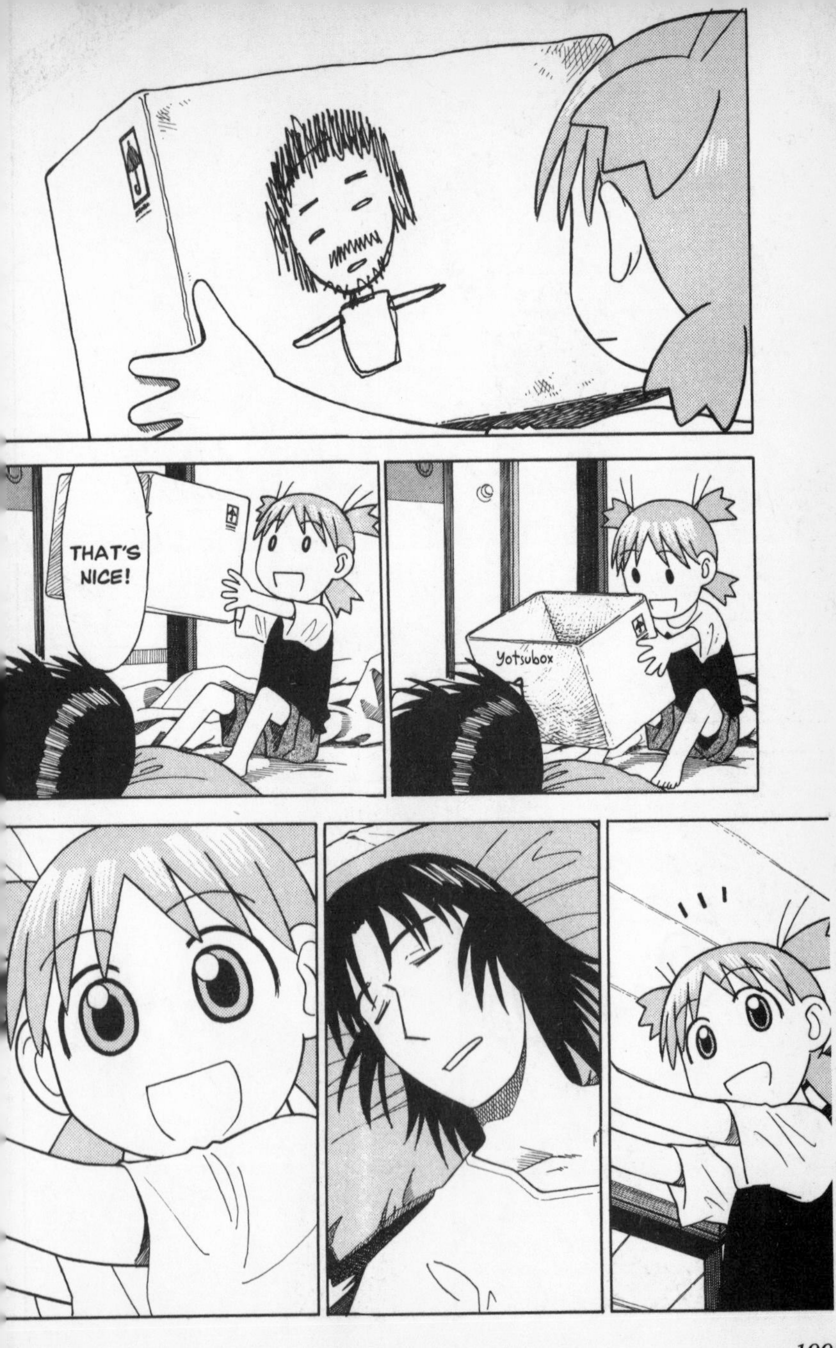
THAT'S NICE!
yotsubox

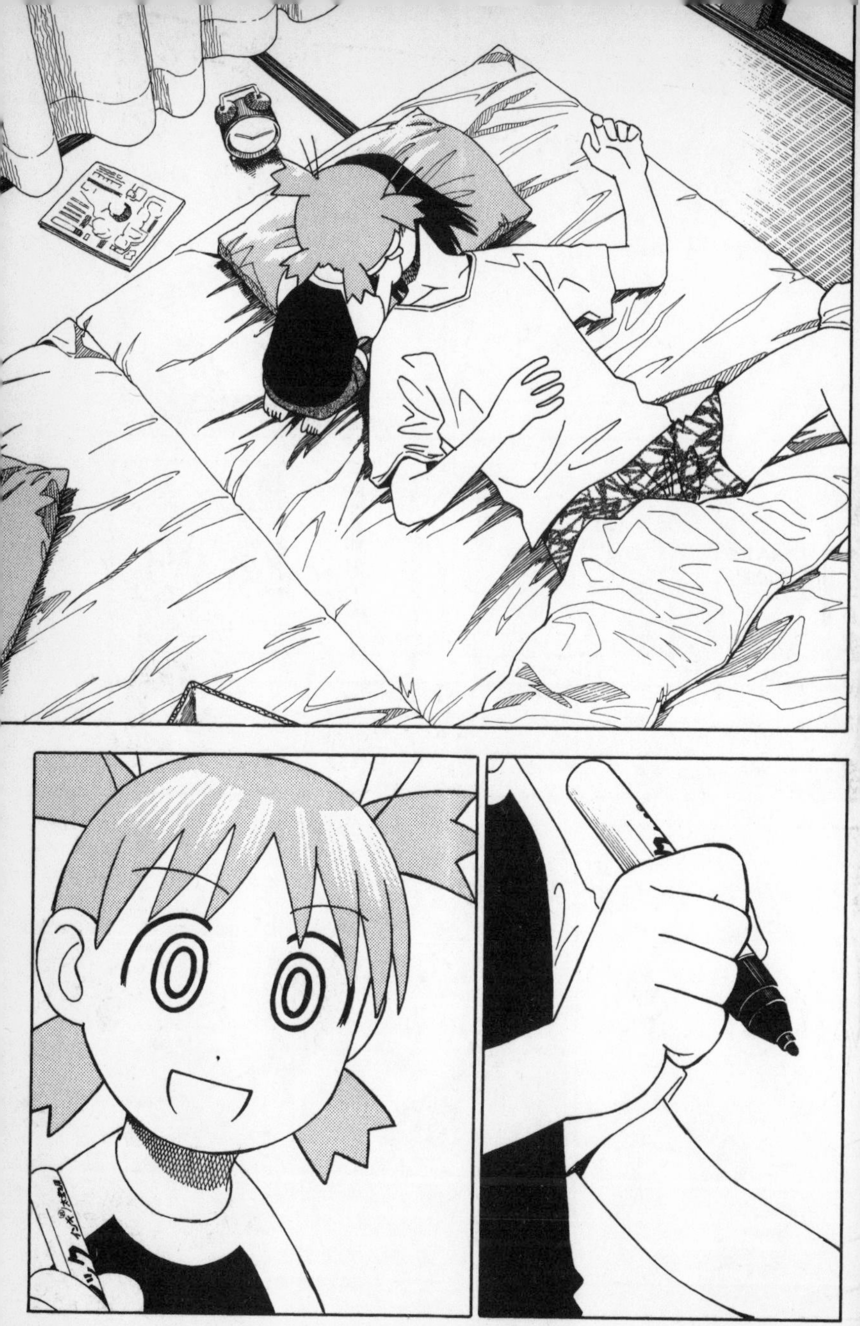

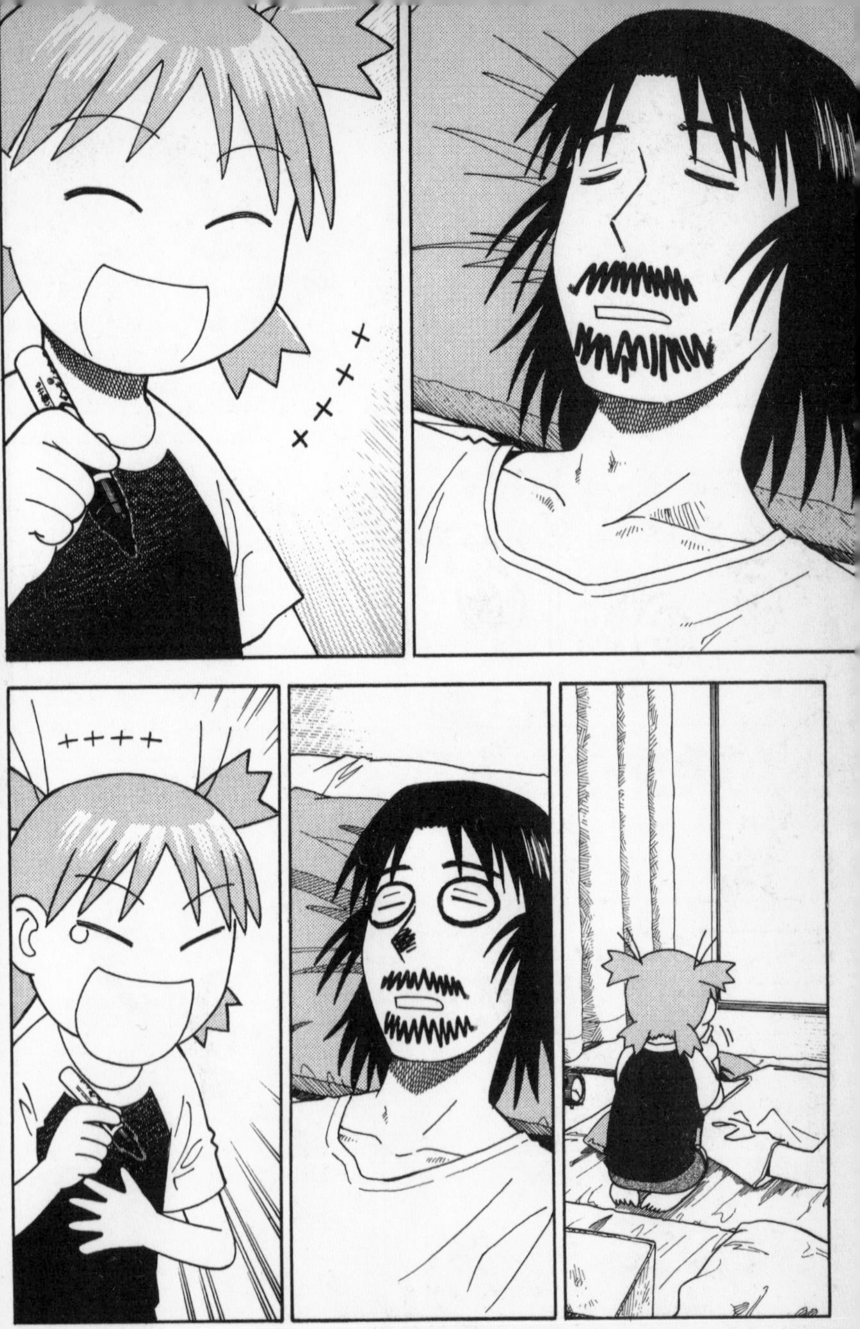

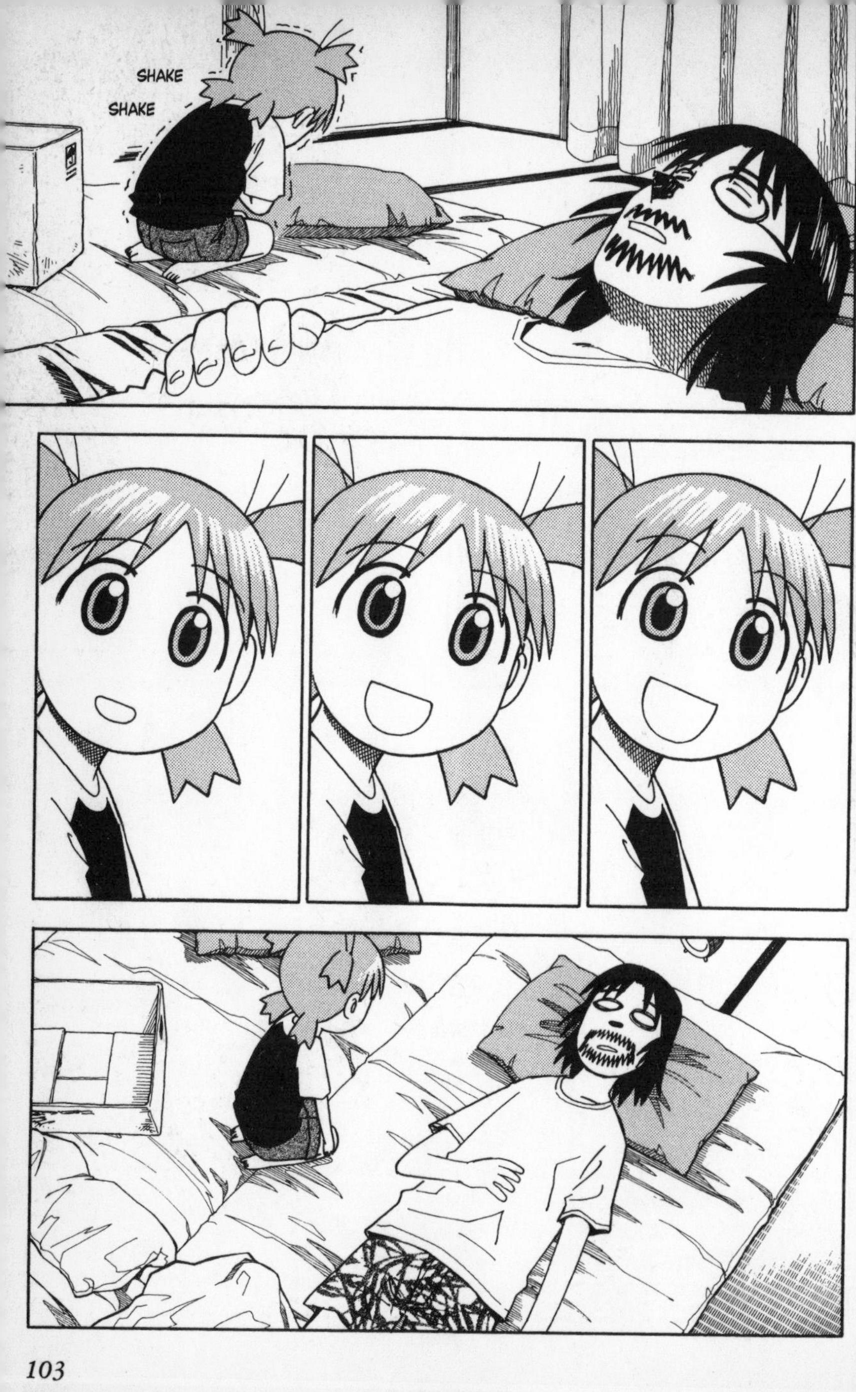
SHAKE
SHAKE

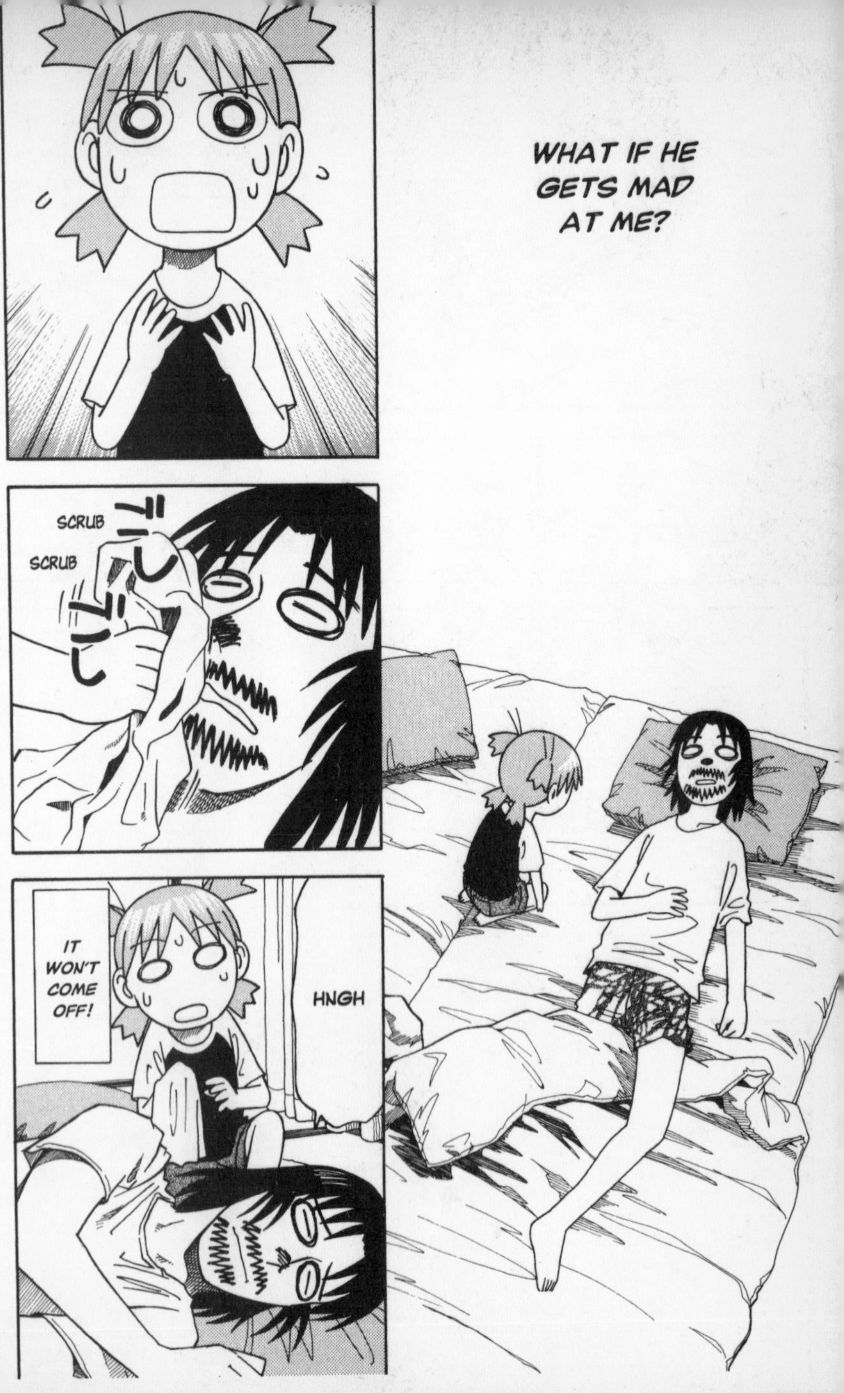
WHAT IF HE GETS MAD AT ME?
SCRUB
SCRUB
HNGH
IT WON'T COME OFF!

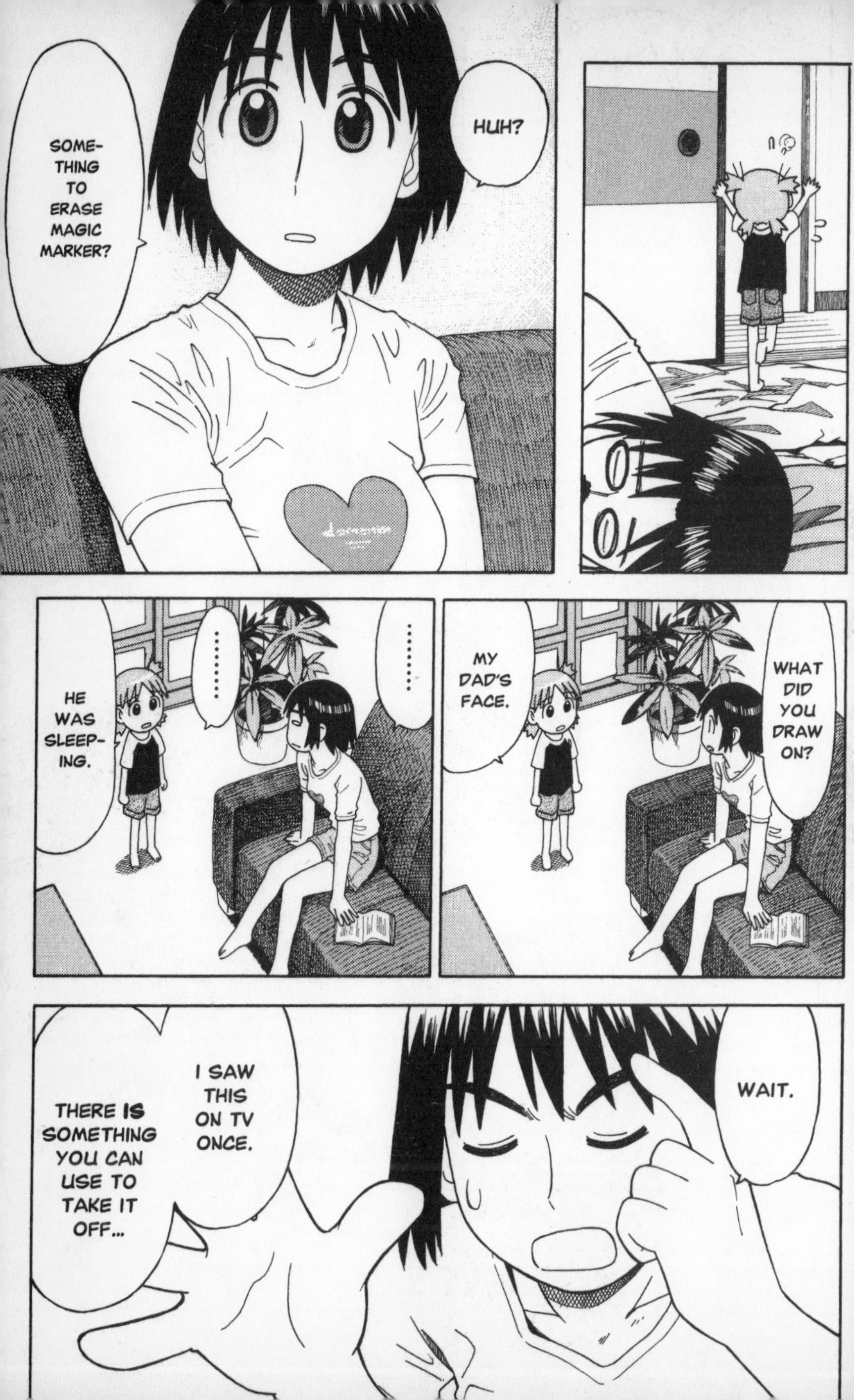
HUH?
SOMETHING TO ERASE MAGIC MARKER?
WHAT DID YOU DRAW ON?
MY DAD'S FACE.
......
......
HE WAS SLEEPING.
WAIT.
I SAW THIS ON TV ONCE.
THERE **IS** SOMETHING YOU CAN USE TO TAKE IT OFF...

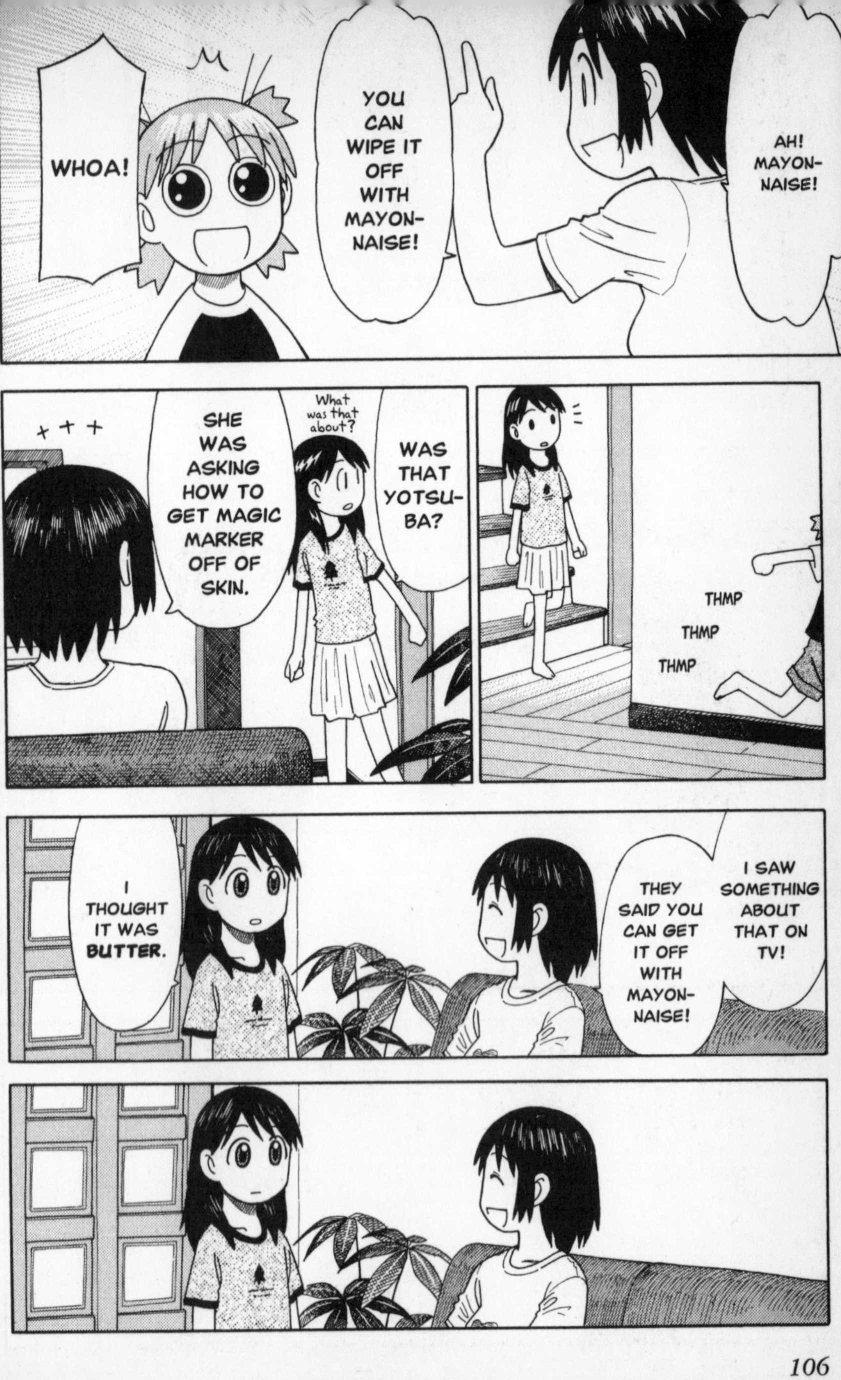
AH! MAYON-NAISE!
YOU CAN WIPE IT OFF WITH MAYON-NAISE!
WHOA!
THMP
THMP
THMP
WAS THAT YOTSU-BA?
What was that about?
SHE WAS ASKING HOW TO GET MAGIC MARKER OFF OF SKIN.
I SAW SOMETHING ABOUT THAT ON TV!
THEY SAID YOU CAN GET IT OFF WITH MAYON-NAISE!
I THOUGHT IT WAS BUTTER.

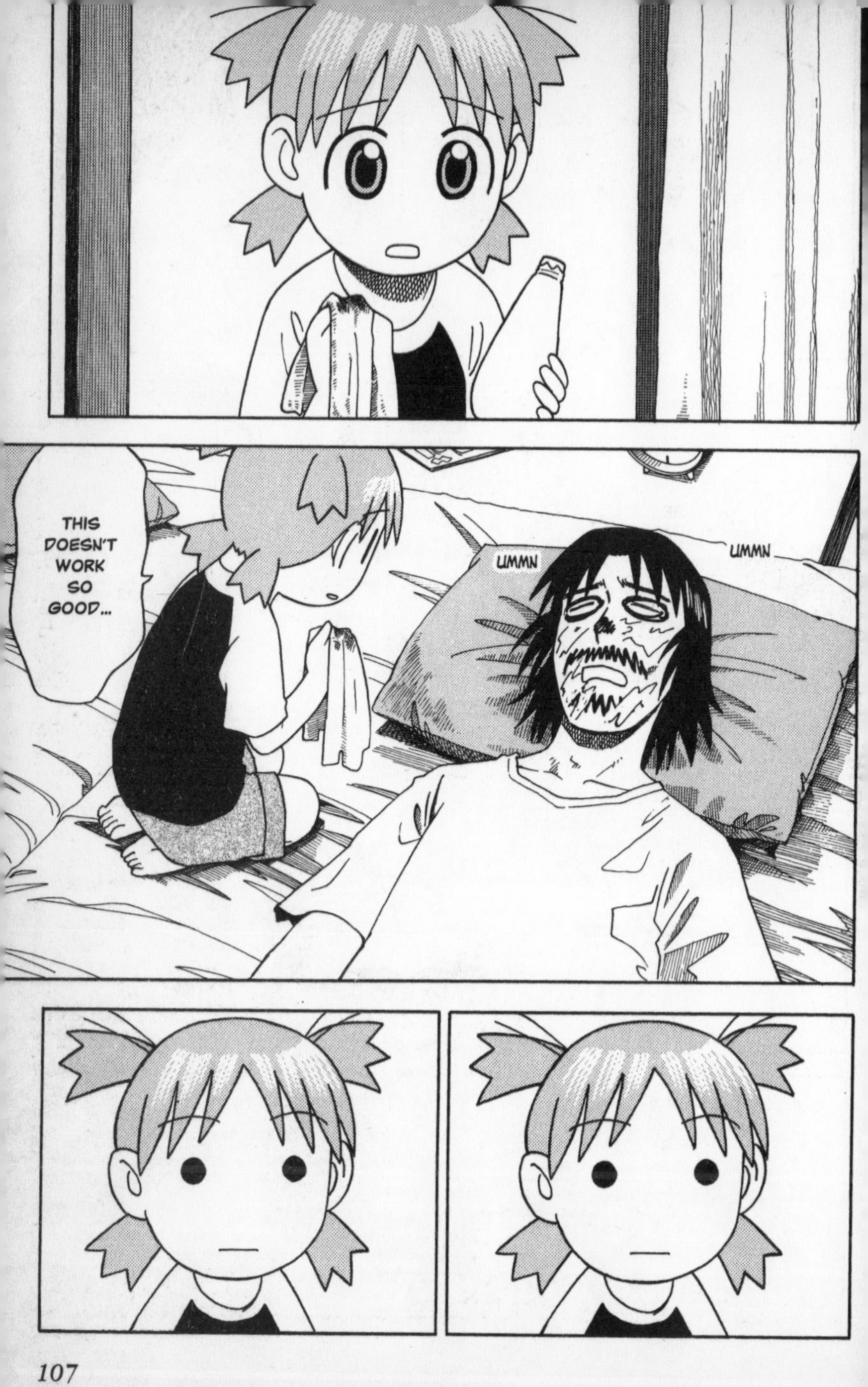
UMMN
UMMN
THIS DOESN'T WORK SO GOOD...

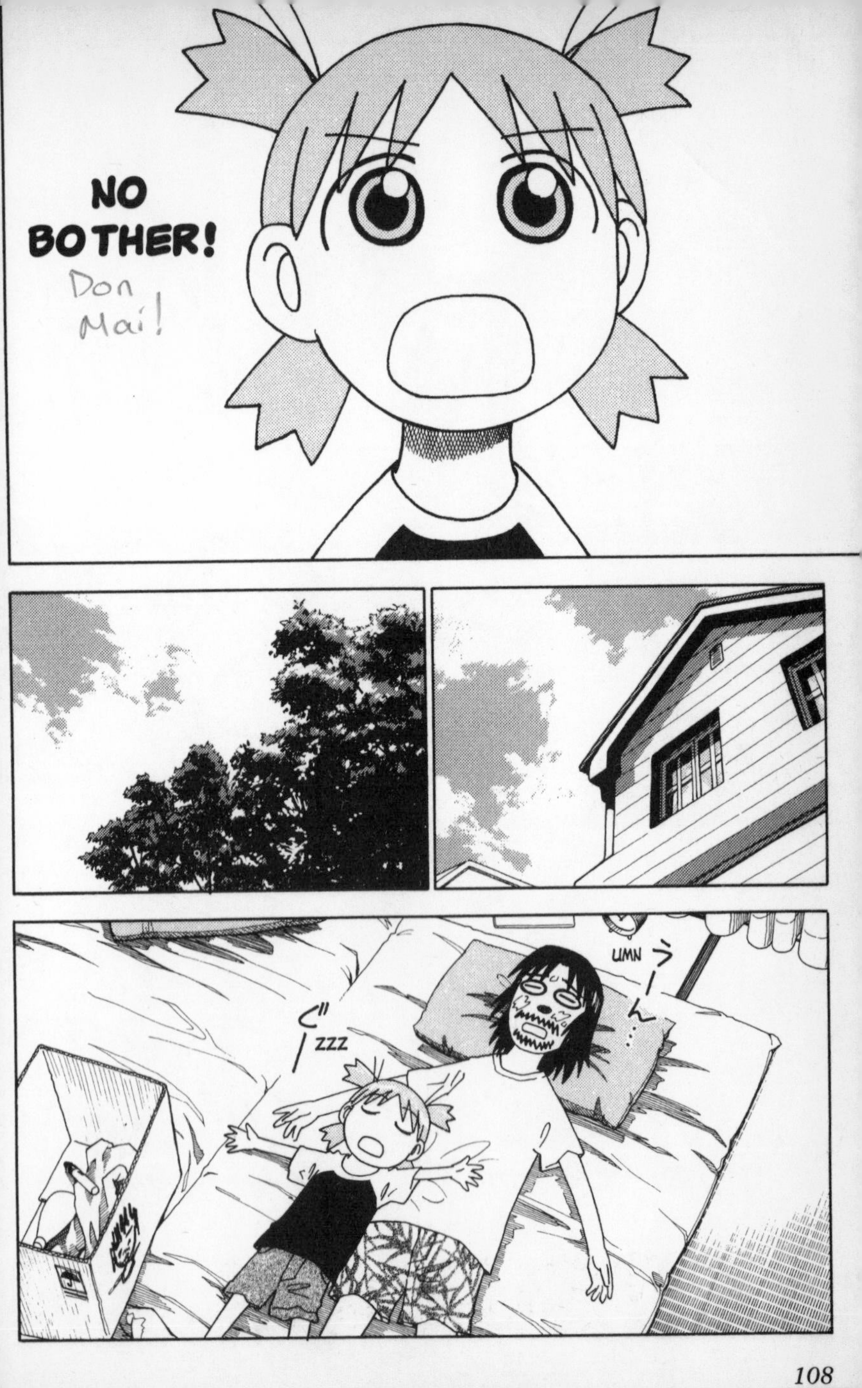
NO BOTHER!
Don Mai!
うーん…
UMN
ぐー
ZZZ

YOTSUBA&!

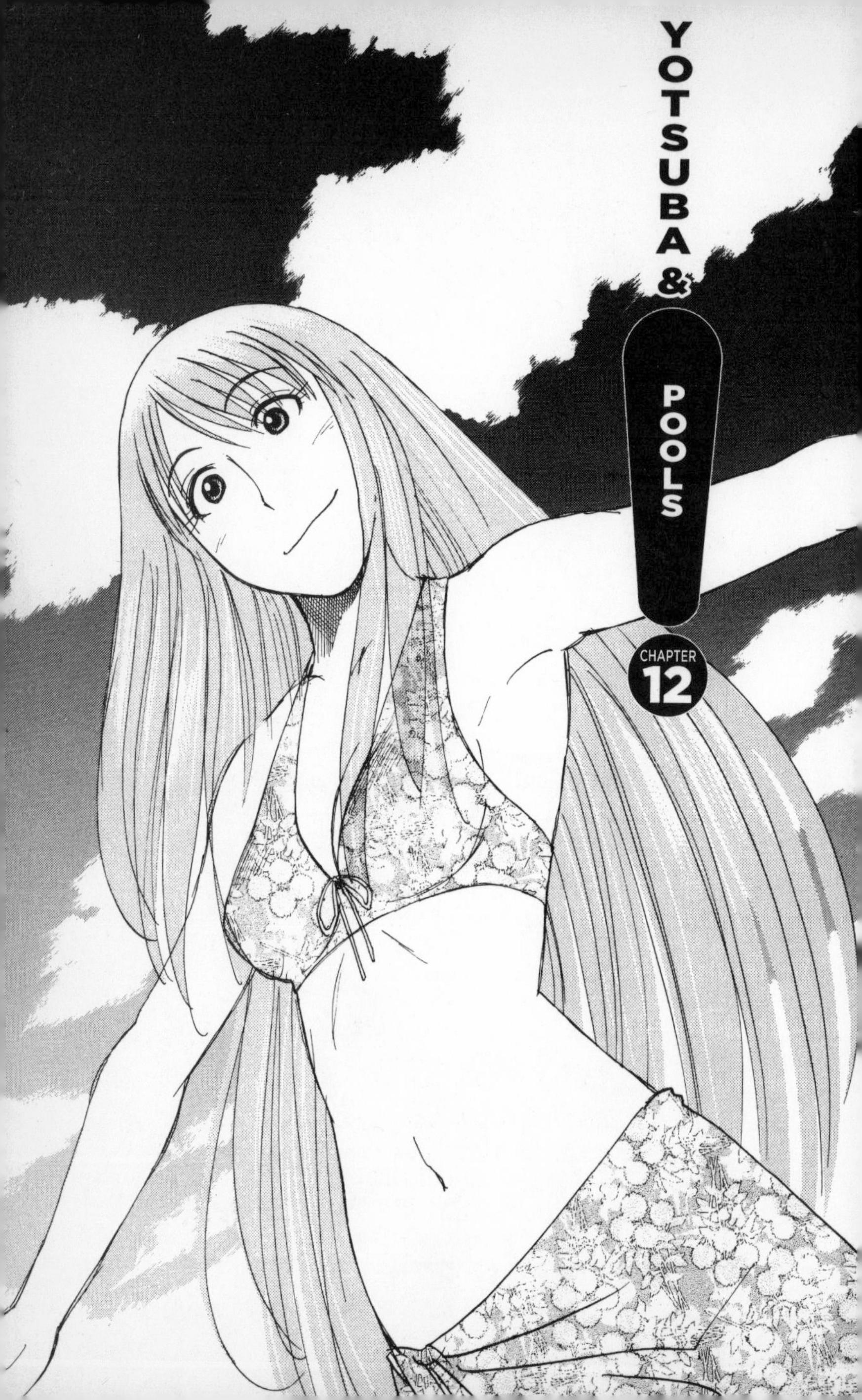
YOTSUBA&
POOLS
CHAPTER 12

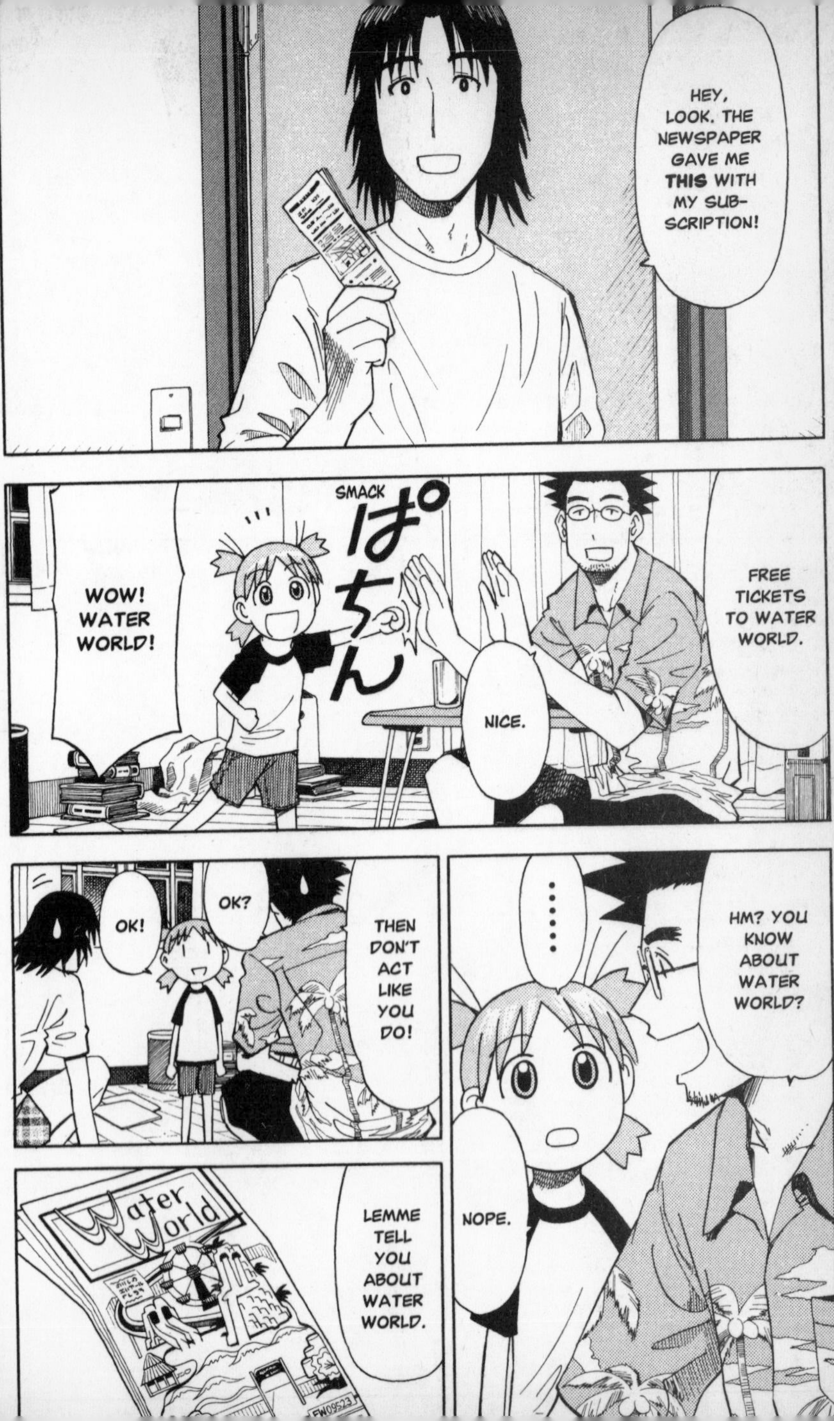
HEY, LOOK. THE NEWSPAPER GAVE ME THIS WITH MY SUB-SCRIPTION!
FREE TICKETS TO WATER WORLD.
NICE.
SMACK
ぱちん
WOW! WATER WORLD!
HM? YOU KNOW ABOUT WATER WORLD?
......
NOPE.
THEN DON'T ACT LIKE YOU DO!
OK?
OK!
LEMME TELL YOU ABOUT WATER WORLD.
Water World
FW09523

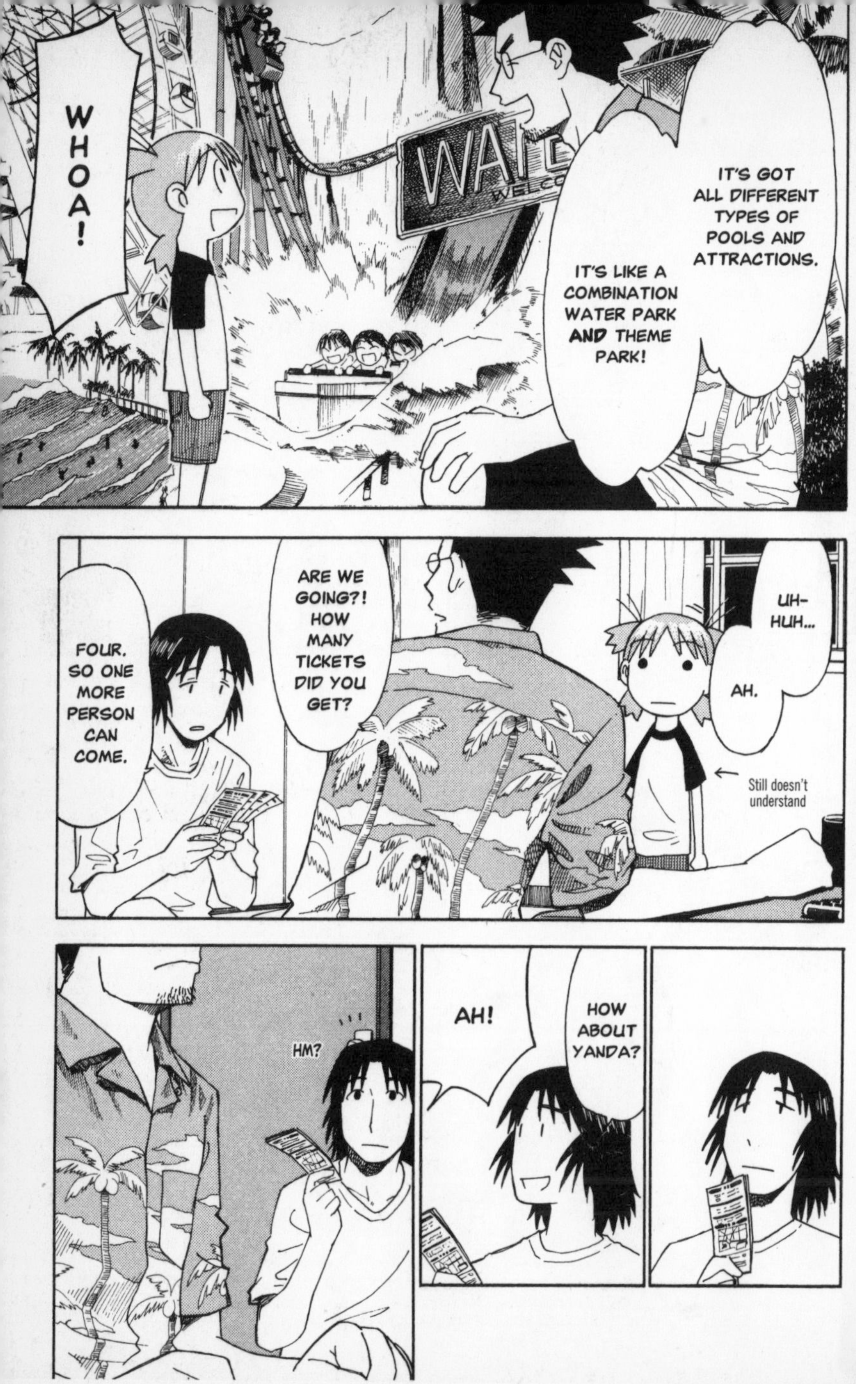
WHOA!
IT'S GOT ALL DIFFERENT TYPES OF POOLS AND ATTRACTIONS.
IT'S LIKE A COMBINATION WATER PARK **AND** THEME PARK!
WA
WELC
ARE WE GOING?! HOW MANY TICKETS DID YOU GET?
FOUR. SO ONE MORE PERSON CAN COME.
UH-HUH...
AH.
Still doesn't understand
HM?
AH!
HOW ABOUT YANDA?

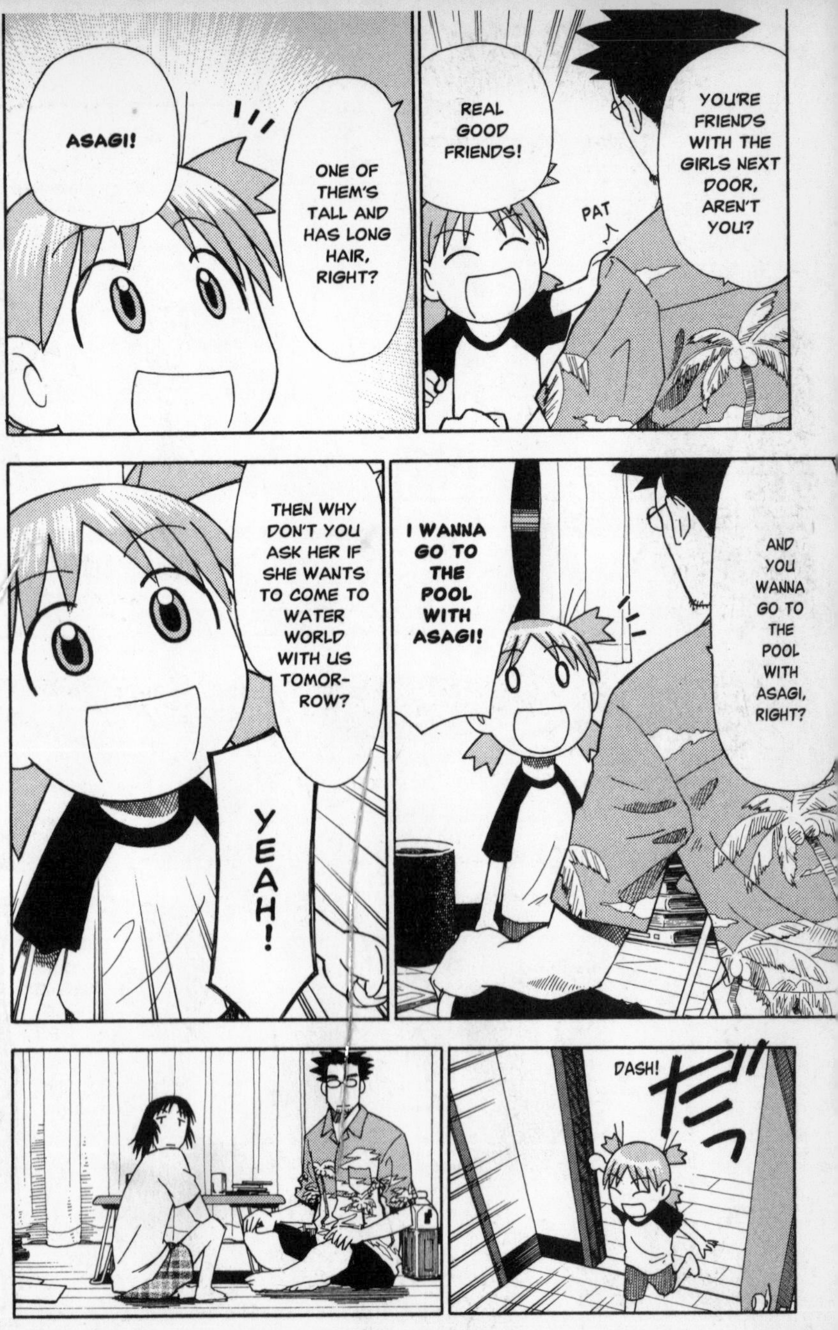
YOU'RE FRIENDS WITH THE GIRLS NEXT DOOR, AREN'T YOU?
PAT
REAL GOOD FRIENDS!
ONE OF THEM'S TALL AND HAS LONG HAIR, RIGHT?
ASAGI!
AND YOU WANNA GO TO THE POOL WITH ASAGI, RIGHT?
I WANNA GO TO THE POOL WITH ASAGI!
THEN WHY DON'T YOU ASK HER IF SHE WANTS TO COME TO WATER WORLD WITH US TOMORROW?
YEAH!
DASH!

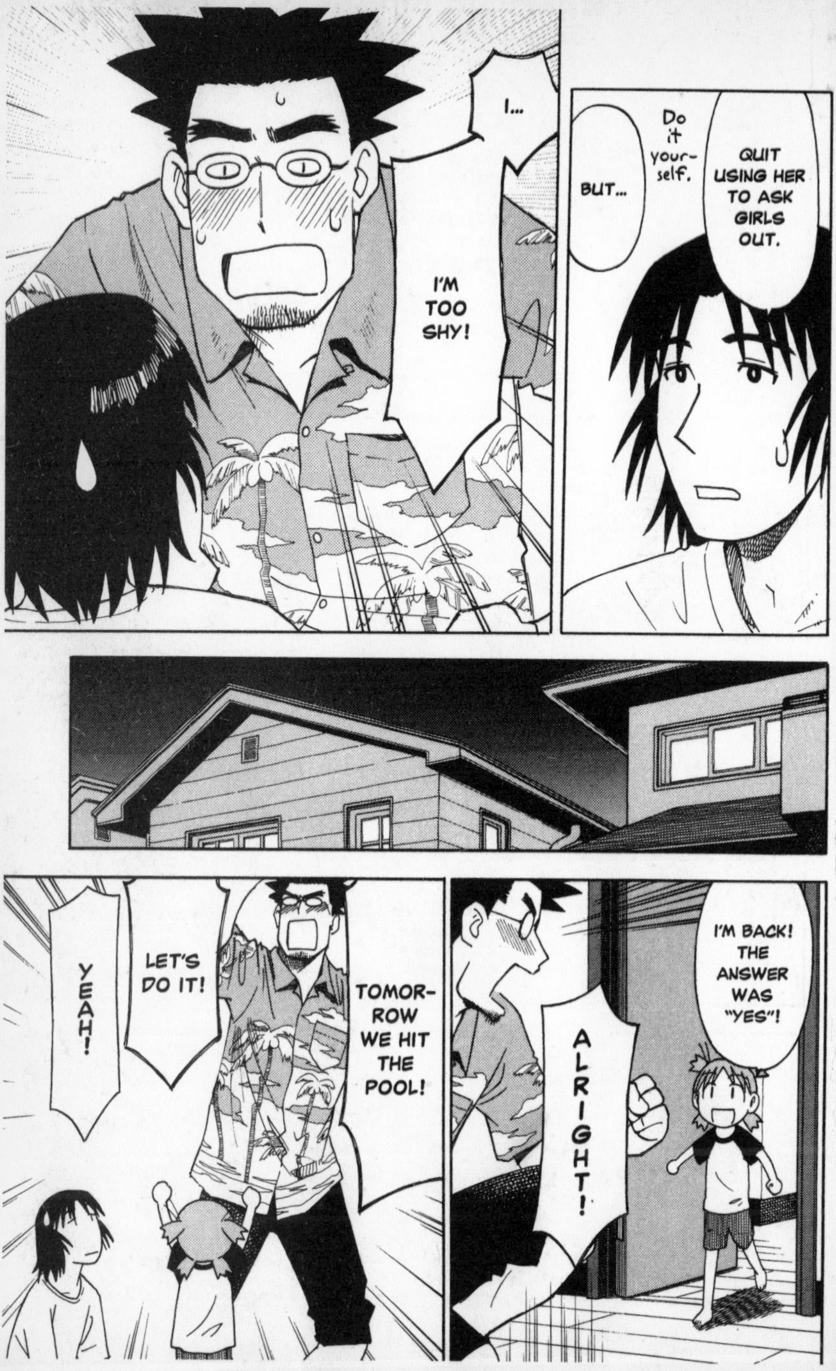
QUIT USING HER TO ASK GIRLS OUT.
Do it yourself.
BUT...
I...
I'M TOO SHY!
I'M BACK! THE ANSWER WAS "YES"!
ALRIGHT!
TOMORROW WE HIT THE POOL!
LET'S DO IT!
YEAH!

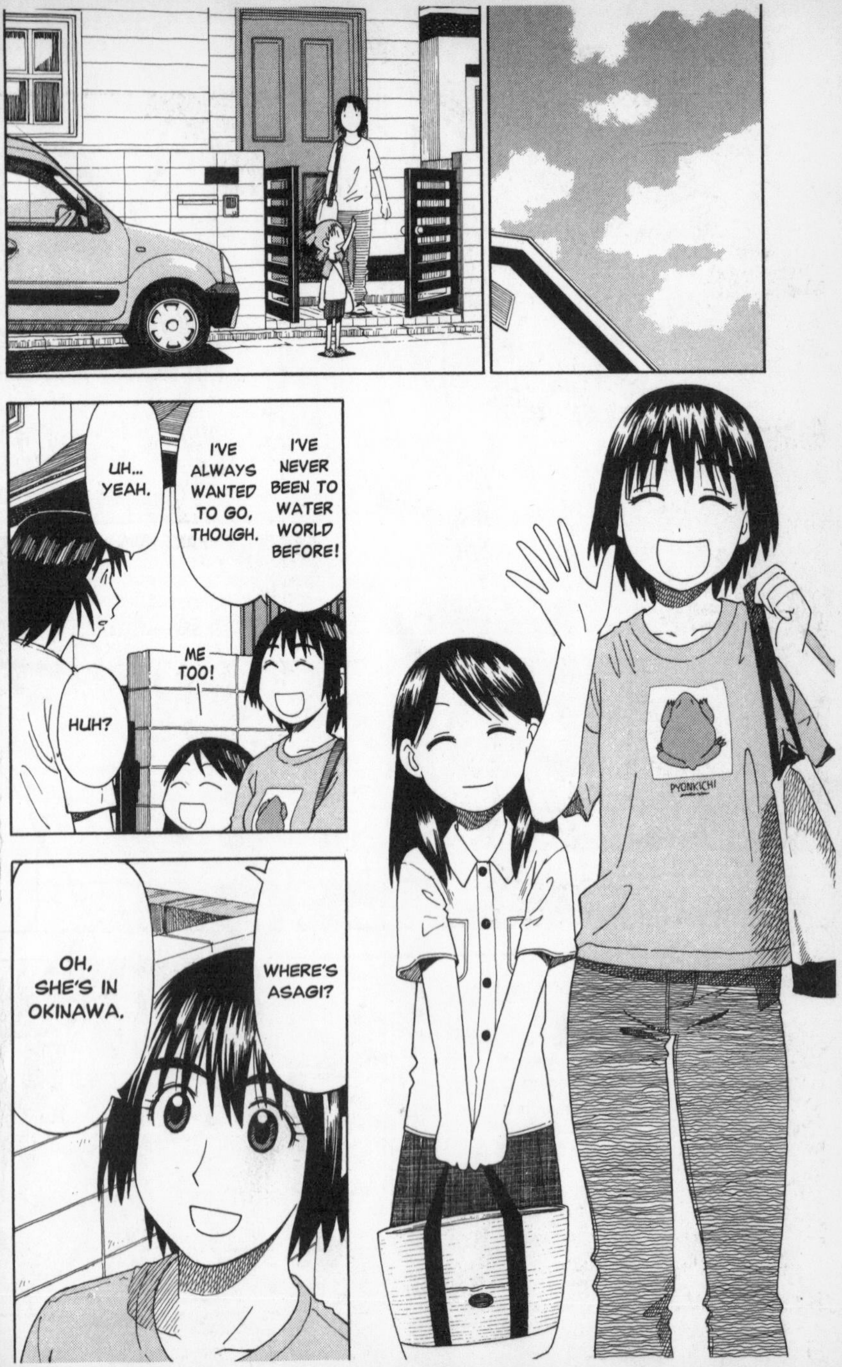
I'VE NEVER BEEN TO WATER WORLD BEFORE!
I'VE ALWAYS WANTED TO GO, THOUGH.
UH... YEAH.
ME TOO!
HUH?
PYONKICHI
WHERE'S ASAGI?
OH, SHE'S IN OKINAWA.

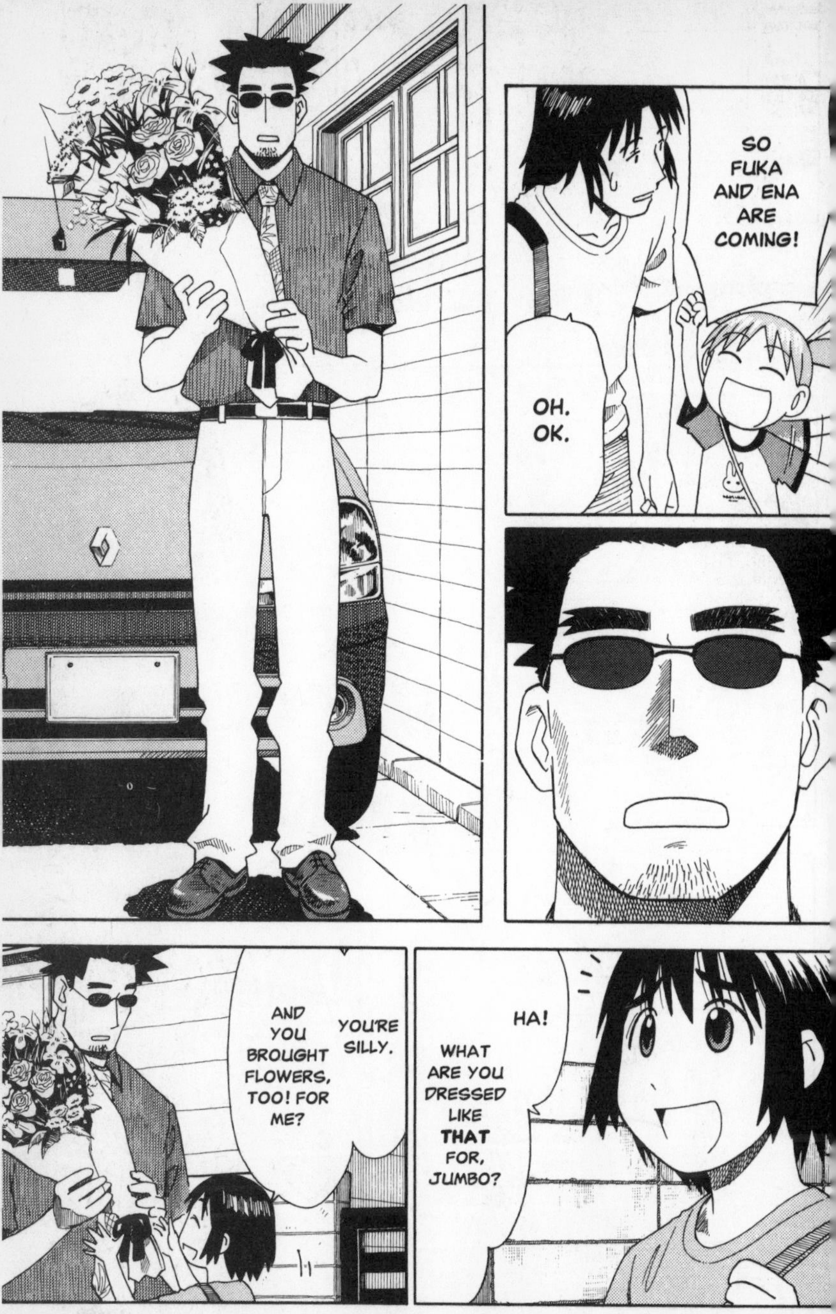
SO FUKA AND ENA ARE COMING!
OH. OK.
HA!
WHAT ARE YOU DRESSED LIKE THAT FOR, JUMBO?
YOU'RE SILLY.
AND YOU BROUGHT FLOWERS, TOO! FOR ME?

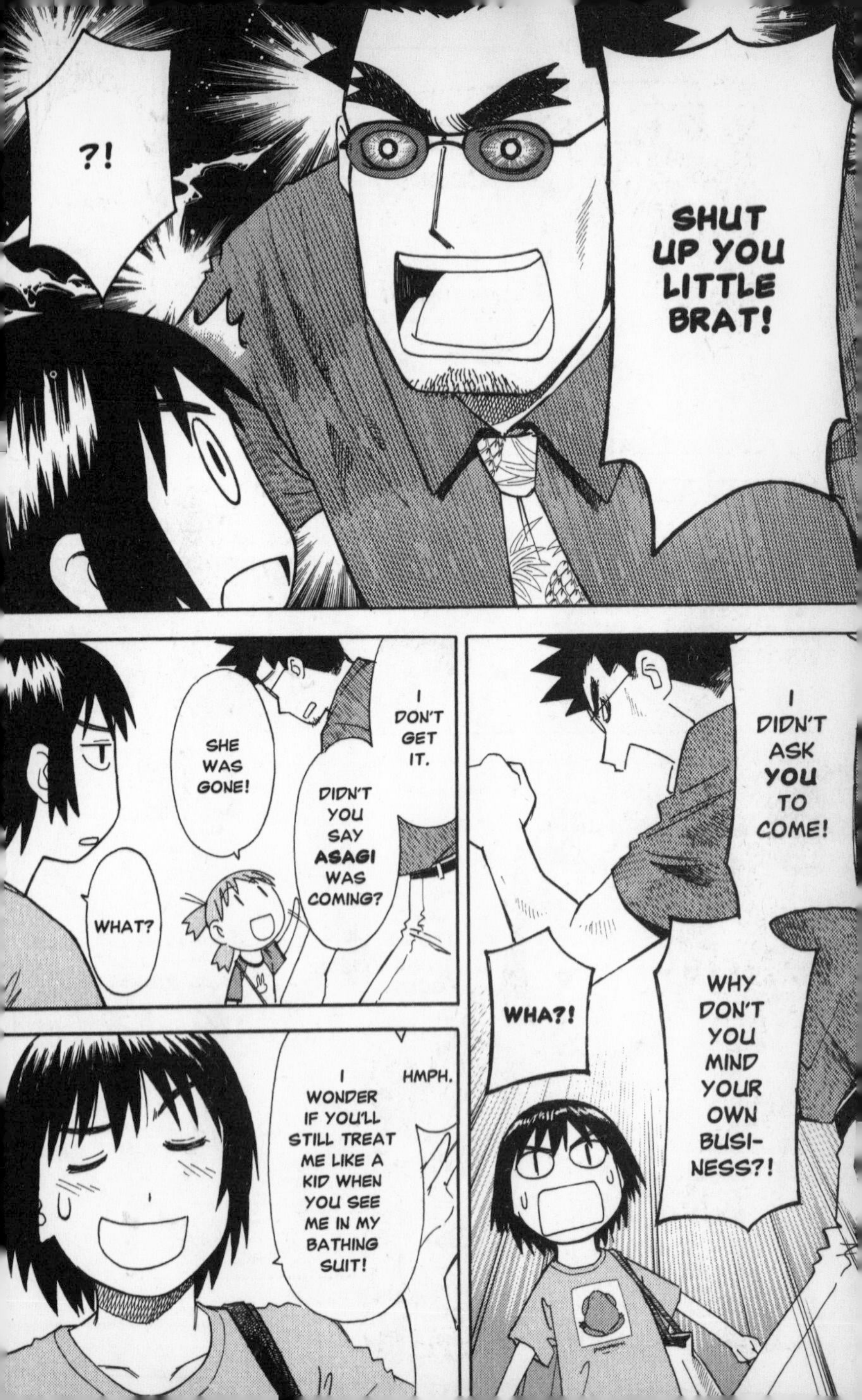
SHUT UP YOU LITTLE BRAT!
?!
I DIDN'T ASK YOU TO COME!
WHY DON'T YOU MIND YOUR OWN BUSINESS?!
WHA?!
I DON'T GET IT.
DIDN'T YOU SAY ASAGI WAS COMING?
SHE WAS GONE!
WHAT?
HMPH.
I WONDER IF YOU'LL STILL TREAT ME LIKE A KID WHEN YOU SEE ME IN MY BATHING SUIT!

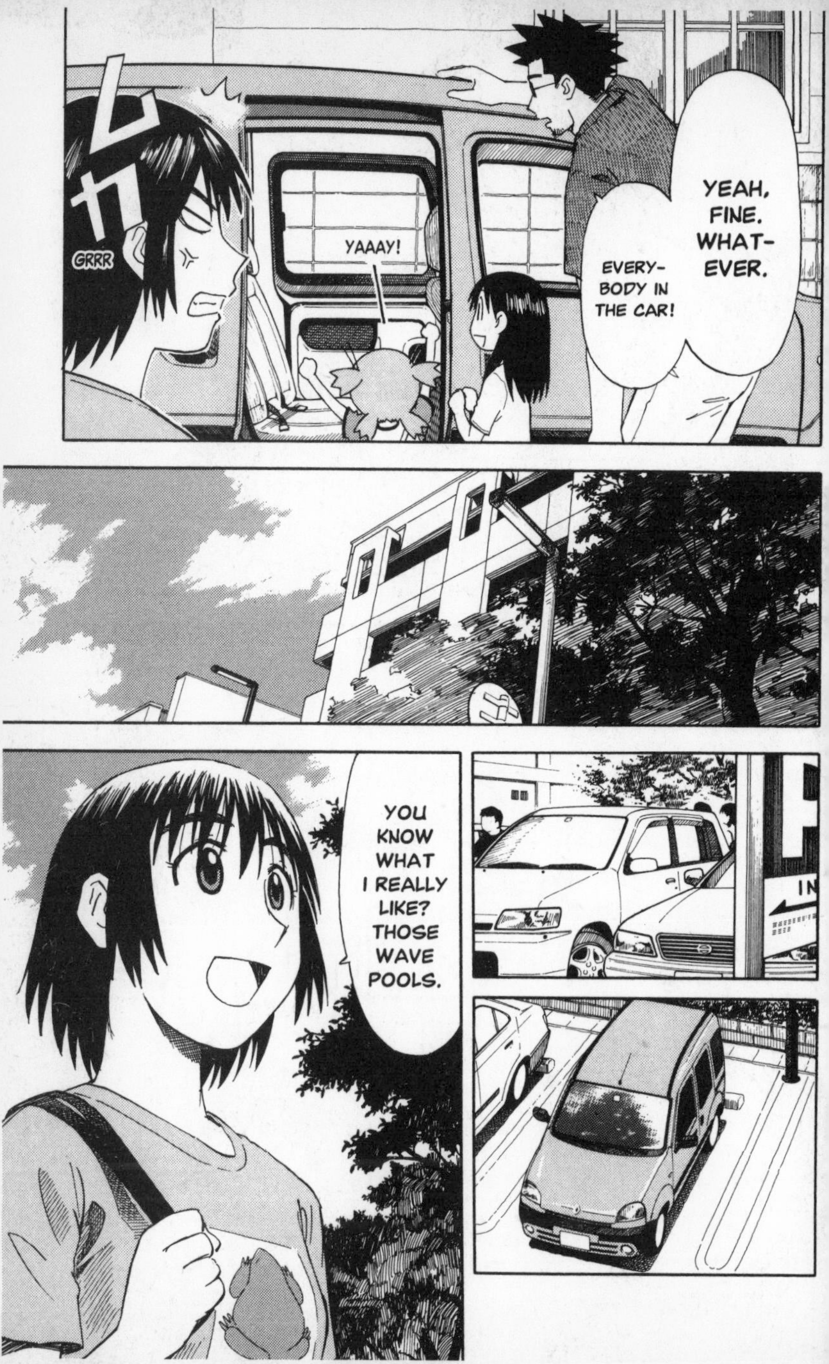
YEAH, FINE. WHATEVER.
EVERYBODY IN THE CAR!
YAAAY!
ムカ
GRRR
IN
YOU KNOW WHAT I REALLY LIKE? THOSE WAVE POOLS.

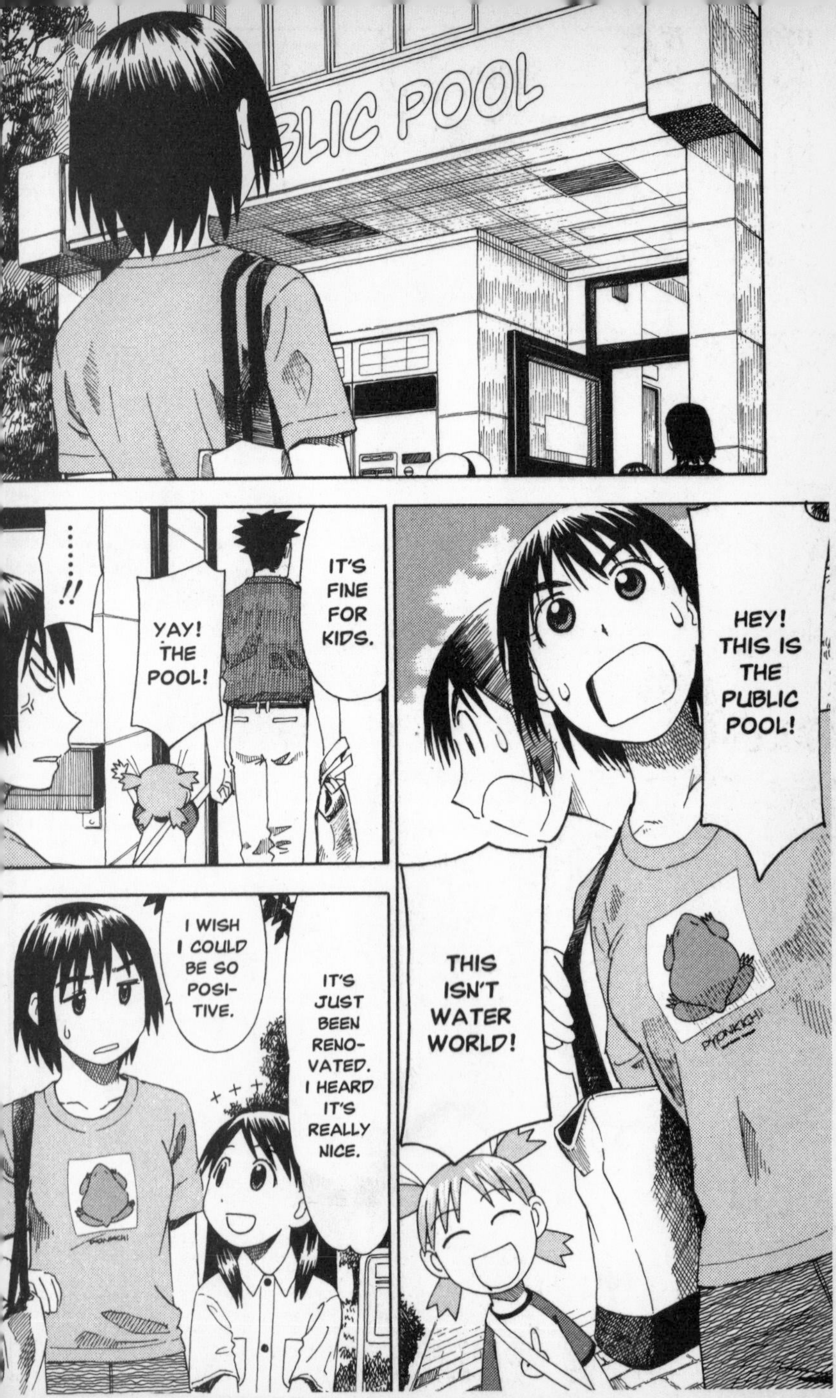
BLIC POOL
HEY! THIS IS THE PUBLIC POOL!
THIS ISN'T WATER WORLD!
IT'S FINE FOR KIDS.
YAY! THE POOL!
......!!
PYONKICHI
IT'S JUST BEEN RENOVATED. I HEARD IT'S REALLY NICE.
I WISH I COULD BE SO POSITIVE.

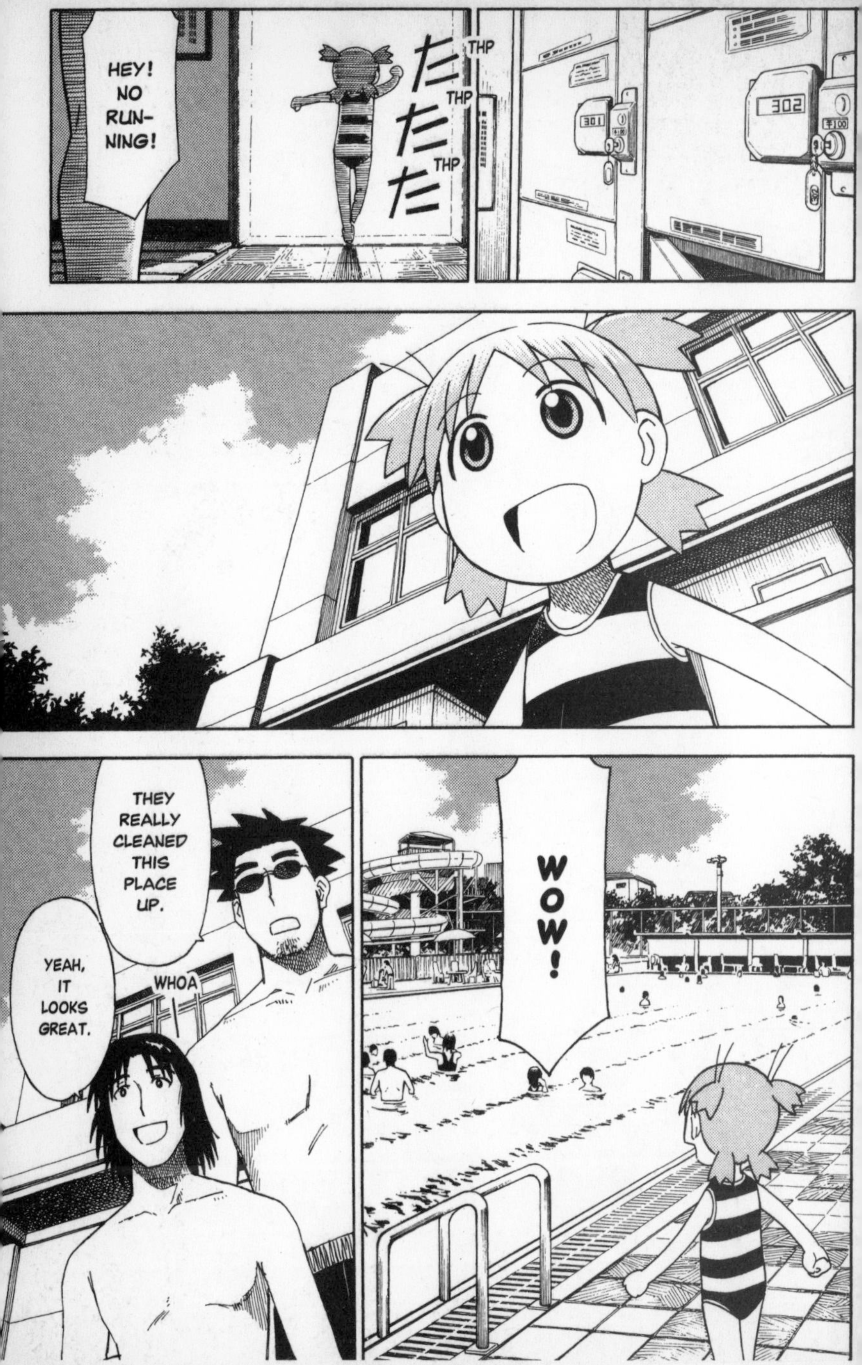

301
302
たたた
THP
THP
THP
HEY! NO RUN-NING!
WOW!
THEY REALLY CLEANED THIS PLACE UP.
WHOA
YEAH, IT LOOKS GREAT.

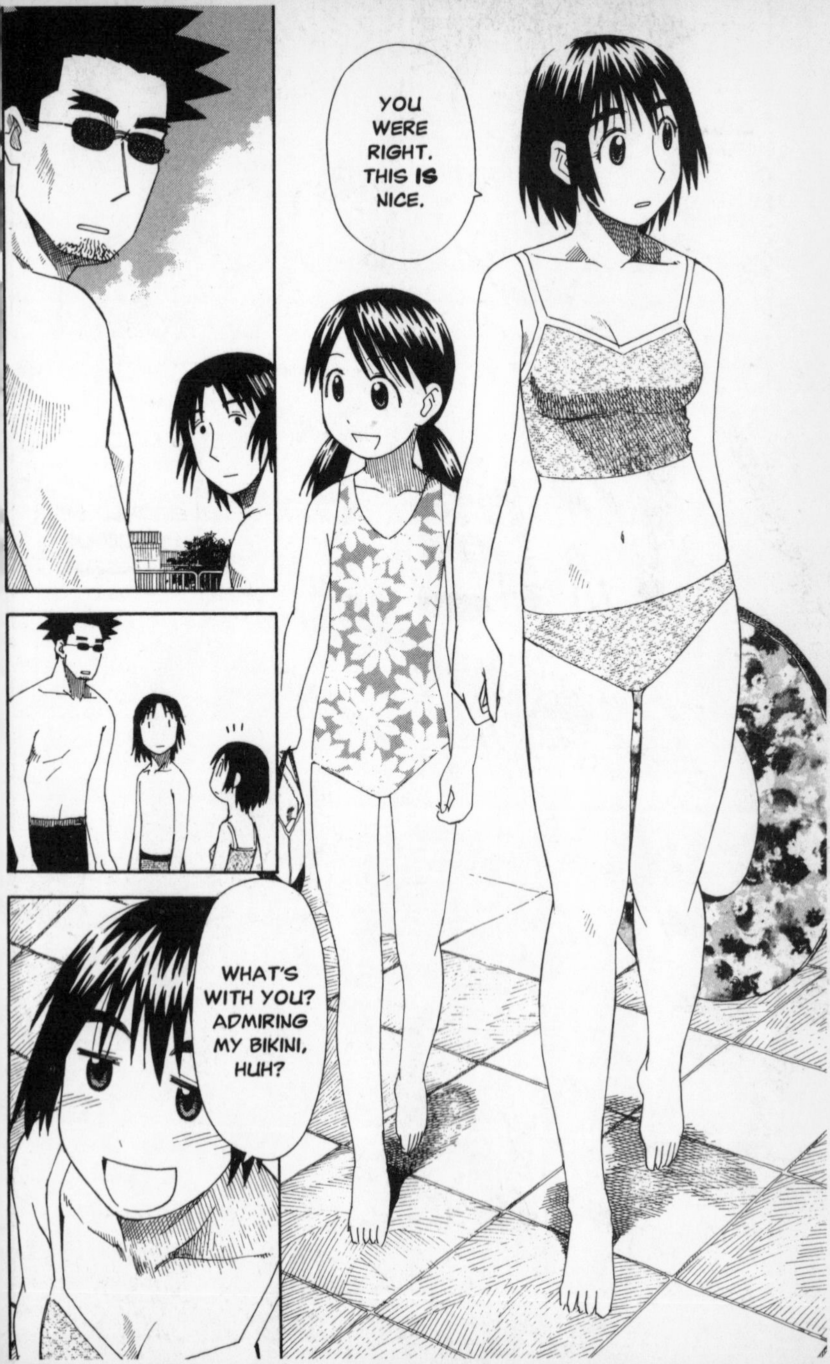
YOU WERE RIGHT. THIS IS NICE.
WHAT'S WITH YOU? ADMIRING MY BIKINI, HUH?

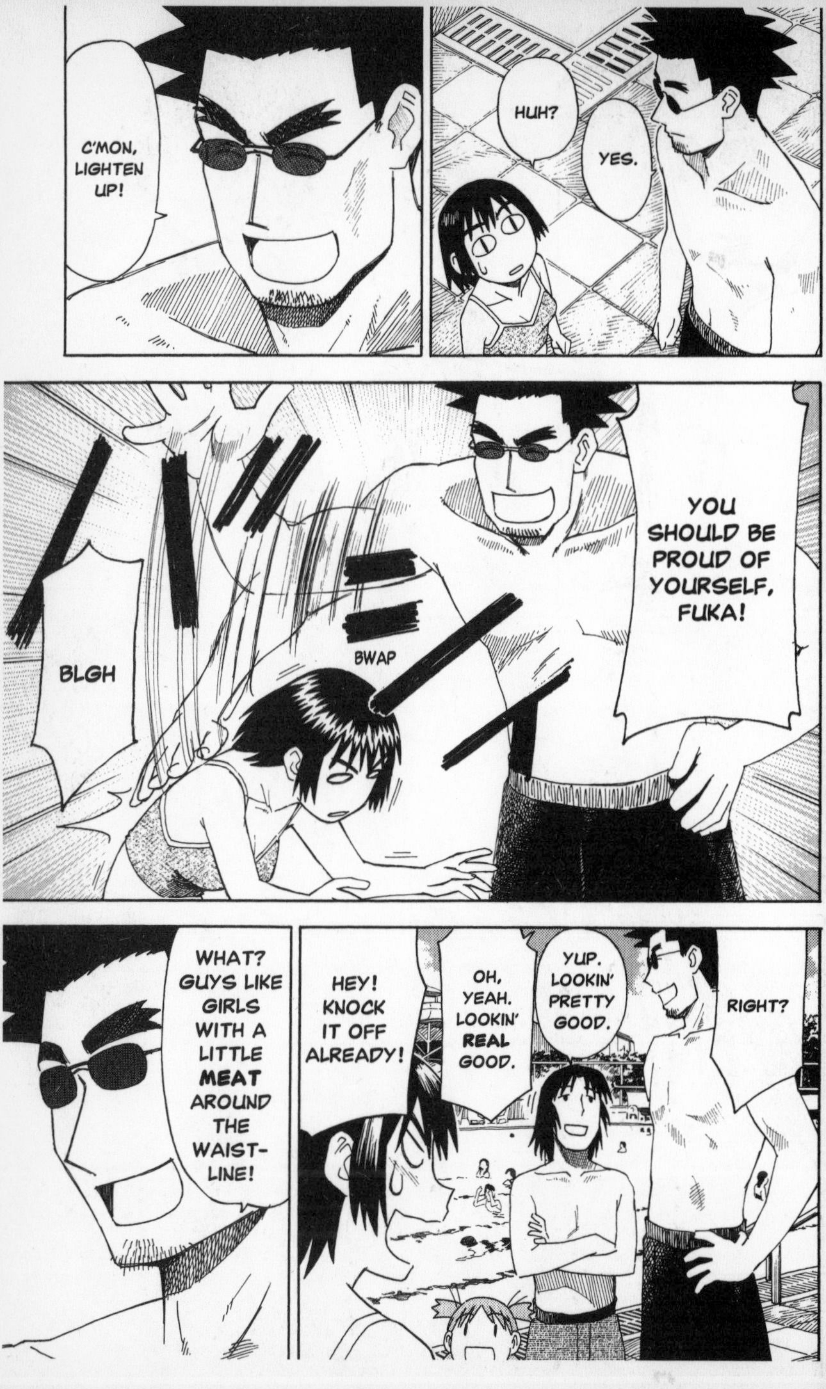
YES.
HUH?
C'MON, LIGHTEN UP!
YOU SHOULD BE PROUD OF YOURSELF, FUKA!
BWAP
BLGH
RIGHT?
YUP. LOOKIN' PRETTY GOOD.
OH, YEAH. LOOKIN' **REAL** GOOD.
HEY! KNOCK IT OFF ALREADY!
WHAT? GUYS LIKE GIRLS WITH A LITTLE **MEAT** AROUND THE WAIST-LINE!

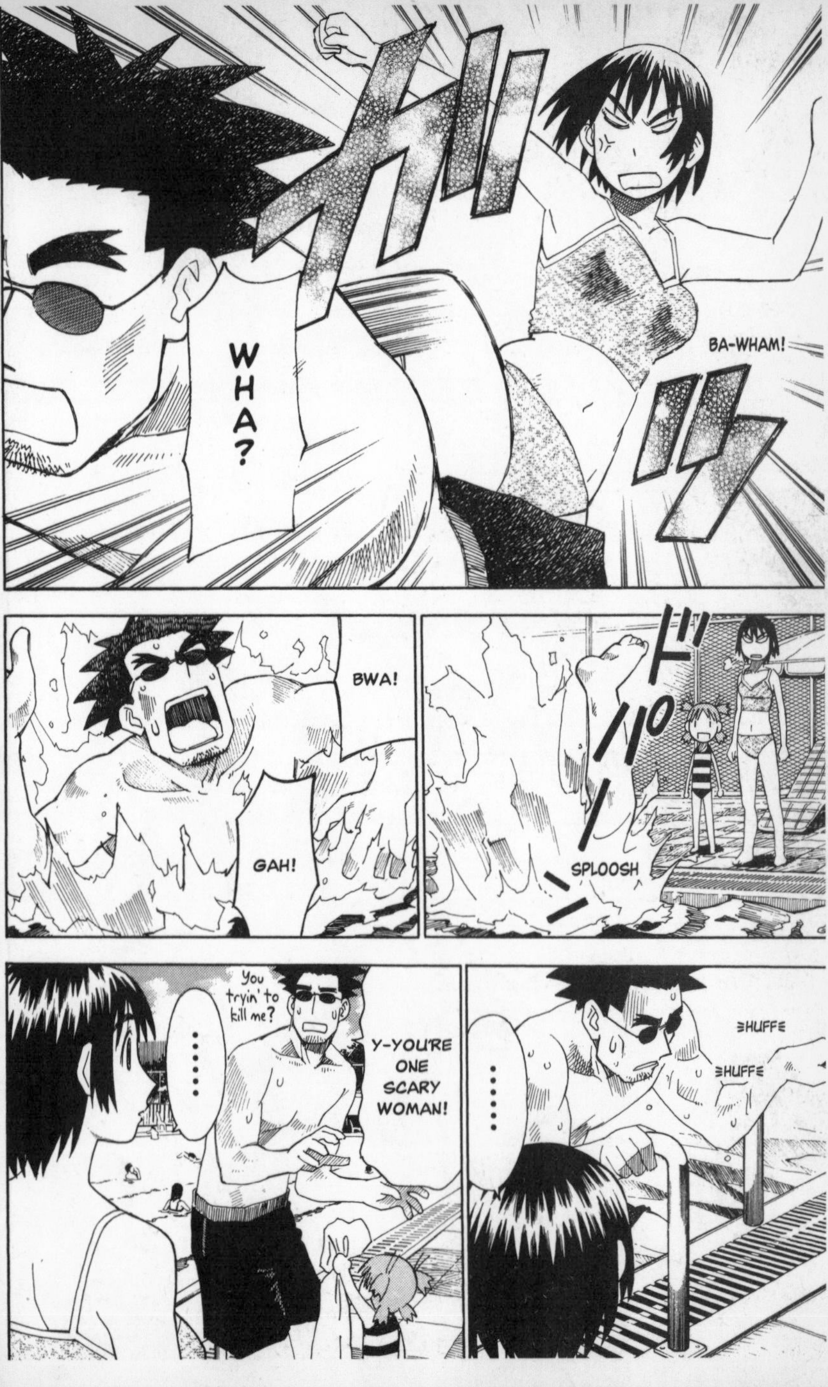

BA-WHAM!
WHA?
ドパ
SPLOOSH
BWA!
GAH!
≡HUFF≡
≡HUFF≡
......
Y-YOU'RE ONE SCARY WOMAN!
You tryin' to kill me?
......

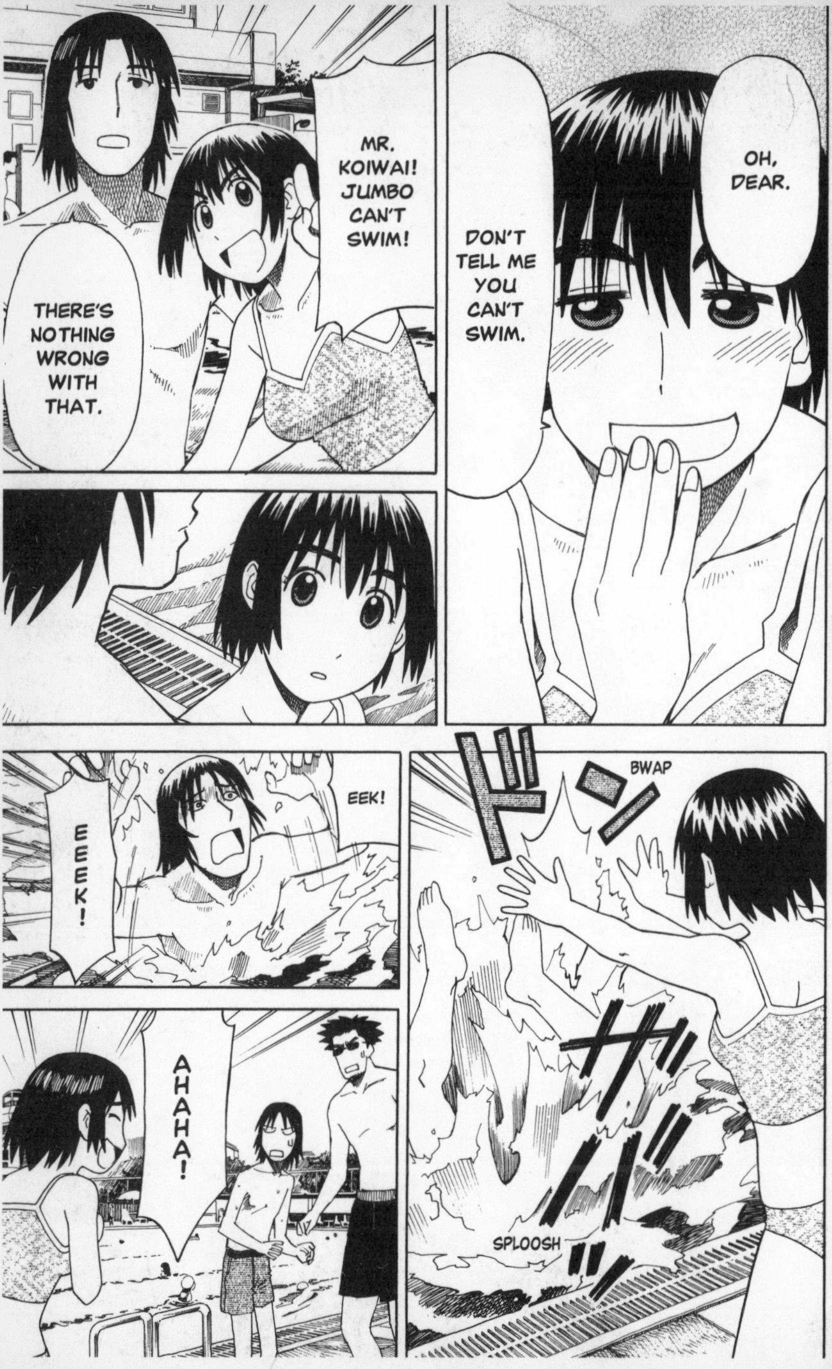
OH, DEAR.
DON'T TELL ME YOU CAN'T SWIM.
MR. KOIWAI! JUMBO CAN'T SWIM!
THERE'S NOTHING WRONG WITH THAT.
BWAP
SPLOOSH
EEK!
EEEEK!
AHAHA!

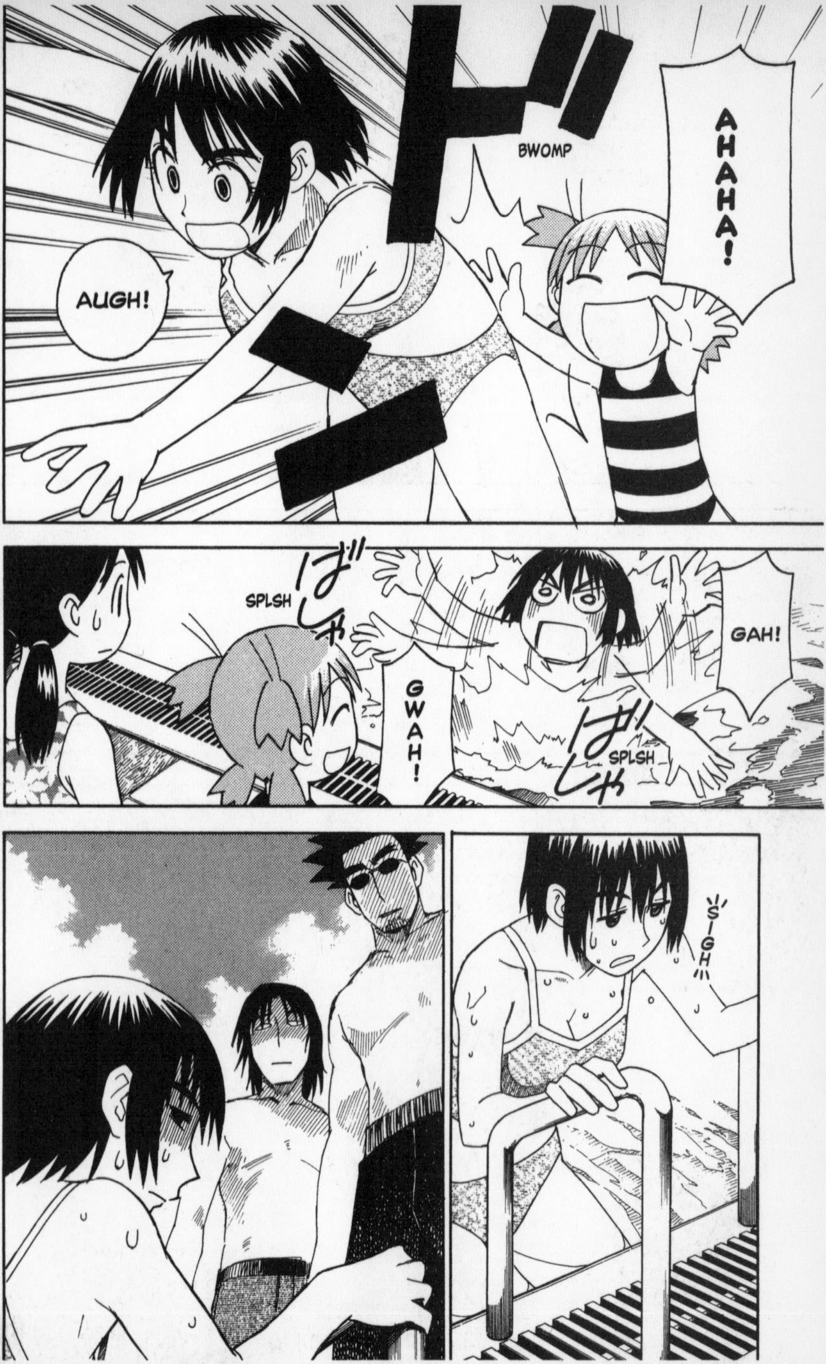
AHAHA!
BWOMP
AUGH!
GAH!
SPLSH
ばしゃ
GWAH!
ばしゃ
SPLSH
SIGH

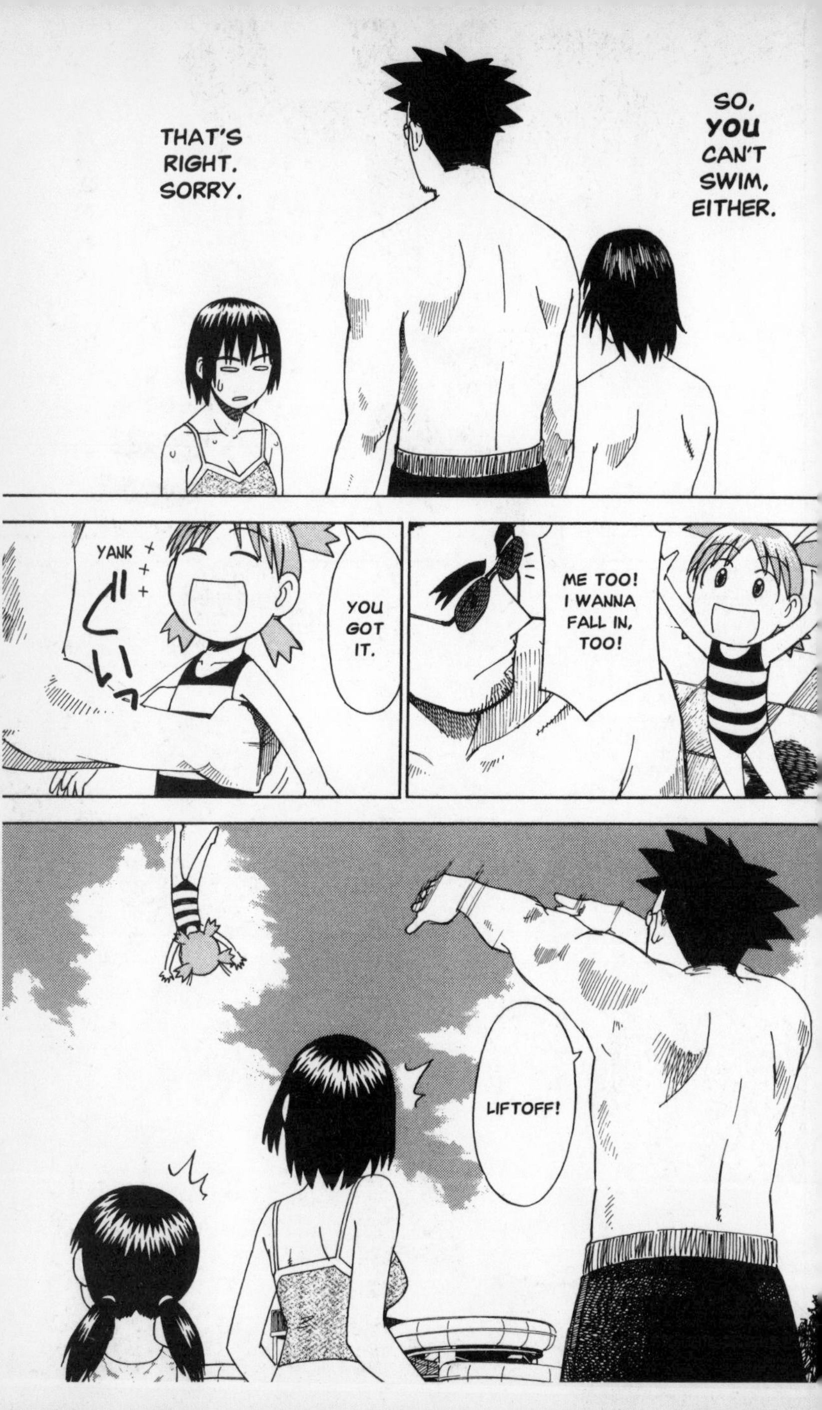

SO, YOU CAN'T SWIM, EITHER.
THAT'S RIGHT. SORRY.
ME TOO! I WANNA FALL IN, TOO!
YOU GOT IT.
YANK
LIFTOFF!

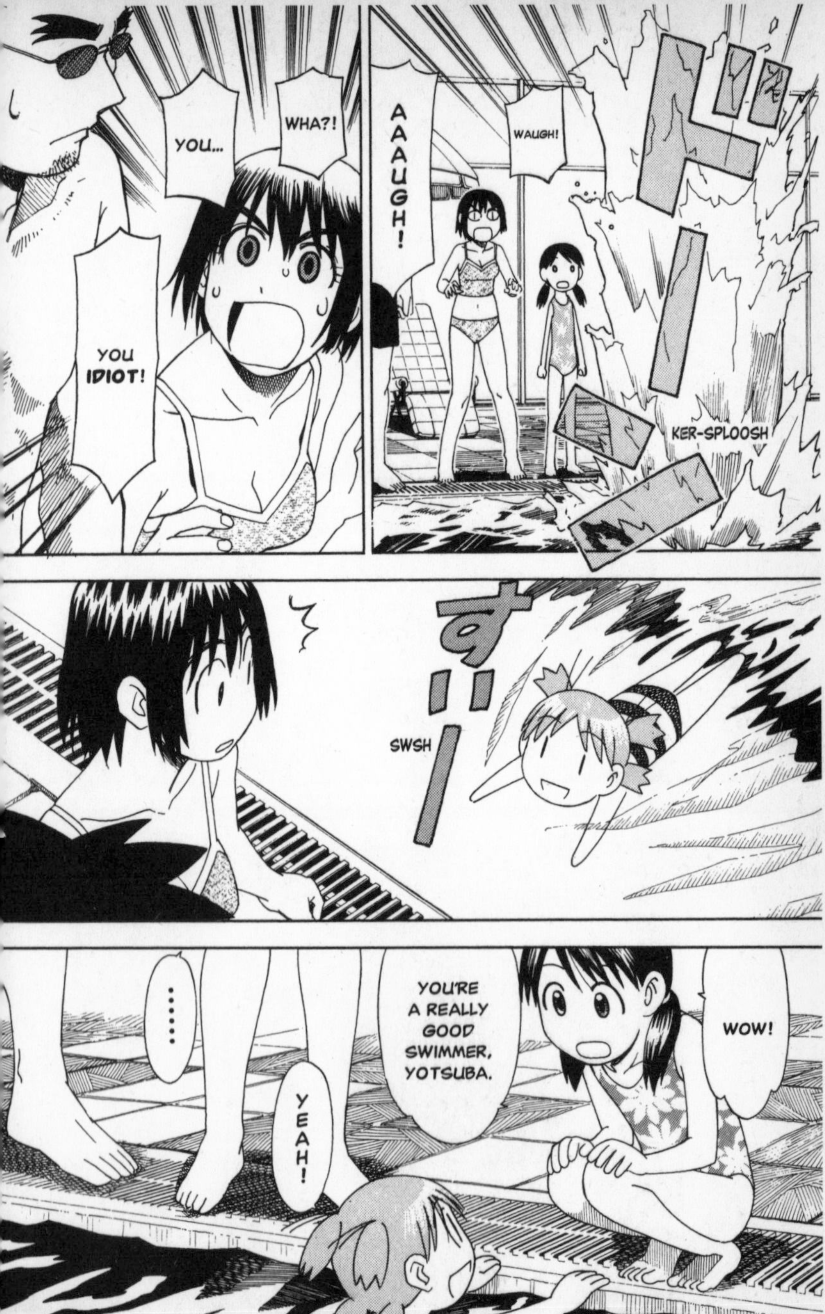
KER-SPLOOSH
WAUGH!
AAAAUGH!
WHA?!
YOU...
YOU IDIOT!
SWSH
WOW!
YOU'RE A REALLY GOOD SWIMMER, YOTSUBA.
YEAH!
......

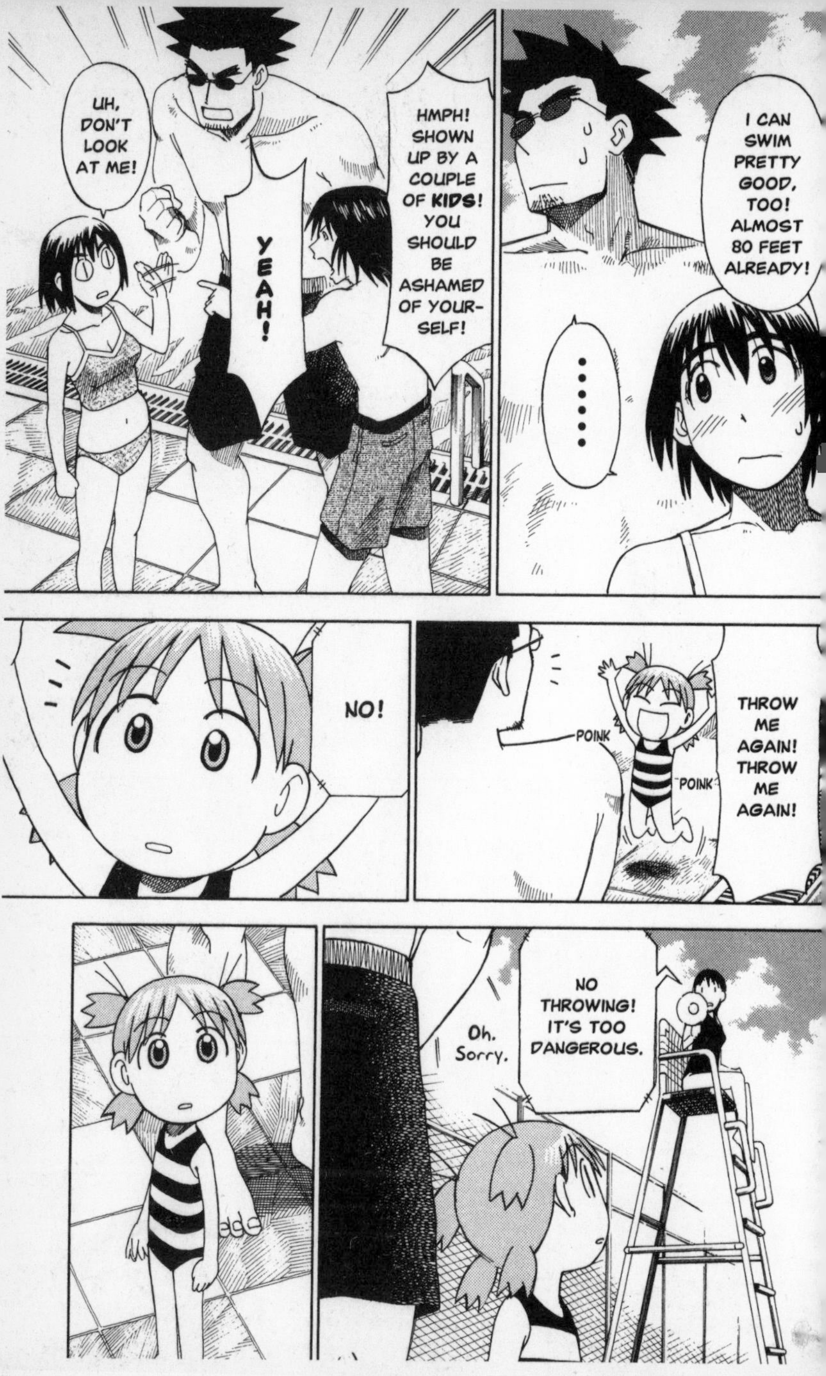
HMPH! SHOWN UP BY A COUPLE OF KIDS! YOU SHOULD BE ASHAMED OF YOURSELF!
YEAH!
UH, DON'T LOOK AT ME!
I CAN SWIM PRETTY GOOD, TOO! ALMOST 80 FEET ALREADY!
......
NO!
POINK
POINK
THROW ME AGAIN! THROW ME AGAIN!
NO THROWING! IT'S TOO DANGEROUS.
Oh. Sorry.

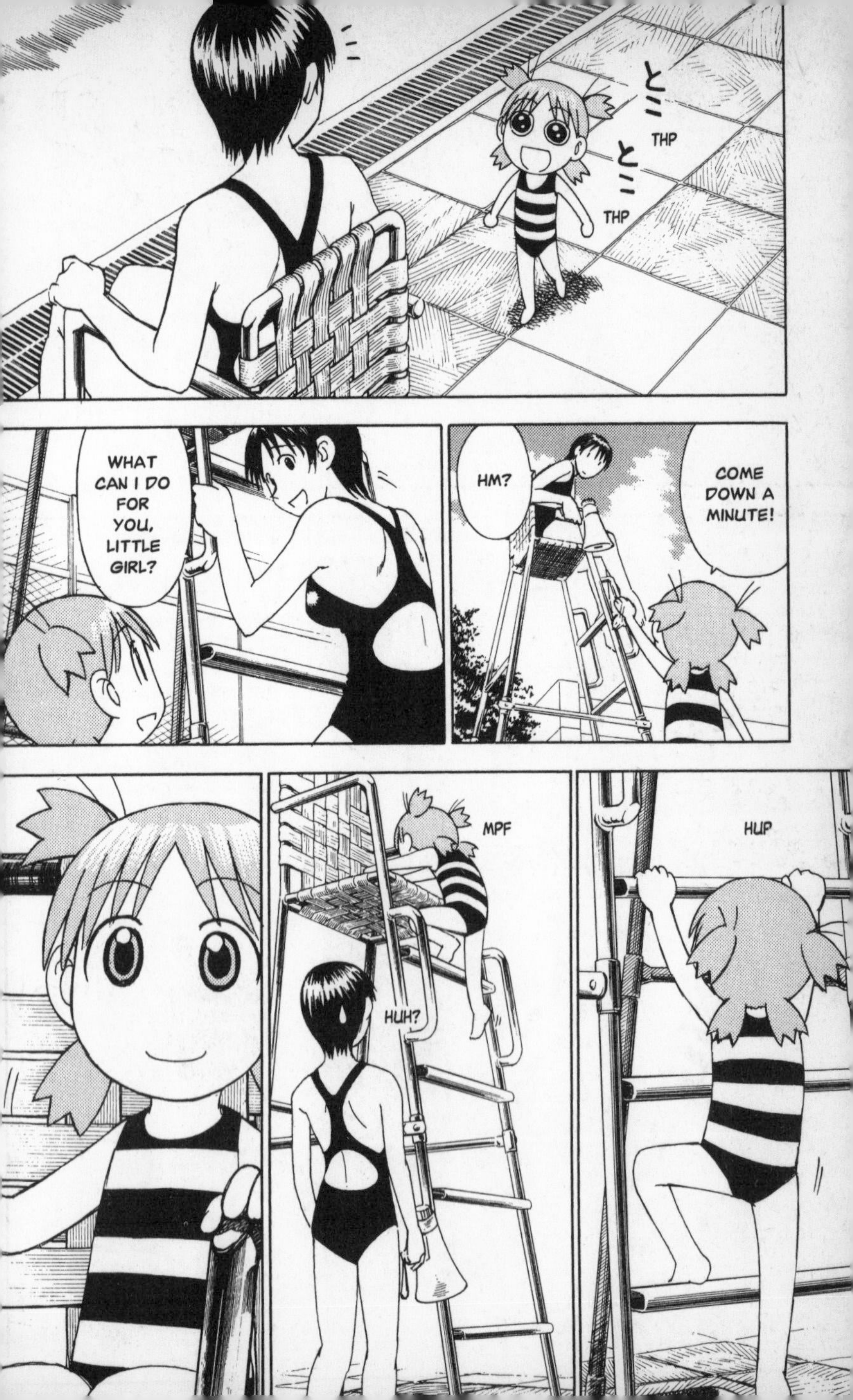
とこ
THP
とこ
THP
COME DOWN A MINUTE!
HM?
WHAT CAN I DO FOR YOU, LITTLE GIRL?
HUP
MPF
HUH?

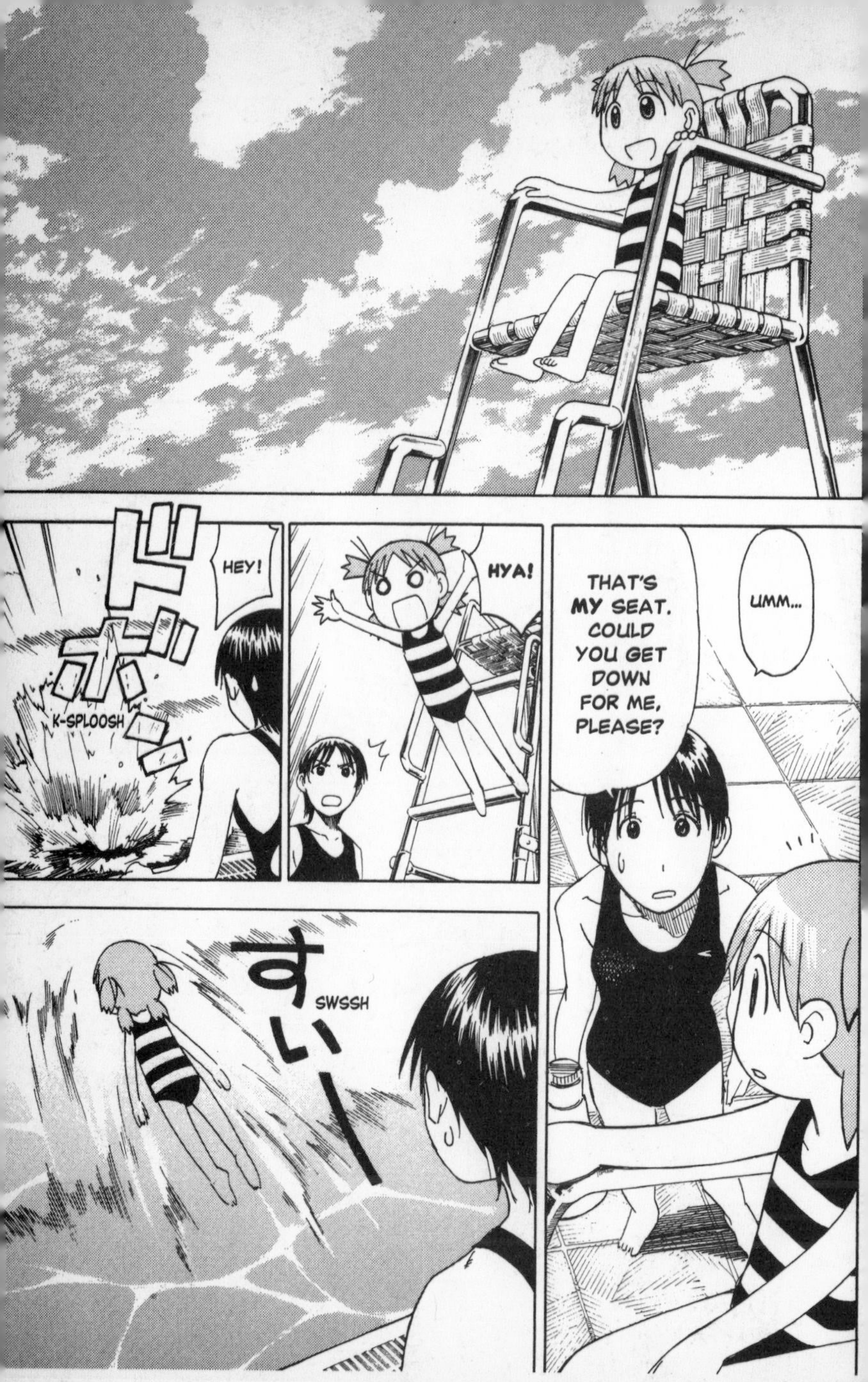
UMM...
THAT'S MY SEAT. COULD YOU GET DOWN FOR ME, PLEASE?
HYA!
HEY!
ドボ
K-SPLOOSH
すいー
SWSSH

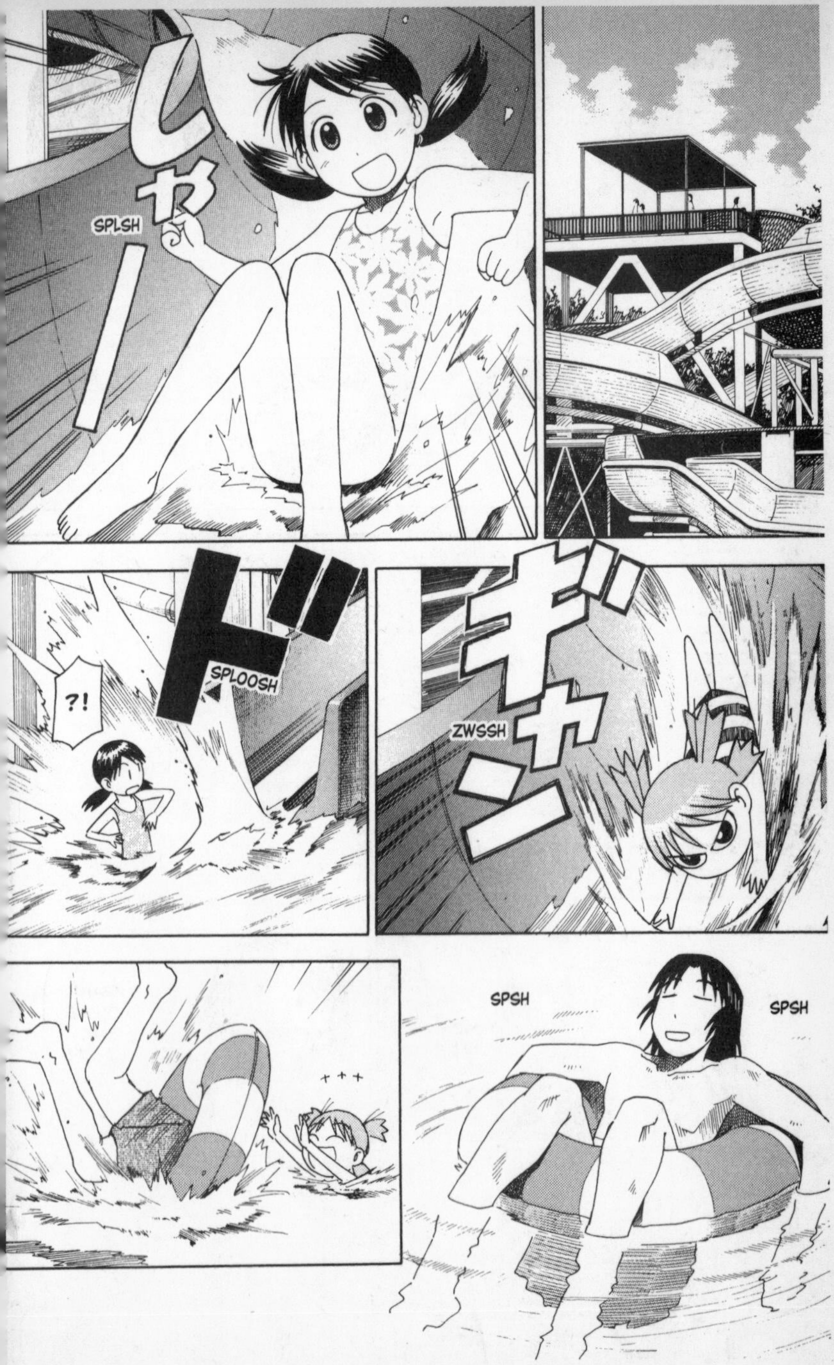
SPLSH
ZWSSH
SPLOOSH
?!
SPSH
SPSH

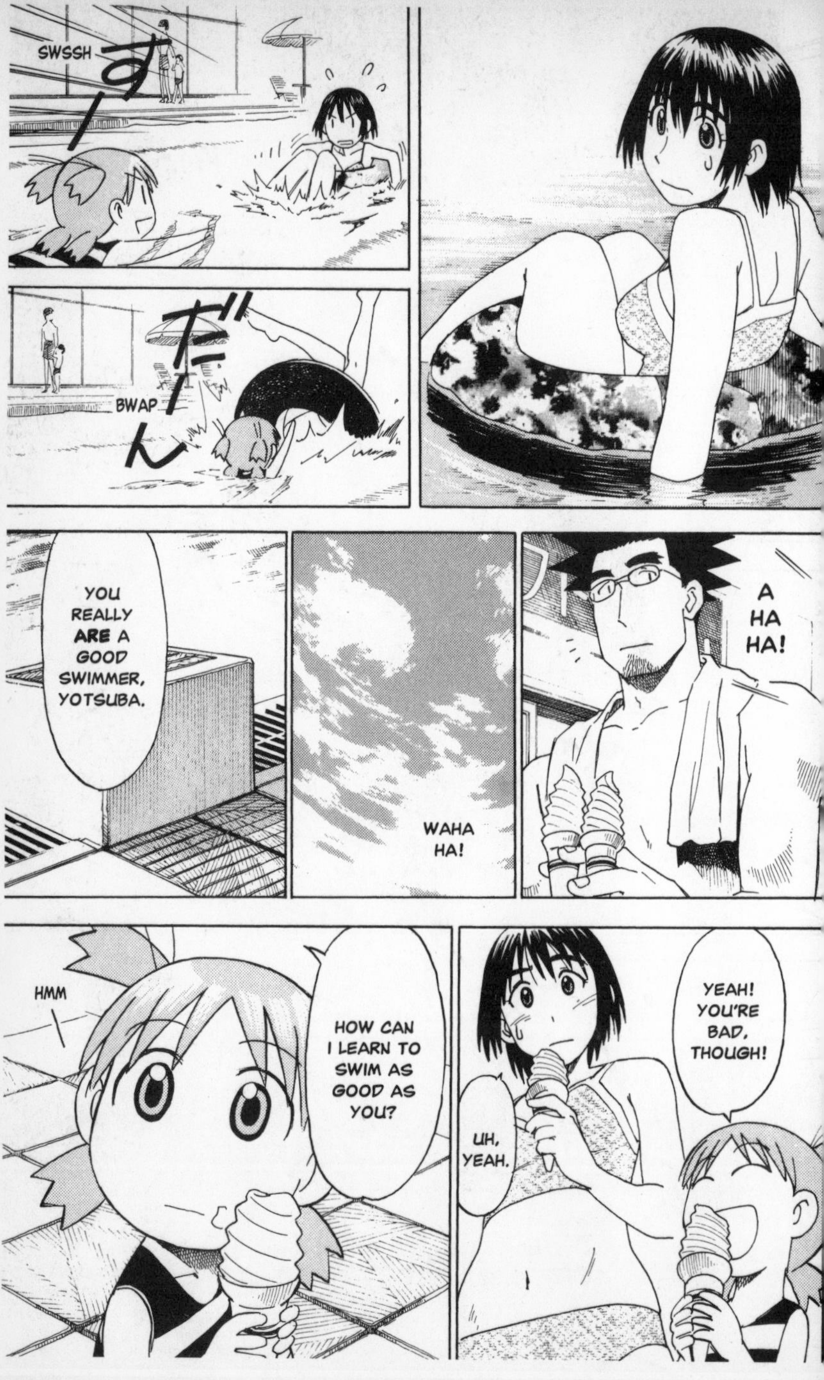
SWSSH
BWAP
YOU REALLY ARE A GOOD SWIMMER, YOTSUBA.
WAHA HA!
A HA HA!
HMM
HOW CAN I LEARN TO SWIM AS GOOD AS YOU?
UH, YEAH.
YEAH! YOU'RE BAD, THOUGH!

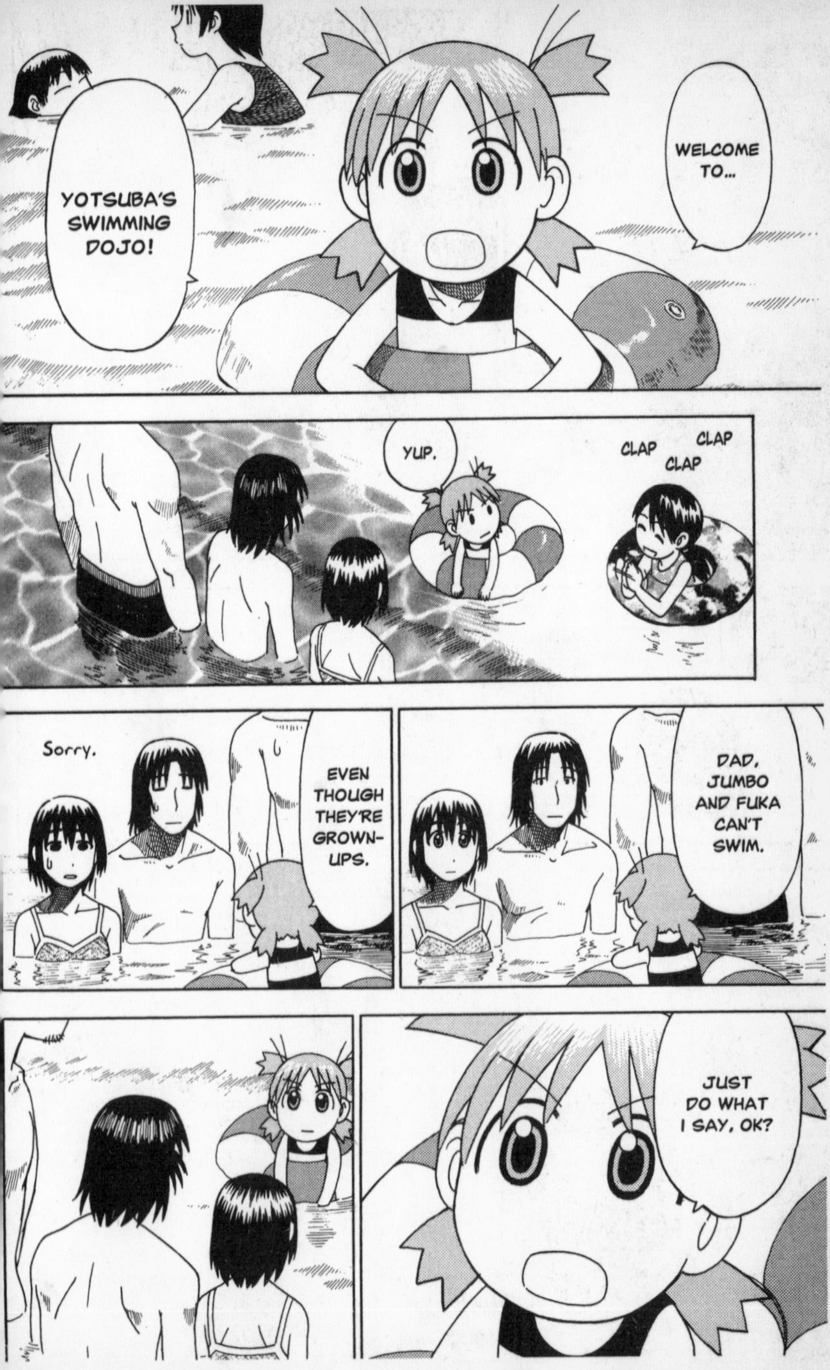
WELCOME TO...
YOTSUBA'S SWIMMING DOJO!
CLAP
CLAP
CLAP
YUP.
DAD, JUMBO AND FUKA CAN'T SWIM.
EVEN THOUGH THEY'RE GROWN-UPS.
Sorry.
JUST DO WHAT I SAY, OK?

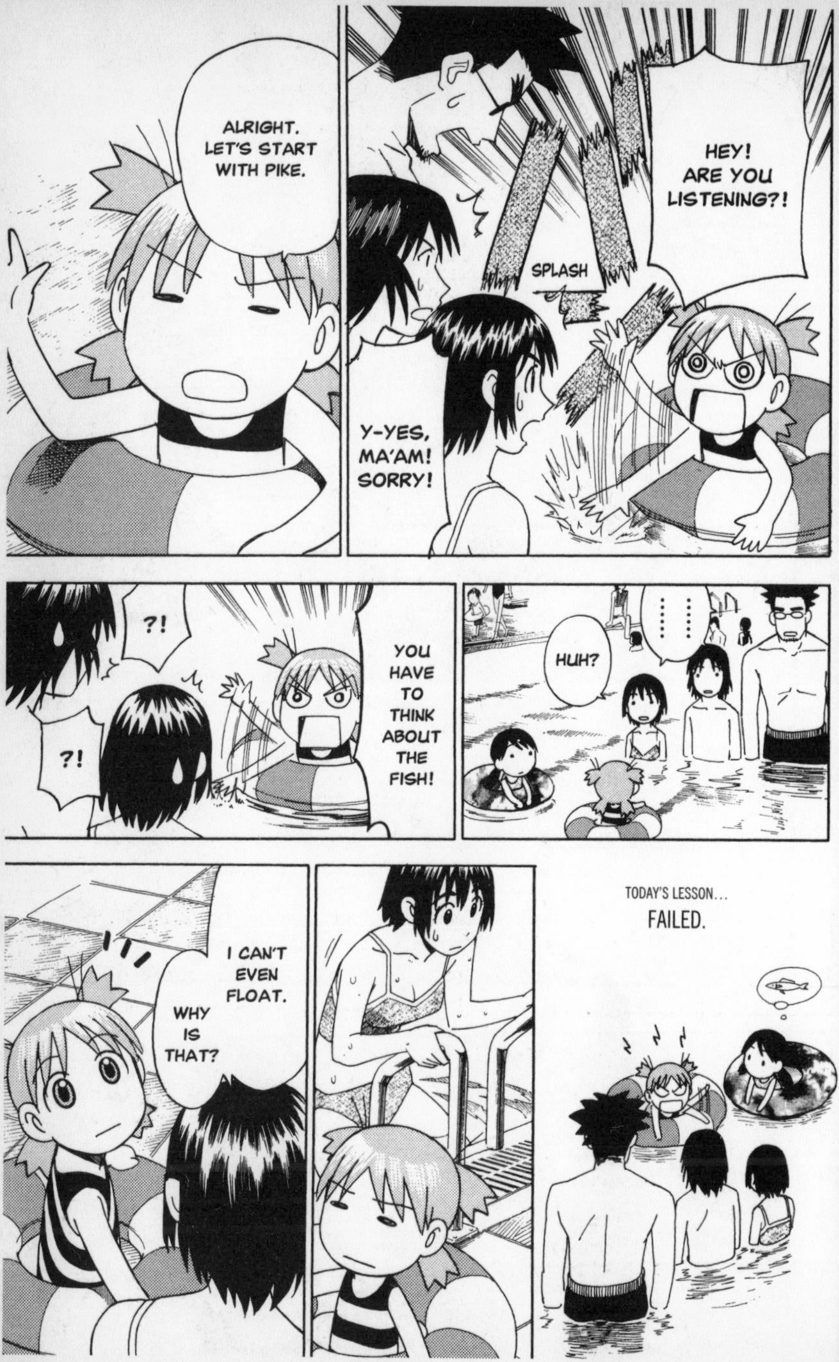

ALRIGHT. LET'S START WITH PIKE.
HEY! ARE YOU LISTENING?!
SPLASH
Y-YES, MA'AM! SORRY!
?!
?!
YOU HAVE TO THINK ABOUT THE FISH!
HUH?
......
I CAN'T EVEN FLOAT.
WHY IS THAT?
TODAY'S LESSON...
FAILED.

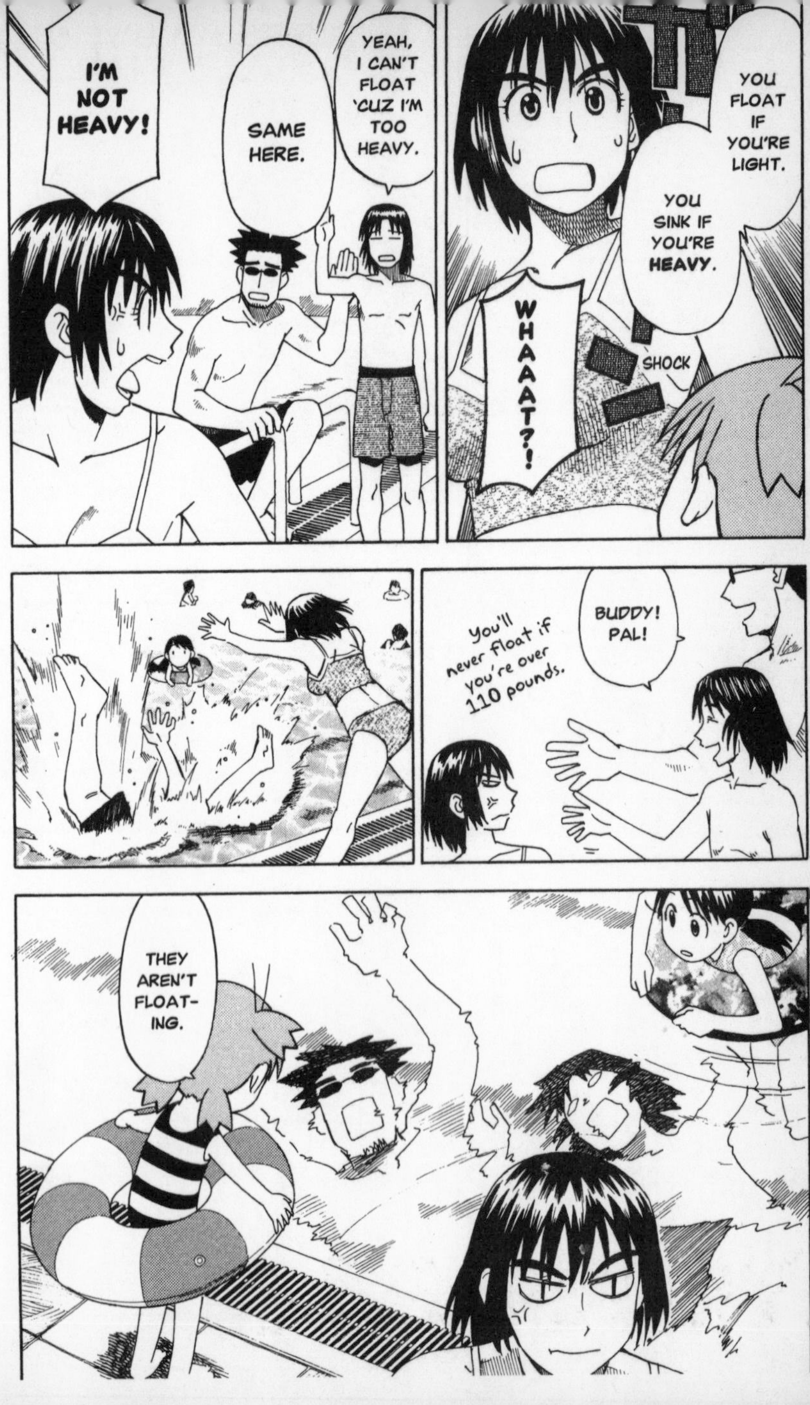

YOU FLOAT IF YOU'RE LIGHT.
YOU SINK IF YOU'RE HEAVY.
SHOCK
WHAAAT?!
YEAH, I CAN'T FLOAT 'CUZ I'M TOO HEAVY.
SAME HERE.
I'M NOT HEAVY!
BUDDY! PAL!
You'll never float if you're over 110 pounds.
THEY AREN'T FLOAT-ING.

YOTSUBA&!

YOTSUBA & THE FROG

CHAPTER 13

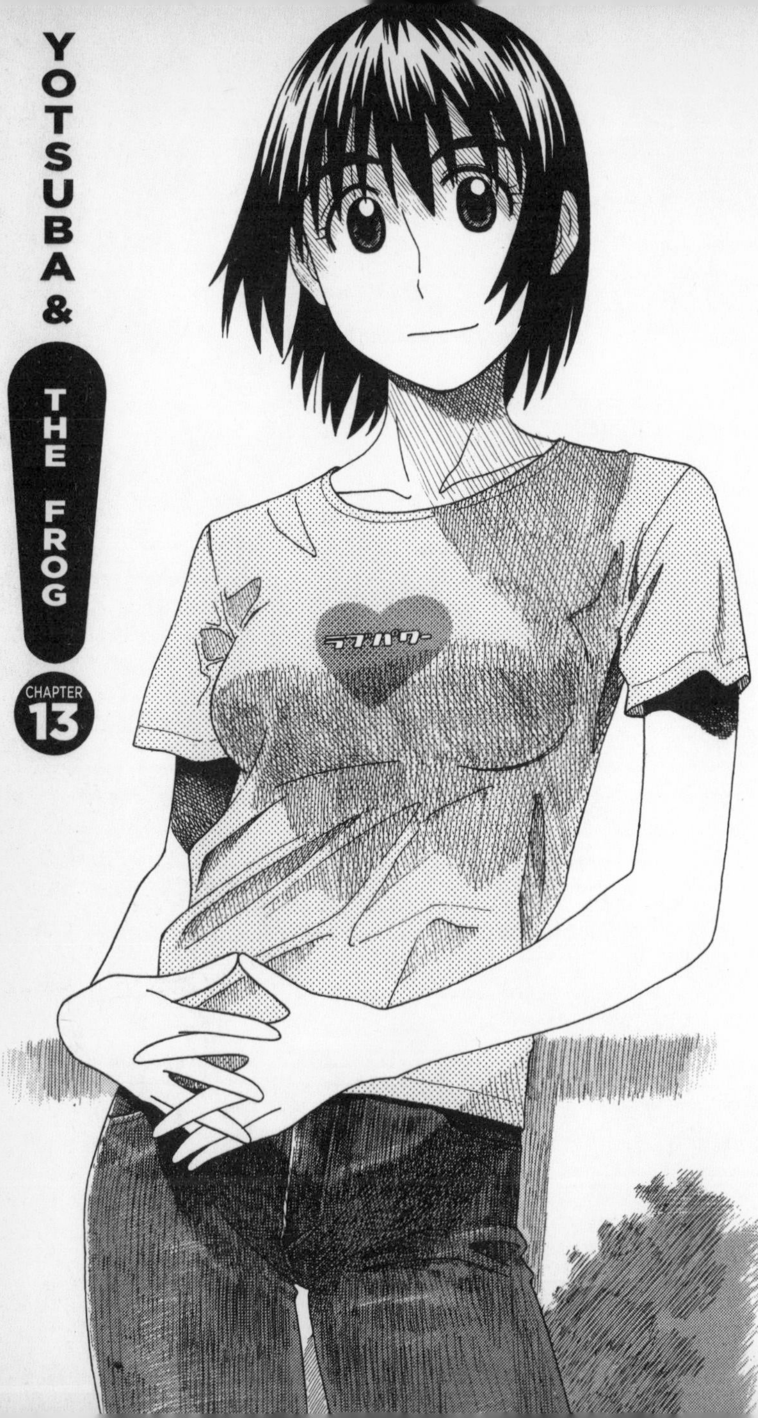
ラブパワー

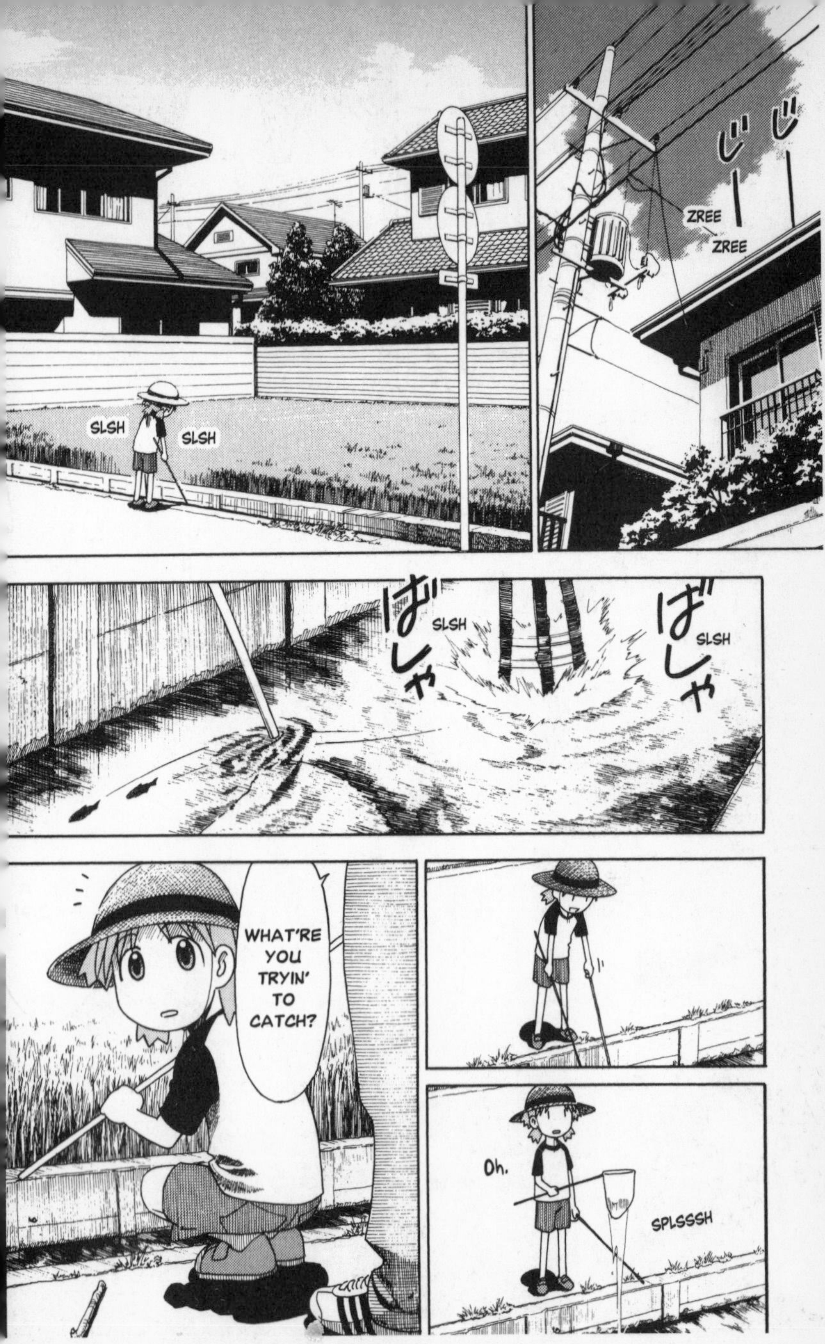
じー
じー
ZREE
ZREE
SLSH
SLSH
ばしゃ
SLSH
ばしゃ
SLSH
WHAT'RE YOU TRYIN' TO CATCH?
Oh.
SPLSSSH

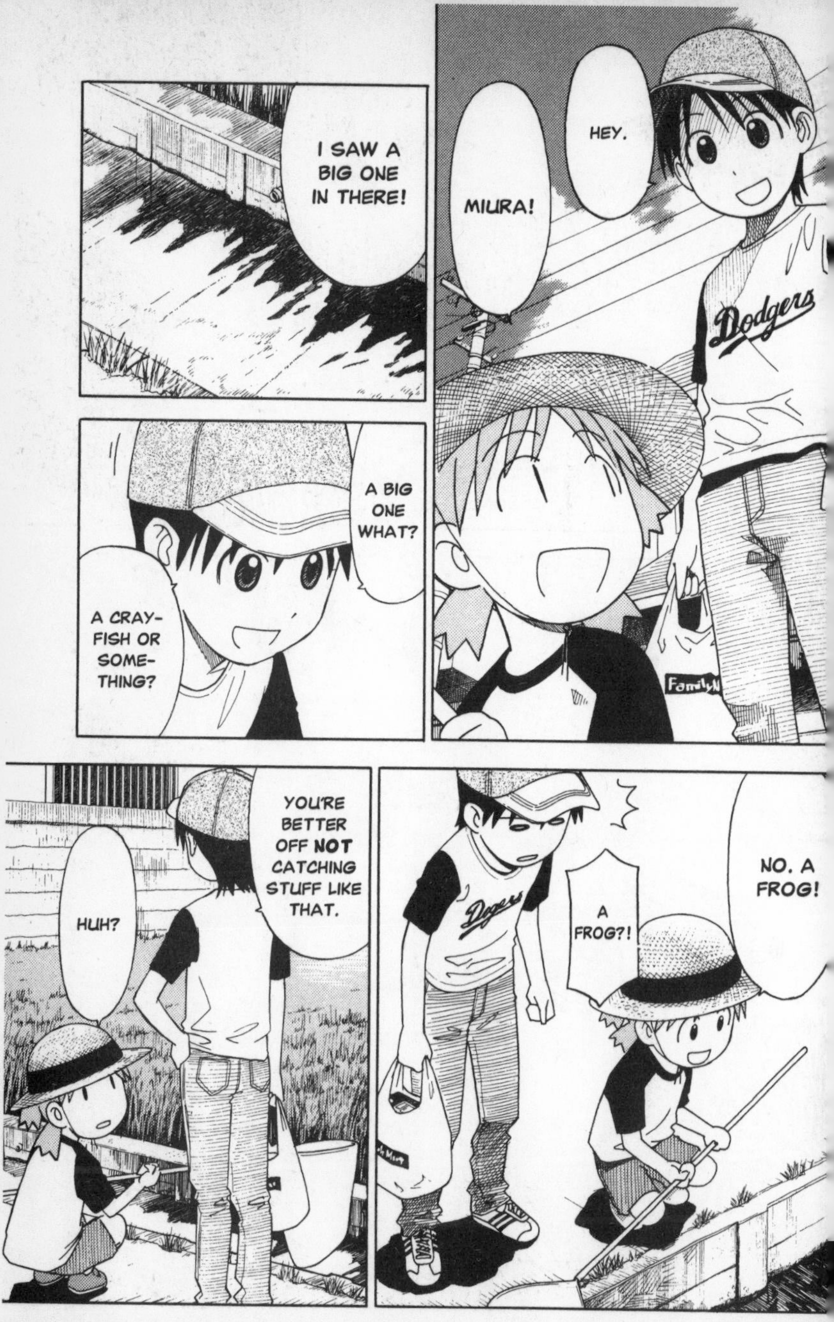
HEY.
MIURA!
I SAW A BIG ONE IN THERE!
A BIG ONE WHAT?
A CRAY-FISH OR SOME-THING?
NO. A FROG!
A FROG?!
YOU'RE BETTER OFF **NOT** CATCHING STUFF LIKE THAT.
HUH?

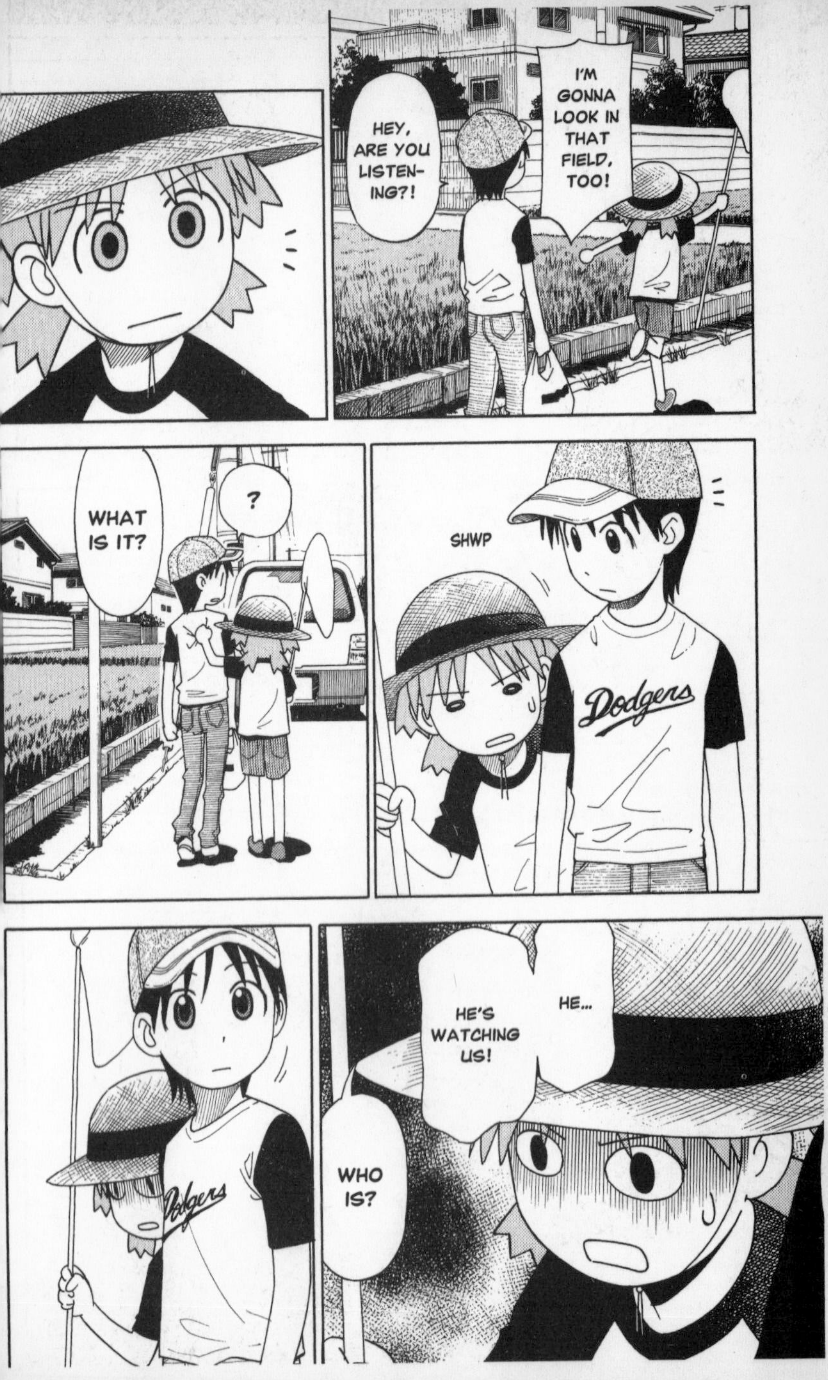

HEY, ARE YOU LISTEN-ING?!
I'M GONNA LOOK IN THAT FIELD, TOO!
WHAT IS IT?
?
SHWP
Dodgers
HE...
HE'S WATCHING US!
WHO IS?
Dodgers

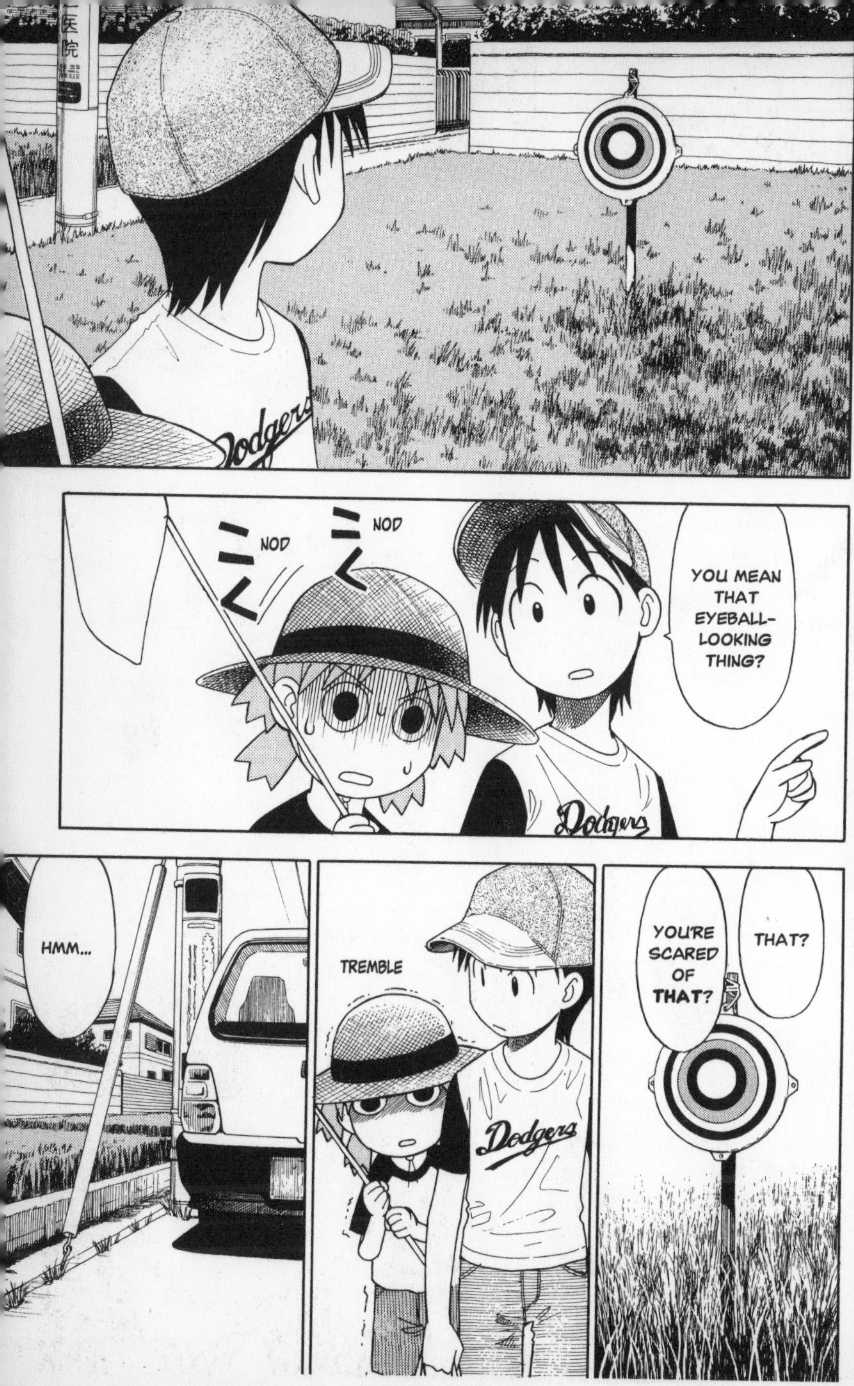
YOU MEAN THAT EYEBALL-LOOKING THING?
NOD
NOD
THAT?
YOU'RE SCARED OF THAT?
TREMBLE
HMM...

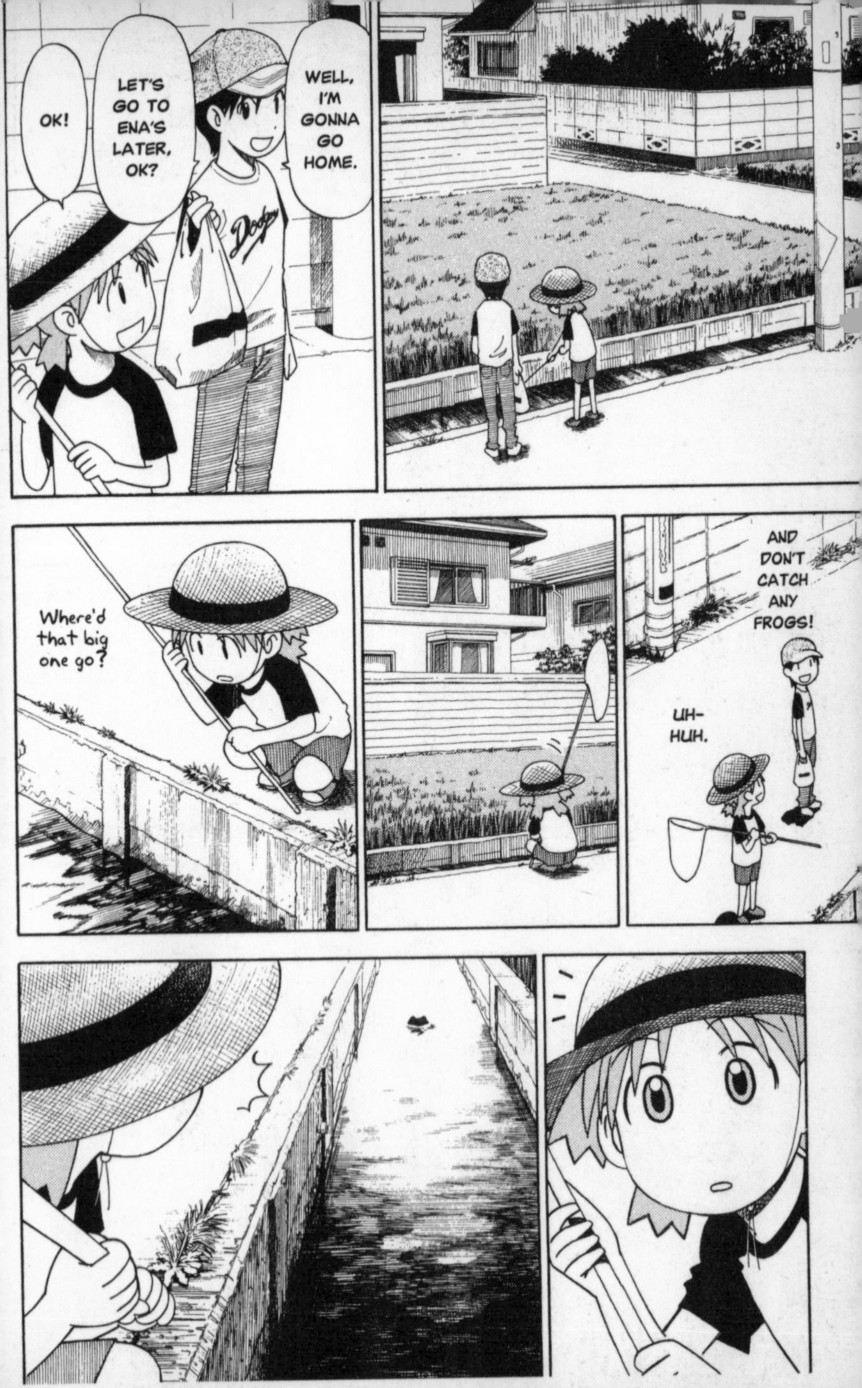
WELL, I'M GONNA GO HOME.
LET'S GO TO ENA'S LATER, OK?
OK!
AND DON'T CATCH ANY FROGS!
UH-HUH.
Where'd that big one go?

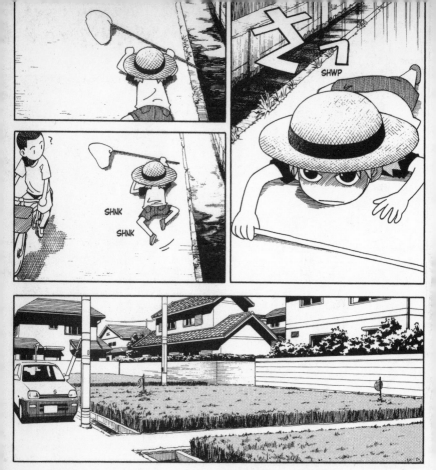

SHWP

SHNK

SHNK

ANY-
ONE
HOME?!

HELLOOO!

THMP

THMP

THMP

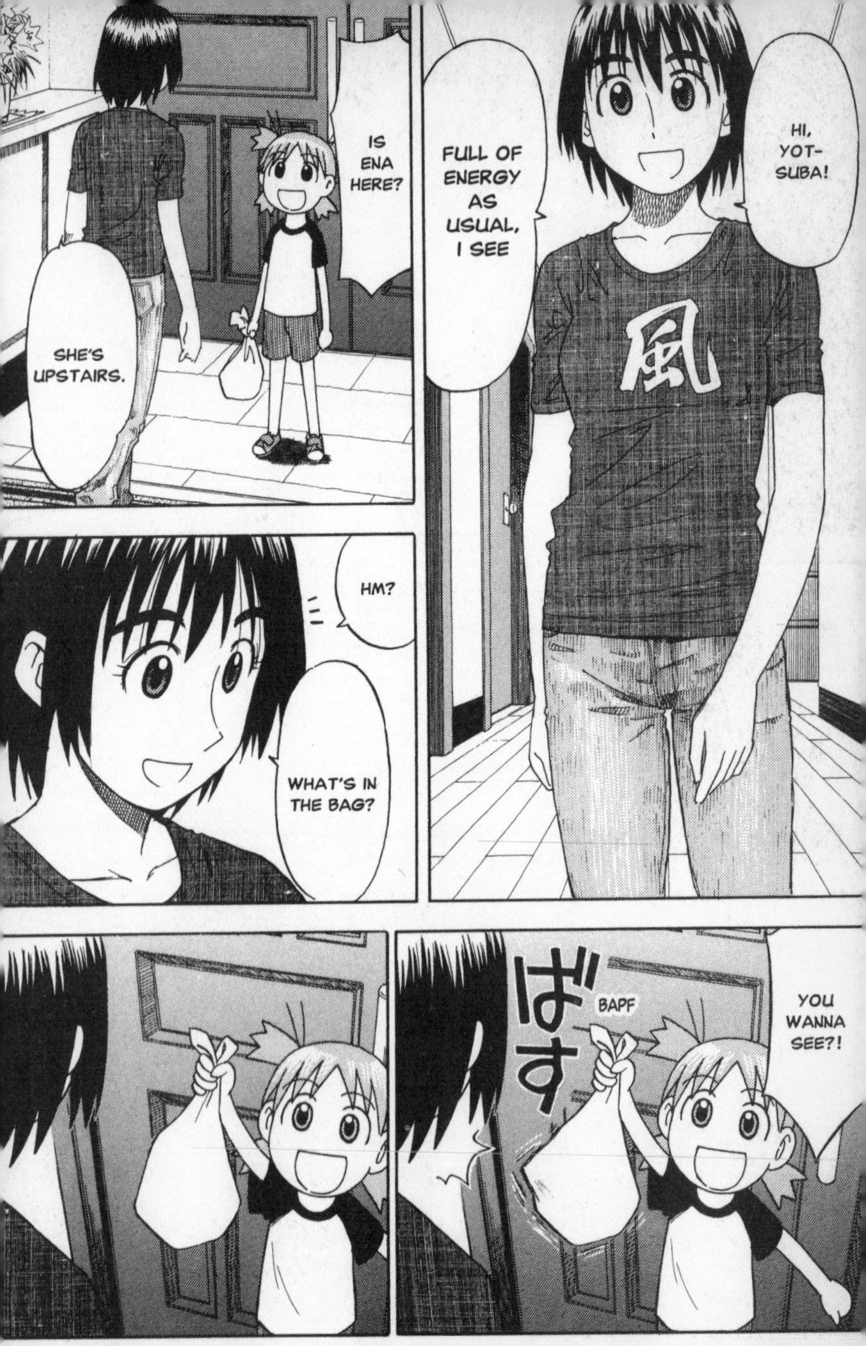
HI, YOT-SUBA!
FULL OF ENERGY AS USUAL, I SEE
IS ENA HERE?
SHE'S UPSTAIRS.
HM?
WHAT'S IN THE BAG?
ばす
BAPF
YOU WANNA SEE?!

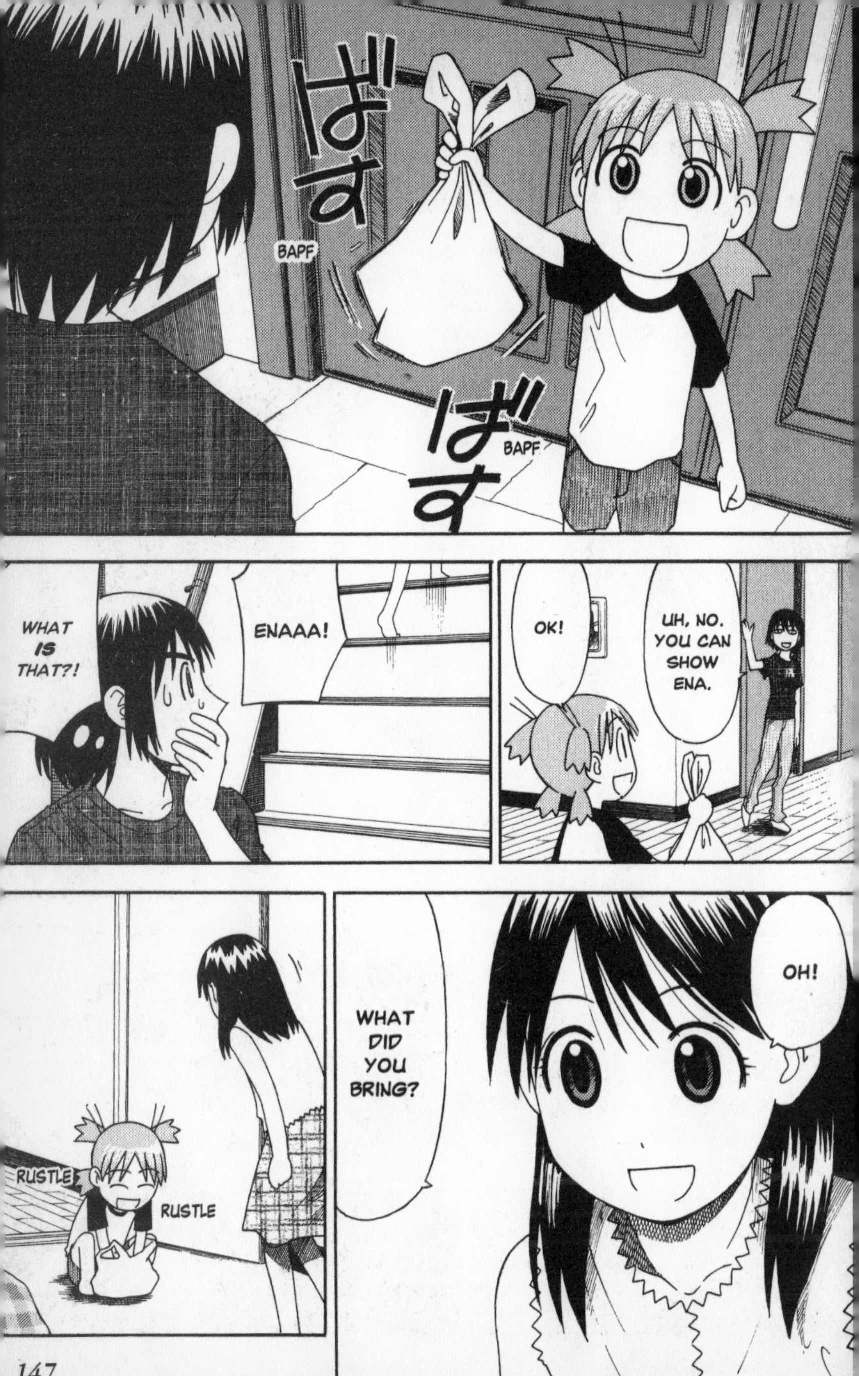

ばす
BAPF
ばす
BAPF
UH, NO. YOU CAN SHOW ENA.
OK!
ENAAA!
WHAT IS THAT?!
OH!
WHAT DID YOU BRING?
RUSTLE
RUSTLE

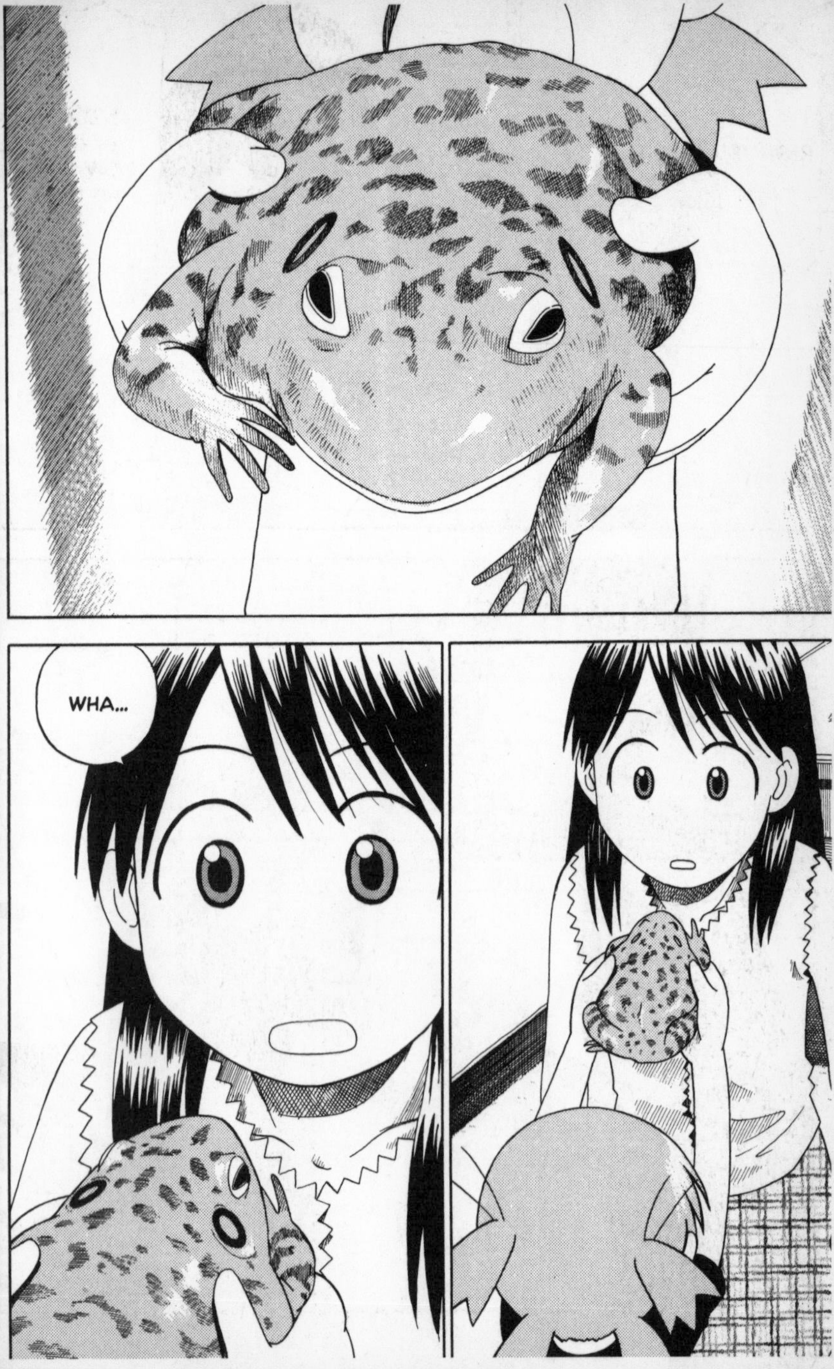
WHA...

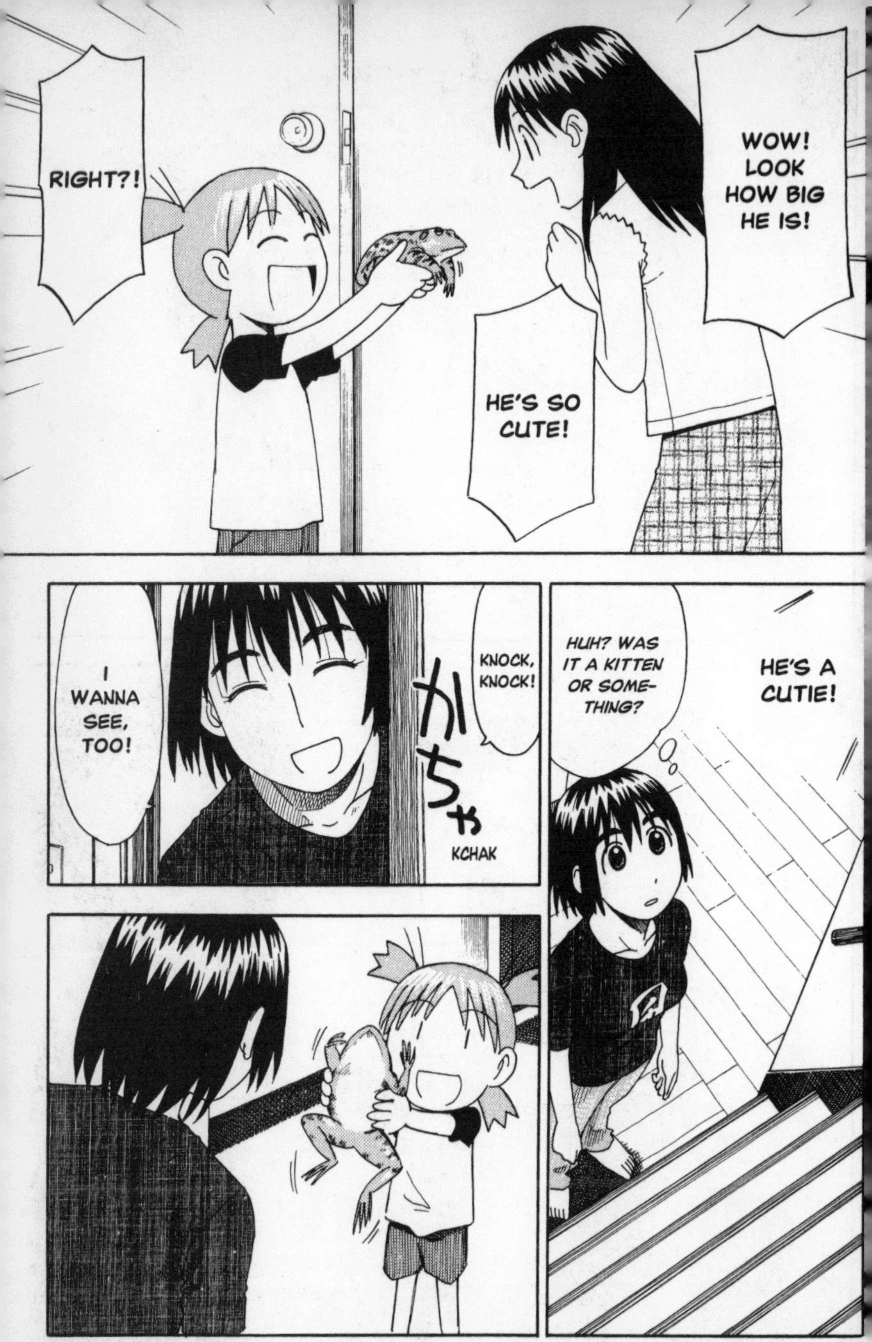
WOW! LOOK HOW BIG HE IS!
HE'S SO CUTE!
RIGHT?!
HE'S A CUTIE!
HUH? WAS IT A KITTEN OR SOME-THING?
KNOCK, KNOCK!
かちゃ
KCHAK
I WANNA SEE, TOO!

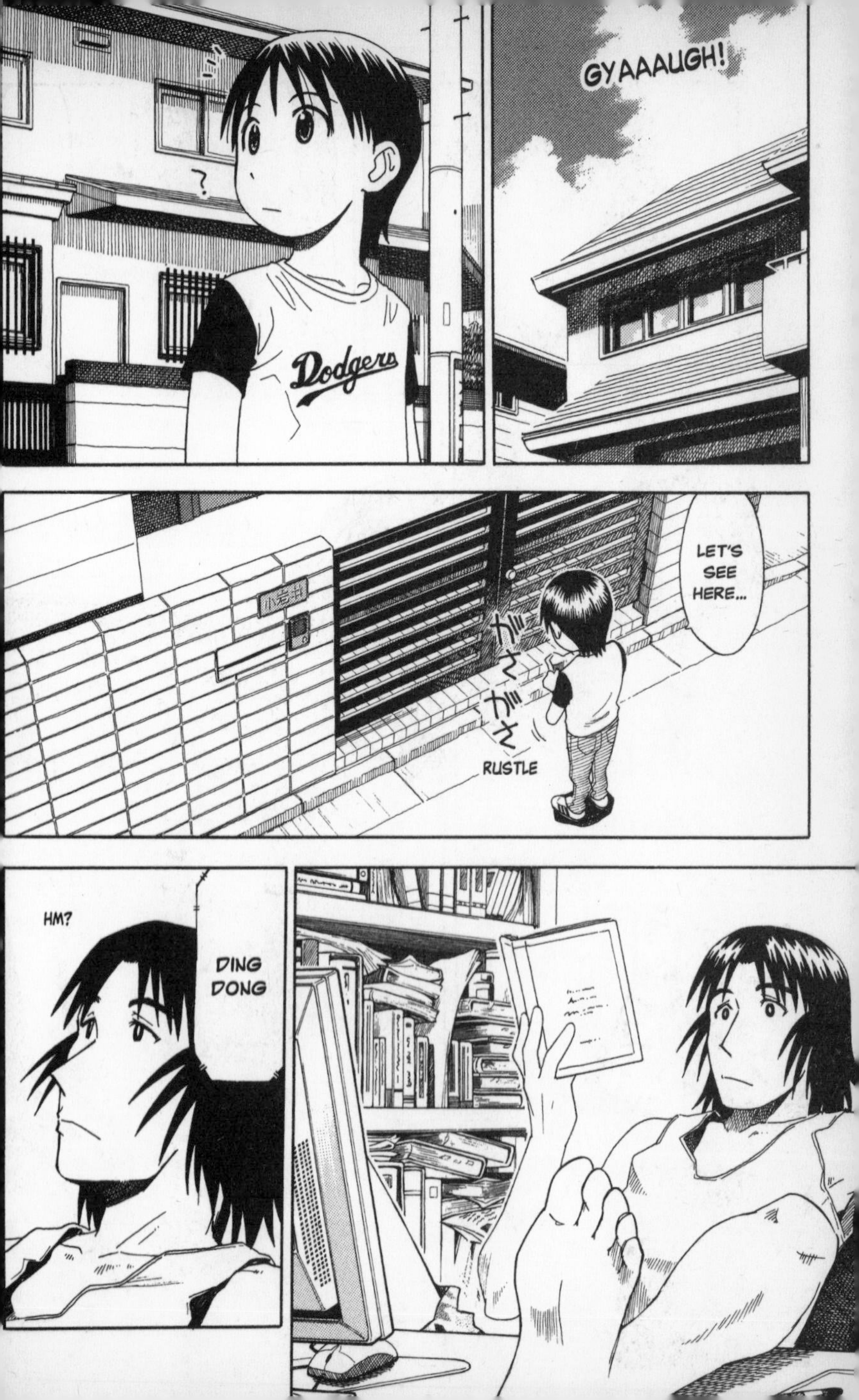
GYAAAUGH!
?
LET'S SEE HERE...
がさ がさ
RUSTLE
DING DONG
HM?

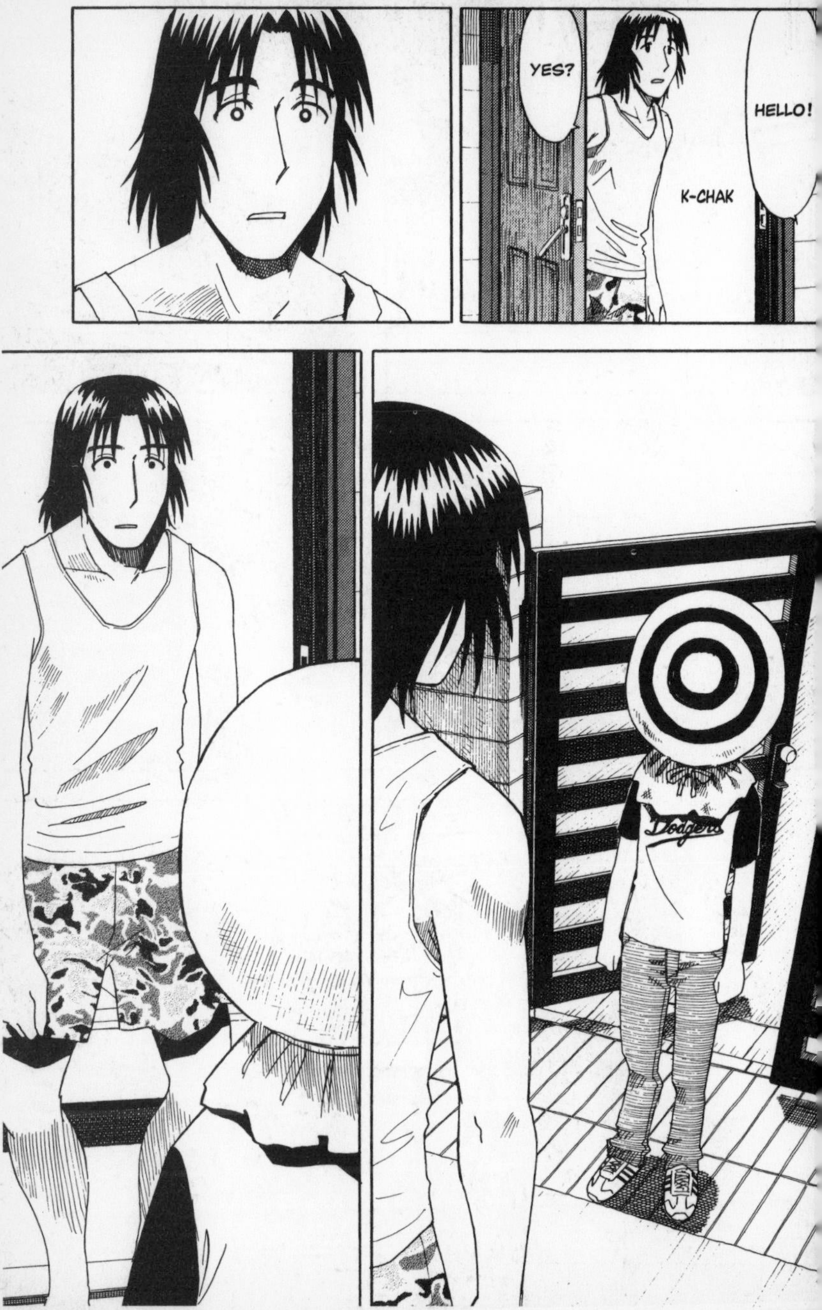
HELLO!
K-CHAK
YES?

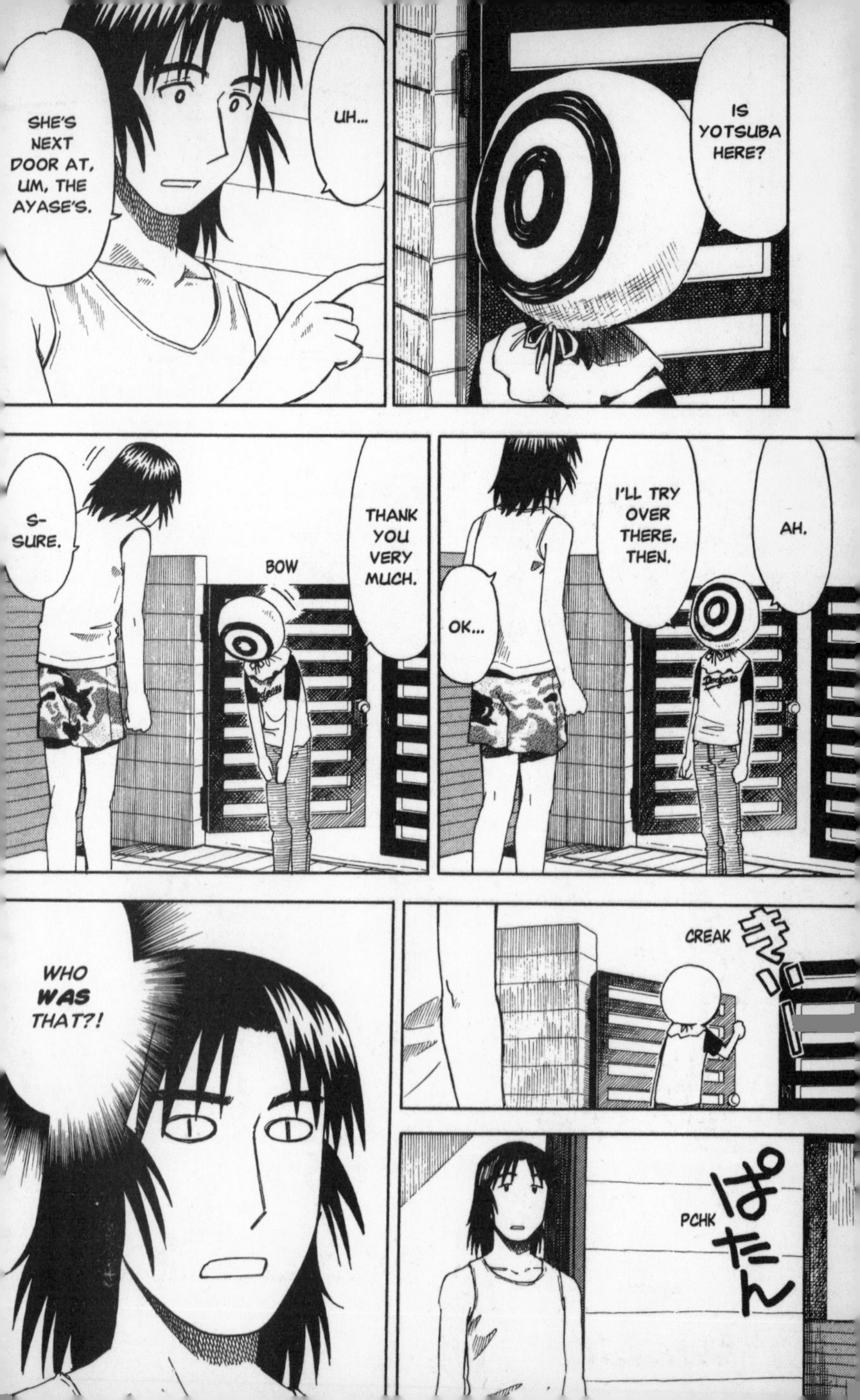
IS YOTSUBA HERE?
UH...
SHE'S NEXT DOOR AT, UM, THE AYASE'S.
AH.
I'LL TRY OVER THERE, THEN.
OK...
THANK YOU VERY MUCH.
BOW
S-SURE.
CREAK
PCHK
ぱたん
WHO **WAS** THAT?!

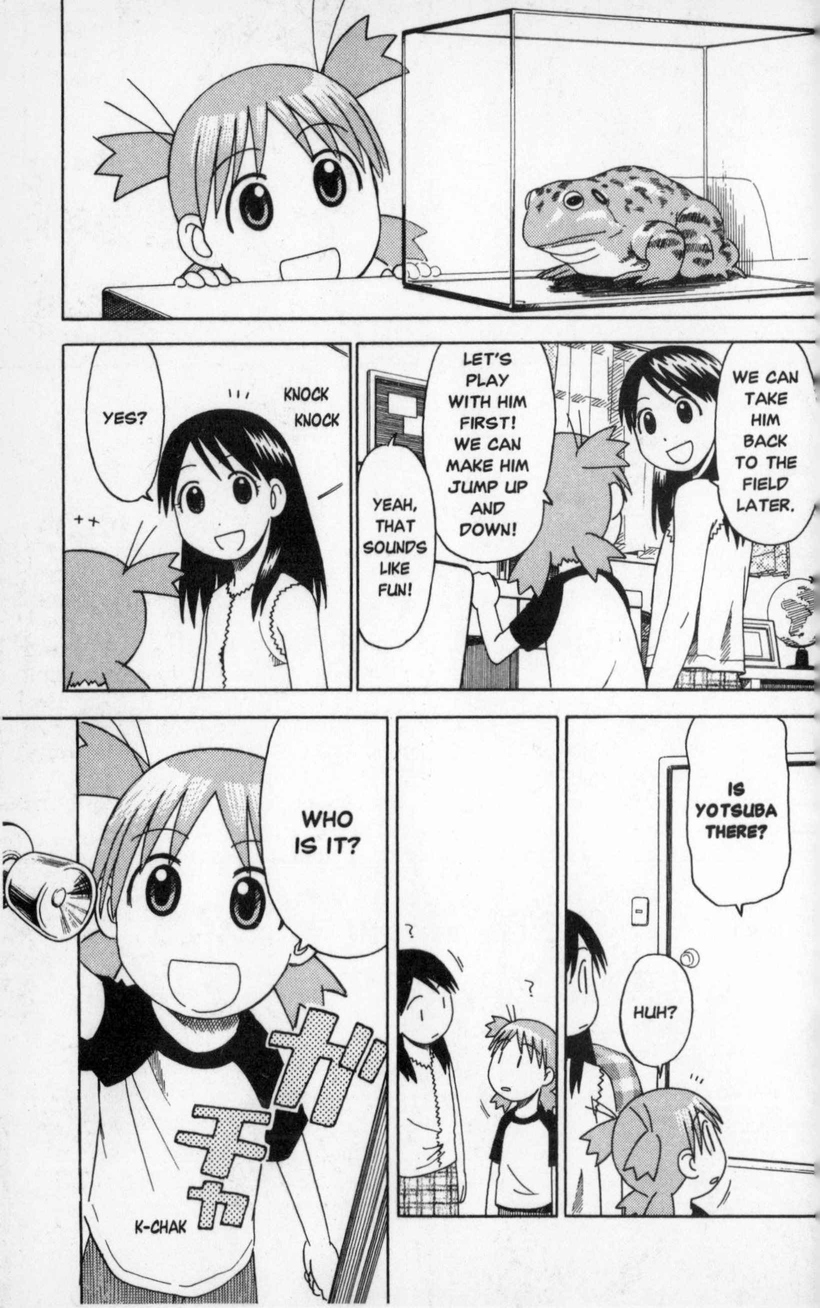
WE CAN TAKE HIM BACK TO THE FIELD LATER.
LET'S PLAY WITH HIM FIRST! WE CAN MAKE HIM JUMP UP AND DOWN!
YEAH, THAT SOUNDS LIKE FUN!
KNOCK KNOCK
YES?
IS YOTSUBA THERE?
HUH?
WHO IS IT?
K-CHAK

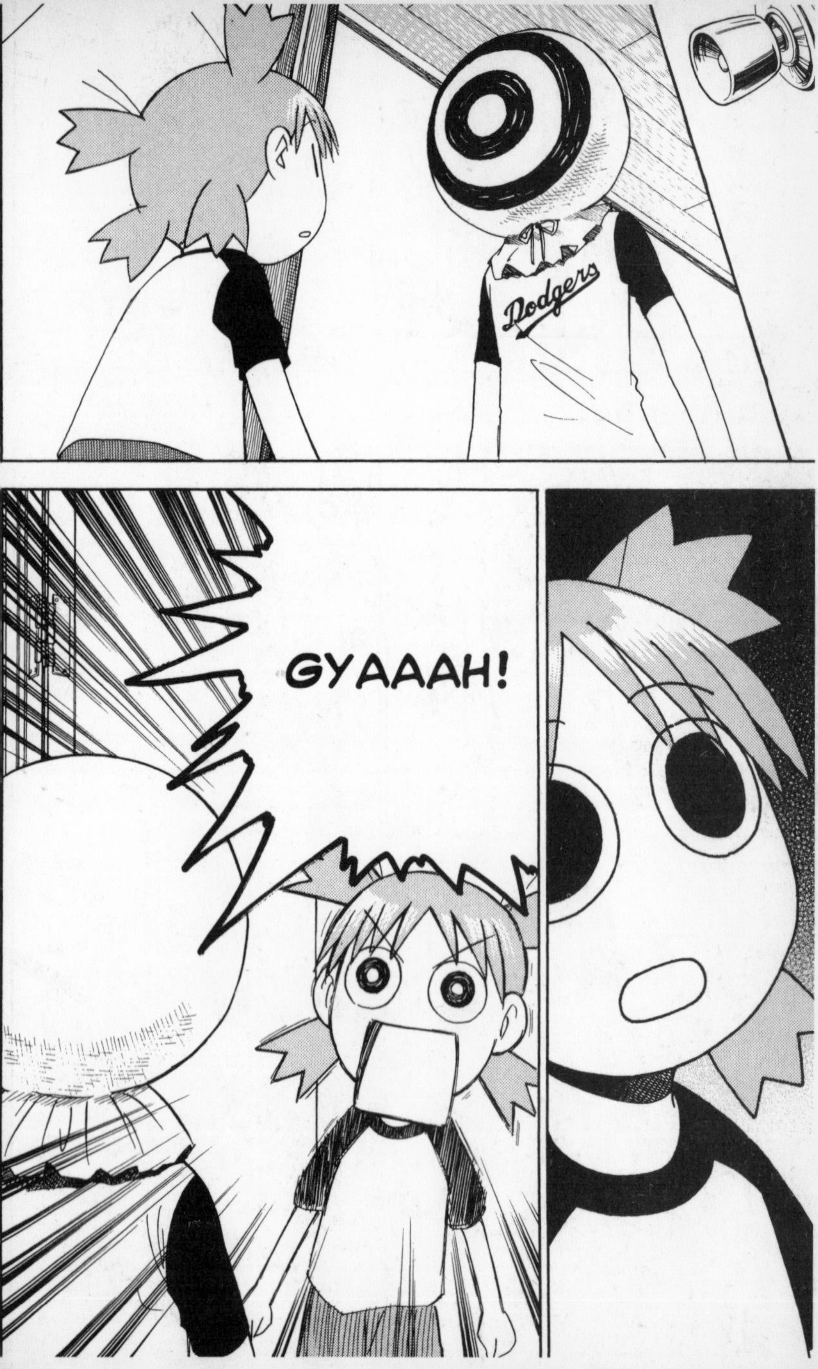
Dodgers
GYAAAH!

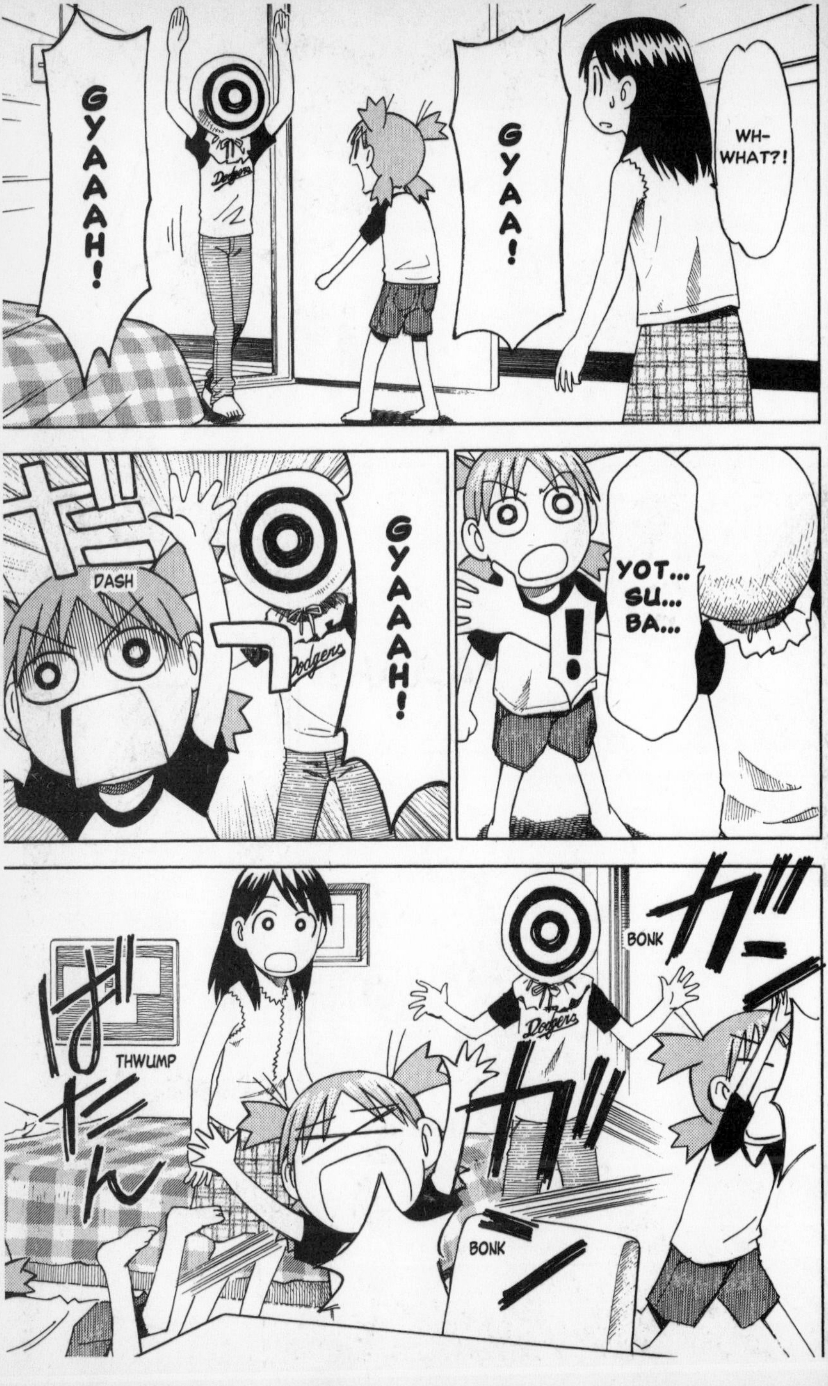
WH- WHAT?!
GYAAA!
GYAAAAH!
YOT... SU... BA...
GYAAAAH!
DASH
BONK
BONK
THWUMP

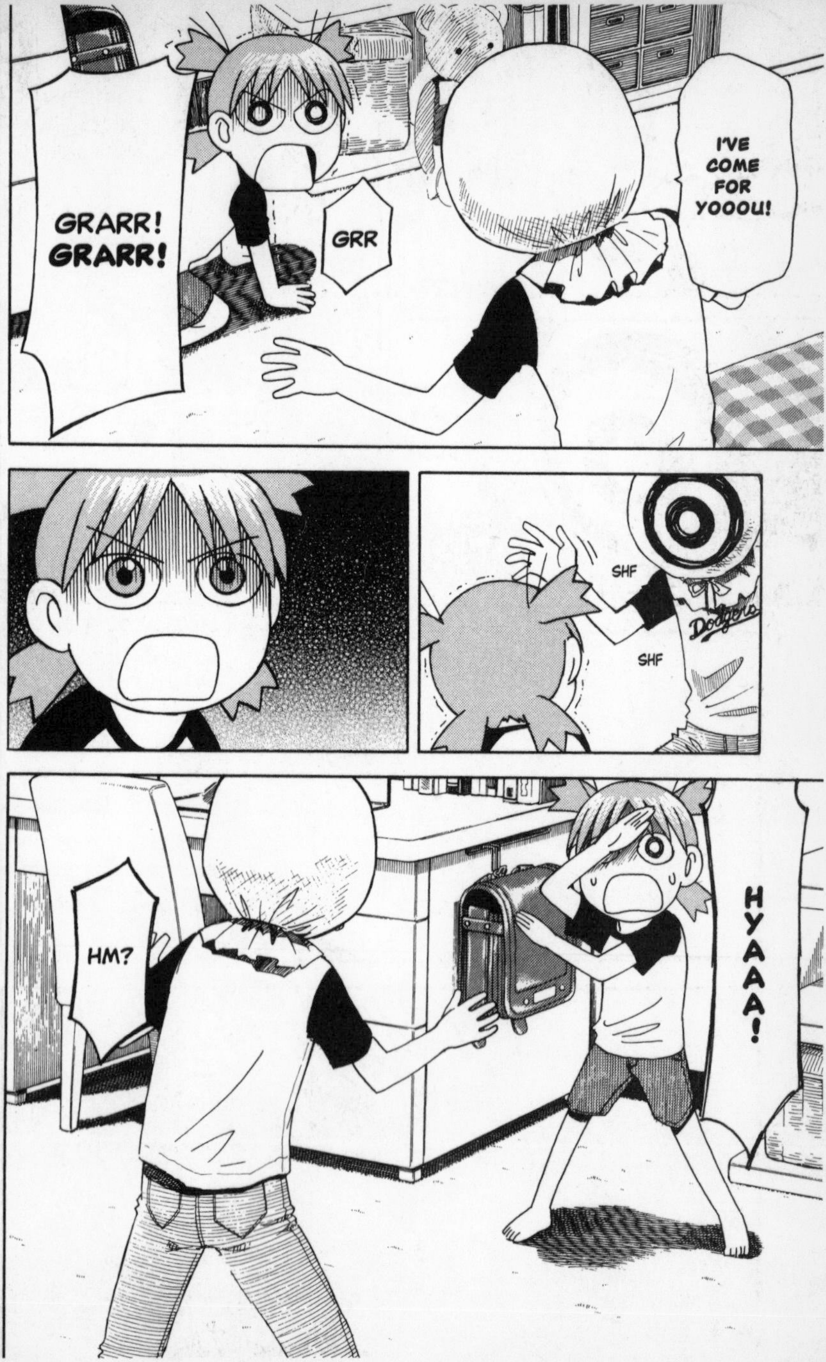
I'VE COME FOR YOOOU!
GRR
GRARR! GRARR!
SHF
SHF
Dodgers
HYAAA!
HM?

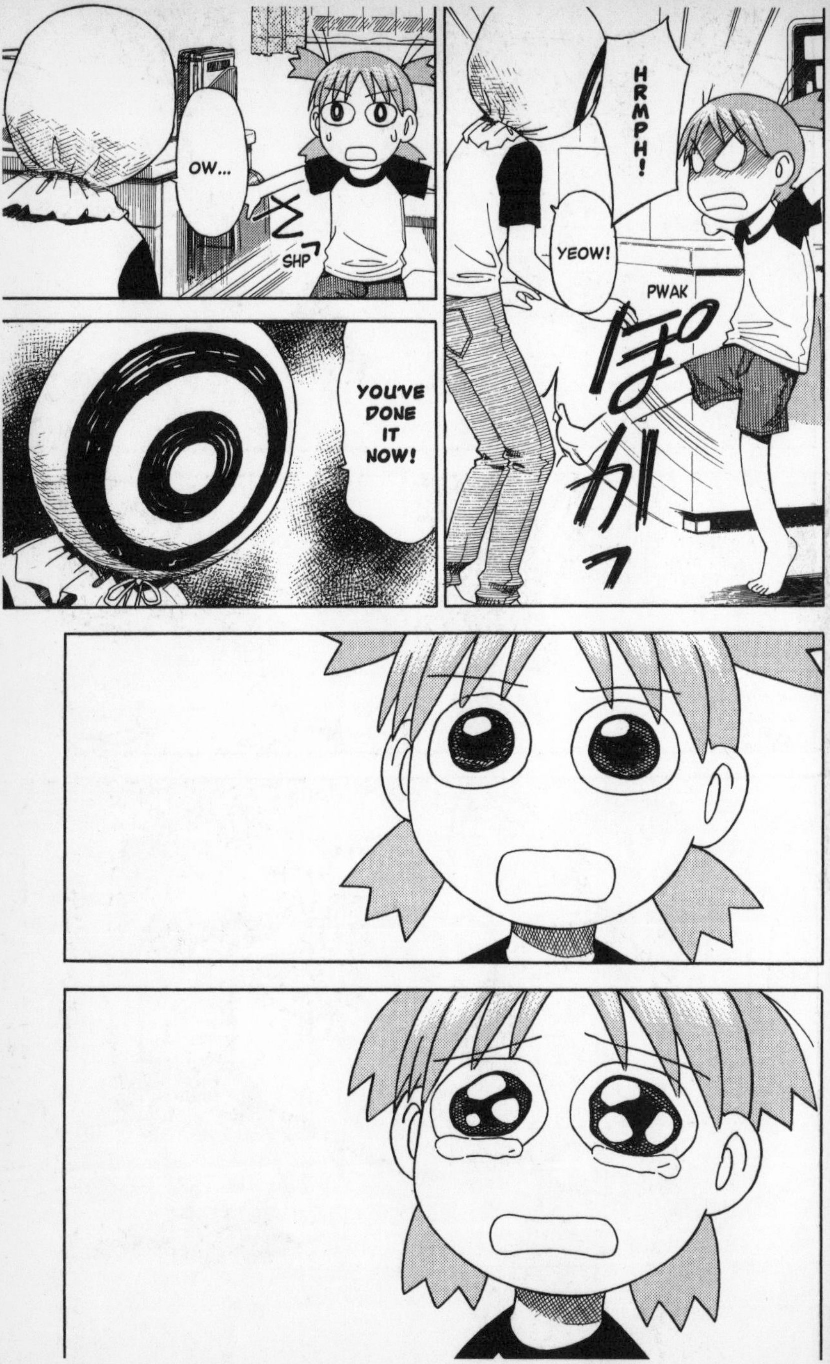
HRMPH!
YEOW!
PWAK
ぽかっ
OW...
SHP
YOU'VE DONE IT NOW!

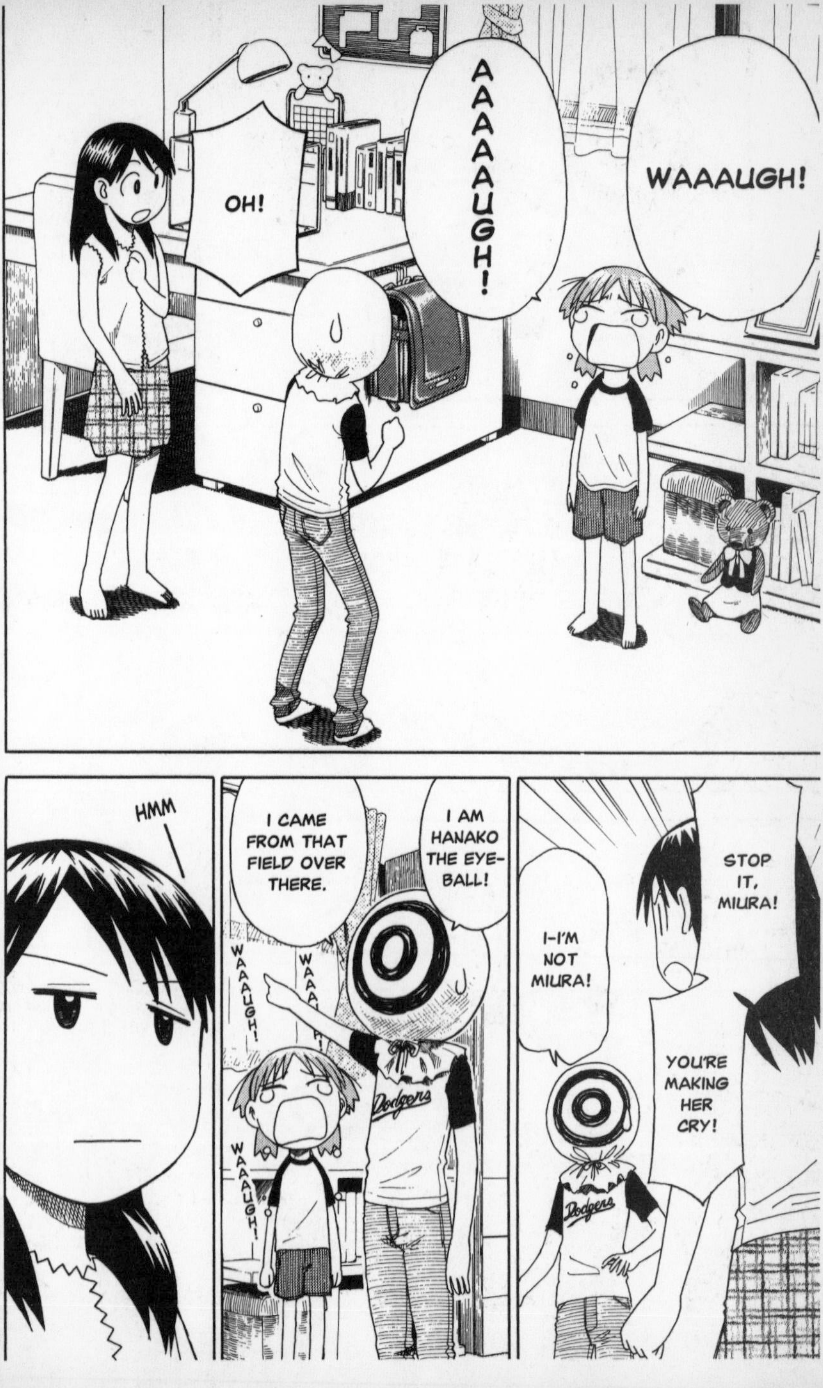
WAAAUGH!
AAAAAUGH!
OH!
STOP IT, MIURA!
I-I'M NOT MIURA!
YOU'RE MAKING HER CRY!
I AM HANAKO THE EYE-BALL!
I CAME FROM THAT FIELD OVER THERE.
WAAAUGH!
WAAAUGH!
HMM

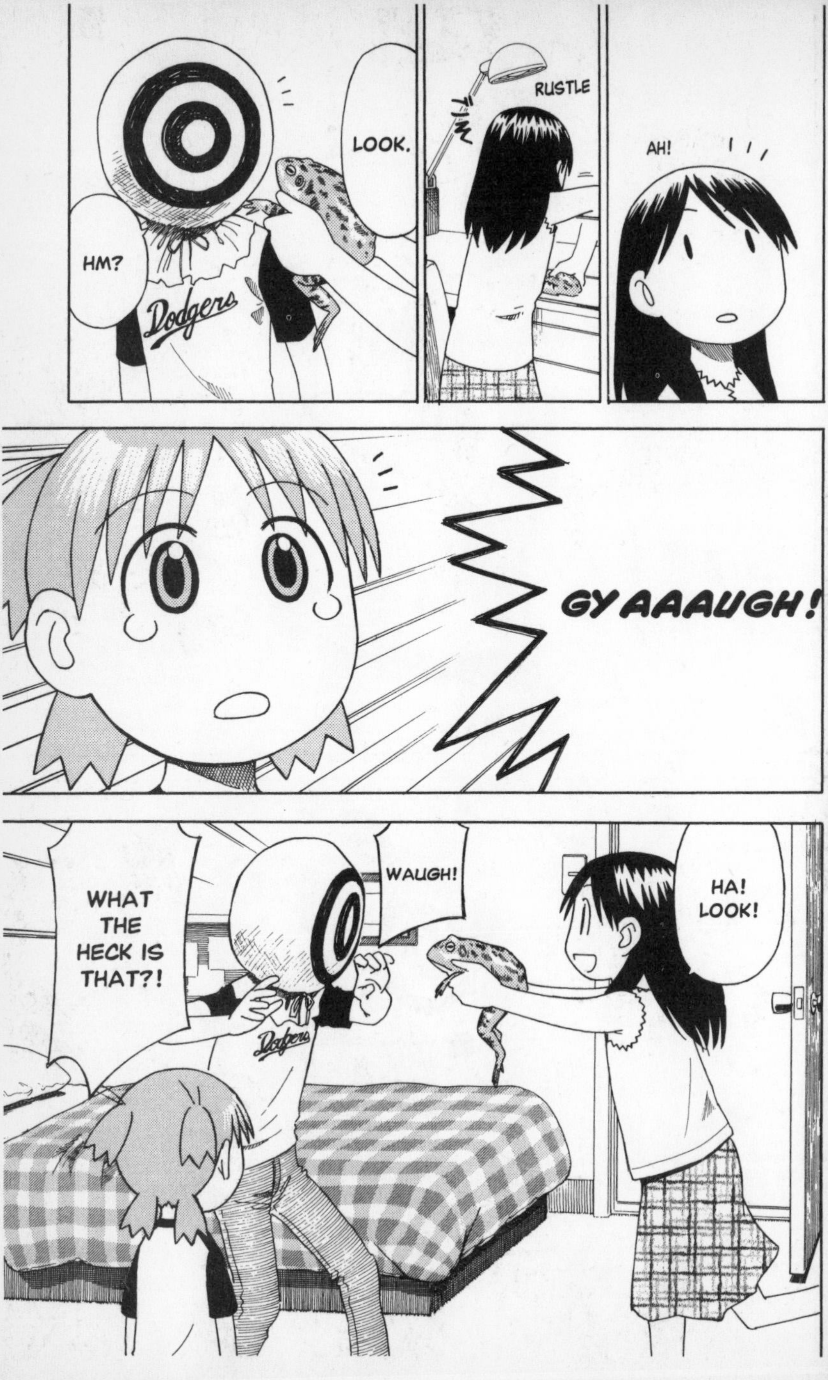
AH!
RUSTLE
LOOK.
HM?
Dodgers
GYAAAAUGH!
HA! LOOK!
WAUGH!
WHAT THE HECK IS THAT?!
Dodgers

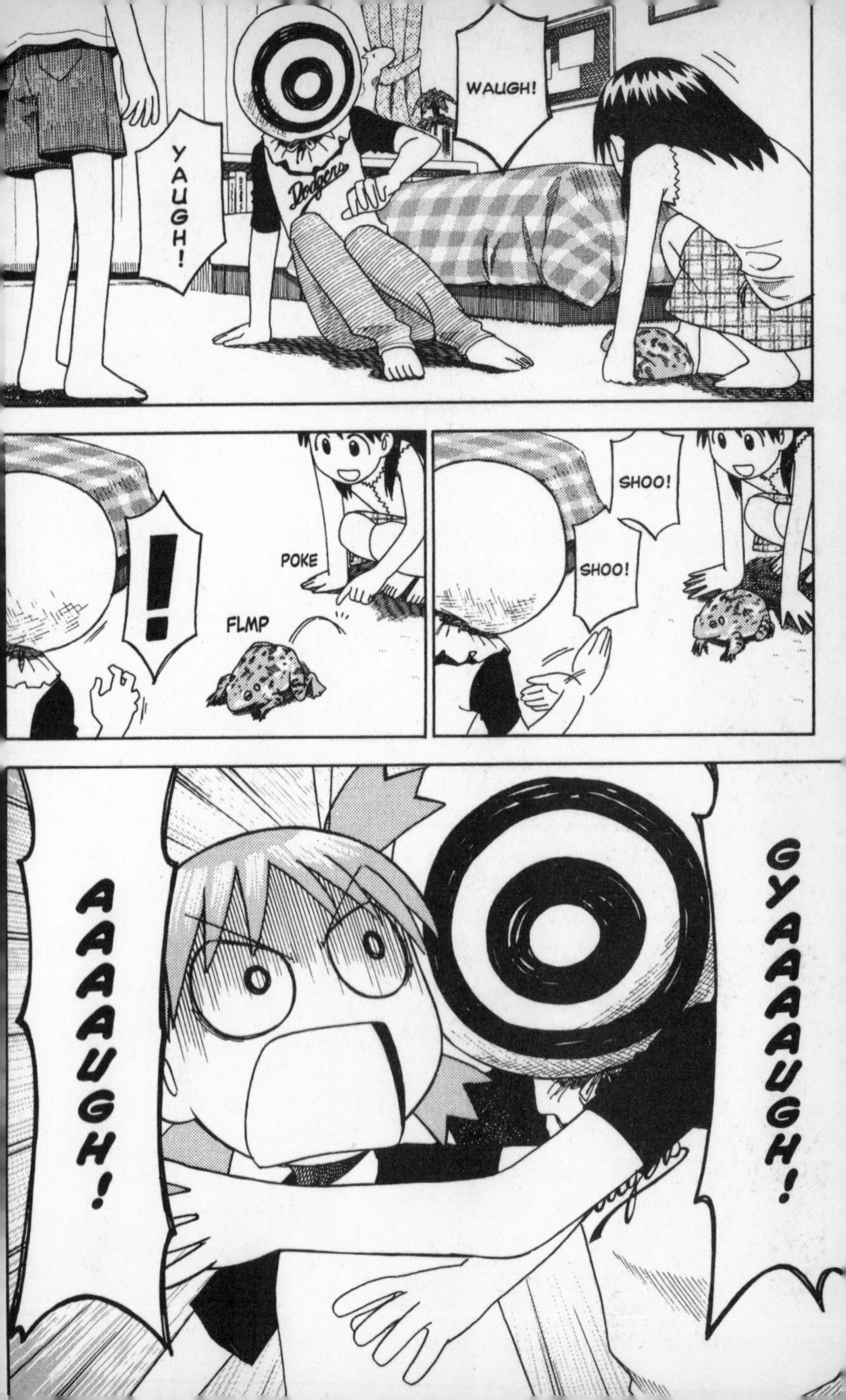

YAUGH!
WAUGH!
Dodgers
!
POKE
FLMP
SHOO!
SHOO!
AAAAAUGH!
GYAAAAAUGH!

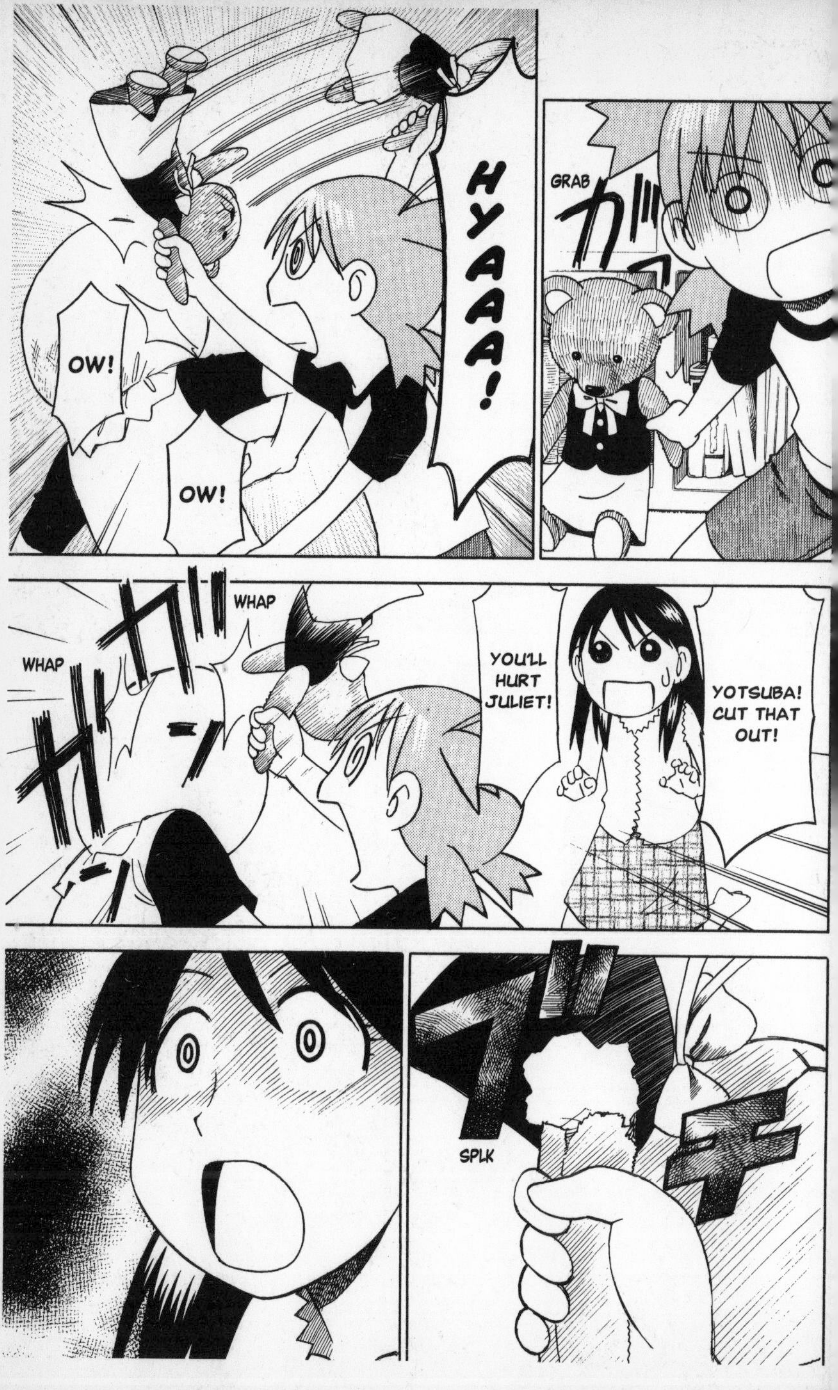
GRAB
HYAAAA!
OW!
OW!
YOTSUBA! CUT THAT OUT!
YOU'LL HURT JULIET!
WHAP
WHAP
SPLK

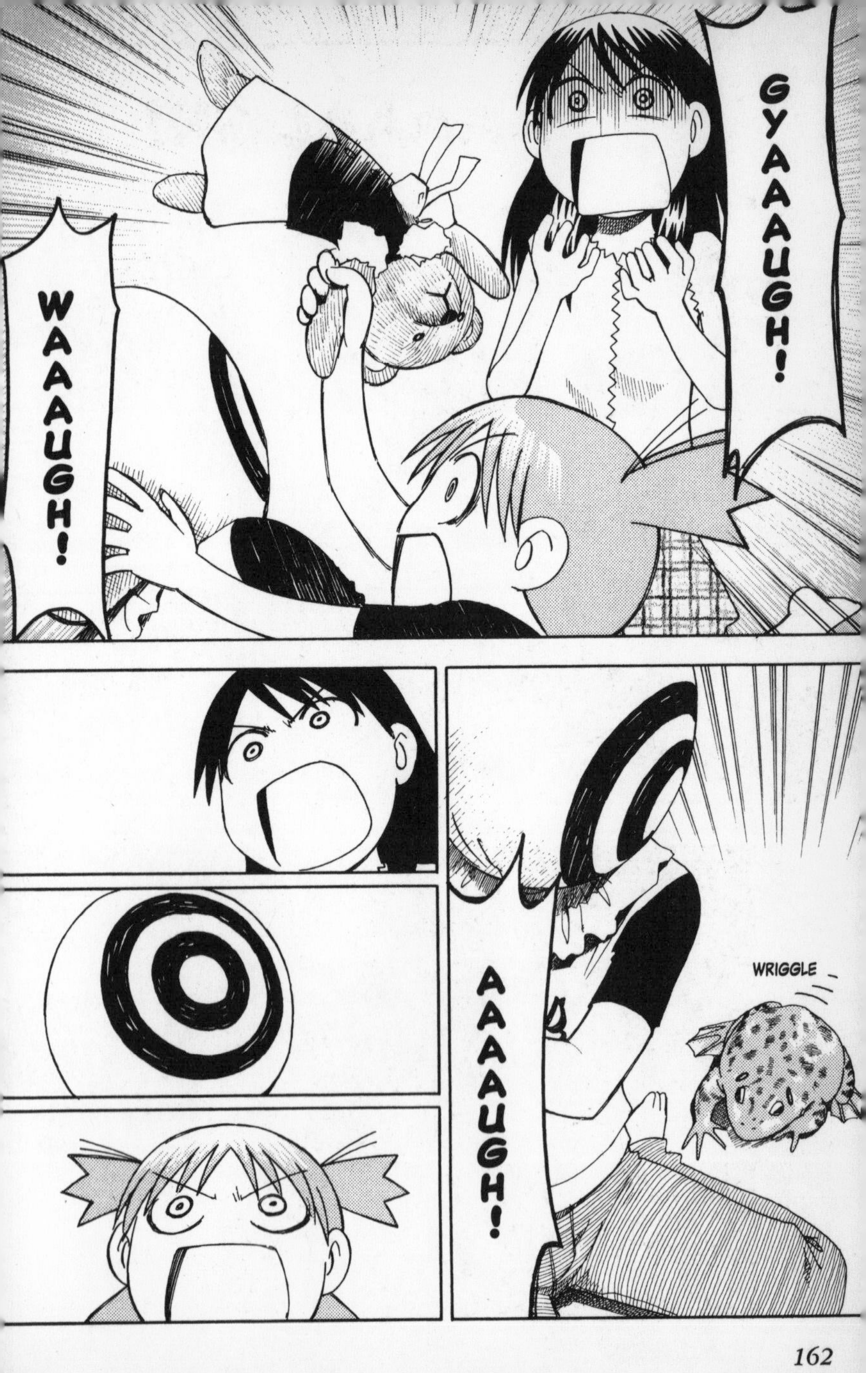
GYAAAAUGH!
WAAAAUGH!
AAAAAUGH!
WRIGGLE

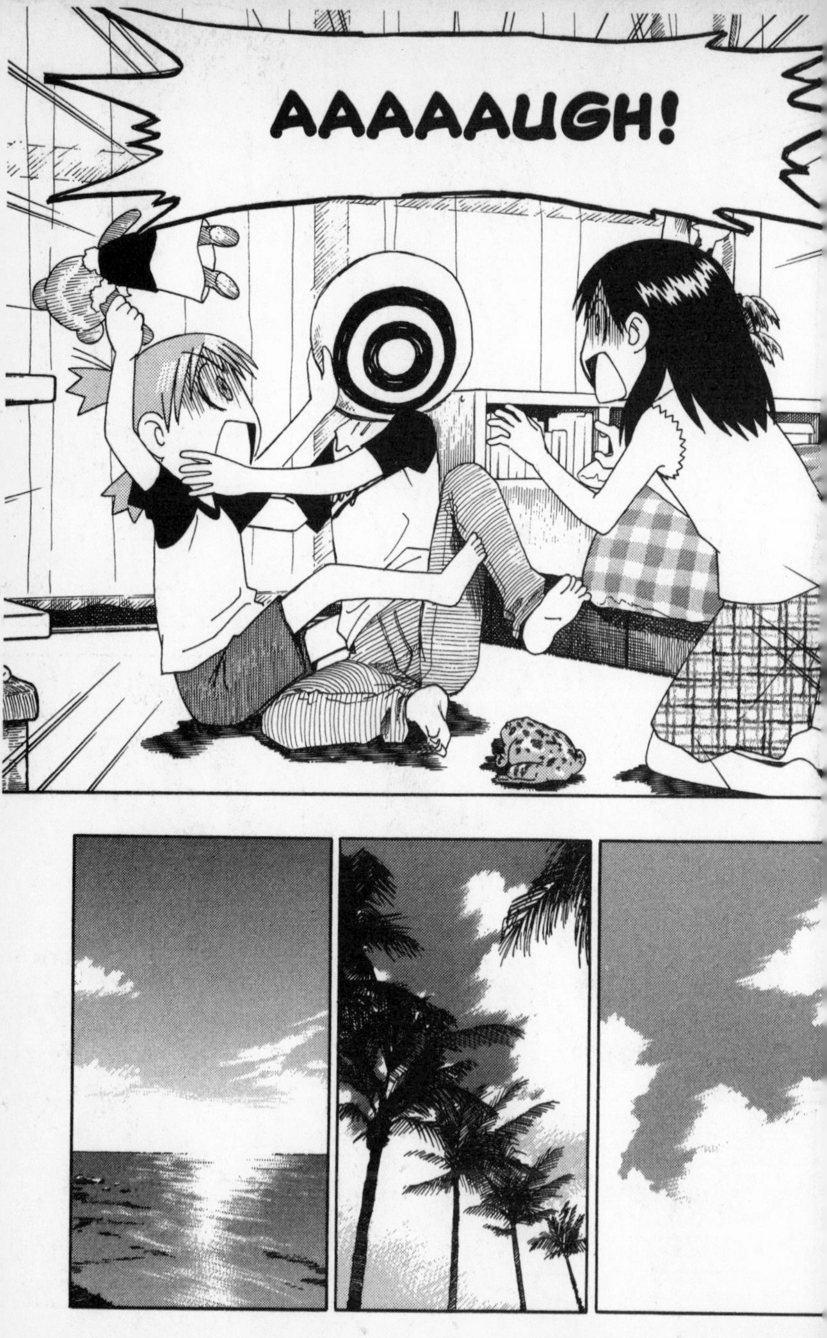
AAAAAAUGH!

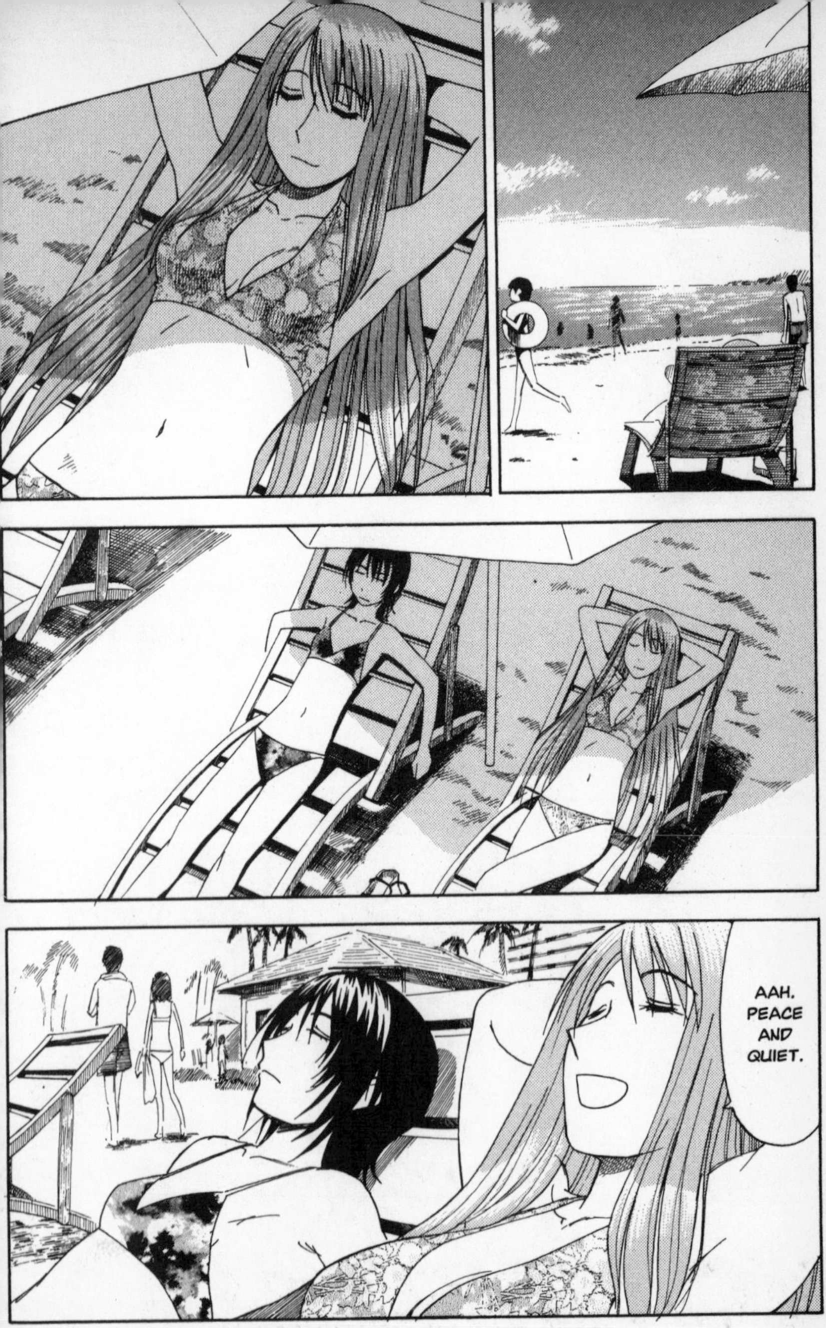
AAH. PEACE AND QUIET.

YOTSUBA&!

ASAGI & SOUVENIRS

CHAPTER 14

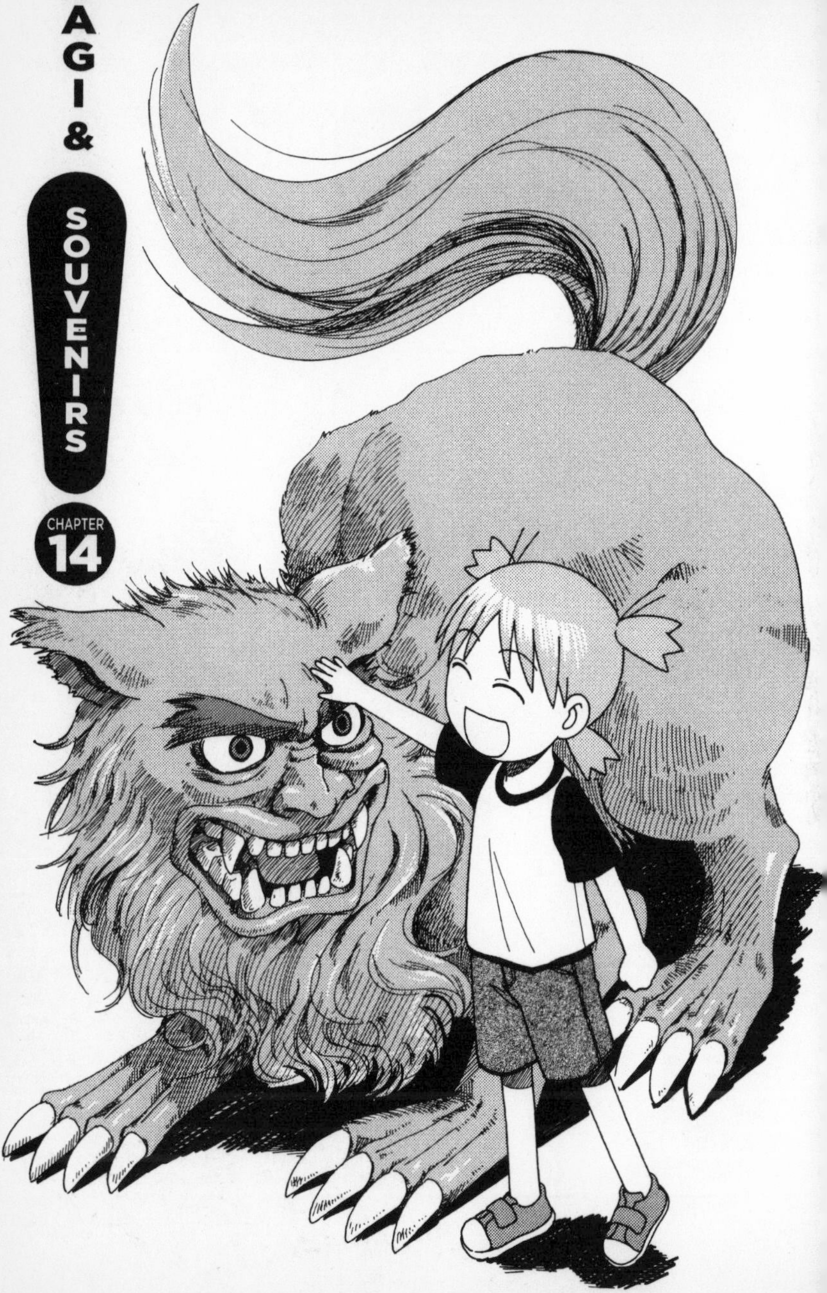

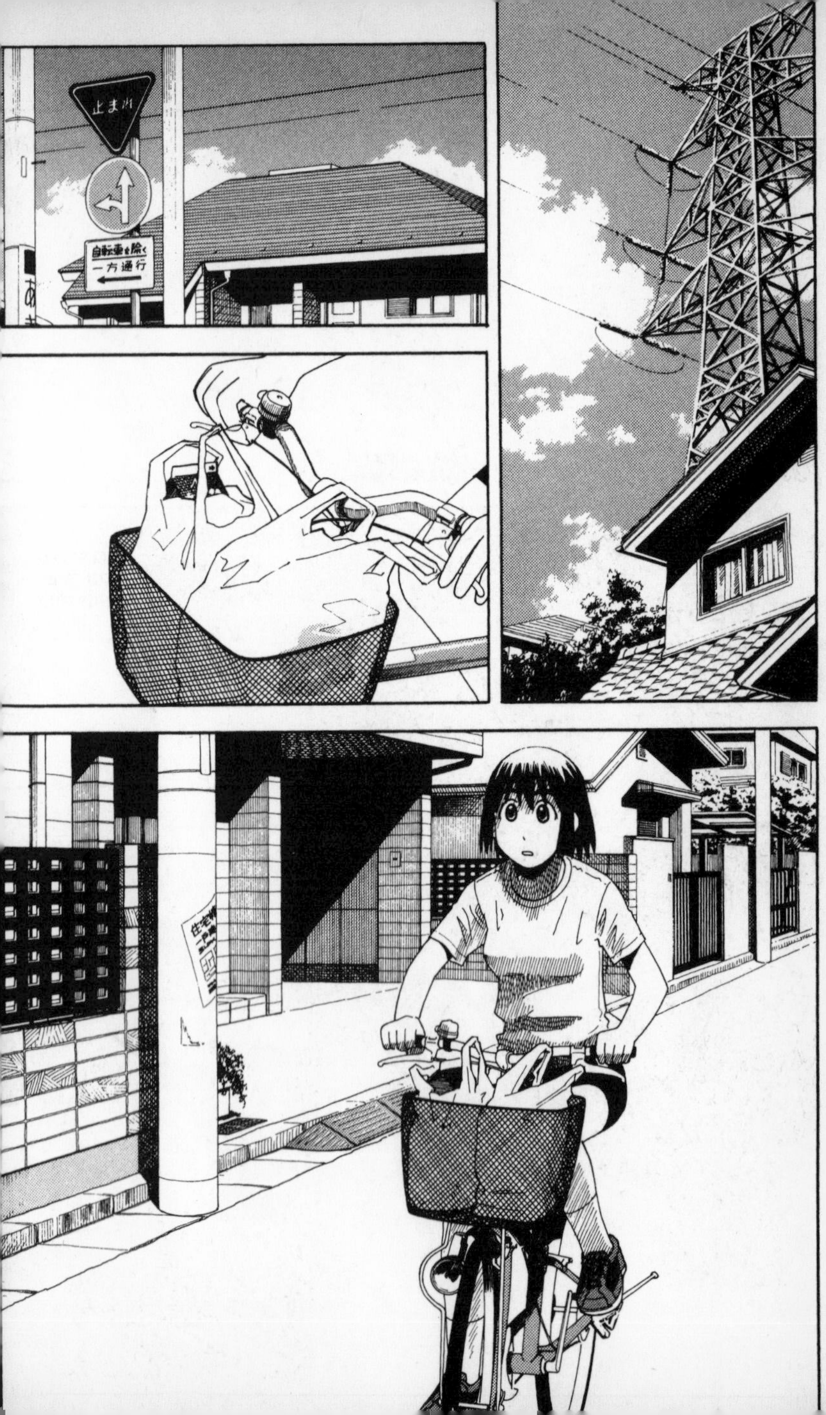
止まれ
自転車を除く
一方通行

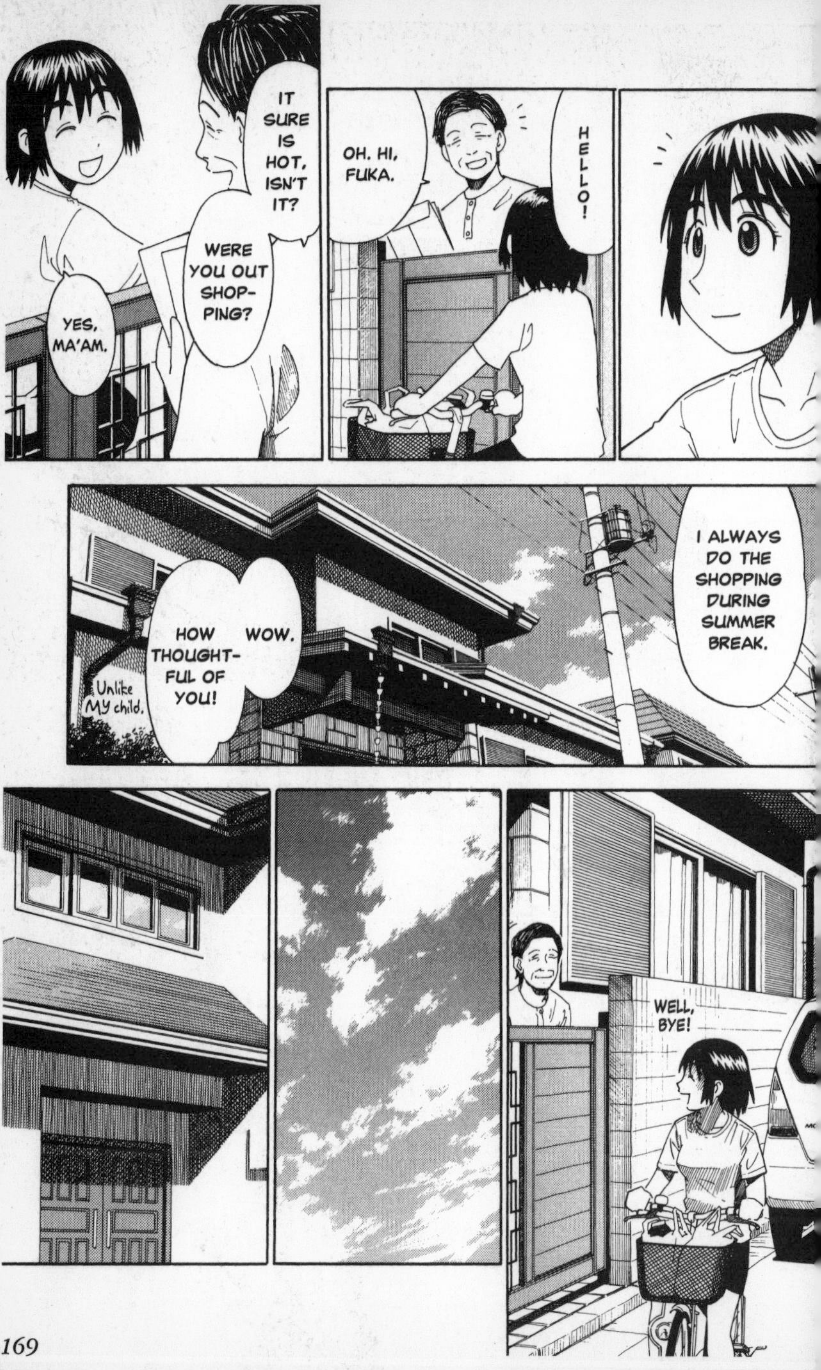
HELLO!
OH. HI, FUKA.
IT SURE IS HOT, ISN'T IT?
WERE YOU OUT SHOPPING?
YES, MA'AM.
I ALWAYS DO THE SHOPPING DURING SUMMER BREAK.
WOW.
HOW THOUGHTFUL OF YOU!
Unlike MY child.
WELL, BYE!

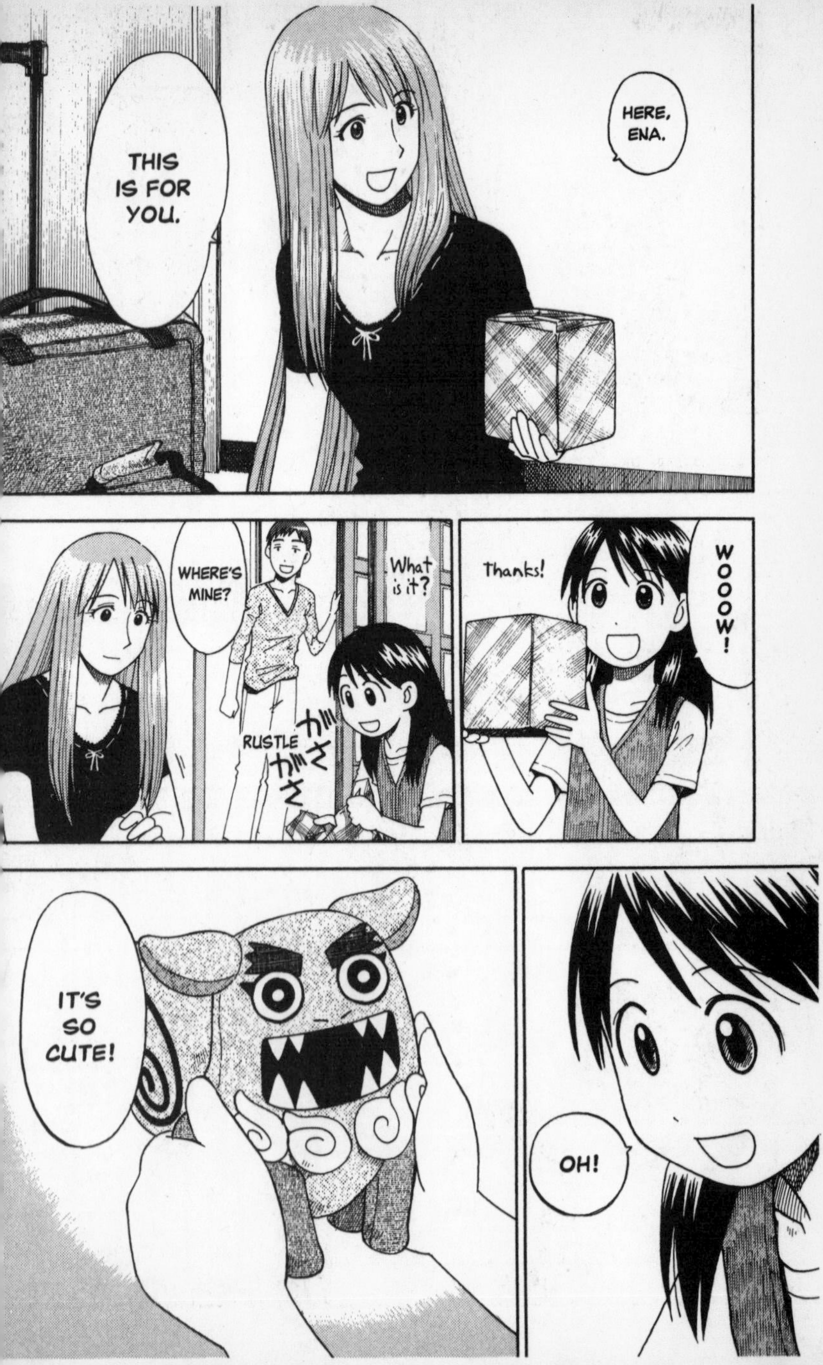
HERE, ENA.
THIS IS FOR YOU.
WOOOW!
Thanks!
What is it?
WHERE'S MINE?
RUSTLE
がさ がさ
OH!
IT'S SO CUTE!

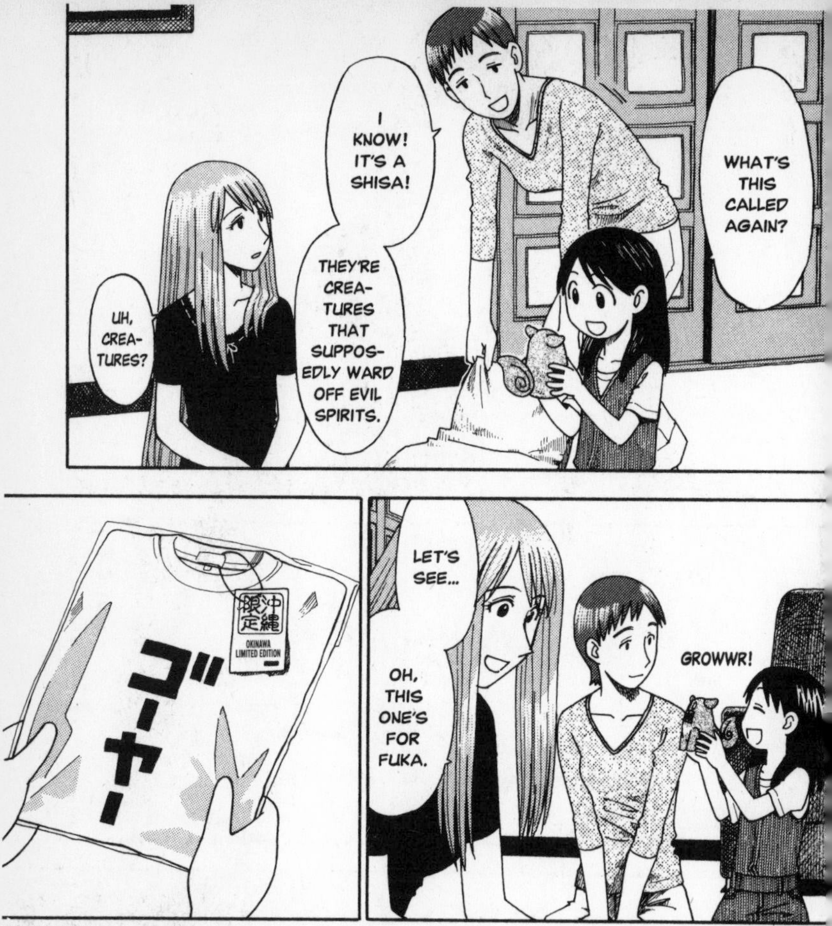
WHAT'S THIS CALLED AGAIN?
I KNOW! IT'S A SHISA!
THEY'RE CREATURES THAT SUPPOSEDLY WARD OFF EVIL SPIRITS.
UH, CREATURES?
GROWWR!
LET'S SEE...
OH, THIS ONE'S FOR FUKA.
沖縄限定
OKINAWA LIMITED EDITION
ゴーヤー

*On shirt: GOYA

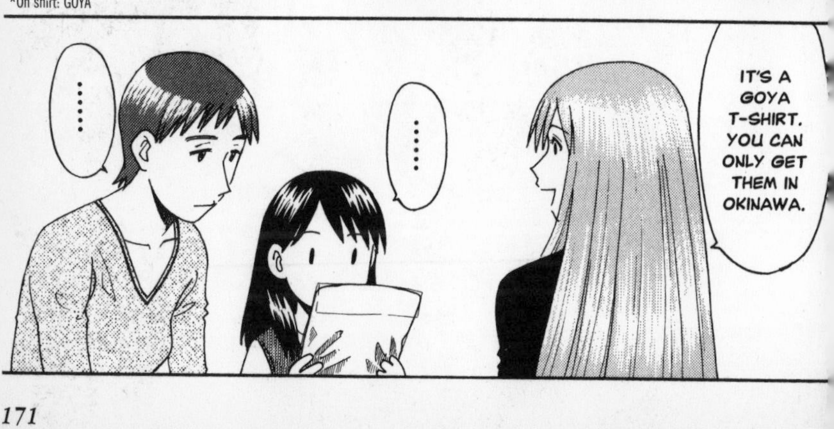
IT'S A GOYA T-SHIRT. YOU CAN ONLY GET THEM IN OKINAWA.
......
......

SHE'S BACK!

I'M HOME!

Yeah, but...

FUKA'S ALWAYS WEARING STRANGE T-SHIRTS AROUND THE HOUSE, RIGHT?

OH!

ASAGI'S BACK, AND SHE BROUGHT SOUVENIRS!

FUKA!

IT'S SO HOT!

A/C...

ICED TEA...

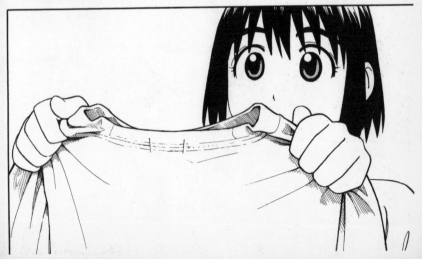

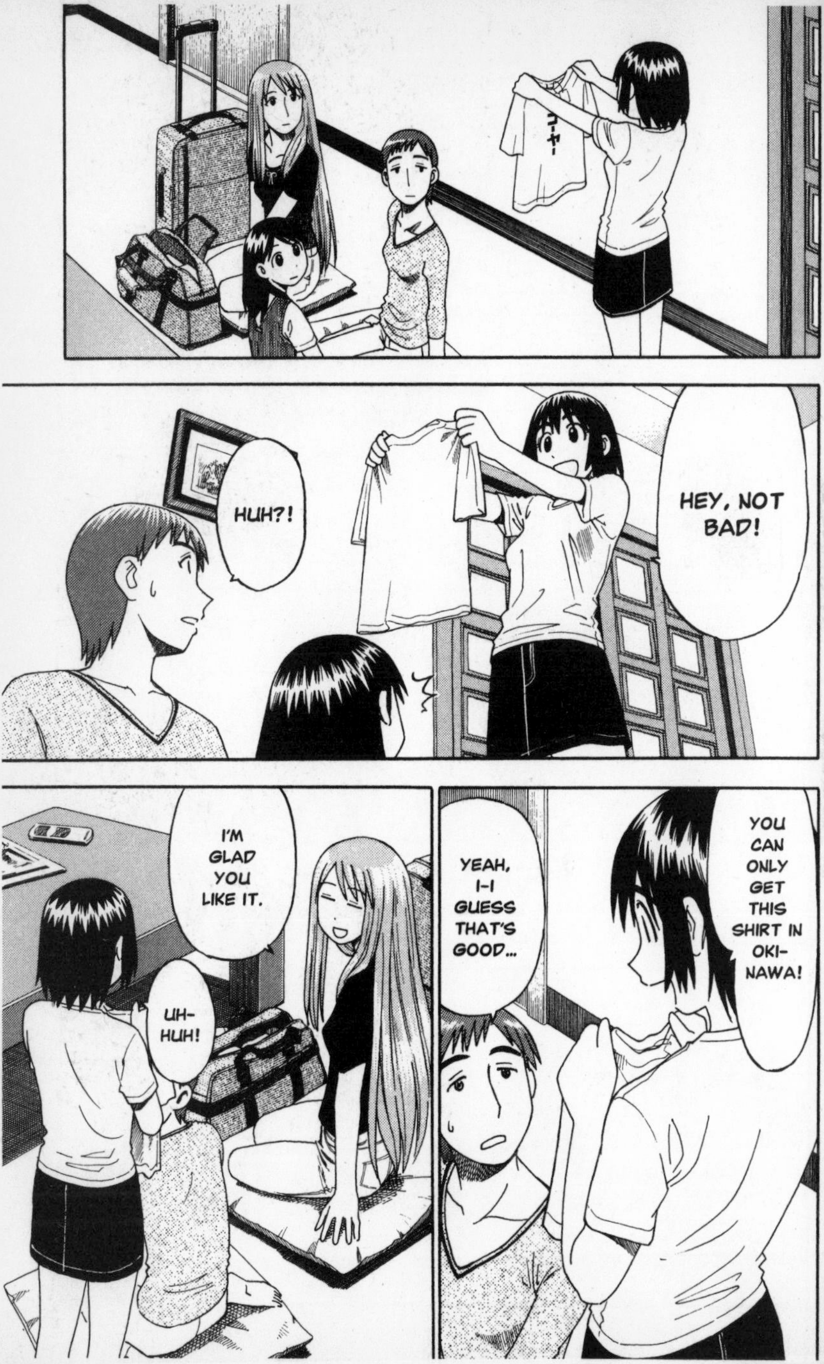

コーヤー
HEY, NOT BAD!
HUH?!
YOU CAN ONLY GET THIS SHIRT IN OKI-NAWA!
YEAH, I-I GUESS THAT'S GOOD...
I'M GLAD YOU LIKE IT.
UH-HUH!

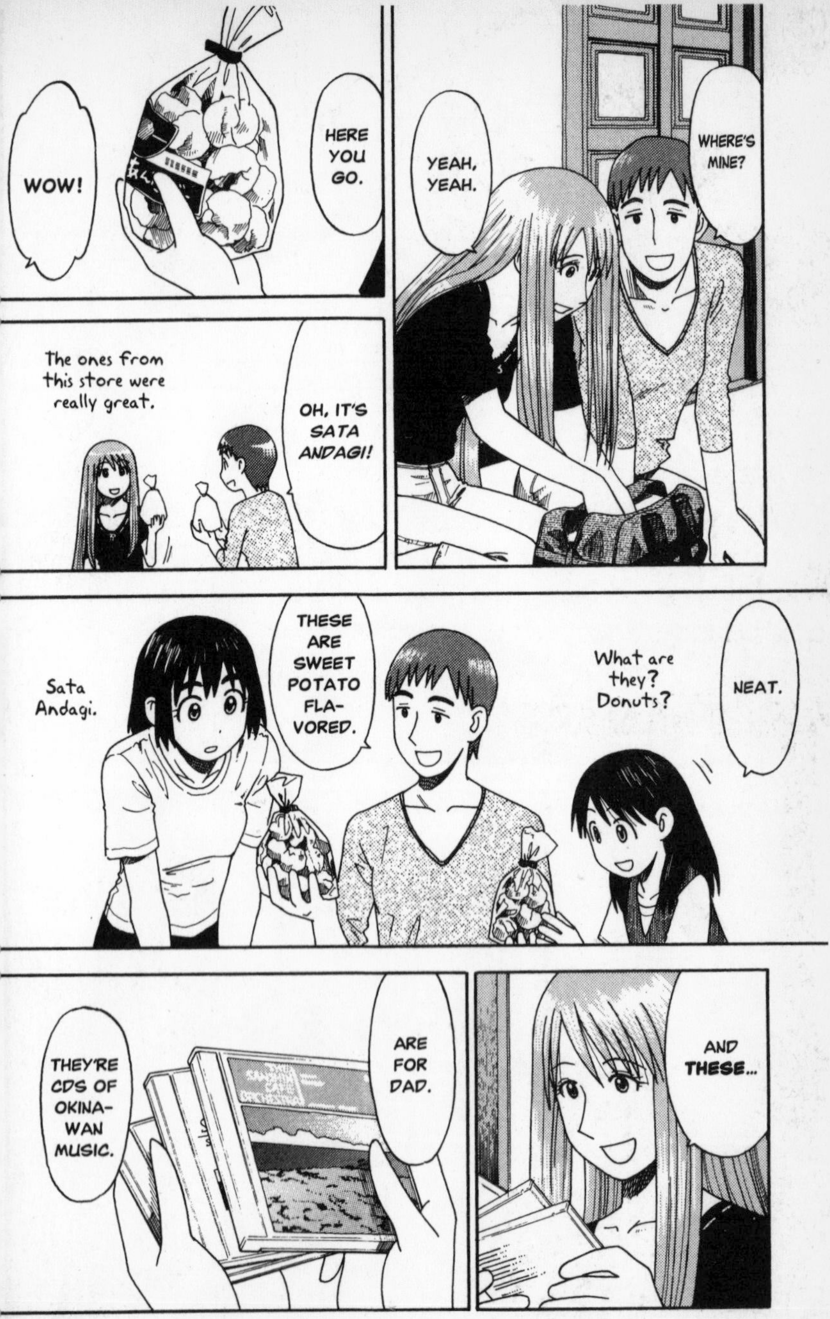
WHERE'S MINE?
YEAH, YEAH.
HERE YOU GO.
WOW!
OH, IT'S SATA ANDAGI!
The ones from this store were really great.
NEAT.
What are they? Donuts?
THESE ARE SWEET POTATO FLA-VORED.
Sata Andagi.
AND THESE...
ARE FOR DAD.
THEY'RE CDS OF OKINA-WAN MUSIC.

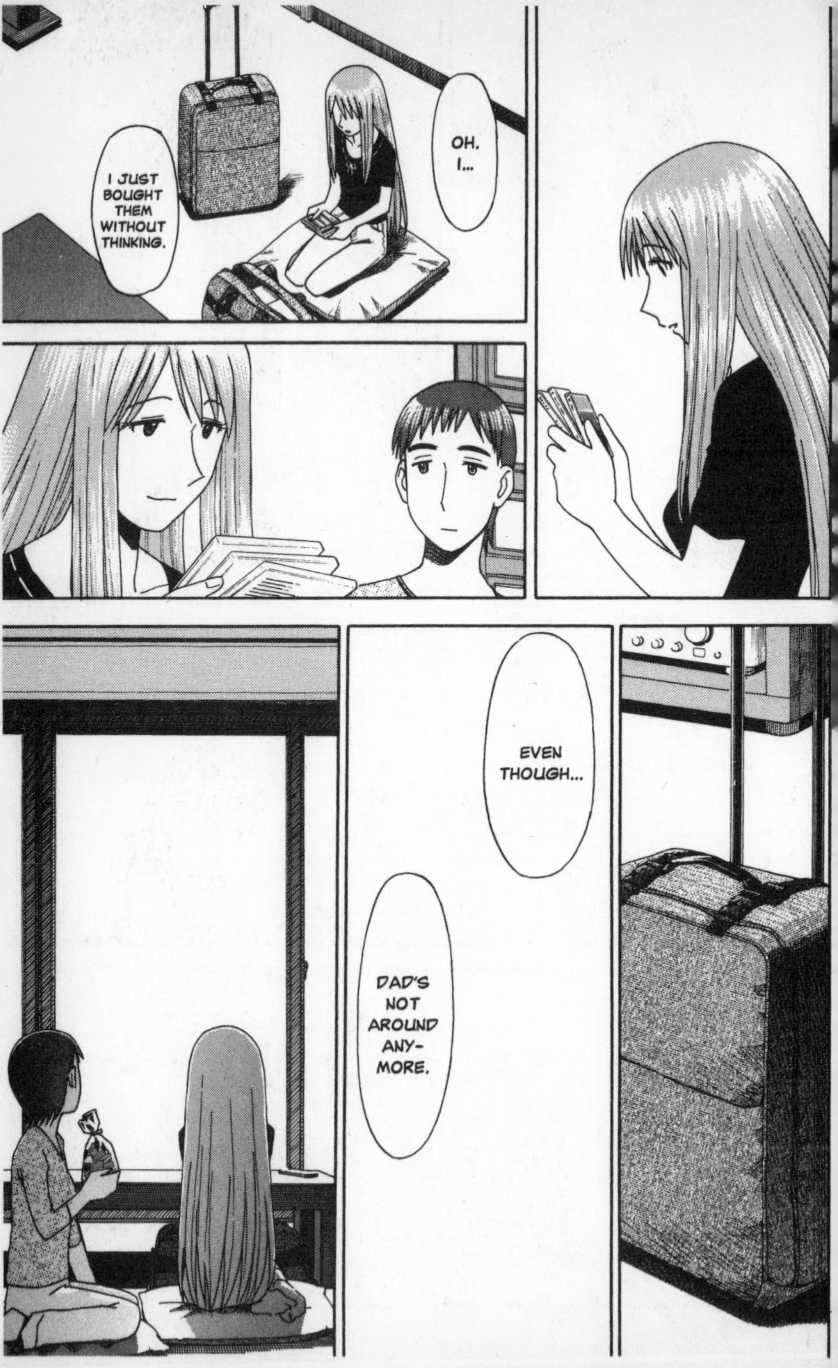
OH. I...
I JUST BOUGHT THEM WITHOUT THINKING.
EVEN THOUGH...
DAD'S NOT AROUND ANY-MORE.

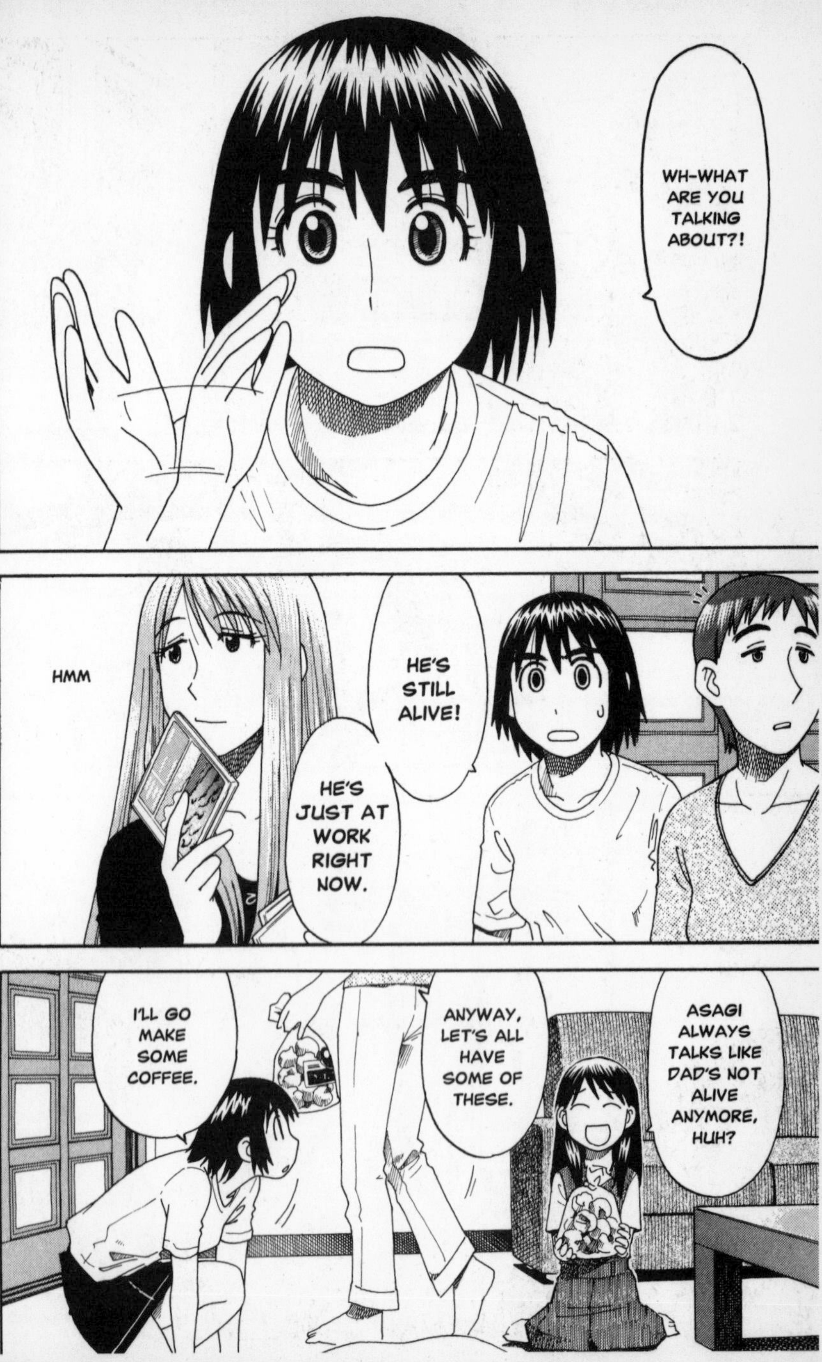
WH-WHAT ARE YOU TALKING ABOUT?!
HE'S STILL ALIVE!
HE'S JUST AT WORK RIGHT NOW.
HMM
ASAGI ALWAYS TALKS LIKE DAD'S NOT ALIVE ANYMORE, HUH?
ANYWAY, LET'S ALL HAVE SOME OF THESE.
I'LL GO MAKE SOME COFFEE.

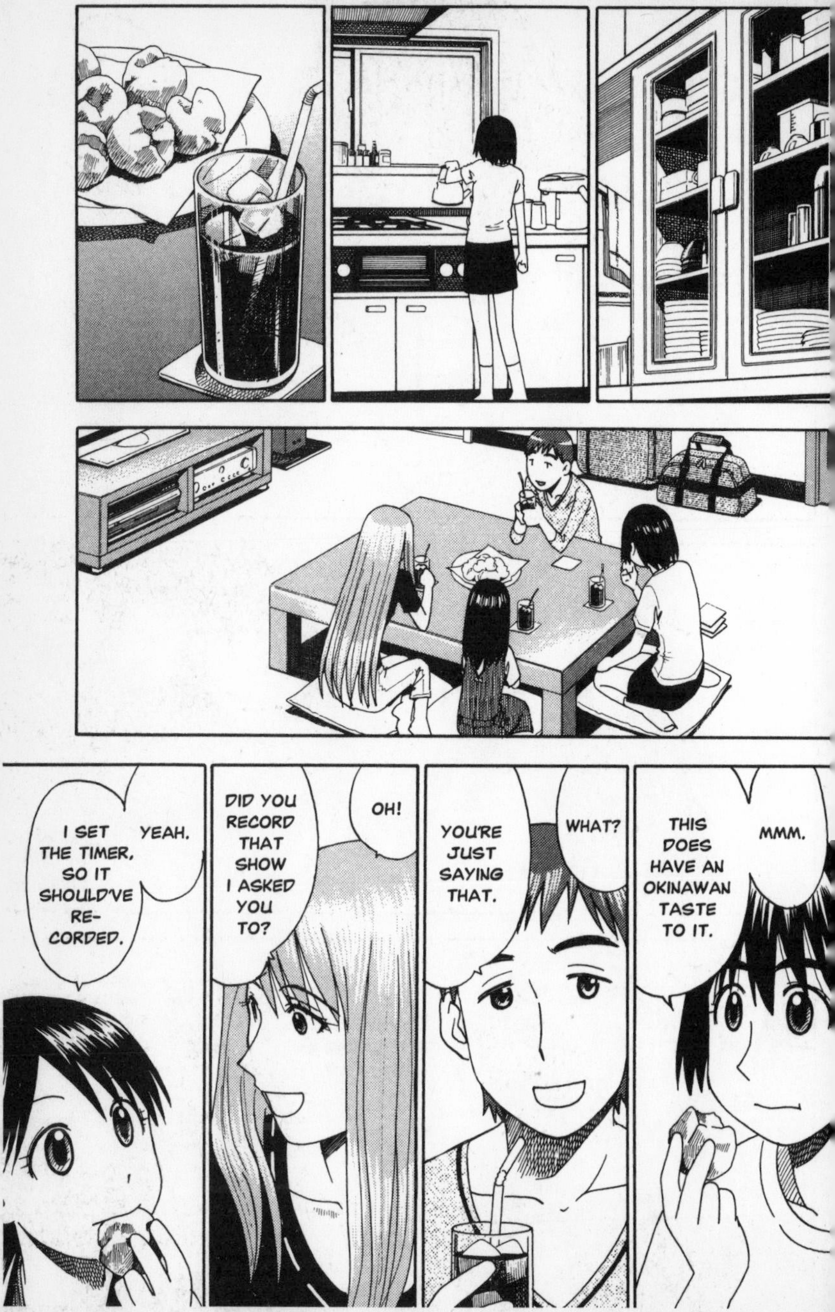
MMM.
THIS DOES HAVE AN OKINAWAN TASTE TO IT.
WHAT?
YOU'RE JUST SAYING THAT.
OH!
DID YOU RECORD THAT SHOW I ASKED YOU TO?
YEAH.
I SET THE TIMER, SO IT SHOULD'VE RE-CORDED.

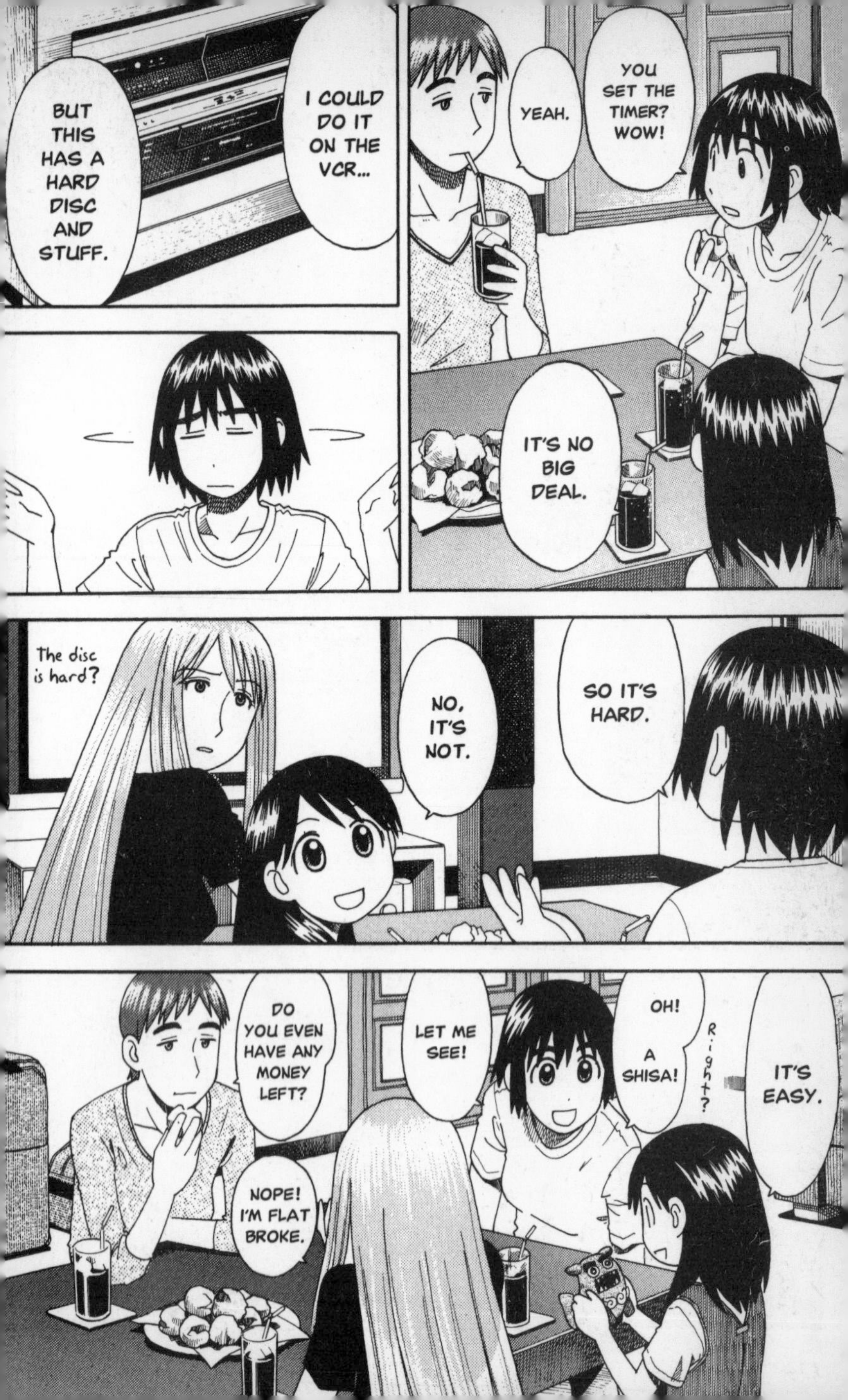
YOU SET THE TIMER? WOW!
YEAH.
I COULD DO IT ON THE VCR...
BUT THIS HAS A HARD DISC AND STUFF.
IT'S NO BIG DEAL.
SO IT'S HARD.
NO, IT'S NOT.
The disc is hard?
IT'S EASY.
Right?
OH!
A SHISA!
LET ME SEE!
DO YOU EVEN HAVE ANY MONEY LEFT?
NOPE! I'M FLAT BROKE.

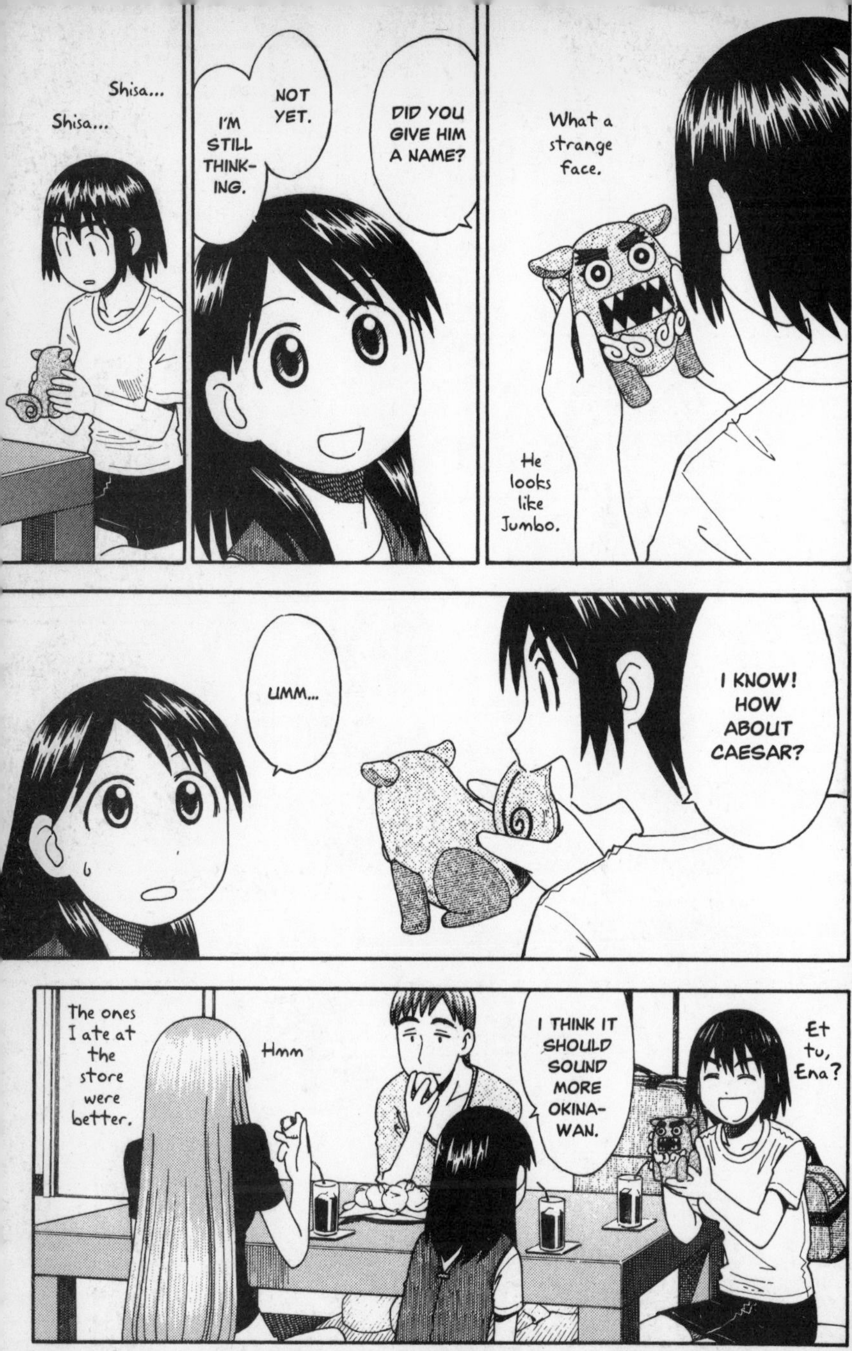
What a strange face.
He looks like Jumbo.
DID YOU GIVE HIM A NAME?
NOT YET.
I'M STILL THINKING.
Shisa...
Shisa...
I KNOW! HOW ABOUT CAESAR?
UMM...
Et tu, Ena?
I THINK IT SHOULD SOUND MORE OKINAWAN.
Hmm
The ones I ate at the store were better.

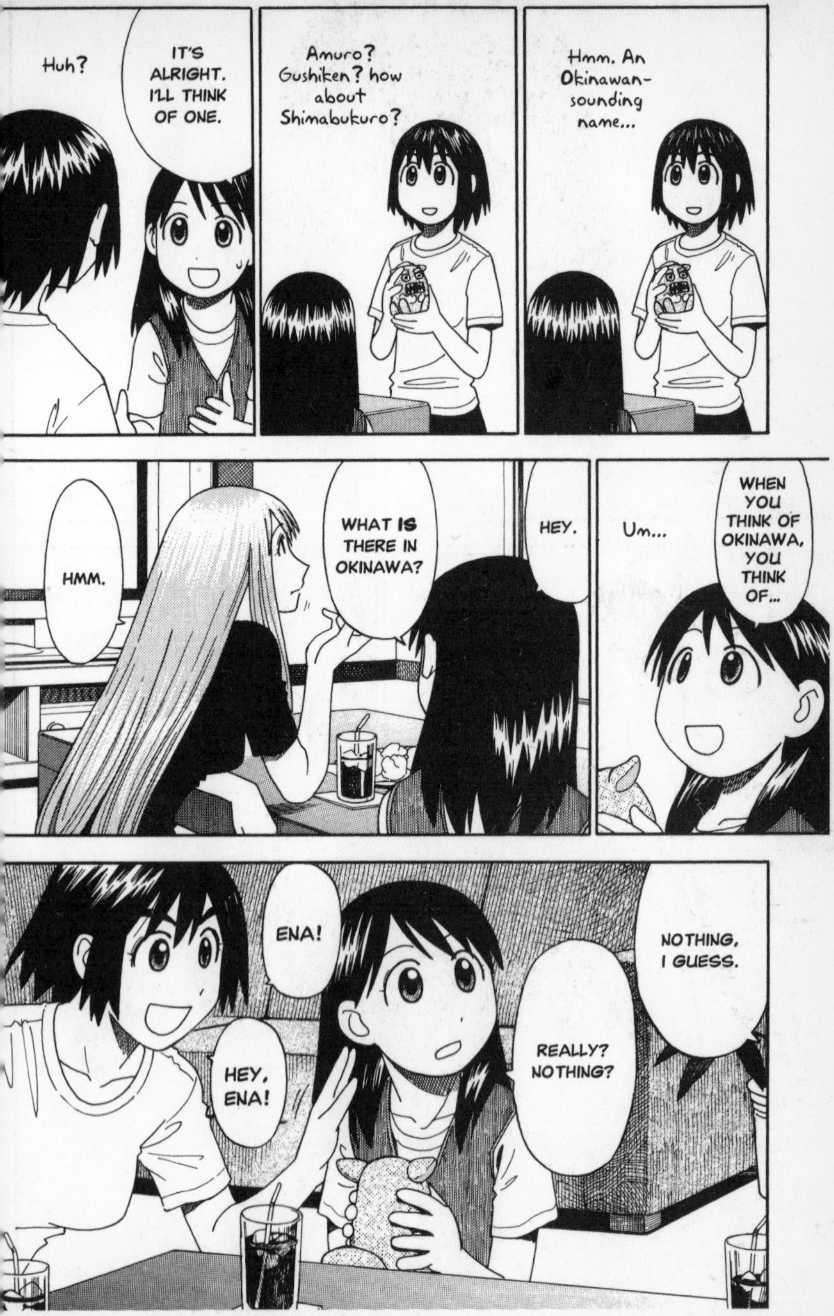
Hmm. An Okinawan-sounding name...
Amuro? Gushiken? how about Shimabukuro?
IT'S ALRIGHT. I'LL THINK OF ONE.
Huh?
WHEN YOU THINK OF OKINAWA, YOU THINK OF...
Um...
HEY.
WHAT IS THERE IN OKINAWA?
HMM.
NOTHING, I GUESS.
REALLY? NOTHING?
ENA!
HEY, ENA!

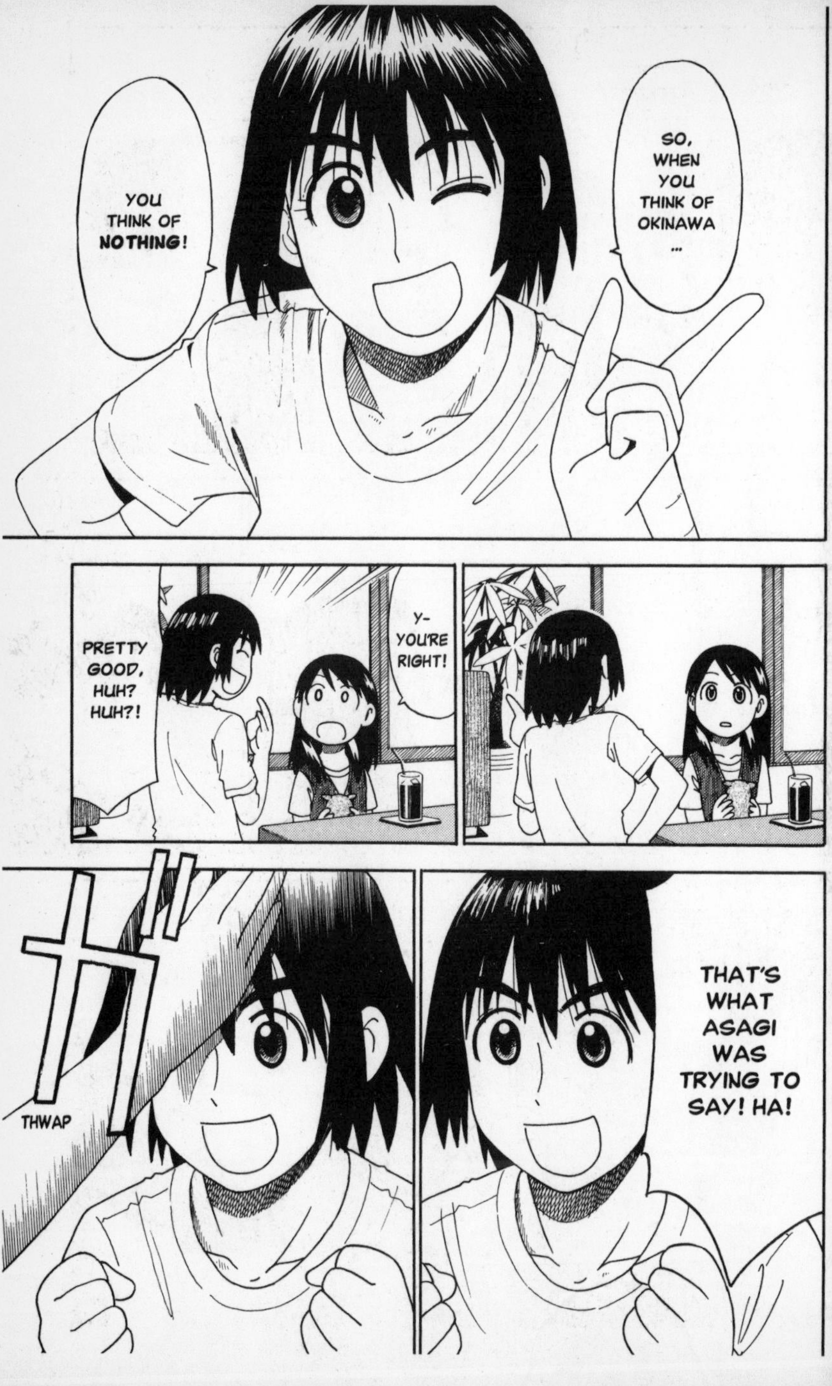
SO, WHEN YOU THINK OF OKINAWA ...
YOU THINK OF NOTHING!
Y- YOU'RE RIGHT!
PRETTY GOOD, HUH? HUH?!
THAT'S WHAT ASAGI WAS TRYING TO SAY! HA!
THWAP

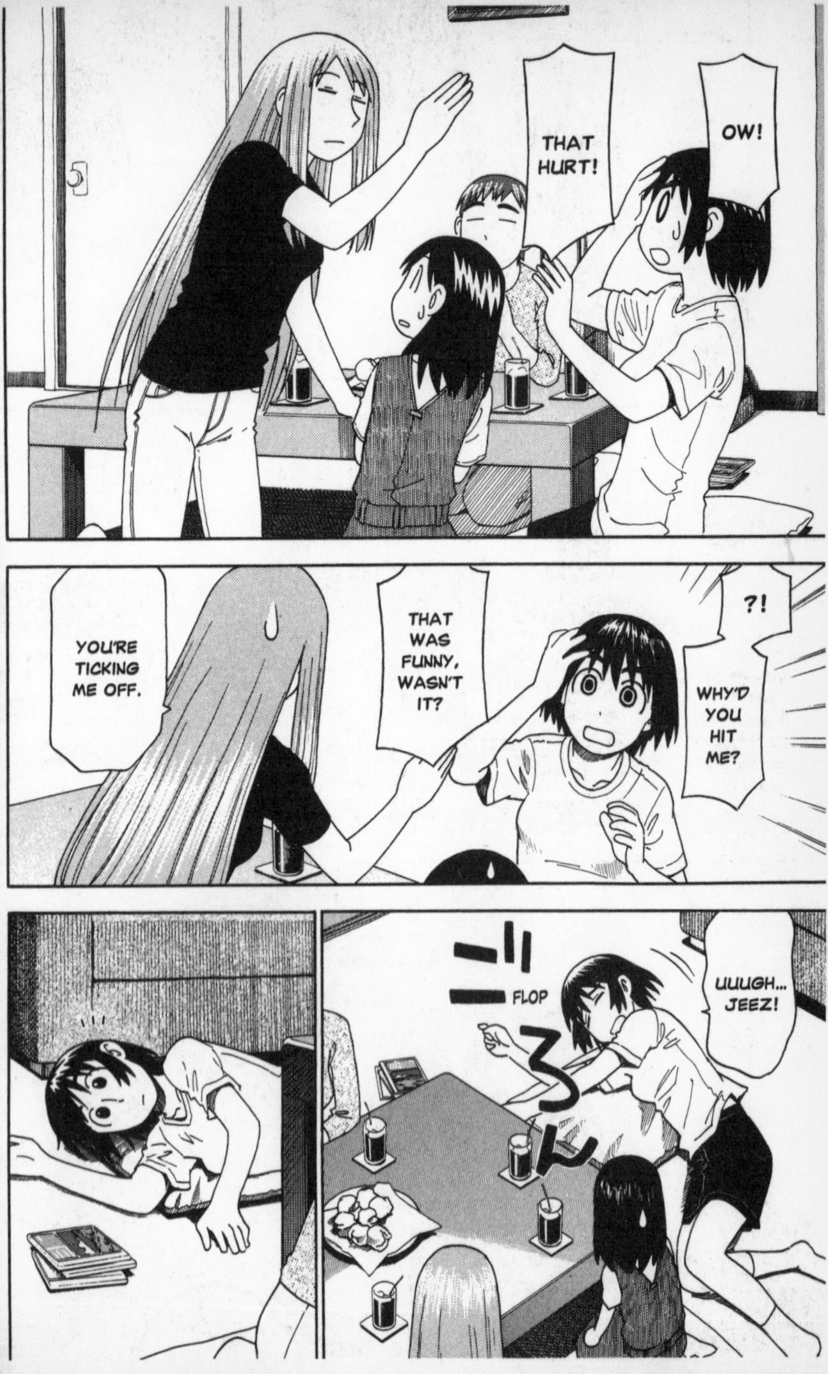
OW!
THAT HURT!
?!
WHY'D YOU HIT ME?
THAT WAS FUNNY, WASN'T IT?
YOU'RE TICKING ME OFF.
UUUGH... JEEZ!
FLOP

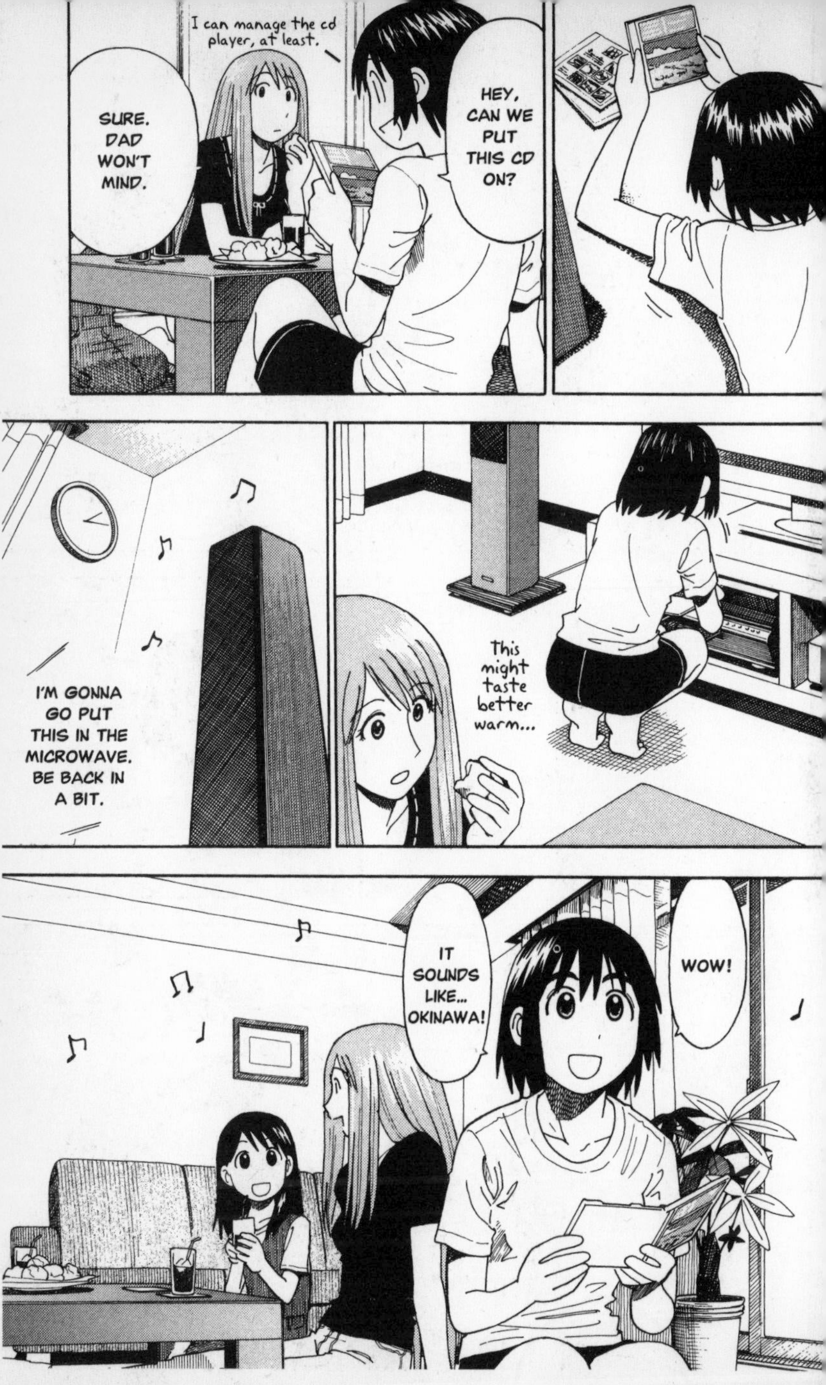
HEY, CAN WE PUT THIS CD ON?
SURE. DAD WON'T MIND.
I can manage the cd player, at least.
This might taste better warm...
I'M GONNA GO PUT THIS IN THE MICROWAVE. BE BACK IN A BIT.
WOW!
IT SOUNDS LIKE... OKINAWA!

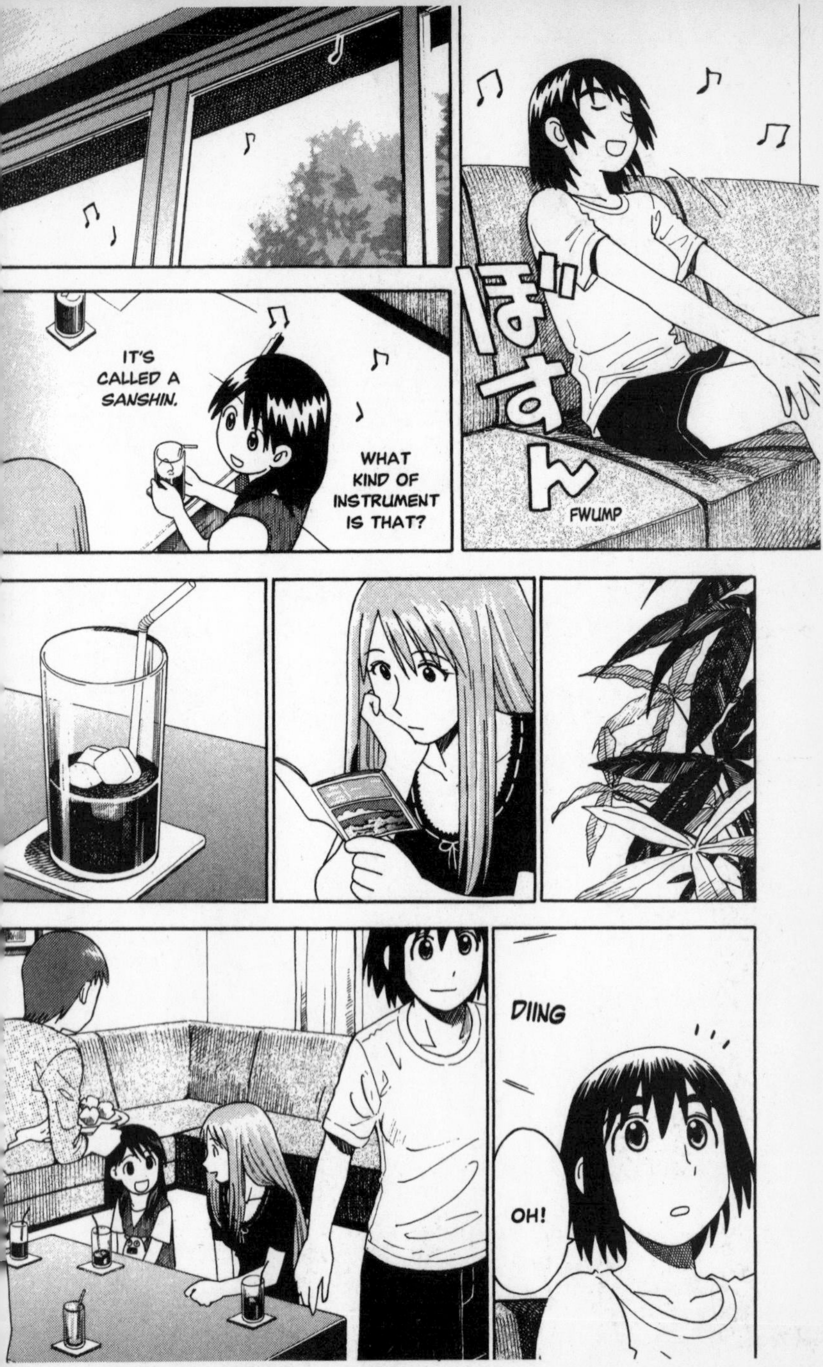
ぼすん
FWUMP
WHAT KIND OF INSTRUMENT IS THAT?
IT'S CALLED A SANSHIN.
DIING
OH!

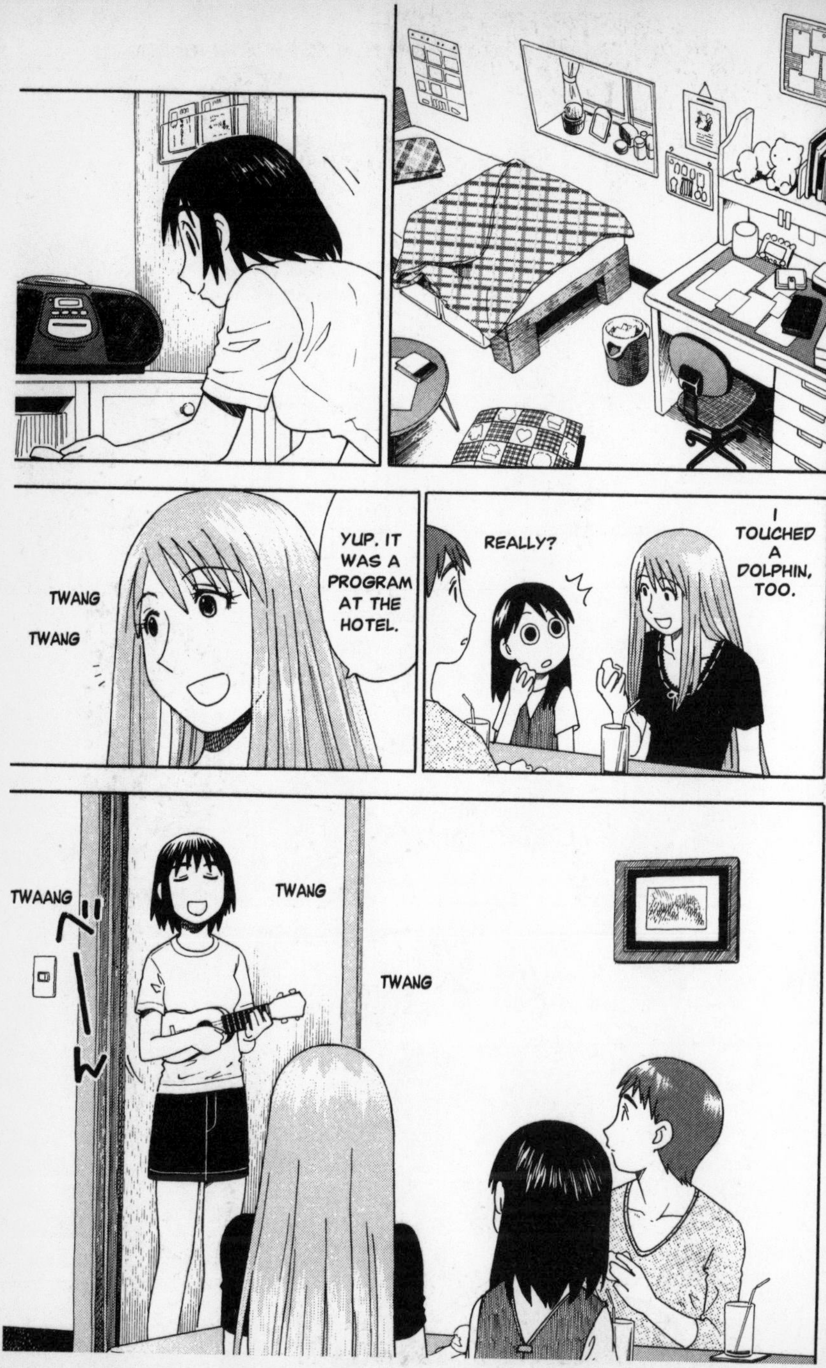
I TOUCHED A DOLPHIN, TOO.
REALLY?
YUP. IT WAS A PROGRAM AT THE HOTEL.
TWANG
TWANG
TWANG
TWANG
TWAANG

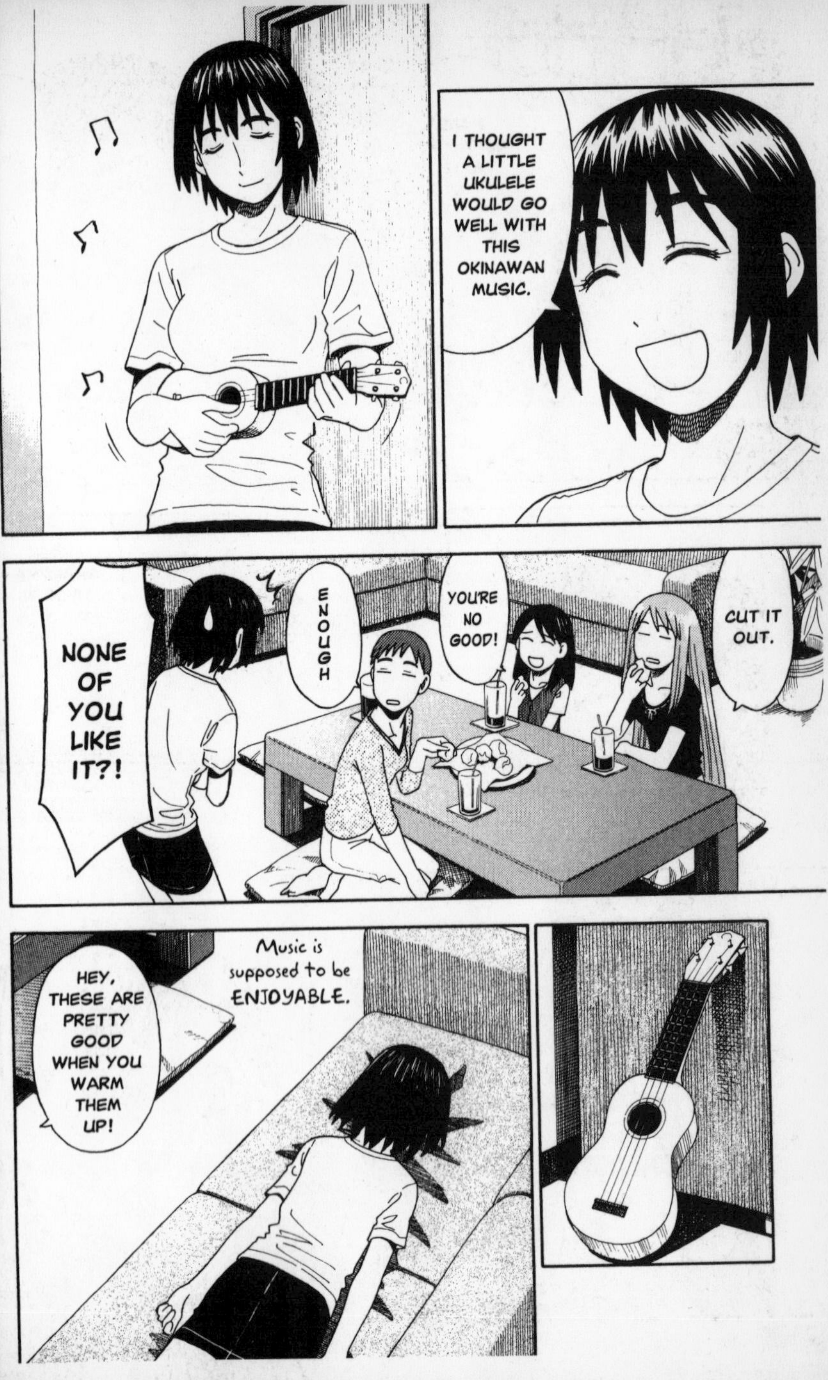
I THOUGHT A LITTLE UKULELE WOULD GO WELL WITH THIS OKINAWAN MUSIC.
CUT IT OUT.
YOU'RE NO GOOD!
ENOUGH
NONE OF YOU LIKE IT?!
Music is supposed to be ENJOYABLE.
HEY, THESE ARE PRETTY GOOD WHEN YOU WARM THEM UP!

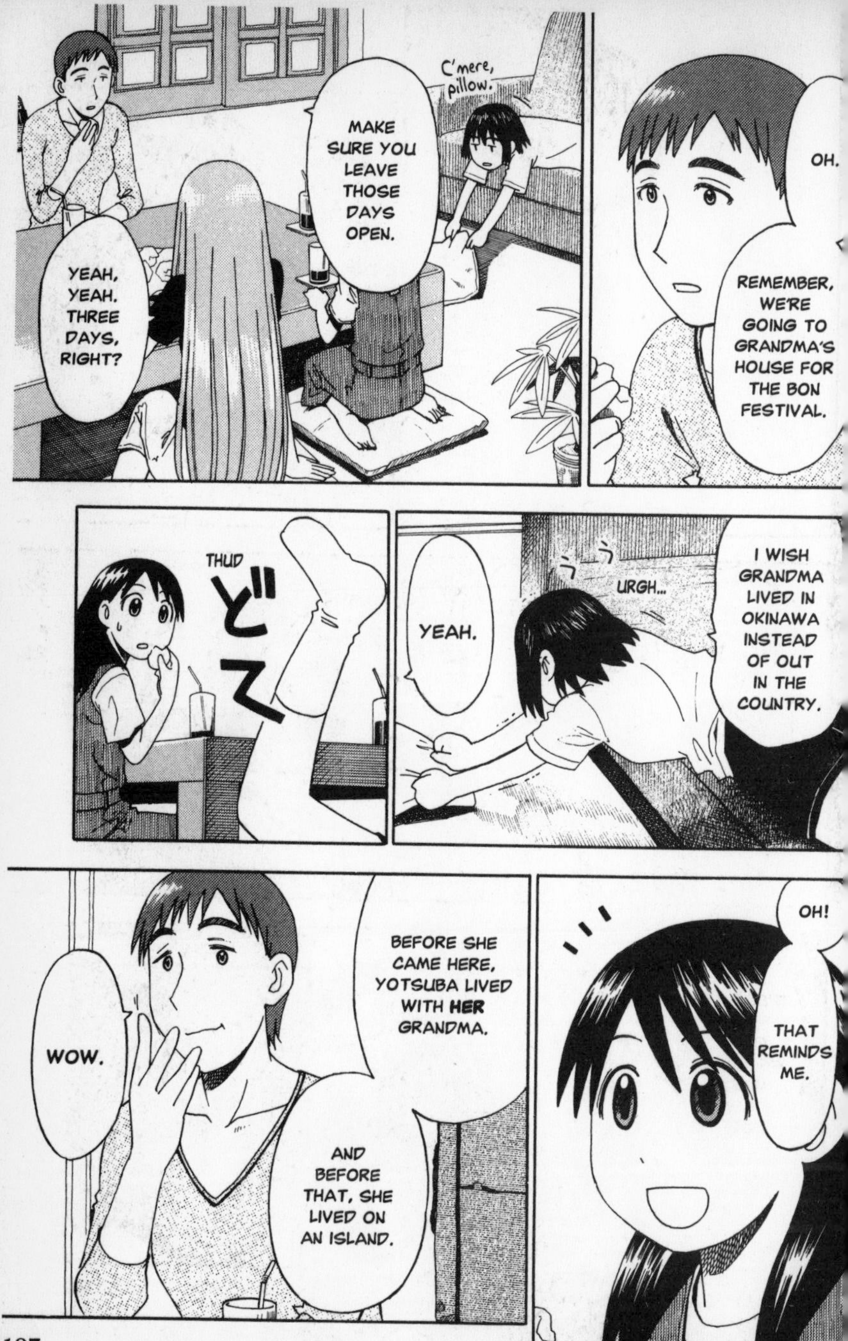
OH.
REMEMBER, WE'RE GOING TO GRANDMA'S HOUSE FOR THE BON FESTIVAL.
MAKE SURE YOU LEAVE THOSE DAYS OPEN.
C'mere, pillow.
YEAH, YEAH. THREE DAYS, RIGHT?
I WISH GRANDMA LIVED IN OKINAWA INSTEAD OF OUT IN THE COUNTRY.
うう
URGH...
YEAH.
THUD
どて
OH!
THAT REMINDS ME.
BEFORE SHE CAME HERE, YOTSUBA LIVED WITH **HER** GRANDMA.
AND BEFORE THAT, SHE LIVED ON AN ISLAND.
WOW.

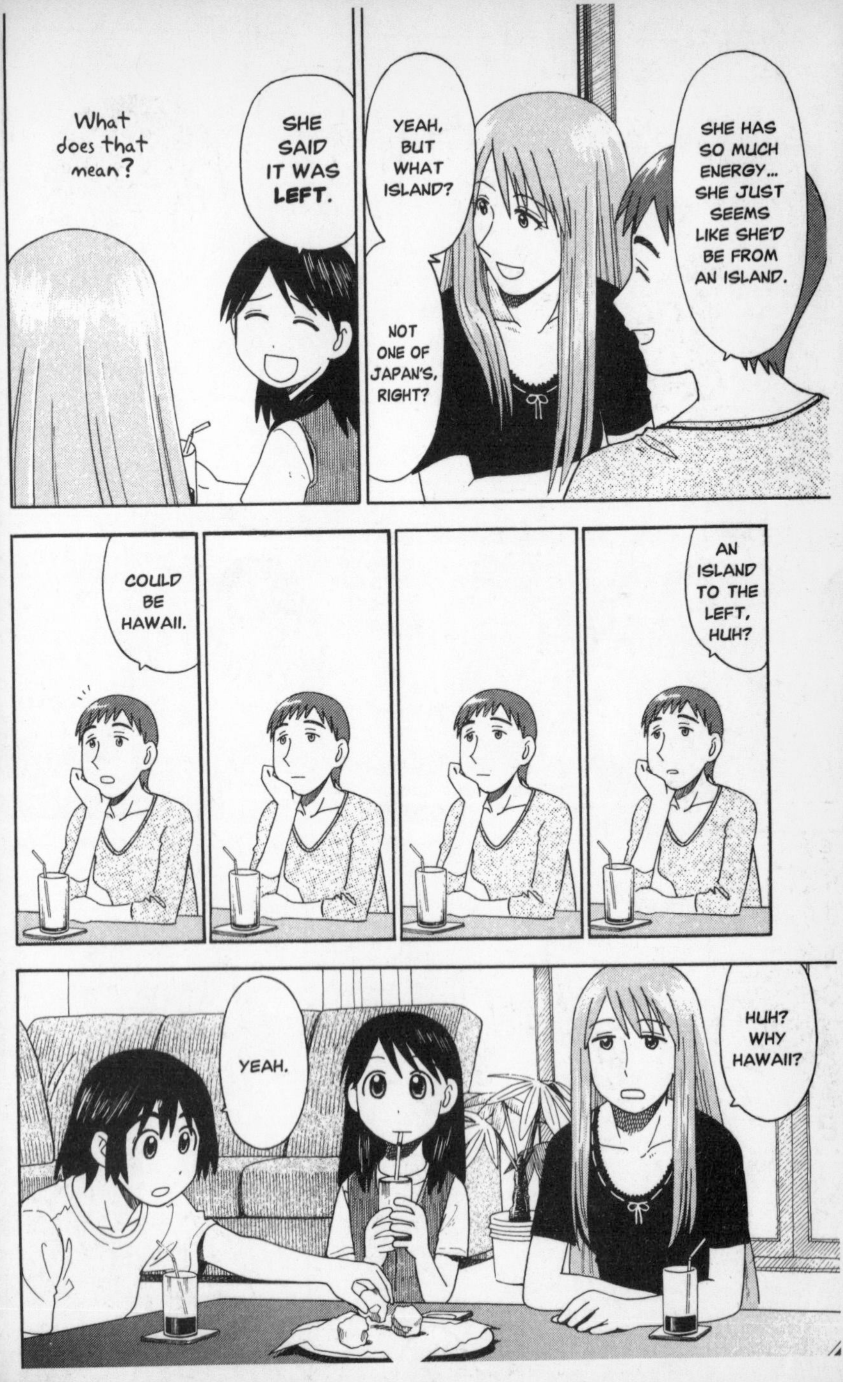
What does that mean?
SHE SAID IT WAS LEFT.
YEAH, BUT WHAT ISLAND?
NOT ONE OF JAPAN'S, RIGHT?
SHE HAS SO MUCH ENERGY... SHE JUST SEEMS LIKE SHE'D BE FROM AN ISLAND.
COULD BE HAWAII.
AN ISLAND TO THE LEFT, HUH?
YEAH.
HUH? WHY HAWAII?

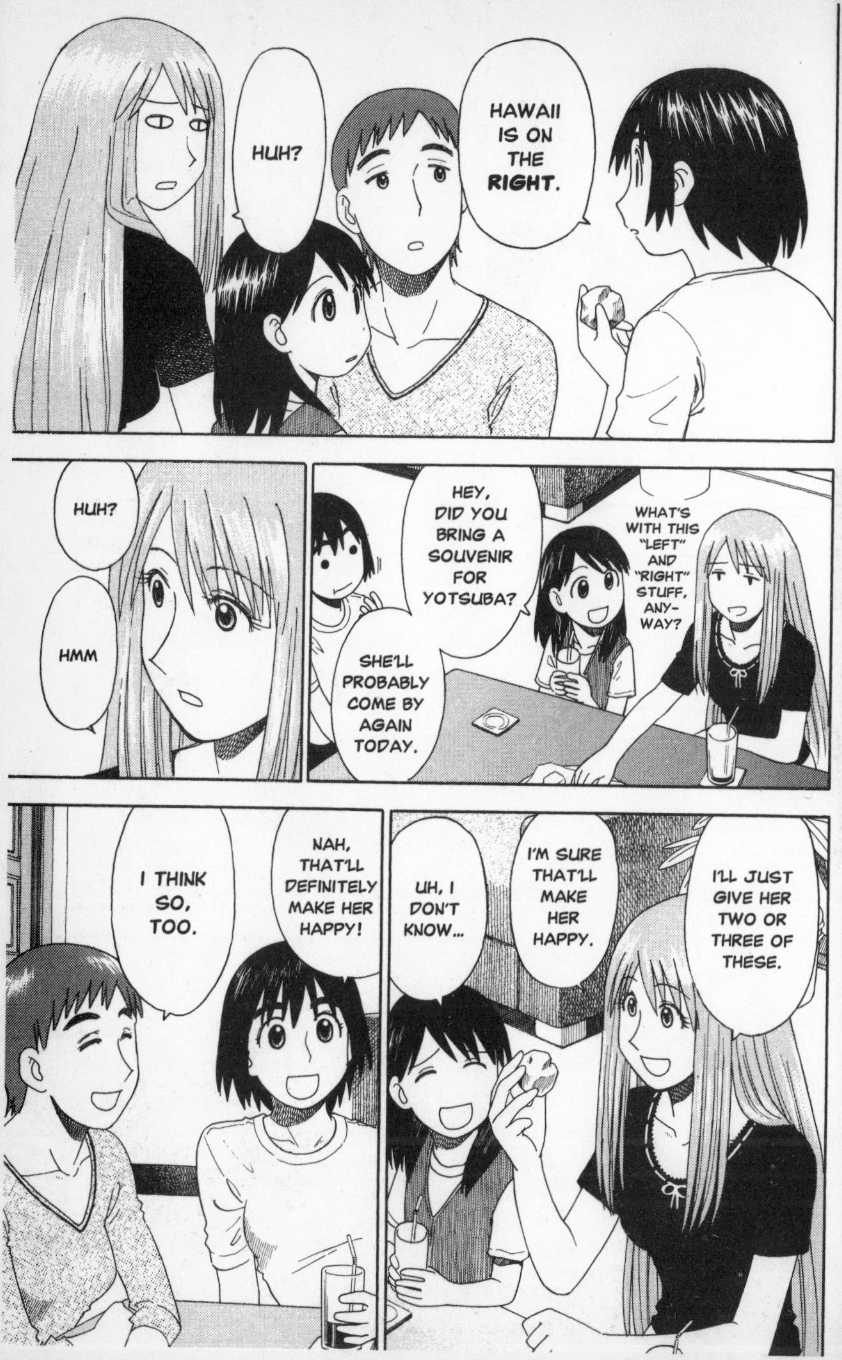
HAWAII IS ON THE RIGHT.
HUH?
WHAT'S WITH THIS "LEFT" AND "RIGHT" STUFF, ANYWAY?
HEY, DID YOU BRING A SOUVENIR FOR YOTSUBA?
SHE'LL PROBABLY COME BY AGAIN TODAY.
HUH?
HMM
I'LL JUST GIVE HER TWO OR THREE OF THESE.
I'M SURE THAT'LL MAKE HER HAPPY.
UH, I DON'T KNOW...
NAH, THAT'LL DEFINITELY MAKE HER HAPPY!
I THINK SO, TOO.

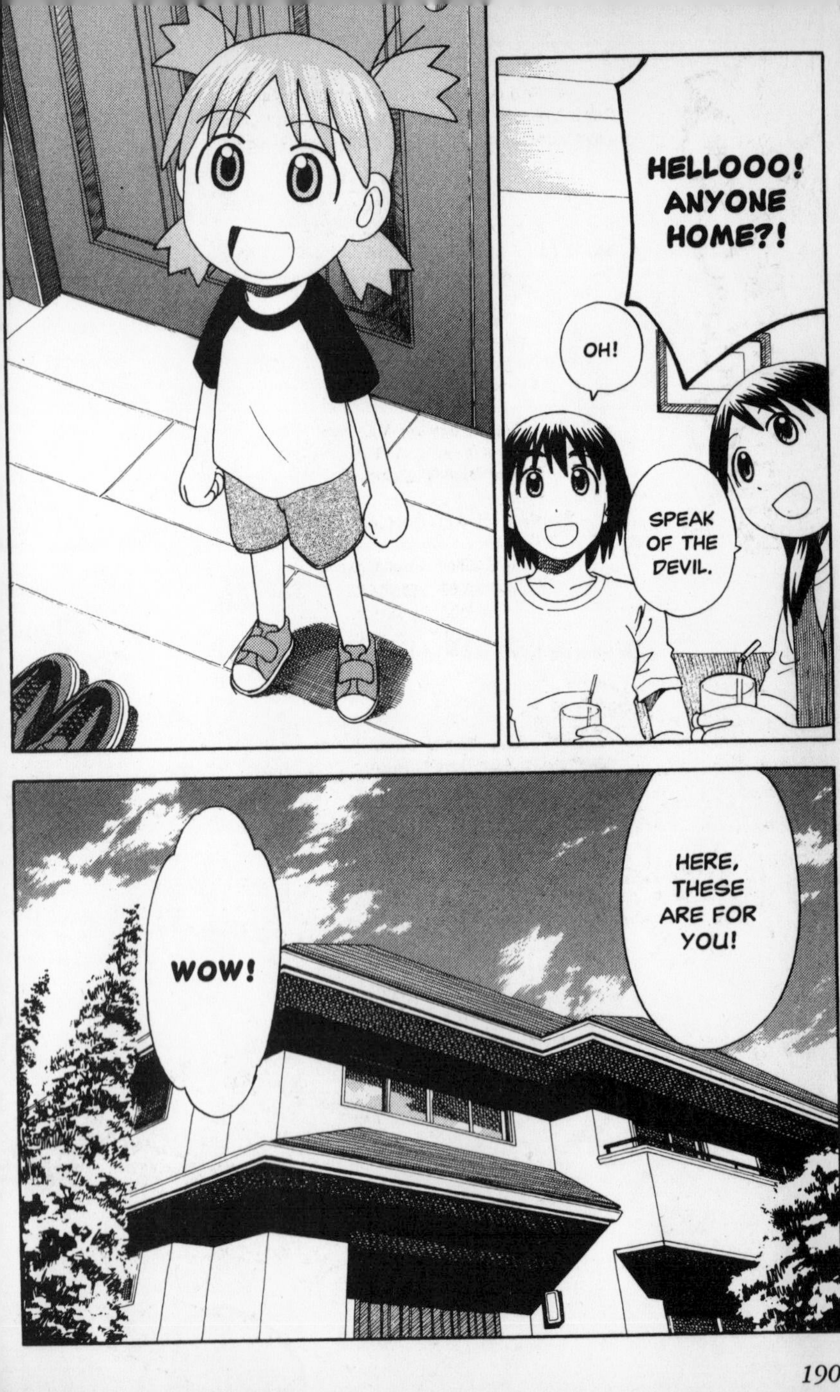
HELLOOO! ANYONE HOME?!
OH!
SPEAK OF THE DEVIL.
HERE, THESE ARE FOR YOU!
WOW!

© KIYOHIKO AZUMA/YOTUBA SUTAZIO 2004
First published in 2004 by Media Works Inc., Tokyo, Japan.
English translation rights arranged with Media Works Inc.

Editor **JAVIER LOPEZ**
Translator **AMY FORSYTH**
Assistant Editor **SHERIDAN JACOBS**
Graphic Artists **HEATHER GARY AND NATALIA REYNOLDS**
Graphic Intern **MARK MEZA**

Editorial Director **GARY STEINMAN**
Creative Director **JASON BABLER**
Print Production Manager **BRIDGETT JANOTA**
Sales and Marketing **CHRIS OARR**

Production Coordinator **MARISA KREITZ**
International Coordinators **TORU IWAKAMI,
KYOKO DRUMHELLER AND AI TAKAI**

President, CEO & Publisher **JOHN LEDFORD**

Email: editor@adv-manga.com
www.adv-manga.com
www.advfilms.com

For sales and distribution inquiries please call 1.800.282.7202

ADV MANGA™ is a division of A.D. Vision, Inc.
5750 Bintliff Drive, Suite 210, Houston, Texas 77036

English text © 2005 published by A.D. Vision, Inc. under exclusive license.
ADV MANGA is a trademark of A.D. Vision, Inc.

ISBN: 1-4139-0318-5
First printing, August 2005
10 9 8 7 6 5 4 3 2 1
Printed in Canada

ENJOY EVERYTHING

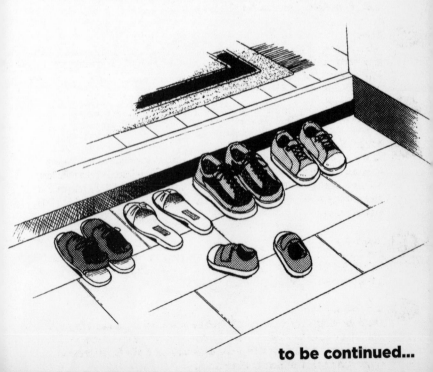

to be continued...

Yotsuba&! Vol. 02

PG. 8 Fuka's shirt
Fans of author Kiyohiko Azuma's work will no doubt recognize the strange-looking creature on Fuka's shirt as Chiyo-chan's dad from *Azumanga Daioh*.

PG. 68 *Taiyaki*
Taiyaki is a kind of thick pancake shaped like a fish and stuffed with sweet red bean paste, custard, or even chocolate creme. The same thing made into a smallish oval shape is called *obanyaki*.

PG. 75 Mont Blanc
A Mont Blanc is a type of Italian pastry consisting of meringue, whipped cream and sweet chestnut cream. Traditionally, the cream is piled high in the shape of a mountain, which is why Yotsuba remarks that it looks like mud.

PG. 171 Shisa
Shisa are the traditional "lion-dogs" of Okinawa. Originally imported from China, Shisa tend to come in pairs—one with its mouth open to let out the evil spirits, and the other with its mouth closed to keep in the good spirits.

PG. 174 *Sata Andagi*
A type of Okinawan fried donut hole.

PG. 180 Amuro, Gushiken and Shimabukuro
Amuro is a reference to Namie Amuro, a famous Japanese pop singer from Okinawa. Gushiken is a distinctively Okinawan surname (possibly a reference to Yoko Gushiken, a boxer known as the "Okinawan Eagle"), while Shimabukuro could be a reference to Masao Shimabukuro, a master of classical Okinawan music who was designated a living national treasure.

PG. 184 *Sanshin*
The *sanshin* is a traditional Okinawan instrument. It's somewhat similar to a guitar, but has only three strings, which were originally made of silk. Traditionally, the base of the instrument was covered with snake skin.

PG. 187 Bon festival
This is the festival of the dead, which is celebrated every summer (some areas celebrate it on July 15, others on August 15). It's said that this is the one time of year when the dead can return to the world of the living. It is a tradition to offer food to the dead, and to light lanterns to guide them on their journey.

EDITOR'S PICKS

IF YOU LIKE *YOTSUBA&!* THEN YOU'LL LOVE THESE!

PICK 1

AZUMANGA DAIOH

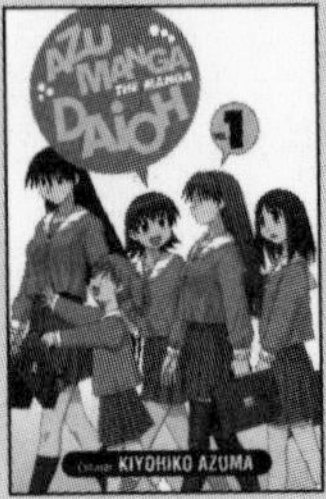
AZU MANGA DAIOH
1
KIYOHIKO AZUMA

It's not manga, it's Azumanga! Created by Kiyohiko Azuma, the madcap genius behind *Yotsuba&!*, Azumanga Daioh is smart, funny and totally out of control! Featuring kooky characters who meander through their everyday lives, *Azumanga Daioh* takes the reader through the daily tribulations of Miss Kurosawa, Miss Yukari, the wild Tomo, hair-triggered Yomi, ditzy Osaka, brash Kagura, cute Chiyo-chan and sporty Sakaki. It's seriously silly, and completely addictive!

PICK 2

BY THE SWORD

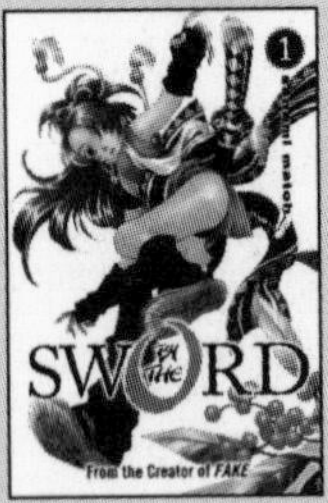
1
SWORD
From the Creator of FAKE

The Demon Hunter Asagi was born with a mysterious inner force, but his only means of releasing it has shattered the steel of countless swords. His search for the ultimate weapon leads him to the Moegi, a blade forged with the power of a hundred and one Demon Orbs. There's only one problem—the spirit of one girl's father is trapped within it. Asagi will have to lead this dysfunctional family on a journey to release his spirit and secure the sword—but he better beware: If Asagi isn't careful, his new young charge and her extremely hearty appetite might land him in the poorhouse!

PICK 3

PRINCESS TUTU

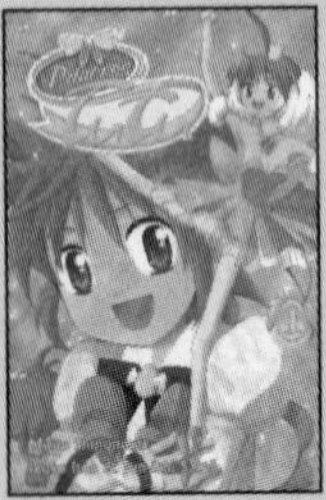

Ahiru wants to be a ballerina, but her two left feet always get in the way of her dreams. All of that changes when she's given a magical pendant and is suddenly transformed into the graceful Princess Tutu. But not all is well for the princess of pirouettes. The boy of her dreams has a broken heart, and she'll have to do more than dance to repair his shattered spirit!

CHECK'EM OUT TODAY!

ADV Manga™

www.adv-manga.com

IN PURSUIT OF A PRESENT!

SINCE ASAGI
SURPRISED HER WITH
A SOUVENIR FROM OKINAWA,
YOTSUBA IS DETERMINED
TO RETURN THE FAVOR,
AND SHE'LL LEAVE NO
STONE-OR TIRE-UNTURNED
IN HER FRANTIC SEARCH!
AND WITH FIREWORKS SEASON
HOT ON THEIR TAILS, SPARKS
WILL FLY (AND SO WILL JUMBO)
IN THE NIGHTTIME SKIES OF
YOTSUBA&! Volume 3!

© KIYOHIKO AZUMA/YOTUBA SUTAZIO 2004

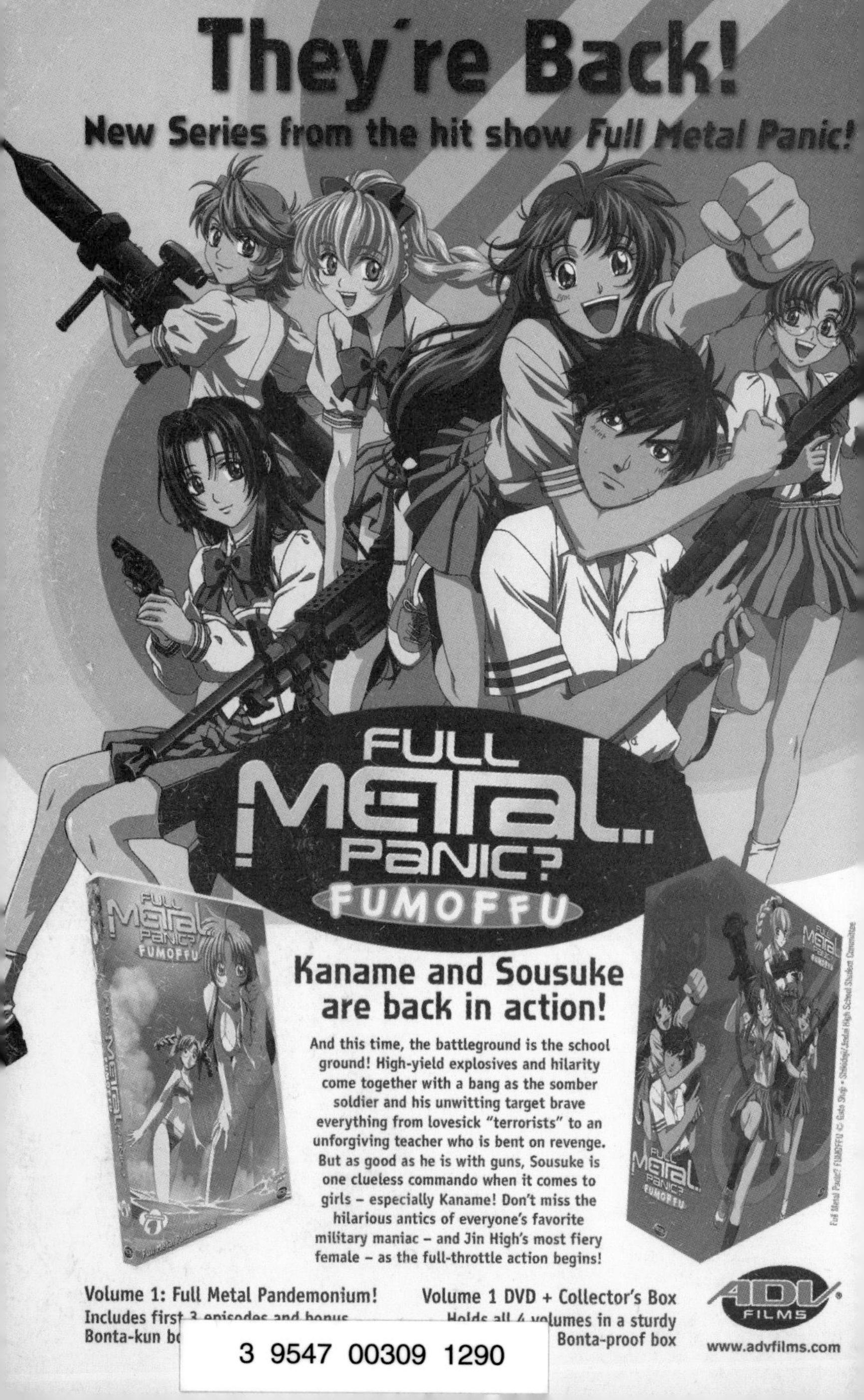

They're Back!
New Series from the hit show Full Metal Panic!
FULL METAL PANIC?
FUMOFFU
Kaname and Sousuke are back in action!
And this time, the battleground is the school ground! High-yield explosives and hilarity come together with a bang as the somber soldier and his unwitting target brave everything from lovesick "terrorists" to an unforgiving teacher who is bent on revenge. But as good as he is with guns, Sousuke is one clueless commando when it comes to girls – especially Kaname! Don't miss the hilarious antics of everyone's favorite military maniac – and Jin High's most fiery female – as the full-throttle action begins!
Volume 1: Full Metal Pandemonium!
Includes first 3 episodes and bonus
Bonta-kun bo
Volume 1 DVD + Collector's Box
Holds all 4 volumes in a sturdy
Bonta-proof box
ADV FILMS
www.advfilms.com
Full Metal Panic? FUMOFFU © Gato Shoji • Shikidouji/Jindai High School Student Committee

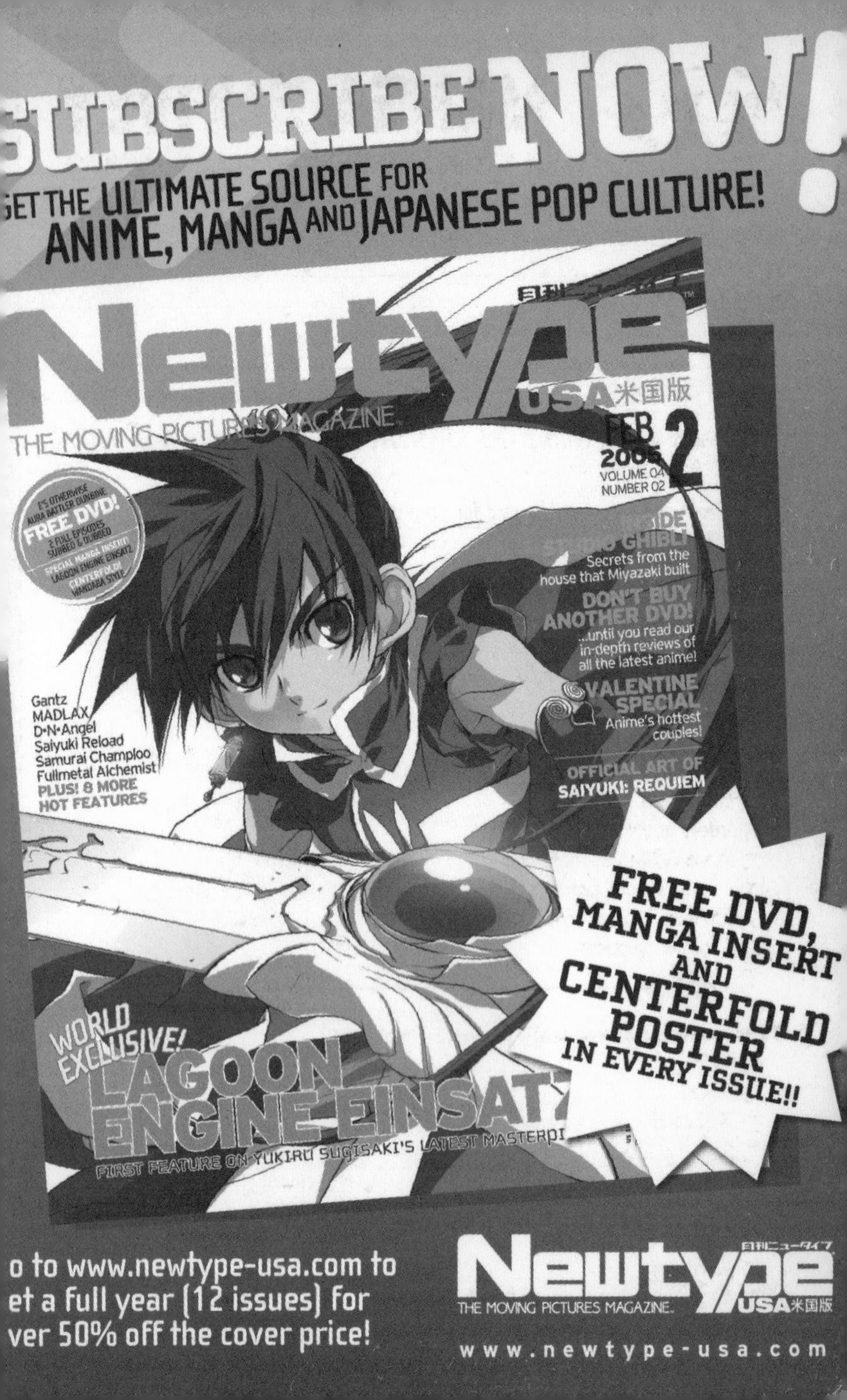

SUBSCRIBE NOW!
ET THE ULTIMATE SOURCE FOR
ANIME, MANGA AND JAPANESE POP CULTURE!
Newtype USA 米国版
THE MOVING PICTURES MAGAZINE
FEB 2005 2
VOLUME 04
NUMBER 02
FREE DVD!
Secrets from the house that Miyazaki built
DON'T BUY ANOTHER DVD!
...until you read our in-depth reviews of all the latest anime!
VALENTINE SPECIAL
Anime's hottest couples!
OFFICIAL ART OF
SAIYUKI: REQUIEM
Gantz
MADLAX
D•N•Angel
Saiyuki Reload
Samurai Champloo
Fullmetal Alchemist
PLUS! 8 MORE HOT FEATURES
WORLD EXCLUSIVE!
LAGOON ENGINE EINSAT
FIRST FEATURE ON YUKIRU SUGISAKI'S LATEST MASTERPI
FREE DVD, MANGA INSERT AND CENTERFOLD POSTER IN EVERY ISSUE!!
o to www.newtype-usa.com to
et a full year (12 issues) for
ver 50% off the cover price!
Newtype USA 米国版
THE MOVING PICTURES MAGAZINE.
www.newtype-usa.com

MANGA SURVEY

PLEASE MAIL THE COMPLETED FORM TO: EDITOR – ADV MANGA
℅ A.D. Vision, Inc. 10114 W. Sam Houston Pkwy., Suite 200 Houston, TX 77099

Name: ______________________________
Address: ______________________________
City, State, Zip: ______________________________
____
E-Mail: ______________________________
Male ☐ Female ☐ Age: ______________

☐ ***CHECK HERE IF YOU WOULD LIKE TO RECEIVE OTHER INFORMATION OR FUTURE OFFERS FROM ADV.***

All information provided will be used for internal purposes only. We promise not to sell or otherwise divulge your information.

1. Annual Household Income (*Check only one*)
- ☐ Under $25,000
- ☐ $25,000 to $50,000
- ☐ $50,000 to $75,000
- ☐ Over $75,000

2. How do you hear about new Manga releases? (*Check all that apply*)
- ☐ Browsing in Store
- ☐ Internet Reviews
- ☐ Anime News Websites
- ☐ Direct Email Campaigns
- ☐ Magazine Ad
- ☐ Online Advertising
- ☐ Conventions
- ☐ TV Advertising
- ☐ Online forums (message boards and chat rooms)
- ☐ Carrier pigeon
- ☐ Other: ______________________________

3. Which magazines do you read? (*Check all that apply*)
- ☐ Wizard
- ☐ SPIN
- ☐ Animerica
- ☐ Rolling Stone
- ☐ Maxim
- ☐ DC Comics
- ☐ URB
- ☐ Polygon
- ☐ Official PlayStation Magazine
- ☐ Entertainment Weekly
- ☐ YRB
- ☐ EGM
- ☐ Newtype USA
- ☐ SciFi
- ☐ Starlog
- ☐ Wired
- ☐ Vice
- ☐ BPM
- ☐ I hate reading
- ☐ Other: ______________

4. Have you visited the ADV Manga website?
- ☐ Yes
- ☐ No

5. Have you made any manga purchases online from the ADV website?
- ☐ Yes
- ☐ No

6. If you have visited the ADV Manga website, how would you rate your online experience?
- ☐ Excellent
- ☐ Good
- ☐ Average
- ☐ Poor

7. What genre of manga do you prefer?
(*Check all that apply*)
- ☐ adventure
- ☐ romance
- ☐ detective
- ☐ action
- ☐ horror
- ☐ sci-fi/fantasy
- ☐ sports
- ☐ comedy

8. How many manga titles have you purchased in the last 6 months?
- ☐ none
- ☐ 1-4
- ☐ 5-10
- ☐ 11+

9. Where do you make your manga purchases? (*Check all that apply*)
- ☐ comic store
- ☐ bookstore
- ☐ newsstand
- ☐ online
- ☐ other:_____
- ☐ department store
- ☐ grocery store
- ☐ video store
- ☐ video game store

10. Which bookstores do you usually make your manga purchases at?
(*Check all that apply*)
- ☐ Barnes & Noble
- ☐ Walden Books
- ☐ Suncoast
- ☐ Best Buy
- ☐ Amazon.com
- ☐ Borders
- ☐ Books-A-Million
- ☐ Toys "Я" Us
- ☐ Other bookstore:
  _____

11. What's your favorite anime/manga website? (*Check all that apply*)
- ☐ adv-manga.com
- ☐ advfilms.com
- ☐ rightstuf.com
- ☐ animenewsservice.com
- ☐ animenewsnetwork.com
- ☐ Other
- ☐ animeondvd.com
- ☐ anipike.com
- ☐ animeonline.net
- ☐ planetanime.com
- ☐ animenation.com

All information provided will be used for internal purposes only. We promise not to sell or otherwise divulge your information.